Leaving Readers Behind

Leaving Readers Behind

THE AGE OF CORPORATE NEWSPAPERING

Gene Roberts

Editor in Chief

Thomas Kunkel and Charles Layton

General Editors

THE UNIVERSITY OF ARKANSAS PRESS
FAYETTEVILLE
2001

05   04   03   02   01   5   4   3   2   1

DESIGNED BY ELLEN BEELER

⊗ The paper used in this publication meets the minimum requirements of the
American National Standard for Permanence of Paper for Printed Library Materials
Z39.48-1984.

Library of Congress Cataloging-in-Publication Data

Leaving readers behind : the age of corporate newspapering / Eugene Roberts, editor
in chief ; Thomas Kunkel and Charles Layton, general editors.
     p. cm.
     ISBN 1-55728-709-0 (alk. paper)
        1. Journalism—United States. 2. Journalism—Economic aspects—United
     States. I. Roberts, Gene. II. Kunkel, Thomas, 1955– III. Layton, Charles.
     PN4867 .L38 2001
     071'.3—dc21   2001000486

     Revised

This book is dedicated to Rebecca W. Rimel,

with our thanks and admiration.

Acknowledgments

The editors are indebted to all the people who helped make the Project on the State of the American Newspaper a reality, but a handful warrant special mention—chief among them Rebecca W. Rimel, president and chief executive officer of the Pew Charitable Trusts; Donald Kimelman, director of Pew's Venture Fund; and Tom Rosenstiel, director of the Project for Excellence in Journalism. Their vision made the series possible, and their unwavering support, even in the face of industry criticism, was a constant and valued source of strength to us.

At *American Journalism Review*, editor Rem Rieder was an ideal partner, unselfish in opening up his magazine and unfailingly helpful in making the pieces better. Art director Lissa Cronin and her predecessor, Jann Alexander, gave the series its distinctive look and wrestled our data-heavy charts into attractive, accessible packages. Reese Cleghorn, longtime dean of the University of Maryland College of Journalism, was instrumental in bringing about the Project. And *AJR* vice president Frank Quine, as always, managed to make the crooked roads straight.

The unsinkable Carolyn White, associate editor of the Project, masterfully edited many of the pieces in the series, including some appearing here. Researchers Rachel Powers Kelson and David Allan were true collaborators, putting in untold hours making sure that our facts were correct and compiling most of the data that undergirded the series. And Penny Bender Fuchs worked diligently to update much of that material for the book.

Our thanks go out to Lawrence Malley, director of the University of Arkansas Press, and to his able staff, most especially Brian King, managing editor, and John Coghlan, production manager.

Finally, we would like to thank the writers. To a one they love newspapers —so much so that they were willing to endure months of reporting, kibitzing, writing, rewriting, and editing to produce these complex stories. It took virtually all of them longer than they expected, but there were no complaints. For them it was a labor of love, as it has been for us.

Contents

Foreword

By Gene Roberts

In the past twenty-five years, the American press has paid increasing attention to reporting on itself and on television, but for the most part it has
focused on the larger newspapers and on network coverage. It also has
been oriented to spot news and to the controversy of the moment and not
to the major trends in newspaper ownership and direction or to the hap-
penings in the great mass of American newspapers—those in small and
mid-sized cities. *American Journalism Review* and *Columbia Journalism
Review* have shown more interest than the newspapers, other than the *Los
Angeles Times* and its David Shaw, in in-depth coverage. But as tight-
budget operations, they lacked the resources to do much about it.

What it added up to was this: American newspaper chains were steadily
becoming larger and more dominant, owning 80 percent of the nation's
nearly fifteen hundred daily newspapers; but the goings-on in the chains
went largely unreported. Some of the chains de-emphasized coverage of
state governments and dismissed coverage of local government as boring,
and this went unnoticed by the press. And little attention was paid to sharp
cutbacks by the chains in international coverage and in beat coverage in
Washington.

By the mid-1990s I had become sufficiently concerned over the information gaps to decide I would help *AJR* raise money for in-depth coverage. It was a daunting task. To begin with, you could not ask the newspaper
chains for the money to cover them. This would be a conflict-of-interest
and could taint the coverage. As for foundations, most of the larger ones
had shown little interest in journalism reviews.

What was needed was an ambitious undertaking that would be called
the Project on the State of the American Newspaper. It would produce up
to twenty articles on American journalism, with a heavy emphasis on the
patterns and directions of newspaper corporations and their impact on
news coverage. The articles would appear in *AJR* and then become the
foundation for two books. The need was clear. But where to get the
money? And a sizeable amount would be needed. A minimum of three
months, and sometimes up to six months, of a writer's time would be

needed for each article to provide depth and clarity. And in writing about a chain, a writer would need to spend a minimum of a week in no fewer than five towns in which the chain operated newspapers. The travel budget must be ample if the project was to produce stories that shed new light on American newspapers.

I contacted foundations. One became interested, but offered to put up only a fraction of the money needed for the undertaking. Then Tom Rosenstiel, formerly of the *Los Angeles Times,* hooked up with the Pew Charitable Trusts and began roving the country looking for ideas that might improve American journalism. We talked; and he put me in touch with Rebecca W. Rimel, Pew's president and chief executive officer. She was immediately interested in the idea. She agreed to take a formal proposal to her board. The board approved. The project was funded.

Next came the job of selecting editors and writers. Ideally, the project needed editors who understood both small-town and big-city journalism. The editorship went to Tom Kunkel, formerly a key editor of the *San Jose Mercury News,* who had once run a small city daily, the *Ledger-Enquirer* in Columbus, Georgia. And the associate editorship went to Carolyn White, whose work experience included both the *Philadelphia Inquirer* and the *Daily Tribune* in Columbia, Missouri.

Then came the writers. They could not, because of conflict concerns, currently work on newspapers. But it was important that they had *once* worked on newspapers. That way they would know their subjects, know where to push the buttons for information from a newsroom. This made this search complicated, but far from impossible. We came up with seventeen, who alone and in teams produced eighteen articles that averaged fifteen thousand words. All the writers had professionally rich backgrounds. From those appearing in this volume, for example, William Prochnau wrote the definitive book on coverage in Vietnam; syndicated columnist Geneva Overholser once edited the *Des Moines Register;* Ken Auletta is the respected media writer for the *New Yorker;* and Pulitzer Prize–winner Buzz Bissinger is an acclaimed author and contributor to *Vanity Fair.*

The project lasted two years. It culminated in this book and a companion volume, which will be published later this year. This volume probes the corporatization of newspapers. The next one will deal with newspaper content, and how newspapers too often fall down in their coverage of government.

Everywhere, during this two-year study period, our writers encountered change. The corporatization of newspapers was moving so fast that, at times, companies were transforming themselves—sometimes getting bigger, sometimes smaller—even as the writers were gathering the material for their stories. But whatever the change in a specific company, the overall thrust in the newspaper industry was never in doubt: Fewer and fewer newspaper companies are owning more and more newspapers. And the distance is growing between the corporate decision-makers and the readers of their newspapers.

Ethics and standards questions also were heavy on the minds of the writers. Three large newspaper companies were controlled by ownership interests from outside the newspaper industry. Still other companies brought in managers who were experienced in business, but untutored in journalistic values and practices.

There was, for example, Community Newspaper Holdings Inc., which was controlled by a state employees' pension fund and which owned more than one hundred newspapers. There was the Liberty chain, bankrolled by a leverage-buyout king. And there was Mark Willes, former executive of a cereal company, brought in to head Times Mirror, one of the nation's most prestigious newspaper companies. What did this portend? Could these new newspaper leaders understand, for instance, where the line should be drawn between advertising and news? One of the ironies in the project was that the first company we dealt with—Chicago's Tribune—bought the last company featured in the series, Times Mirror. This, of course, dramatically illustrated the immensity of the changes occurring in newspaper ownership.

In between the first and last story, both of which are in this book with updated statistics and charts, the writers showed us the toll that a never-ending drive for corporate profits is taking on the news. In Cumberland, Maryland the police reporter had so many duties piled upon him he no longer had time to go to the police station for the daily reports. But newspaper management had a cost-saving solution: Put a fax machine in the police station, and let the cops send over the news they thought the paper should have. In New Jersey, the Gannett chain bought the *Asbury Park Press,* then sent in a publisher who slashed the staff from 240 to 185 and cut the space for news, and was rewarded by being named Gannett's Manager of the Year. But these are just two of a thousand glimpses into America's newspaper companies that this book provides.

It is the most comprehensive account to date of America's changing newspaper scene.

Contributors

MARY WALTON is a former *Philadelphia Inquirer* reporter and magazine writer. She has also written freelance articles for the *New York Times* and other publications and is the author of four books, most recently *Car: A Drama of the American Workplace.*

BUZZ BISSINGER won a Pulitzer Prize for his reporting at the *Philadelphia Inquirer.* He is a contributing editor at *Vanity Fair* and the author of two books, *Friday Night Lights* and *A Prayer for the City.*

JACK BASS has covered politics, taught journalism, and published his own weekly newspaper. The most recent of his six books is *Ol' Strom: An Unauthorized Biography of Strom Thurmond.* He is a professor of humanities at the College of Charleston.

GENEVA OVERHOLSER was editor of the *Des Moines Register* for six-and-a-half years, during which time the paper won a Pulitzer Prize for public service. She was the *Washington Post*'s ombudsman for three years and now writes a syndicated column.

WILLIAM PROCHNAU, a former reporter for the *Seattle Times* and the *Washington Post,* is a contributing editor at *Vanity Fair.* His most recent book is *Once Upon a Distant War,* an account of the first American journalists in Vietnam.

KEN AULETTA has written extensively for the *New Yorker* about Microsoft, Time Warner, Disney, and other corporate giants of the news and entertainment world. The most recent of his eight books is *World War 3.0: Microsoft and Its Enemies.*

ROY REED has been a foreign and national correspondent for the *New York Times* and taught journalism for eighteen years at the University of Arkansas. His recent book, *Faubus: The Life and Times of an American Prodigal,* is about former Arkansas governor Orval Faubus.

CYNTHIA GORNEY was a reporter for the *Washington Post* in San Francisco and was the paper's South America bureau chief for three years. She is the author of *Articles of Faith: A Frontline History of the Abortion Wars*. She teaches journalism at the University of California at Berkeley.

JAMES V. RISSER was director of the John S. Knight Fellowships program at Stanford University for fifteen years. As a Washington correspondent for the *Des Moines Register* he won Pulitzer Prizes in 1976 and 1979 for distinguished reporting on agricultural and environmental issues.

1 | Leaving Readers Behind

I believe in the profession of journalism. I believe that the public journal is a public trust; that all connected with it are, to the full measure of
their responsibility, trustees for the public; that acceptance of lesser service
than the public service is a betrayal of this trust.

—WALTER WILLIAMS, "The Journalist's Creed," 1914.

We stand for excellent service to customers and communities, a fair,
respectful and learning environment for all our employees and a strong
return for our shareholders. This responsibility is shared by each of us in
Knight Ridder, regardless of title or function.

—KNIGHT RIDDER "Statement of Strategic Intent," 1997.

NEWSPAPER OWNERS AND PUBLISHERS like to say that ink courses
through their veins, but it's really paranoia. They are world-class
worriers, and with decades of practice is it any wonder? After all,
they were persuaded Hollywood was going to kill them off, then radio,
then television, then cable. Now the Internet has them fretting about New
Media and personal data appliances the same way they once worried about
Teamsters and direct mail. To be a newspaper publisher is to know perpet-
ual angst. You can't enjoy it when advertising is up because you know it
will go down, just as you can't enjoy it when the cost of newsprint is down
because you know it will go up. A boom is nothing but a bust waiting to
happen.

So you worry—all the way to the bank. The American newspaper
industry today is a $60-billion-a-year, diversified colossus with profit mar-
gins triple the norm for U.S. industry as a whole. As writer William
Prochnau put it not long ago, "A funeral for newspapering? It would draw
more stretch limos than lined up for Elvis."

Despite what you might have heard, then, it's not a genuine question
whether newspaper companies will survive in our ever-shifting, hyper-
competitive communications landscape. They will, their genius for adap-
tation and self-preservation evolved to a level that Darwin would relish.
They are that well tested—and, it should not be forgotten, even better
bankrolled.

Meantime, a far more compelling question goes unasked: As this evolution plays out, what might it ultimately cost us, the newspaper-reading public?

Judging from the evidence so far, the answer is: A lot.

The simple fact is that the American newspaper industry finds itself in the middle of the most momentous change in its three-hundred-year history, a change that is diminishing the amount of real news available to the consumer. A generation of relentless corporatization is now culminating in a furious, unprecedented blitz of buying, selling, and consolidating of newspapers, from the mightiest dailies to the humblest weeklies. Intended to heighten efficiency and maximize profits, this activity is at the same time reducing competition and creating new ownership models. Perhaps most alarming, it is revolutionizing, to the point of undermining, the traditional nature and role of the press. Today's thoroughly modern newspaper executive sees himself less the "public trustee" of Walter Williams's famous creed than the New Age guardian of shareholder value described in Knight Ridder's committee-written "Statement of Strategic Intent." Roll over, Ben Bradlee.

This is not to say that all the change in the industry has been bad, or that there aren't wonderful newspapers out there. There are, from the *New York Times* and *Washington Post* on one coast to the *Los Angeles Times* and *San Jose Mercury News* on the other. In between are dozens of good, some exceptionally so, papers. But many of these metropolitan regionals—still the key disseminators of information for tens of millions of Americans— are not as good as they should be, or in the case of such papers as the *St. Louis Post-Dispatch* and *Des Moines Register,* as good as they once were. Indeed, one can argue that considering there are nearly fifteen hundred daily papers in the United States, and considering that most of these are handsomely profitable, the percentage of excellence is abysmally low. Today's typical daily is mediocre, with a strong overlay of provincialism. And industry trends are only making matters worse.

That may help explain why newspapers largely failed to report the seismic activity shaking up their own backyard. Or at least they did until, in early 2000, a tremor out of Southern California was too big to be ignored. This was the takeover of mighty Times Mirror Co.—publishers of the *L.A. Times, Newsday,* the *Baltimore Sun,* and other respected papers—by Chicago's Tribune Co. With Wall Street having decreed to corporate America that you either Get Big or Get Out, the industry and its analysts generally applauded the $8 billion deal, which also included a handful of lucrative television stations. And they practically salivated over the synergistic possibilities; imagine what an enlightened conglomerate could do with these combined resources in print, broadcast, online, and cable!

But few addressed what the takeover said about the increasingly quaint notion of local ownership; the most important outlet for news in our second-largest and most sociologically complex metropolis would now be governed out of a skyscraper two thousand miles away in a city that can be fairly characterized as the *anti*-L.A. Nor did they speculate much about how it might fuel the industry's increasingly monopolistic practices, nor how in recent years the government's antitrust watchdogs have been fairly blasé about this whole business of media consolidation. (In acquiring Times Mirror, Tribune also got television stations in virtually all its major newspaper markets. As such, it was gambling that the Federal Communications Commission will be more permissive than in the past about cross-ownership—a bet that at this writing certainly seems well-placed.)

Nor did they assert what the Times Mirror acquisition *really* represented: the absolute triumph of corporate newspapering. Simply put, it was the biggest, baddest deal in a world that has become a deal-maker's paradise.

This is a world where conglomerates now rule unchallenged. Where independent papers, once as ubiquitous on the American landscape as water towers, are nearly extinct. Where small hometown dailies in particular are being bought and sold like hog futures. Where chains, once content to grow one property at a time, now devour other chains whole. Where they are effectively ceding whole regions of the country to one another, further minimizing competition. Where money is pouring into the business from interests with little knowledge and even less concern about the special obligations newspapers have in our society.

The amount of activity is simply dizzying.

Just look at giant Gannett Co. After a multibillion-dollar burst of acquisitions in the first half of 2000, Gannett, which already was the nation's largest newspaper company in terms of circulation and sales, grew itself from seventy-four daily newspapers to ninety-nine. Most conspicuous was its swallowing of the Pulliam family's Central Newspapers Inc., which if nothing else practically guarantees that consumers of Phoenix's *Arizona Republic* and the *Indianapolis Star* will *never* get the kind of papers they have long deserved. Regardless, Gannett can now brag that it produces one out of every seven newspapers sold in America. Along with Knight Ridder and the newly fattened Tribune, these three chains now claim a quarter of all the daily newspaper circulation in the nation.

Consider the phenomenon that is Community Newspaper Holdings

Inc. Bankrolled by that First Amendment bastion the Alabama state employees' pension fund, CNHI didn't even *exist* until 1997, but it already owns 112 daily newspapers reaching from Alamagordo, New Mexico, to Tonawanda, New York. The year 1998 saw the emergence of another instant chain, Liberty Group, created by a leveraged-buyout king whose other holdings have included bus companies, pharmacy chains, and home-improvement centers. Liberty has acquired 68 dailies. It's too soon to know what will happen with these two newborn companies, but so far they have paid more attention to rigorous bottom-line management than to distinguished journalism.

The nonstop trading of small-town dailies may seem creative and exciting to newspaper brokers and financial analysts, but think how unsettling it is for those who actually subscribe to these papers, or work for them. Consider the *Northwestern* (circulation 23,500) in Oshkosh, Wisconsin. Here is a paper that prided itself on being in hometown hands since the Johnson administration—the Andrew Johnson administration. But in 1998 it was sold not once but twice, within the space of two months. Two years later it was sold *again*. Four owners in less than three years.

But more than the transactions themselves, it is the thinking underlying them that is having such a profound impact. Most of these sales are being driven by a relatively new concept known as clustering, in which a company purchases properties in close proximity to one another, or to its existing papers. This allows the company to consolidate a number of functions, chiefly on the business side but sometimes editorial as well, for maximum efficiency. So it is that in populous New Jersey, the Newhouse and Gannett chains between them now own thirteen of the state's nineteen dailies, or 73 percent of all the circulation of New Jersey–based papers. (It may be our most monopolized state—a new license-plate slogan, perhaps?—although it would be given a run by not-so-populous Oklahoma, where CNHI alone owns twenty-four of the state's forty-three dailies.)

To date there are at least 125 major newspaper clusters around the country, involving more than a fourth of our daily papers. These clusters may be as small as two papers but typically involve five or six, and not uncommonly as many as eight. There are countless others if you throw in weeklies, which lend themselves more naturally to the cluster concept. Proponents point out, correctly, that in some (unusual) cases a clustering arrangement has kept alive an otherwise failing newspaper. But even then the clustered management removes major decisions from that town, which is to say puts them one step farther away from its readers.

By definition clustering reduces competition, with fewer companies operating in the same area, and taken to its logical conclusion it can dramatically reduce the number of editorial voices as well. This was seen recently in suburban Westchester County, just outside New York City. Over the years Gannett had collected ten small local dailies there and operated them as a cluster, though it maintained their individual nameplates and identities. But in 1998 the company yielded to temptation and melded them into one vanilla-flavored metro, the *Journal News*. Now, the *Journal News* without doubt is a better paper than any of its small predecessors. Yet would anyone argue that this consolidation wasn't a severe blow to those communities' respective identities? Does anyone beyond its corporate minders really believe that the confederated *Journal News* "cares" about, say, Tarrytown more than the old *Tarrytown Daily News* did?

No matter. The *Tarrytown Daily News* was sacrificed on the altar of efficiency, and other luckless nameplates are sure to follow.

But when it comes to media efficiency, the absolute *latest* new thing is not consolidation or clustering but synergy, which is the leveraging of different kinds of media holdings to enhance one another. Tribune Co., as was evident in its Times Mirror takeover, has established itself as a pioneer in this field, using its newspapers as content factories for online sites, local television stations, and cable news outlets, all under common ownership. "I am not the editor of a newspaper," declared Howard Tyner, then editor of the *Chicago Tribune* and subsequently promoted to oversee all the company's papers. "I am the manager of a content company. That's what I do. . . . We gather content."

Such an observation is *de rigueur* for modern newspaper editors; to say otherwise is to speak heresy. Never mind that the *Chicago Tribune*'s circulation has eroded steadily from its peak of 1 million decades ago to 658,000 today, or that the daily once fond of calling itself "The World's Greatest Newspaper" is no longer even considered in the top ten in America. (There are days, some Chicagoans argue, when it isn't even the best paper in town.) It doesn't matter if the obligation of feeding an omnivorous hydra-headed news machine may have helped take the edge off the paper, because this synergy idea is catching real fire. Down in Tampa, Media General has gone so far as to put its newspaper, the *Tribune*, in the same building with its local television station and online operation, the better to exchange stories and, ostensibly, resources. (It's still unclear what the newspapers get out of the bargain other than garish weather maps sponsored by the local TV meteorologist.) Tampa's has become the most sophisticated model for this kind of thing, and as such is drawing enormous interest from other newspaper companies.

Under the Tampa model—and presumably in many major city rooms of the future—news decisions for all these outlets are made in a coordinated way, sometimes in the same meeting. In effect the same group of minds decides what "news" is, in every conceivable way that people can get their local news. This isn't sinister; it's just not competition.

But you'd better get used to it because the real momentum is just beginning. Indeed, should the consolidation of the newspaper industry continue at its current fevered pace, it won't be long before the nation effectively is reduced to half a dozen major print conglomerates. The flamboyant William Dean Singleton, CEO of MediaNews Group, one of the chains that has championed this new order, flatly predicts, "You will see a lot fewer newspaper companies in five years." No one has contradicted him.

T HIS IS NOT another pointless lamentation on the Citicorping and Wal-Marting of America. All change has implications. Some are intended, some not; some are beneficial, some not. If it is regrettable that the corner five-and-dime and your neighborhood S&L have been driven out of business by the giants, it's also likely that at the end of the day you have more banking services and button selection at your disposal than ever before.

News, however, is a different commodity. It is unique to any given place; what happens in Portland, Maine, is of little consequence in Portland, Oregon. But unlike other realms of business, in the newspaper industry, consolidation—in tandem with the chains' desperation to maintain unrealistic profit levels (most of these big companies now being publicly traded)—is actually reducing the amount of real news being gathered and disseminated, most conspicuously at the local and state levels where consumers need it most. This is because consolidation has resulted in far fewer news outlets, and the economic pressures have resulted in fewer reporters with fewer inches in the paper to say anything.

Concentration has other ramifications, less easy to document but no less real. For starters, it too readily facilitates a kind of corporate group mindset. Sometimes this is a good thing; in recent years, for instance, it has resulted in a doubling of sports coverage and a fourfold increase in space devoted to business news. More often than not, however, notions turn into convictions with no supporting rationale. Years back the idea took hold in the industry that readers found coverage of government "boring," and that foreign news was hopelessly "irrelevant," even though empirical evidence shows both suggestions to be canards. Coverage of government at every level has since been in retreat—about which more in a moment—and for-eign news is quietly disappearing from mainstream newspapers. Indeed, most of the nation's dailies—perhaps 95 percent—practice journalistic iso-lationism. They devote twice the space to comics as they do to interna-tional news. They take the weather almost as seriously as momentous events from abroad.

This new media environment also fosters a kind of creepy coziness, where activity that once would have been dismissed as preposterous is now commonplace. Times Mirror can lend Dean Singleton $50 million to help MediaNews purchase the *Los Angeles Daily News*—hometown rival to TM's own *L.A. Times*—so that a stronger competitor won't. The publisher of Hearst's *San Francisco Examiner* promises to stem his paper's criticism of Mayor Willie Brown if Hizzoner doesn't oppose Hearst's takeover of the rival *Chronicle*. The entire business side of the *L.A. Times* can climb into bed with a major advertiser, the Staples Center, and no one in a leadership position appreciates its blatant impropriety. At a time when rank-and-file journalists are being held to higher standards of conduct than ever, what kind of screwy, hypocritical message does such activity convey?

Meanwhile, budgetary strictures and multimedia demands leave news-rooms more sorely pressed than ever. Our favorite example—and maybe a poster child for the beleaguered journalistic fraternity—is the police reporter for the paper in tiny Cumberland, Maryland, where the staff was stretched so thin that he had to have the local police fax him the day's crime reports—the ones they *wanted* him to see, of course, as opposed to the ones he might really need to see. This sort of thing isn't as uncommon as one might suppose.

In other words, what's happening in the newspaper world is more than inside baseball, of interest only to journalists and Wall Street analysts. It has a cost to average Americans that grows increasingly clear. And that cost, in the form of diluted and less serious, less substantive news, could be high for a nation whose democracy literally depends on an informed citizenry.

I N AN EFFORT to assess what is happening, an enterprise calling itself the Project on the State of the American Newspaper spent over two years conducting the most comprehensive examination of the industry in his-tory. Underwritten by the Pew Charitable Trusts, the work was an initiative of the Project for Excellence in Journalism, a Washington-based organiza-tion, led by media critic Tom Rosenstiel, committed to bringing about accountability and reform in the news business.

The Project's goal was simple: Hire some of the nation's top journalists to apply the same scrutiny to the newspaper industry that newspapers have historically applied to other business sectors. These correspondents, virtually all of them newspaper junkies who came of age at major metros themselves, spent an average of six months reporting and writing. They traversed the nation from New York to San Francisco, from Oklahoma City to beleaguered little Oshkosh. Their reports—eighteen in all and most running to fifteen thousand words or more—were published serially in *American Journalism Review.* Given the megadeal that was presently to follow, it was fitting that the series debuted in the spring of 1998 with Ken Auletta's profile of Tribune Co. and concluded in early 2000 with William Prochnau's examination of the *Los Angeles Times,* where a highly touted effort to build a "newspaper without walls"—that is, without the traditional barrier between business and editorial—had just collapsed in the rubble of the Staples Center fiasco.

The point of the series was to get past the city rooms and into the business suites, to analyze the people and the forces that, for better and worse, are remaking the newspaper landscape. Where possible, the reporters were asked to quantify these changes. Beyond that, they were to discuss their implications, for industry and customer alike.

Some of their specific findings were unutterably sad. A good example was the story of the *Asbury Park Press,* New Jersey's second-largest newspaper. Over the years the *Press* had carved out a reputation as one of the most enterprising independent papers in the nation. It did this by deploying an editorial staff of 240, quite robust for a paper with a circulation of 159,000, and by approaching its patch of the Jersey Shore with the amalgam of concern and affection that generally is possible only under local ownership.

Then in 1997, the *Press* was sold to Gannett. As is typical in such cases, the company promised no diminution of editorial quality. Just as typically it moved to effect precisely that. Within a year the Gannett-appointed publisher, Robert Collins, had slashed the newsroom staff from 240 to 185, significantly reduced the space available for serious news (though plenty was available for a new weekly pets section), and presided over the exodus of many of the *Press*'s most talented people to its competitors. Hewing to well-documented Gannett principles, the paper shortened stories, de-emphasized government news, and ordered reporters to "localize" pieces to the point of absurdity.

The year after his emasculation of the paper, Collins was named Gannett's manager of the year, and praised by his corporate bosses for remaking the Press "into a decisive, results-oriented enterprise."

What happened in Asbury Park was a blunt but not especially exceptional example of what is occurring around the country. Prosperous Gannett applies the knife in this way because that is its corporate culture. But other companies doing such cutting say they have no choice, and often that is true. Why? Simple economics. One reason the newspaper market has been so heated is that properties are fetching record prices. The high prices put tremendous pressure on new owners to pare costs in order to make their debt payments. And as anyone in the business can tell you, there really are only two major cost centers in newspapering: people and paper.

Which helps explain the eviscerations at the papers of Journal Register Co., whose primary owner is the Warburg, Pincus investment bank. The company has squeezed properties like its *Times Herald* in Norristown, Pennsylvania, so hard that today the paper runs about half as many pages as it did before Journal Register acquired it. A paper that once prided itself on comprehensive coverage of local government now lets many important meetings go uncovered, and accounts of others often appear days after the fact. "I have nothing good to say about it," Mayor Ted LeBlanc says of the *Times Herald*. He has stopped subscribing.

Other examples abound. Out in California, Knight Ridder hacked away at newsroom positions and salaries after it acquired the feisty little *Monterey County Herald*, while MediaNews did the same in its highly contentious acquisition of the *Long Beach Press-Telegram*. Thomson Co. was notorious for its knife work at *all* its papers, before it abandoned them recently for the even more profitable and infinitely less messy world of online information.

In Atlanta, meanwhile, Cox's cost-cutting showed up not only in the consolidation of the *Journal* and *Constitution* editorial staffs, but in how they were used. This became clear in 1998 when the Project conducted the first-ever comprehensive survey of newspaper coverage of state capitals. The Project documented a strong nationwide retreat from such coverage throughout the decade of the '90s—sometimes to the point of near abandonment—at precisely the time when state government was gaining new power and exerting more impact than ever on the average American. The survey of full-time reporters at all fifty state capitols found a total of only 513. To put that in perspective, more than three thousand media credentials are issued each year for the Super Bowl. And more than fifty thousand lobbyists are registered with state governments. That's about one hundred lobbyists for every overworked, underpaid press watchdog. The survey revealed that, over a decade, newspaper commitment to state-house coverage fell in twenty-seven states, among them New York, Michigan, Connecticut, and Illinois.

In fast-growing Georgia, state coverage had almost disappeared off the radar. This was particularly distressing because the *Journal* and *Constitution* had a proud legacy of blanketing the statehouse like kudzu. A generation ago when the legislature was in session, ten or twelve reporters, columnists, and editorial writers could be found trolling the capitol's marble corridors. By the spring of 1998 the combined Atlanta papers were down to three full-time state government reporters. Things reached such a pass that reporters with little background or expertise had to be parachuted in to cover stories on an emergency basis—with predictable results. As Rick Dent, then press secretary to Gov. Zell Miller, explained, "They'll get assigned a welfare piece. I'll have to spoon-feed the information to them. . . . But I'm an advocate. I'm not going to give you the whole side of the story. . . . They say, 'Who else should I talk to?' Well, hell, I'm not going to tell them to talk to the people who are on the other side."

The statehouse survey garnered considerable national attention, and followups the next two years revealed a discernible though modest increase in full-time statehouse reporters: up to 543, or nearly a 6 percent increase. But the *Journal* and *Constitution* still had only three reporters on the beat.

A similarly disturbing situation was found to exist in Washington. A 1999 survey of nineteen key departments and agencies showed a wholesale retreat in coverage of the federal government. Regular reporting of the Supreme Court and the State Department, for instance, dropped off considerably throughout the '90s. At the Social Security Administration, whose activities affect literally every American, only the *New York Times* was maintaining a full-time reporter. And incredibly, at the Interior Department, which controls 500 million acres of public land and oversees everything from the national park system to the Bureau of Indian Affairs, there were no full-time reporters around.

What was happening here? Why had government reporters gone from being newsroom stars to pariahs?

Mostly it was because their editors, under financial pressure from their publishers and under industry pressure to do more expansive lifestyle coverage, allowed themselves to believe that readers found "incremental" government news inherently boring. Of course, that kind of coverage *does* result when witless reporters are allowed to approach it that way, but in truth readers have never stopped, nor will they stop, appreciating intelligent reporting of public affairs.

The foreign story suffered the same fate as the government story—which is to say it wound up deep inside the paper, or out of it altogether. The *Indianapolis Star,* a fairly typical mainstream paper, published 23 percent less foreign news in November of 1997 than in the same month twenty years earlier. In a comparative survey of ten metro newspapers, the Project found that the percentage of newshole devoted to international events dropped from 5 percent in the mid-'60s to just 3 percent in the late '90s—by which time the United States had become the world's lone superpower, globalization and Internet communications were ubiquitous, and events overseas were having a more direct impact on the average American than ever before.

Another issue the series brought to light was the incredible vulnerability of our hometown papers. Half the newspapers in America have a circulation below thirteen thousand, and they are a precious national heritage. But these small dailies are being especially whipsawed by the new ownership models. After documenting every newspaper sale from 1994 through July of 2000—719 transactions in all—the Project found that two-thirds of the time it was one of these community papers that was changing hands. In that six-and-a-half-year window, 47 percent of *all* hometown papers turned over—many of them, like Oshkosh, three and four times. And since with each swap a paper typically is more highly leveraged, budgets got tighter, and content of necessity became expendable.

Nor has the selling frenzy been confined to daily papers. It has also spread to the nation's eight thousand weekly newspapers. Weeklies once were too small and parochial for the major chains to bother with, but the big boys have gotten over that attitude in a hurry. When Pulitzer Inc. recently bought the thirty-eight Suburban Journal weeklies and niche publications that ring its flagship *St. Louis Post-Dispatch*, it was only the latest big company to turn a nuisance into a synergistic opportunity. In city after city—Washington, Baltimore, Cleveland, and Dallas, to name just a few— metro papers have been purchasing the community weeklies that surround them. Today, major owners of daily newspapers—such chains as CNHI, Gannett, Journal Register, and Liberty—are also among the largest holders of weeklies. Times Mirror even purchased the weekly in Hartford, Connecticut, that was begun years ago precisely to give readers there an alternative to the daily paper, Times Mirror's *Hartford Courant*. The point is, the corporatization of the weeklies further erodes the number and diversity of editorial voices.

Other changes in the industry are much less noticeable to the public but are proving no less harmful. For instance, the chains increasingly are pressuring top editors—primarily through their wallets—to focus more and more on corporate goals, and less and less on the news. At too many papers these days, the editor is just another replaceable face in a management constellation. The business side is in clear control, and its influence is being felt in unwelcome ways in the news pages. Decisions about editorial emphasis, the size of reporting staffs, special sections, newshole—more and more these are being made either by committee or by corporate fiat. The diminution of editorial authority has resulted in great frustration, and many editors simply have left. "I think in that process a lot of editors were really beaten down," said John Carroll, former editor of the *Baltimore Sun* and the person Tribune brought in to run the *L.A. Times.* "They were demoralized. And some of them just never got back up off the canvas."

It wasn't ever thus. Once it was the norm in chains that a paper's chief business executive was called general manager or business manager, or more rarely, president, and usually this person had no authority over the newsroom. When the formidable John S. Knight was building the newspaper empire that was the forerunner of Knight Ridder, his editors and general managers reported separately to corporate headquarters. This arrangement began to fade in the late '70s, but it didn't disappear totally until the late '80s. Under the new system, a local publisher served as the top official of each paper, and he or she was the ultimate authority over both the news and business sides. Even then, to minimize the risk of the business side running roughshod over newsrooms, Knight selected many of his publishers from the editor ranks. But within a decade, with the founder dead and buried, the business-side executives were filling the top roles. In Gannett and other companies a similar process played out, albeit swifter and more sweepingly.

Knight, legendary curmudgeon and Pulitzer Prize–winning columnist, not only tolerated but actively *supported* argument and debate among editors and businessmen; he believed he would more likely get the truth if all felt free to have their say. But times change. A few years ago, when the editor of Knight Ridder's paper in Columbia, South Carolina, differed with his publisher about the direction of local coverage, he was told point-blank that dissent was not in his job description. And Gannett circulated a memo to its editors that put it succinctly: "The publisher is responsible for the entire newspaper, including the quality of the news report."

So much for the walls between news and business.

O F COURSE, there is nothing inherently evil about corporate newspaper owners, any more than there is anything inherently angelic about local ones. Most any print journalist old enough to remember typewriters —and it wasn't that long ago when an IBM Selectric was the epitome of high tech—has worked for at least one independent owner with the scruples of a loan shark. (Ask readers in Oklahoma City about the "blessings" of independent ownership, as their *Oklahoman* enters its ninth decade of benighted leadership under the Gaylord family.) Besides, newspaper chains are hardly a new phenomenon. Hearst, Pulitzer, Scripps—to a one the glorious, notorious print titans of the early twentieth century made their fortunes and consolidated their immense influence by stringing metropolitan papers together, and Adolph Ochs couldn't invent the *New York Times* as we know it until he had first turned around the lowly *Chattanooga Times*.

Nevertheless, for the first half of the twentieth century these chains, while inordinately powerful, were more the exception than the rule. Independent newspapers dominated the nation. A community of any size might have two or even three. Were many of these operated by boosters, shills, and scalawags? Absolutely. But others were courageous and civic-minded. And even in the worst cases competition could be counted on as the great leveler, feeding the community's vitality and ensuring that at least a modicum of honest information reached the populace.

By the '60s, however, that was changing—slowly at first, then with the vigor of a Goss Metroliner whirring to life. The story of the modern newspaper industry is one of relentless chain-building, consolidation, and corporate centralization.

It should be said that in the beginning, this development was not necessarily a bad thing. One can make a strong argument that as the large chains mushroomed, they very often improved the newspapers they bought, sometimes sharply. Certainly this was the case in Philadelphia, Miami, Macon, Lexington, and other cities where Jack Knight took control of papers. Long Island's *Newsday*, already a fine paper when it was acquired by Times Mirror in 1970 from Harry Guggenheim, blossomed and matured under its Los Angeles owners. Applying steadily evolving technological improvements and other efficiencies to their new properties, such chains in a couple of decades were able to ratchet up their profit margins while simultaneously bolstering editorial content.

Along the way society was changing, and so was the industry. The automobile, the booming suburbs and television altered commuting and reading patterns, and the marginal big-city papers began to fall by the wayside. (Not *all* that worry we talked about earlier was heedless, you understand.) As afternoon dailies especially became expendable, more and more communities suddenly found themselves one-newspaper towns. And those who survived this great shakeout realized something that the oil and steel crowd had known for years: A monopoly can be a beautiful thing.

Philip Meyer, a longtime industry executive who now holds the Knight chair in journalism at the University of North Carolina, and other industry critics have made this point before, but it's worth revisiting. The economic model of a newspaper, all things being equal, should resemble that of a supermarket—high volume, low margin. You make money because you produce something inexpensively that the masses consume day after day after day. But suddenly newspapers were no longer in a conventional situation. If yours were the only supermarket in Atlanta, you could surely charge whatever you wanted for milk and eggs. Likewise, because they became monopoly institutions, newspapers got to the point where they could boost profit margins to 20, 30, and in some usurious cases 40 percent. These are dizzyingly high margins for any type of commerce. They are also addictive, to owners and stock analysts alike. "That easy-money culture has led to some bad habits that still haunt the industry," Meyer observed. "If the money is going to come in no matter what kind of product you turn out, you are motivated to turn it out as cheaply as possible. If newspapers are under pressure, you can cheapen the product and raise prices at the same time. And, most important, innovation is not rewarded."

Certainly that became the industry's default position, especially in economic downturns. Newspapering has traditionally been considered a cyclical industry, doing better when times are better—and advertising, therefore, is stronger. And while the analysts didn't expect growth from newspaper companies when the economy was weak, they did expect their executives to tighten their belts.

Then a dynamic new kind of newspaper CEO arrived on the scene to demonstrate to Wall Street and the world that such cycles could be defied. And damned if he didn't do it.

Al Neuharth had grown up on the editorial side of the newspaper business, earning a reputation for being as tough as he was flamboyant. As the influential leader of Gannett, he was less interested in Pulitzers and editorial excellence than in financial performance. And he managed to string together an astounding eighty-six consecutive quarters in which every period had higher profits than in the same quarter of the preceding year. Neuharth's performance radicalized profit expectations. But he had constantly expanded his company, carefully buying noncompetitive papers usually in cities with booming growth. The rule for his publishers was simplicity itself: Make your quarterly profit goals and prosper; miss them and you'd better start looking around.

The message spread through the industry like a new gospel. Before long even newspaper companies in stagnant or non-monopoly markets were being pressed to duplicate Neuharth's profit performance. The result in some cases were draconian cuts in the newshole and news staffs. Editors, who found more and more of their compensation tied to the company's financial performance, became all too proficient with the scalpels. "The first time you have to take a hundred thousand out of payroll, it's a fascinating exercise," said former *Milwaukee Journal* editor Sig Gissler. "The fifth time you have to do it, it's lost its allure. . . . You come in and start killing the nearest snake."

In Neuharth's wake, there was no longer any ambiguity about priorities for the publicly traded companies. News was no longer the paramount value, simply a vehicle to achieve the paramount value, which was financial return. Talking about Jack Knight's old company, a Merrill Lynch analyst in 1998 nicely summed up the new paradigm: "KRI's historic culture has been one of producing Pulitzer Prizes instead of profits," she wrote, "and while we think that culture is hard to change, it does seem to be happening."

So in newsroom after newsroom, the cutting continued. If a paper was large enough, it might operate in this fashion for quite a while before anyone but journalists would notice the difference in the product. But by the late '80s, and even more dramatically in the '90s, it became clear that there was a limit to how long you could pile annual earnings gains upon annual earnings gains without damaging newspaper quality. Naturally, newspaper executives didn't want to admit that any more than Detroit wanted to admit it was producing inferior automobiles in the 1970s. Still, the business had reached the point where it was threatening to eat its own seed corn in the pursuit of short-term financial performance. And the evidence was there in the paper—in thinner and blander news reports, in the disappearance of a columnist or a statehouse reporter, in the folding of a Sunday magazine, in stories that simply never got covered. In the '90s, daily papers in the main "had become less distinctive institutions, less connected to their communities, more homogenized, often led by people whose only instinct seemed to be to increase shareholder wealth," said David Laventhol, who served as publisher at both the *L.A. Times* and *Newsday.* "Journalistic and community achievements seemed secondary."

A T THE DAWN of a new millennium, this kind of bottom-line pressure shows no sign of abating. On the contrary, newspaper executives wake up most days to stagnant stock prices and Wall Street analysts who, if they mention newspaper companies at all, do so in the dour manner they reserve for "mature" industries—even those staid, unsexy ones that still manage to return 24 percent profits. Off to one side, the print folks look out in awe at the growth of online, trying to figure out whether it represents their future or their demise. To the other they see a white-hot media environment where Microsoft partners with NBC; America Online swallows up Netscape, then Time Warner; CBS merges with entertainment giant Viacom; Yahoo shops for partners, as does AT&T, as do the Baby Bells. It's confusing, migraine-inducing stuff, and newspaper executives are no more immune than the rest of us to a culture that says if you're not moving—somewhere, somehow—you're dead.

So they *are* moving—by merging, by clustering, by cutting, by reorganizing, by synergizing with a vengeance. They are in such a rush that they are sorting out their destinies even as they fulfill them.

Needless to say, that is not exactly the ideal procedure. Were these same executives able to suppress their quarter-to-quarter anxiety and step back for a broader perspective, they might actually see the contemporary newspaper landscape for what it is—a remarkable opportunity. In the great media shakeout, newspapers stand as the last vestige of local news, something that will never go out of demand. One by one the other media players —local TV, local radio—have left the field. The local franchise most newspapers own has never been more valuable.

It's true that no one is exactly sure what will come of the familiar pulp and ink product that lands at the door, though it likely will prove more enduring (romantics might even add endearing) than we are led to expect from the seers, some of whose more outlandish notions of the communications world to come have the ring of those "helicopter in every driveway" predictions of the old Futuramas. Still, it seems a safe bet that newspaper companies will continue to go along as they are now, delivering news and information in a variety of formats—some of which doubtless even the futurists have yet to conjure.

It seems equally clear that such news will be more personalized, faster, and increasingly married to other technologies. In other words, the old media will adapt to complement the new, as has ever been the case. And who knows? The Internet, far from being the villain of the piece, may turn out to be the print media's salvation, allowing newspapers to capitalize on their franchises with maximum efficiency. Now that we're finally getting past the first initial hysterical reactions to dot-com fever, the early signs are somewhat encouraging. It turns out that even on the Internet profit counts more than hype—and newspapers know a thing or two about making profits. There are surveys suggesting that newspapers are actually employing their Web sites more quickly, and more imaginatively, for breaking news than such vaunted Internet "portals" as Yahoo and MSNBC. At the same time, not only hasn't the Web's widely anticipated siphoning of print classifieds occurred, but newspapers are still showing strong *gains* in lineage. And if overall readership is still shaky and slightly eroding, it remains relatively stable, especially in light of the millions of viewers who are abandoning the network news programs.

All in all, then, this may prove to be a golden time for newspapers—if they have the courage to advance rather than retreat, if they invest in content, and if they remain mindful of what made their commodity special in the first place. "Why does a community desire to have its own medium?" asked the publisher of a small weekly in Washington state. "I kind of like the idea of the First Amendment. It's not owned by the press. It's owned by the public."

Not long ago *Washington Post* columnist Richard Cohen addressed the subject of the turmoil in the news media, and the question of what can happen when a newspaper forgets that it has a higher obligation than a satisfying return on investment. "News is not a product like a tire or a paper towel," he wrote. "It is what we journalists say it is. The reader has to believe. . . . A newspaper's 'brand' is trust—trust in its judgment, its independence, its values. That's what remains constant. The news changes every day."

Indeed, what Walter Williams asserted decades ago is still true. A newspaper is a kind of public trust—and to be trusted it has to be there every day, constantly monitoring, constantly watching, constantly providing information that is not only useful but truthful. That is an expensive and ongoing commitment. Radio, television, even digital interlopers like Microsoft and America Online have demonstrated that they are unwilling to make that kind of commitment, in terms of putting enough trained, skilled information-gatherers on the ground. Should newspaper companies be tempted to follow their lead, as some already have, we will wind up with that most terrible of ironies—communities that are, in the middle of the so-called Information Explosion, less informed than ever.

2 | The Selling of Small-Town America

By Mary Walton

I N THE SIXTEEN YEARS that Arlena McLaughlin worked her way up from advertising sales representative to publisher, the *Huntsville Item,* a 6,100-circulation East Texas daily, had four different owners. When she arrived in 1980 it was held by Harte-Hanks. In 1986 MediaNews Group bought the *Item,* then turned around two years later and sold it to Thomson Newspapers. In 1995 it was sold again, to Hollinger International.

As publisher, McLaughlin became accustomed to showing the paper to prospective buyers. "I'd give them the market tour," she says, "and talk about our marketing plans. And business plans. And talk about the community, the stability of the employees and that sort of thing. Some days you would almost feel more like a real estate broker than you would a newspaper publisher."

Had she hung around, McLaughlin might still be entertaining buyers. In 1998 the *Item* was peddled a fifth time, to the fastest-growing chain in the country, Community Newspaper Holdings Inc., of Birmingham, Alabama. But by then McLaughlin had taken a new job as publisher of the *Courier* (circulation twelve thousand) in Conroe, Texas, and several weeklies on the northern outskirts of Houston.

Two years later, *that* paper got new owners.

America's hometown papers are a precious national resource. They render up on a daily basis the events that matter most to their readers: births, retirements and deaths, school plays and football plays, sewer excavations and pothole repairs, drunk driving arrests, and, these days, even the addresses of the sex offenders among us. If the papers sometimes sidestep controversy—best look for that in the popular letters to the editor columns—they cover the staples: school boards, zoning boards, town councils.

These newspapers are indispensable in another way—as local citizens, heading up annual United Way drives, championing local business, and generally lending their communities a sense of stability in an unstable world. Just about half the nation's 1,483 daily papers are under thirteen thousand circulation; they help form the backbone of an America seldom featured in glossy magazines or on the evening news.

But deeply rooted as they may be, the nation's hometown papers are vulnerable to outside forces. And these days, they are changing hands like used cars at an auction. Of the 564 U.S. newspapers sold from January of 1994 through July of 2000, about two-thirds had circulations under 13,000. One hundred and eleven of these small papers were sold two, three, or even four times during this six-and-a-half year period.

In one of the biggest shifts in newspaper ownership since chains began devouring independent papers more than a generation ago, big-city businessmen with deep pockets are flocking to the industry, lured by small papers with generous margins. These new owners are highly leveraged and itching to make money. Indeed, often built into their financial arrangements are "exit strategies" that force the companies either to sell or go public, generally within five to seven years.

Often the new owners retain the local publishers. Some, like Community Newspaper Holdings, also keep their companies' names off the masthead. As a result, small-town readers may be only dimly aware that the rampant "chain-store" phenomenon has claimed yet another local enterprise—their newspaper.

As these first-time owners trade places with profit-taking sellers wise to the vagaries of newspaper publishing, the road ahead is unmarked and filled with potential hazards. Consider some of the realities of today's newspaper world order:

- Since 1994, about 40 percent of all the nation's daily newspapers have been sold at least once. Small papers accounted for 70 percent of the total.
- Two of the top three newspaper companies in the country, ranked by the number of dailies they own, didn't even exist until a few years ago. Community Newspaper Holdings, which debuted in 1997, topped the list in 2000 with 112 daily papers. Third-ranked was Liberty Group Publishing, which popped up in early 1998 by purchasing 55 dailies from Hollinger. By 2000 it had expanded to 68 dailies plus 252 weeklies and shoppers. Another new player is Paxton Media, which in six years grew from one small Kentucky daily, the Paducah Sun, to a chain of 26 papers in nine states.
- With prices for many small papers at record highs, media empires

like Hollinger, Thomson, and Donrey, which once appeared likely to gobble up every newspaper in the country, are instead eagerly shedding properties. Thomson no longer owns any newspapers in the United States.

- The frenzy of buying and selling has produced a new breed of "financial owner" for whom small newspapers are just another business. Community Newspaper Holdings, or CNHI, is bankrolled by a pension fund. Liberty is owned by a Los Angeles leveraged buyout company. Journal Register Co., with twenty-four dailies and two hundred nondailies, is publicly held, but a Wall Street investment firm owns three-quarters of the stock.

- These new companies typically start out deeply in debt, with rigorous payment schedules based on expectations of steady profits. In the event of an economic downturn, these debt-laden companies have few options beyond cutting costs—which in some cases they've already done with a vengeance.

- When a paper is destined for the block, as is so often the case these days, an owner is more likely to trim costs and less likely to add new equipment or employees.

- The new owners tend to be highly acquisitive. Because the bulk sales from old to new chains typically have involved a large number of leanly run "mature papers" in no- to slow-growth communities, the only way the new owners can increase revenue is to find fresh properties and cut costs.

- As buyers look for papers that can be clustered around a single printing plant, community weeklies have become as important to the equation as dailies. For instance, Boston-based Community Newpaper Co., owned by Fidelity Capital, has just one daily paper, but eighty-eight weeklies and fourteen shoppers.

Perhaps, as some executives suggest, the economies of chain ownership have saved the occasional fragile paper from an almost certain demise. But it is not enough that little papers merely survive. The broader concern is that they continue as institutions that are crucial to a sense of community.

In St. Marys, Pennsylvania (pop. 14,000), in rural Elk County, former mayor Ann Grosser says the *Daily Press* has not covered a sensitive rift in the police department. But she reads it anyway. "It holds the community together," she tells me over coffee one frosty winter morning at the Bavarian Inn, whose name evokes the area's German heritage. "If we had a big newspaper that covered a large area, it wouldn't have the closeness."

The *Daily Press,* circulation five thousand, was sold to Liberty in 1997.

If this buying spree has surprised a lot of newspaper people, perhaps it shouldn't have. The desirability of these properties is no mystery. From 1994 to 1997, when Hollinger owned the papers that now belong to Liberty, their already high margins increased from 27.2 percent to 30.6 percent. "For every dollar of sales, your profit is 15 to 30 cents to the bottom line of real cash," says Kenneth J. Hanau of Weiss, Peck & Greer's Private Equity Group, which has bankrolled Texas-based Lionheart Newspapers. "They can go as high as 40 percent for good strong dailies. Even on the low end of 15, those are very attractive margins compared to most industries you'll see. A lot of manufacturing sectors or distributions are battling it out for single digits."

Unlike large metros that must compete for news and advertising with suburban dailies, radio and television stations, direct mail, and now the Internet, many smaller papers are genuine monopolies. "Our average newspaper is over 100 years old," says Peter J. Nolan of Leonard Green & Partners, which owns Liberty. "And there's a reason for that. . . . It's really unlikely somebody's going to operate a competing daily to a paper that's been around since the 1800s." When it comes to advertising dollars, he says, most of their papers are in communities that don't have TV stations. "We ask these guys who's your competition, and they say matchbook covers."

Because they have fewer pages than metros, small-town newspapers require far less newsprint per copy. Unions are rare, labor is cheap. It is not uncommon to find reporters earning as little as $7 an hour. (The federal minimum wage in 2000 was $5.15.) And most new owners group their properties into money-saving clusters.

Moreover, unlike big papers that are vulnerable to economic cycles, little papers have a more stable base. Their advertisers have nowhere else to turn, and "even in bad times, people can afford 50 cents for a newspaper," says Kevin Murphy of SunTrust Equitable Securities Corp., a Nashville investment bank. "And they're very hard to supplant. Someone just can't throw up a newspaper next door to you. People get in habits. The paper could be terrible but people still get it."

So why would the big chains part with such highly profitable properties? In a word, money. With so many companies competing to buy small papers, "prices are at an all-time high right now," says Liberty's CEO, Kenneth L. Serota. According to a 1998 study by the newspaper brokerage firm Dirks, Van Essen & Associates, the average price of a community daily in a stand-alone market rose to 3.6 times annual revenues, up from 3.41 in 1997 and well above a 2.03 nadir in 1992.

"There's a size below which it requires very intense management to build profitability, and when it gets profitable it doesn't add up to much," explained an executive at another major newspaper company. He spoke on background, lest his company's smaller papers jump to the conclusion they were for sale. "A paper of 10,000 circulation might produce $4 or $5 million in revenue. One third [profit] would be $1.5 million. For a company like Gannett, how many $1.5 million things have to add up to what a larger paper makes, especially when you have all the accounting and other kinds of overhead? Also, big companies tend to pay more benefits. It can add up to a significant amount of money."

When Gannett owned the twelve-thousand-circulation *Saratogian* in Saratoga Springs, New York, says former publisher Monte Trammer, "we were . . . I hesitate to say 'ignored.' But the general attitude was, 'You're out there in Saratoga, try not to bother us.' When you're this size in Gannett, you understand there's a big company out there and it's not about you." The paper was sold in 1998 to the smaller Journal Register Co., and Trammer says it was suddenly a different story. CEO Robert Jelenic called frequently, and Trammer says he could always get him on the phone if he needed him. "You learn very quickly that you matter."

It is not unusual these days for a good property to attract four or five bidders, says broker Owen Van Essen. When owner Wayne T. Patrick put the *Palestine Herald-Press* on the block, he quietly contacted ten companies, says publisher Larry Mayo. Although Palestine, Texas, was a boom-or-bust oil town in the middle of a bust phase, the paper there was nonetheless highly desirable. The nearest big paper was in Tyler, fifty miles away, and radio and TV offered negligible competition. It's said of papers like these that they "own their territory." Patrick received six bids.

I T WOULD BE TEMPTING but wrong to lament the passing of an era when local proprietors put out spirited, independent dailies and the dawn of another when financial owners publish homogenized products that squeeze costs. Some of the most miserable little papers in the country are published by independents. Moreover, most sales these days are from one chain to another, most of which are respected more for their profit margins than their journalism.

Besides, what newspaper company hasn't been swept up in the race to increase profits? In cutting 25 employees at the *Times Herald* in Norristown, Pennsylvania, or 33 at the *Bristol Press* in Connecticut, the Journal Register Co. was scarcely more ruthless than Dean Singleton when his MediaNews Group acquired the *Press-Telegram* in Long Beach, California, and lopped 120 employees off the payroll, or Tony Ridder, CEO of the Knight Ridder chain, whose takeover farther north in Monterey cost 28 workers their jobs, or John Curley, on whose watch 55 editorial positions at the *Asbury Park Press* were abolished after Gannett bought that New Jersey daily. Still, JRC's cuts have hardly been limited to layoffs of low-level employees. And numerous Journal Register managers who have quit or been fired say that CEO Jelenic's relentless push for profits has infected the company with a callousness that goes beyond the norm.

These new ownership trends raise troubling questions. Newspapers have long been looked to as hometown boosters. Is that role in jeopardy? Before the Journal Register bought the *Norristown Times Herald* in 1993, "the publisher was active in every facet of the community," says Payson W. Burt, executive vice president of the Montgomery County Chamber of Commerce. No more, he says. The paper still sponsors the area's spelling bee, "but it's not high on [its] priority list. It doesn't contribute to the bottom line."

Unschooled in First Amendment values, will the new owners pay more than lip service to the historic watchdog role of the press? State newspaper associations have seen participation dwindle as busy corporate executives stick to their own problems. "The decision is a financial one," says Tim Williams, executive director of the Pennsylvania Newspaper Association. "They're not compensated on the basis of support" for journalistic causes. Attendance at PNA meetings is down, Williams says, and so is help with efforts to strengthen state access laws to government information. "Our laws haven't been changed since the late '50s. They don't include computer or digital information." But with fewer and fewer people to lobby, he says, "it hurts." (Yet the big chains do find time to lobby Washington for looser regulation of monopolistic practices in the corporate media.)

And what of the possibilities for conflict of interest, when papers are backed by widely diversified financial corporations? Stephens Group, which acquired the Donrey chain in 1993, is run by the powerful and politically connected Stephens family of Little Rock, Arkansas. It is the parent of Stephens Inc., a large investment firm. It is also the largest stockholder in Alltel Corp., the Little Rock telecommunications giant. Founder and chairman Jackson T. Stephens, No. 138 on the 1998 Forbes magazine list of richest Americans, recently donated $5 million to a youth golfing program. Less wholesome is his longtime association with Indonesian mogul Mochtar Riady, whose Lippo Group made headlines in 1996 for its attempts to win influence with the Clinton administration. Lippo's man in

Washington, John Huang, camped out in Stephens's Washington office during that period. Jackson Stephens's son Warren is the CEO of Stephens Inc. and turns up with wife Harriet on lists of Republican campaign contributors. Another son, Jackson T. Stephens Jr., founded a conservative think tank.

Although Stephens has recently sold many of its newspaper properties, it elected to keep four Arkansas papers, including one in Fort Smith, where the company markets the city's municipal bonds. Stephens Production Co., which engages in oil and gas exploration and drilling, also is headquartered there, and has wells within the city limits.

Are these the people you want to be your community watchdog?

The fact is that many hometown papers belong now to companies whose executives can't remember all their names. And as for the weeklies they own, forget about it.

So how will these new, nontraditional owners acquit themselves? Will they behave like real estate speculators, buying properties, milking them for profits, and then auctioning them off? Or will they demonstrate a lasting stability and commitment? Frankly, it's too soon to know.

But as to how they practice journalism on a daily basis, it is not too early to look at the three biggest companies, the deals they have struck, and the papers they publish. After a decade of newspaper ownership, Journal Register, whose major stockholder is the New York investment firm Warburg, Pincus & Co., has had a cash flow margin of over 34 percent in recent years, far above the industry average. Liberty has the tiniest papers in the country and boasts some of the highest margins. And CNHI claims to be a different breed, more focused on building revenues than cutting costs, owing in part to its financial backing from Retirement Systems of Alabama.

But before I scheduled my first interview with those companies, I needed to know how Will Jarrett got rich.

EARLY INTO MY RESEARCH on today's new breed of owners, I came across a *Business Week* article that described the 1997 sale of a small Texas newspaper company called Westward Communications. One of the founders, Will D. Jarrett, was said to have walked away from the deal "with millions."

As it happened, Jarrett had been one of my editors at the *Philadelphia Inquirer* more than two decades ago. He was one of Knight Ridder's bright young executives, but scarcely what you'd call the entrepreneurial type. I also remembered him as friendly and cheerful. These days he is just as friendly, certainly cheerful—and wearing a golf course tan.

Jarrett, it turns out, was a pioneer of sorts in a new mode of buying and selling rural dailies and weeklies. Over lunch at the Regency Hyatt in the Dallas-Fort Worth International Airport, he tells me how he did it.

In 1985 the native Texan was at the top of his profession as executive editor of the *Dallas Times Herald.* But at heart Jarrett wanted something more—newspaper equity of his own. So that year, on his fiftieth birthday, he resigned. Teaming up with another former *Times Herald* editor, Ken Johnson, Jarrett formed Westward Communications. Johnson, who also had been an assistant general manager at the *Washington Post,* knew something about finance. Together the pair developed what they called their "Wal-Mart strategy." Sam Walton "saw a lot of money in small towns," Jarrett explains. "And luckily for us, we saw the same thing."

Jarrett and Johnson looked for markets where an owner whose newspaper had a printing press might be willing to sell out and retire. Then they would buy surrounding weeklies that had no presses and print them all at the central plant—a "hub-and-spoke" approach. Printing and accounting costs could be centralized. Margins could always be improved in other ways at papers that had been privately held. Sometimes there were surplus family members on the payroll. Hometown proprietors were often reluctant to raise ad rates to their friends in the business community or risk flak from readers over higher subscription prices. Later, according to Jarrett, when he and Johnson executed their plan, "We were pretty insistent on raising circulation and advertising rates."

It was the mid-'80s, and there was then, as there is now, "a lot of money in America looking for managers, and a lot of managers like myself looking for money." Jarrett and Johnson approached five venture capital companies, and "four said they would do the deal." Playing them against one another, Jarrett says, they were able to negotiate favorable terms with MVenture, a division of MBank of Dallas, which with a smaller venture group put up an initial $2 million for 49 percent of the new newspaper company. The two former editors retained a controlling interest of 51 percent—which I would later learn was an unusually generous arrangement, in light of more recent deals. "My feeling is if you're a journalist or an editor," Jarrett says, "you want to have control over your company, not the financial people."

The two newspapermen each put in $50,000. With the MVenture cash for equity, they borrowed an additional $5 million from a Rhode Island bank to make acquisitions. It is typical, Jarrett says, to have "two layers of debt—a layer put in by equity folks. You take that layer of debt and then you leverage it. You go to the bank and say, 'I've been given a down pay-ment by these equity players, and they're willing to put this all at risk if you lend the company money.'" In this fashion, Westward eventually took out an additional $20 million in bank loans.

Money in hand, the pair bought two Texas dailies, in Pasadena and Conroe, plus five semiweeklies and forty-three weeklies. The venture capi-talists had two people on the five-member board to watch over their investment. Each year, Jarrett told me, there are "formulas with cash flows and multiples, and you have to keep hitting the marks."

As Westward realized cash gains, it paid down the bank loans. Jarrett and Johnson collected salaries and bonuses. But neither they nor their equity partners profited personally until the business was sold in 1997. That Westward would change hands in just a few years came as no surprise to anyone, except perhaps some employees. The money that equity part-ners invest comes from individuals and institutions who have placed it in a fund with a targeted life span. At the end of that period they expect returns. How a partnership is terminated is known as the "exit strategy," and it generally takes place within five to seven years. Often in these equity deals, the partners plan to resell the properties. But they may also take the company public or refinance the deal. So these venture capitalists gamble that the value of their company will increase more each year.

In the case of Westward they were right. The company was sold to Banc One Capital Partners of Columbus, Ohio, for more than $80 million, according to estimates at the time. (Jarrett wouldn't divulge the price.) Most of the debts had been paid off by then, Jarrett says, and the two for-mer editors had increased their share to 64 percent.

"It's pretty much like a house," Jarrett says. "No matter what you pay, if you're making payments on it every month for 10 years, you can turn around and sell it for more than you paid. The difference is that for the same 10 years, a paper is making money and paying down debt."

Later I do the calculations. It looks to me like Jarrett and Johnson—and the equity partners—walked away with somewhere between $20 million and $25 million apiece. Money beyond an editor's wildest dreams. I call Jarrett. Can this be true? He doesn't confirm it and he doesn't deny it; he just chuckles. "You didn't hear it from me," he says.

I N A TWENTY-TWO-STORY white tower on the west side of Los Angeles, the view is of a pastel cityscape spread over hills and, beyond it, a plain of water, the Pacific Ocean. Off to the north are the boxy white hilltop buildings that comprise the new and much-acclaimed J. Paul Getty Museum. The offices in this suite are carpeted with Orientals and the walls hung with artwork from the collection of Leonard Green, the man *Business Week* has dubbed "The Bottom-Fisher King of Retail." Coming from *Business Week,* this is a compliment. Said the magazine in 1997, "On the heels of a pair of shrewdly crafted leveraged buyouts of chains for home improvement and sporting goods, the courtly sixty-four-year-old Green has emerged as the nation's leading retail buyout specialist."

Green, the article said, has made a fortune buying troubled enterprises such as the Thrifty drugstore chain and Kmart's Payless, turning them around, then selling them or taking them public at a tremendous profit. Reporter Margaret Webb Pressler in the *Washington Post* described Green as a "friendly takeover artist who eschewed the buy-it-and-break-it-up strategy that was so popular" in the 1980s. In addition to being an avid art collector, he is an animal-rights advocate and has contributed hundreds of thousands of dollars to an organization that supports minority college students.

A Rhode Island newspaper offered a less benign view of Green in 1994 on the eve of the collapse of the homegrown Almac supermarket chain. Quoted in the *Providence Journal-Bulletin,* officials of unions representing hundreds of out-of-work supermarket employees blamed two successive LBOs—Green's in 1991 was the second—for depleting Almac's coffers. Sniffing blood, rival chains moved in with superstores. Green's representatives said they had underestimated the threat of competition.

Perhaps it was foreordained that Green, the son of a dress salesman, would end up in retail. But now he has a new company and a new role: Leonard Green, newspaper publisher.

On January 27, 1998, Leonard Green & Partners consummated a $310 million deal with Hollinger that created an instant newspaper company, Liberty Group Publishing. Based in the Chicago suburb of Northbrook, Liberty now owns 68 dailies with a total circulation of 275,000, and another 252 paid and free nondaily publications.

The deal that catapulted Leonard Green into the newspaper business was a quietly executed transaction that began with a few well-placed words. "There was not a for-sale sign in front of these properties," Jerry Strader, head of Hollinger's community newspaper group, told *Editor & Publisher* at the time. As it happened, Peter Nolan, one of five Green partners who troll for investments, learned from an associate at the investment banking firm where he used to work, Donaldson, Lufkin & Jenrette, that one of its clients, Hollinger, was interested in selling a large number of its small papers. Would Green be interested in buying?

"We said, 'Yes, we were,'" says Nolan, who is tall and blond, with blue eyes and a patrician profile. It is casual Friday here in L.A. and he is tieless in a blue V-neck sweater and khaki pants. On the wall facing him is a large gold-framed oil of the storm-roiled Pacific coast, a painting he chose from the boss's collection.

The Green partners invested $60 million; additional funds were raised from junk bonds and bank loans. Green ended up with 90 percent of the company. The remaining 10 percent is divided among senior management. But the ultimate owners could be said to be Green's clients—big banks like First Boston and Citibank, public pension funds in California, Michigan, Pennsylvania. If all goes according to plan, the company will go public after five years, and Leonard Green can sell its stock and recoup its investment—and then some. On Wall Street, that time span is a millennium. "We're long-term, patient investors," Nolan says. They do not involve themselves in the business, he adds. "We're not operators. We don't know how to run anything."

For that, Leonard Green looks to Ken Serota, the $375,000-a-year CEO of Liberty, who had been Hollinger's vice president for law and finance. It turns out Serota doesn't run the papers either. "I'm not an old and grizzled newspaper guy," the thirty-seven-year-old Serota says, almost apologetically. "I'm a CPA and a lawyer. I let my newspaper guys run my newspapers. They hold the thing together."

Publishers like the indefatigable Bill Anderson at the *Punxsutawney Spirit* in western Pennsylvania are what attracted Leonard Green to these papers. Anderson is a lanky, animated man of forty-nine. Seven years ago there was a rare opening in Punxsutawney's elite, fifteen-member "Inner Circle," which runs the famed Groundhog Day festivities, and Anderson, a hometown booster, was invited to join. Every member had a name; his was "Groundhog Scribe."

Like most small-town publishers, Anderson wore a second hat: He was also the *Spirit*'s advertising manager. On the paper's 125th anniversary, he put out a 144-page special edition, filled with historic front pages and $35,000 in ads. He published a lively Groundhog Day history, researching and laying it out himself, that sold even more ads—$65,000 worth. Every month the company printed forty-five thousand ad-filled placemats. He was proud that the circulation numbers had scarcely budged since he went to work there, despite a 15 percent decline in the local population since 1980. In 1995, Hollinger named him Publisher of the Year.

But Punxsutawney sits amid played-out coal mines, its downtown bubble punctured by Wal-Mart and its industrial base so lean that the school district is the largest employer with three hundred people. Meeting Liberty's monthly revenue targets could be a strain in a town this poor. Every day, Anderson said, he had to generate $4,480 simply to pay the bills. "Sometimes it's scary just to open the front door." He added, "We can't go out and sell an ad for $25 an inch like they do in Philadelphia or Pittsburgh. I sell it for $5 an inch and it's a struggle to get it." When he decided in 1999 to raise the price of the paper from 35 cents, he didn't dare add more than a nickel.

Anderson changed page one to a lively, all-local format. What he called "the front-page news"—world and national events—was moved inside. Not for Anderson the plaint I heard from another publisher, that "sometimes in small towns there isn't any local news." On the day I was in Punxsutawney, page-one headlines announced a fatal car crash, a gas line explosion, the closure of a beloved family-run deli, a fund-raising campaign for homeless families, the first 1999 baby born at Punxsutawney Hospital, and the exotic travels of a toy koala bear. Said Anderson, "Without local news there wouldn't be any difference between the *Punxsutawney Spirit* and *USA Today*."

That's a stretch. The *Spirit* was short on graphics and, except for its flag, as gray as granite. Color costs money. "We save color for special occasions," Anderson said. Reporters punched a clock along with everybody else in the building. They were forbidden to work overtime. They took their own pictures and drove their own cars, for which the reimbursement was a meager eighteen cents a mile. A stream of memos from the boss exhorted the editorial staff of eight to show more initiative, work harder, and make fewer mistakes. Anderson demanded two stories a day—although "it's okay to do a story and a photo." He smiled and said with sincerity, "What a great little job." Because so much of the *Spirit*'s daily grist was meeting coverage, most reporters worked 3 P.M. to midnight. If something newsworthy happened during the day, Anderson himself would pitch in. "If there would be a major fire in town," he said, "[you're] looking at the guy who would take the picture right now."

During the post-Watergate era, when reporting was a hot profession, resumés used to land on his desk routinely. Now, though, when Anderson advertised a job opening in the *Spirit* and two nearby papers every day for three weeks, he got one response. The starting pay, Anderson said, was $300 a week, or $7.50 an hour. Two reporters I talked to later confided that they made less. Asked to explain, Anderson pleaded "extenuating circumstances" having to do with the reporters' experience and job duties.

January of 1999 was a difficult month for Anderson. His editor had resigned and so Anderson was wearing a third hat. Asked to edit each other's copy, the reporters were grumbling. And even though he was saving the editor's salary, Anderson told at least one staffer that he was $25,000 below Liberty's expectations for the month. He told others the stress was getting to him.

What happens, I asked, when you don't make budget? Anderson answered, "You work harder."

But in the world of small-town journalism, nothing lasts forever. A few months after my visit, Liberty sold the *Punxsutawney Spirit* to CNHI. Suddenly, the paper had a new set of absentee bosses demanding that people do more with less. Anderson left the paper to publish a monthly advertising magazine.

A newsroom staff member who also left explained why. "Too many problems. They wanted me to work 55–60 hours a week for $20,000 a year."

IN SPITE OF EVERYTHING, you have to love little papers like these for all the blood and sweat that goes into them, and for all their idiosyncrasies. Perhaps only at a five-thousand-circulation paper like the *Daily Press* in St. Marys, Pennsylvania, could Dick Dornisch, sixty-nine, a retired supermarket manager and liberal activist, find employment as a combination reporter, reviewer, historian, and cartoonist. How many young J-school grads could evoke a hunting camp this way, as Dornisch did in the *Daily Press*: "A combination of sour, uncured hemlock, old coffee grounds, kerosene lamps, musty rooms and dusty bedding, woodsmoke . . . all camps have a smell and the smell is unmistakable."

But ambitious J-school grads are rare in Dornisch's neck of the woods. The *Daily Press,* clustered with two other Liberty dailies, dutifully covers the local meetings, but not much else appears to happen, at least outside hunting season. Page one is often laden with wire copy. Though roughly the same size as the *Punxsutawney Spirit,* the *Daily Press* has three fewer editorial employees—and it shows.

At the nearby *Ridgway Record,* with a circulation of just 3,100 and an editorial crew of four, everybody types obits, covers night meetings, lays out pages, and takes photographs of accidents. "There are no prima donnas," says editor Bekki Guilyard, thirty-eight, who is small with flowing brown hair that reaches to her hips. "This is like a little machine. Everyone has their part in keeping it running."

After putting the afternoon paper to bed at 10:30 one morning, Guilyard dispatches her newest reporter, twenty-five-year-old Jon R. Serianni, to the town's handsome old brick courthouse. In the clerk's office, he peers nearsightedly at a wall calendar where upcoming trials are noted by hand. He's trying to decipher the code. "What's the difference between blue ink and black ink?" he asks one of the three women now eating lunch at their desks. She nods toward another woman. "It's whatever pen she picked up."

Back at the paper, Guilyard recognizes one of the cases. It will be the county's first trial in a Megan's Law case—one involving a sexually violent predator. She immediately phones a local psychologist who is an expert on sex offenders. "How many times do I have to call you before you call me back?" she asks, in a plaint heard in newsrooms the world over.

She tells her sports reporter, Todd Hughes, twenty-nine, who has been dragging his feet on a tip about a new golf course, "I don't want to open the *Bradford Era* and find a big story on a golf course that's going to go into Bridgeton Township. Capiche?"

Guilyard, who has a degree in environmental science, struggles daily to turn out a professional paper. "The community here deserves good, thorough news coverage as much as they do in Pittsburgh or Baltimore or anywhere," she says. If a wedding story contains a mistake, she'll correct it and run it again. "People cut those things out and save them."

Things were a little easier for the *Record* staff before the court reporter left a few months ago. The publisher, Joseph C. Piccirillo, has been putting off the hire because a major advertiser, the chain that owns some of the local supermarkets, is teetering on the edge of bankruptcy. No advertising dollars, no courthouse reporter. Other than that, it's been business as usual since Liberty bought out Hollinger. Liberty's CEO, Ken Serota, did tour the paper. "He talked to Todd about sports," Guilyard says. And of course, Piccirillo handed out those nifty T-shirts, the ones with the red, white, and blue Liberty logo, just before Christmas.

I N MID-1990, when the United States had just toppled one dictator in Panama and was about to take on another in Iraq, a seven-month-old tabloid crashed and burned in the heartland. The splashy *St. Louis Sun* had been a misguided mission from the start. Estimated to have lost nearly $30 million, the *Sun* foundered, at least in part, because of an almost comical miscalculation—that a paper could build circulation on heavy street sales in a suburban area with no mass transit. But the owner, Ralph Ingersoll II, made an even greater mistake when he spent the last half of the 1980s acquiring newspaper after newspaper in deals financed with $500 million in junk bonds marketed by his close friend Michael Milken.

By early 1990, amid an industrywide downturn in advertising revenues, Ingersoll had sold ten dailies to raise cash, but it was too late to avoid bankruptcy. The collapse of the *Sun* was followed by the total destruction of the newspaper kingdom Ingersoll had built on a foundation laid by his father, a legendary New York journalist. Ingersoll's silent partner, the investment firm of Warburg, Pincus, stepped in to salvage what it could of its $200 million equity investment. Ingersoll was allowed to keep newspapers he had acquired in Ireland and England during his buying spree but had to surrender all properties in the United States.

Though newspaper prices had plummeted in those recessionary years, many people expected Warburg, Pincus to sell the U.S. properties and take the losses rather than try to run a business it knew little about. Instead, the firm decided to stay in the game. The big losers were the original investors, who had to settle for just over half the value of their bonds. Warburg, Pincus then built a new corporation—the Journal Register Co., or JRC—from the rubble of Ingersoll's kingdom.

Today JRC is run with an iron hand by the man Warburg, Pincus chose in 1990 to nurse its newspaper investments back to health, Robert M. Jelenic, the former president of Ingersoll Publications. The son of a Canadian nickel miner and a former controller of the *Toronto Sun*, Jelenic, forty-eight, has pushed company profits to new highs in the industry, while earning a reputation for ruthlessness and fits of temper.

Under Jelenic's leadership, Journal Register went public in 1997. Three-quarters of its stock is held by Warburg, Pincus. Headquartered in Trenton, New Jersey, the company owns twenty-four dailies, concentrated chiefly in New England, Pennsylvania, and Ohio, with a combined circulation of 613,231, plus about two hundred nondailies. Along the way, Journal Register has accumulated a hefty debt to banks that loaned money for bondholder settlements and acquisitions. The 1998 year-end debt of $765 million, more than the book value of the company, raises eyebrows in an industry where debt ratios usually are held to around 40 percent. "They're probably the only company I know that has a higher debt ratio than I do," says Ralph Martin of CNHI, "and I'm totally leveraged."

"They owe a lot of money," says newspaper analyst John Morton. In 1997, the company's cash flow totaled $133 million, which was more than sufficient to meet combined interest and principal payments of $99 million. In 1998, the company refinanced its long-term debt so that no principal payments would be due until 2000. In the years after that, however, the payments escalate. And there is always the danger that the economy will go into a tailspin. "It's pressure," Morton says. "Obviously they have to keep an eye cocked on the cash flow."

That's Jelenic's job. And so far, say his Wall Street handlers, he's done it extremely well. Even though circulation declines at JRC papers are much higher than the national average, and the company's recent share prices have been below the $14 initial public offering, JRC has led the industry in cash flow margins—37.1 percent in 1997, 34.4 percent in 1998, and 34.2 percent in 1999. "Unlike many newspaper executives, [Jelenic] has a very good financial eye," says Warburg's managing director, Gary Nusbaum, who joined the JRC board in 1999. He stressed that Warburg's decision to "reinvest behind Bob Jelenic" was a mark of confidence. Jelenic has been well rewarded. Normally his compensation is just over $1 million per year, but in 1997 he topped *Advertising Age*'s list of newspaper executive salaries—$11.3 million in salary and bonus, about half of which was in stock.

"Bob is very much a visionary," says Trish Dresser, JRC's former marketing vice president, who left the company in 1997 for personal reasons. "When he believes in something, he is very driven. You're not working for somebody who's wishy-washy. You always know where you stand. If you're a type-A person who's driven also, it kicks open doors for you to be the best you can be."

Managers agree that Jelenic has imposed discipline on sometimes unruly newspaper operations, but his narrow focus on the bottom line has also produced a huge cadre of employee opt-outs and exiles.

Shortly after taking over the company, Jelenic ousted *New Haven Register* publisher Tom Geyer, a respected figure in the industry. Geyer had cut twenty people from the payroll, including eleven newsroom staffers, and refused to lay off more. Jelenic flew to New Haven on the company plane and Geyer met him at the airport. "We had some sort of 'or-else' conversation," Geyer recalls. "I turned to him, I said, 'Are you firing me?' He said I had to go."

After Geyer left, says Gerald Ryerson, who quit his job as chief financial officer at the *Register* in 1992, "it was an extremely hostile environment. If you did a forecast and the answer wasn't what top management—meaning Bob—wanted. . . . You know the story about 'Don't shoot the messenger'? The messenger would get shot."

In addition to minding the books, Ryerson says he had to monitor the amount of film the photographers used, check odometer readings in employees' cars against expense accounts, and lock up the supply cabinet "because people would be stealing tape to take home for Christmas presents."

Kathy Morris, controller at the *Times Herald* in Norristown, Pennsylvania, from 1993 to 1996, recalls the time Jelenic demanded a monthly bottom-line figure by 8:30 P.M. on a Friday night—two days early. She knew the paper's new computer system and a decrepit printer would cause delays, so she left the building before Jelenic could call. "I was afraid to talk to him because I wouldn't have what he wanted. You don't tell Bob no." She received a letter of reprimand, and a recent raise was rescinded. Now chief financial officer at a paper in South Carolina, Morris still believes the Journal Register is "smart—they know how to monitor the newspaper business." But she gives them low marks as an employer. For much of her three years at the Norristown paper, she says she filled two jobs, as comptroller and human resources administrator. "In every instance it was done to save money."

Jules Molenda, publisher of MediaNews' *Bennington Banner* in Vermont, calls the eighteen months he spent at the JRC-owned *Times* in Pawtucket, Rhode Island, in 1994 and 1995 "the single most unpleasant time in a very long career." He has been in newspaper management thirty years and worked for nine companies, he says. "I can live with cautious people looking to cut fat, but not bone and muscle. That's what JRC does."

As we talk, Molenda volunteers that Jelenic fired him—another airport transaction—because a circulation audit disallowed 40 percent of a two-thousand-copy increase. Even so, his specific complaints are consistent with those I would hear from many other JRC veterans. For instance, Molenda tells me about Jelenic and "the flash." The flash is a weekly financial report JRC requires from its publishers. In Molenda's day, it was due at noon Friday. If you had a "bad flash," Molenda says, "at two o'clock you'd get the call." Several times, an angry Jelenic ordered him to fire someone—anyone—now. "'I want somebody out of the newsroom at five o'clock. No severance. I want him out. I want his name.'"

When JRC purchased Rhode Island's *Narragansett Times* and several other weeklies from Capital Cities, the publisher, Frederick J. Wilson, whose family had once owned the *Times,* stayed only five months. "They don't care about the product. They don't care about the customer. They don't care about the employees," Wilson says. "And they don't know anything about the business." He has since launched two weeklies, with money from local backers, that directly compete with JRC papers.

After Wilson was gone, says *Times* former editor Betty J. Cotter, the new publisher broke a longstanding ban against advertising on page one. Soon a shoe ad appeared in one of three top-of-the-page tease boxes. "So instead of having three tease boxes, we had two tease boxes and a shoe." Cotter stuck it out a little longer. Cap Cities had cut her staff in half to fatten the bottom line prior to the sale, she says, and JRC was slow to hire replacements. As in New Haven, she says, the operations manager was ordered to check the odometer readings in reporters' cars. "When you're paying people so little—we paid $17,000—and then you sneak around like that, it makes people feel like dirt." After she rousted her staff on a weekend to cover a major coastal oil spill, she learned their overtime vouchers exceeded the publisher's estimate to Jelenic. Cotter was forced to tell people to reduce their hours. "It was humiliating to me, it was a slap on the face to them. When I called them on a Saturday, they were on it. They dropped everything and did it, because that's what we do. JRC saved 50 bucks by doing that but they pissed people off so bad that everybody in that room eventually left." Including Cotter. She now works for Wilson.

On acquiring new properties, JRC typically whacks payrolls and merges operations with other papers, to form a money-saving cluster. At the same time, it overhauls the format to fit the corporate model. With the exception of two tabloids, the JRC dailies look quite similar, with four sections, a minimum of twenty-two pages and colorful if uninspired graphics. The company shrinks the width of the paper, switches evening papers to mornings, banishes national and world news to inside pages, puts local news out front, launches a Sunday edition, if none exists, and emphasizes sports coverage. Business sections get three pages of stock tables; sports sections get columns of agate box scores. Presses are often upgraded to improve color capacity. The chain likes color and spends $7,000 a year at each paper on a multi-hued daily weather map. "It's their mantra," says a former editor. "All local, all color. All local, all color." Even so, in some papers the color looks washed out and fuzzy.

At the *Saratogian* in prosperous Saratoga Springs, the new JRC format was all for the better, says former publisher Monte Trammer, who left to head up the Gannett-owned *Star-Gazette* in Elmira, New York. The newshole, he says, increased 35 percent. Six pressmen lost their jobs when printing shifted to Troy, New York, but two editorial positions were added. No one seemed to notice that JRC had trimmed the paper to a narrower width, Trammer says, but the increased page count drew compliments.

Under Gannett, says *Saratogian* editor Barbara Lombardo, "There was a lot of talk about Web pages, who would have them. And then we never got it because it required an investment. Journal Register said it on Friday—'You'll have it on Monday.'" And they did. The paper lost the

Gannett News Service but gained Knight Ridder's, which she says "has opened up a whole new world," particularly in its business coverage. On the other hand, she misses the state government news from Gannett's three-person Albany bureau and the New York copy out of Gannett's Washington bureau.

The *Saratogian* is one of three papers I visit in January of 1999 with Diane B. Pardee, then JRC's vice president for public relations. (Pardee would resign several months later to pursue an M.B.A.) My request to go without a chaperon was turned down as "not company policy." On the whole, Lombardo says of JRC ownership, "It's been okay." She adds, "I would say that even if Diane wasn't sitting here."

In central Connecticut, where Journal Register owns three papers, circulation declines suggest that readers aren't happy. From 1995 to 1999, the *Herald* in New Britain fell from 31,344 to 21,172 (a 32 percent drop); the *Bristol Press* from 20,036 to 14,505 (a 28 percent drop), and the *Middletown Press* from 13,019 to 10,034 (a 23 percent drop).

The *Hartford Courant,* a Times Mirror paper, has "been a direct beneficiary" of JRC ownership, says Mark E. Aldam, the *Courant*'s vice president for sales, marketing, and operations. He says the *Courant* increased market share by 3 percent, or eleven thousand readers, at the expense of JRC's papers in New Britain, Bristol, and Middletown and is now the dominant newspaper in all but four ZIP Codes where those papers circulate. Meanwhile, preprint advertising volume in the *Courant* went up 19 percent over a four-year period. Journal Register's "mission is cash-flow generation," Aldam says. "Over time that priority will cost you market share. The reader is making a judgment based on content. They vote with their pocketbook and the advertisers follow."

At the *New Haven Register,* JRC's flagship paper and another that I visit with Diane Pardee, the editor, Jack Kramer has no ready answer to a question about recent stories that made him proud. An investigative piece, perhaps? "We don't look for scandal," he says. He mentions stories on the city's questionable disbursement of HUD funds, an issue also covered by an alternative weekly, the *New Haven Advocate.* (*Advocate* managing editor Carole Bass says the first accounts of mismanagement actually were produced by a New Haven television station. The *Advocate* some months later published a story about a suspicious loan to a mayor's aide, and then the *Register* jumped on the issue. All three continued their coverage, and there was a HUD investigation.)

In New Haven, the editor merely recommends stories for his front page; the publisher has the last word. Says Kramer, "We have two news meetings a day. At the conclusion of the second, I bring the news list to the publisher and we'll discuss [it]." He says, "I respect the boss."

In July of 1998, when JRC took over the *Mercury* in Pottstown, Pennsylvania, four managers lost their jobs immediately, including the publisher and two top editors. The managing editor was not replaced, and the number of reporters assigned to local beats has dwindled from six to three, say newsroom insiders. Crimes and crashes are now less likely to lead the paper, and the "Cheers and Jeers" column on the editorial page has a new name: "Roses and Thorns."

Subscriber Gayle Buckman, who is on the board of the Boyertown Area School District, says she is pleased to no longer encounter "a disgusting wreck on the front page with somebody's body parts sticking out." What she does miss, she says, is the interaction with reporters she knows and trusts, who understand local issues. "It took a while to learn the people and the ins and outs, the undercurrents. A lot of times it's what's not said that's important." She says she would be much less likely to confide in the stringers who cover meetings these days. They tend to "ask surface questions, and they miss stuff," Buckman says. "It comes from not knowing the players."

At the *Daily Freeman* in Kingston, New York, JRC added a Saturday paper without increasing staff, and it also cut back on its use of correspondents. Meetings of county legislatures, once a staple of the paper's coverage, now frequently go uncovered, as do other important local government stories. At its two Rhode Island papers, JRC reduced staff, closed bureaus, and dropped zoned editions that, in Pawtucket at least, had increased circulation, according to former publisher Molenda.

In the Woonsocket suburb of Franklin, the *Woonsocket Call* was once so beloved that the high school field house was named after one of its reporters, says Scott Cole, a sports reporter who recently resigned. The paper has closed three bureaus, Franklin among them, despite strong competition in the area. Both Rhode Island papers have slipped badly in circulation since JRC took over. The *Call* plummeted from 28,774 in 1990 to 16,199 in 1999. The *Pawtucket Times* fell from 24,298 to 15,021.

In the fall of 1998, the *Call* was shaken by several events that suggested Journal Register had lost its grip. The Newspaper Guild successfully organized two small departments at the paper. The day after the second victory, in September, the paper's publisher, T. Paul Mahony, abruptly cleaned out his desk and left, later telling associates that Jelenic had fired him because of the union victories. Mahony had joined Ingersoll in 1989 and had held a number of positions within JRC. He was Woonsocket's third publisher to leave in less than three years. The same day that Mahony left, Jelenic flew in.

Guild official Tim Schick says that Scott Cole, the president of the union local, was called into the managing editor's office that afternoon and told that Jelenic had a statement and a question for him. The statement was, "If you want a war you've got a war"; the question was, "If you don't like the way things are run around here, why don't you just leave?"

In a separate incident that day, the Guild sent a congratulatory floral bouquet to its new members in circulation. A manager threw the flowers in a dumpster. When an employee fished them out and returned them to the building, they ended up in the dumpster again. The Guild alleged in charges filed with the National Labor Relations Board that both the Cole incident and the one with the flowers constitute unfair labor practices.

Cole did leave, as Jelenic had suggested, but he says it was because his job had changed. "I went from a person who used to cover college basketball, minor league baseball, some professional sports and a lot of high school to someone who doesn't get out of the office near as much, to becoming a glorified phone clerk and layout person."

WHILE JOURNAL REGISTER may have merely chipped away at some papers, the *Times Herald* in Norristown, a suburb of Philadelphia, got the ax. On JRC's first day at the helm, September 27, 1993—still known there as "takeover day"—the company fired twenty-five employees. Under family ownership the paper had weathered the lean years of the recession without layoffs, so the cuts shocked employees. "They lined us up in two lines like cattle," recalled Maureen Burk, an advertising sales representative. Each line led to a different set of strangers who would rule on their future. As the top salesperson in her department, Burk was "totally confident" she would keep her job. When she entered a conference room, she said, the new publisher smiled broadly, then told her, "We have no place for you." When she walked out, "people were crying and sobbing. One woman took her arm and swept everything off her desk." Burk, a union activist, filed charges with the NLRB and eventually won a settlement.

The layoffs triggered a one-day walkout by the Guild. Although members returned when the company agreed to recognize the union, a new contract took three years to negotiate. Under its terms a reporter with four years of experience earned $445 a week, $145 less than under the previous contract. In a moonlighting survey in 1998, the Guild found that three of its ad takers were working part time cleaning houses. Robert Carville, chairman of the Guild unit, worked at a convenience store on weekends.

After the takeover, said feature writer Valerie Newitt, her health insurance co-payments increased from $4 a week to $60 every two weeks. But when she developed cervical cancer and required chemotherapy, she realized that the bigger loss was her accrued sick leave of six months. Under JRC, she was only entitled to five days. "I have a biopsy, now I'm down to four days. I go to see the oncologist, now I'm down to three days." Under the company's disability plan, she went on half-pay for the maximum thirteen-week period, but then she had to go back to work for financial reasons. "I was not in great shape and I was bald, but what are you going to do? I stuck a wig on my head and I was back."

Newitt had written a popular weekly restaurant review. One day the new editor demanded to know, "Who pays for the meals?" When told the company picked up the check, he canceled the feature. Readers complained. "We logged over 100 calls," Newitt said. "That's a lot for a paper this size. But they fell on deaf ears." Elsewhere in the paper, the op-ed page was dropped and the number of comics was reduced. Once fifty or sixty pages thick, the *Times Herald* shrank to half its former size.

"We used to cover every meeting," said Newitt. "Before I went to work for the paper, a neighbor told me, 'If there's anything you want to know, you can find it in the *Times Herald.*'" Carville, the Guild leader and a copy editor, said coverage of planning or zoning meetings had been rare since JRC took over, and because space was tight, those municipal meetings that did get covered might get held for a day. "If we get a sensational crime story," he said, "God help the council story."

Norristown mayor Ted LeBlanc said he no longer subscribed to the paper. "I have nothing good to say about it," he said. The *Times Herald* has "ceased to be a Norristown newspaper." Accidents and crime stories, displayed prominently on page one even if they occur in distant townships, gave his city, he said, "an undeserved reputation as a place to stay away from." On the day I talked with him, LeBlanc had bought the paper, looking in vain for a story on a council meeting the night before. It ran a day later.

At the time of my visit, only five people remained on the *Times Herald* editorial staff from pre-JRC days, and the staff had shrunk from thirty-five to twenty-four, according to Guild figures. The librarian lost her job, and no electronic database replaced the clipping she used to do. "The people with institutional knowledge are all gone," Carville said. "Reporters have to depend on what people are telling them right there on the spot and whatever they can gather from the old folks. News becomes more shallow."

Carville, a 1994 hire who now ranked as a newsroom veteran, said the last major enterprise story he could remember was four years ago. "I think we do a decent job," he said. "We know the locals. We get out there, do the interviews. But when it gets to the issues, it becomes a much more difficult thing to do. Reporters are just trying to keep pace with the day-to-day. Even if they had time to do research, who gets a week off to assemble all the data and make sense of it and get it out in a timely fashion?"

The *Times Herald* used to be a place, people said, where employees worked all their lives. But under JRC it had been plagued by turnover at all levels. According to a tally by employees in 1999, after six years the paper was on its third publisher, third editor, sixth comptroller, and eighth advertising director. The sixth circulation manager left in December of 1998, and as of March 1999, the post had yet to be filled. Meanwhile, circulation had fallen 27 percent, from 29,581 in 1993 to 21,515 in 1999.

Former circulation manager Robert Penick, who resigned in 1994 after only six months, said that he got into an argument over draws and returns with a high JRC executive at Penick's first budget meeting. The executive called him "an ignorant moron," Penick said. "I wrote it down. 'Ignorant moron.'" But what triggered his resignation was an incident that took place at another budget meeting—on a Saturday—when he got a message that his son, who lived with his ex-wife in Illinois, had been injured in an automobile accident. He told the group he had to catch a plane. "They said, 'No, you can't leave. How bad is he? Call the hospital.' I said, 'I don't believe you people. I'm leaving right now.'" Penick left to take a job managing home delivery for the *Indianapolis Star.*

Unlike their colleagues on the business side, editors at Journal Register papers rarely hear from the boss. That's the best thing about the company, says one New England editor: "They leave you alone." The only telephone call William M. Caulfield says he received from Jelenic in seven years as editor of the *Daily Local News* in West Chester, Pennsylvania, was when the paper failed to send a reporter to an important Philadelphia Flyers game. Sports coverage is shared among JRC papers, and when the Trentonian, in the city where JRC is headquartered, used a wire story, Jelenic demanded to know why.

Caulfield also received a congratulatory note in 1997 from CFO Jean B. Clifton after the paper fielded a nine-month blitz of articles and editorials exposing widespread cracks in the 911 emergency response system that resulted in substantial reforms. The series won several state awards and was a finalist for the AP Managing Editors' Public Service Award that year. West Chester has been a prosperous franchise for the company, and Caulfield says he always has a big enough newshole. "And if I don't, all I have to do is ask for it. I've never been turned down once."

The casual reader, or a new subscriber, would not necessarily detect gaps in news coverage at JRC papers. They might just find them boring. In reading two weeks' worth of papers from nine JRC communities—well over one hundred papers in all—I was struck by the contrast between the splashy design of the section fronts and the absence of provocative or surprising stories. From time to time, a reporter breaks out of the mold, or a news event produces dramatic coverage. JRC certainly has collected its share of citations from the hundreds that state news organizations award every year. But day in and day out, the news stories are predictable, the features are canned, and there are few idiosyncratic local voices—columnists, reviewers, essayists—to be heard.

BOB JELENIC HAS a lean face with a commanding nose, and short, wispy brown hair. Trim, with broad shoulders, he is said to work out daily. We are in JRC headquarters, in a conference room on the top floor of a Trenton office building that overlooks the state capitol complex.

Flashes of his ego and temper are almost immediately on display. I have mentioned Journal Register and Community Newspaper Holdings in the same breath. "All they're doing is amassing titles," he fumes. "I don't think Community's got a paper bigger than 25,000. [Our interview precedes CNHI's purchase of the 44,000-circulation *Tribune Democrat* in Johnstown, Pennsylvania, or the 34,000-circulation *Terre-Haute Tribune-Star* in Indiana.] I mean, they're totally different than us. I'm just trying to point out to you, we are a public newspaper company. Very substantial in size. We have no similarities at all with Community . . . whatsoever. Zero. Absolutely zero."

Unlike CNHI, he says, "We are looking for areas where there is growth—growth in people, growth in population, growth in retail, in the economy, and we have a plan to add on once we find those areas and totally focus only on those areas. We've been consistent for almost a decade now on that plan, and we've got some of the finest newspaper properties in the country. I think the *New Haven Register* is one of the best newspapers in New England and possibly the country."

Jelenic grabs a copy of the *Register* from a credenza stacked with JRC papers. "You take a look at that paper. That is hands down a phenomenal product. We have 117 people in editorial. By any rule of thumb that's. . . ." He doesn't finish his point but lands on another. "The process color that we run. The graphics." Fully half the front page of the paper he waves at me is devoted to the mayor's unveiling of a developer's plans for a $431 million mall in a section of the city known as Long Wharf. It reads like promotional copy. Only in a separate, inside story does the reader discover that smaller towns and cities with their own agendas have the power and possibly the motive to sabotage the plan.

The *New Haven Register* (circulation 90,416 in 1999, down from 106,000 in 1990) does not quite put Jelenic among the heads of the largest one hundred papers in the country. He tells me that "Andy Barnes"— Andrew Barnes, CEO and editor of the *St. Petersburg Times*—"who is on the NAA [Newspaper Association of America] board with me, commented to me that he had spent some time in Old Saybrook, where he's got some kids, and he told me that we were hands down better than the *Hartford Courant*."

Jelenic says the frequency of management turnover at JRC is exaggerated, and that often managers have just switched to better jobs within the company. He deflects criticism that he dwells on the bottom line. "We're a fine company, we put out great products, we treat our people well. I'm not going to apologize that we're No. 1 in margin. If it wasn't us, it would be Gannett."

I ask about circulation declines at JRC papers. He says what's important is not "circulation for circulation's sake," but rather "quality circulation. . . . We want the right people reading it . . . people who have got the disposable income to shop." He contends that it isn't fair to compare the circulation of JRC properties to national statistics that include thriving Sun Belt papers.

He doesn't want to discuss why T. Paul Mahony cleaned out his desk in Woonsocket. "I decided to make a change. I don't comment on internal matters."

And he says he had no choice about the layoffs in Norristown. "The paper was losing money. The paper was owned by a millionaire . . . a very eccentric millionaire that was funding the losses." How large the losses were, he wouldn't say, but "we're not talking about $50,000. We're talking about hundreds of thousands of dollars."

The interview lasts nearly two hours, and Jelenic appears to hate every question. "It's just so negative," he says. "It bothers me. Turnover. . . . changes. They're just so negative." Maybe the question he hates most of all is whether Warburg, Pincus might consider selling some of the papers, as some industry observers have suggested. "It's so wrong and ludicrous that anybody who says anything like that. . . . It just shows that they have no financial acumen whatsoever. Zero. . . . So wrong that it's laughable. . . . If we've never sold a newspaper since 1990, and Gannett, Knight Ridder,

Thomson, McClatchy, all sold papers since '90, why would there be a rumor that we're selling papers?" He chokes a laugh. "Other than, you've got a bunch of jealous, venomous people out there that try to pull down successful people."

The following year, however, the rumors of impending sales would prove to be absolutely correct. JRC put five daily papers up for sale—one in Illinois and four in Ohio. It also sold the huge Suburban Newspapers of Greater St. Louis, consisting of thirty-eight weeklies.

But that wasn't the only point on which Jelenic's word proved unreliable. A few days after my interview I called Andrew Barnes in St. Petersburg and asked him whether he told Jelenic the *New Haven Register* was a better paper than the *Hartford Courant*. Barnes was flummoxed. "Why do you suppose he said that? That's the last thing I would have said. I can't imagine having said that and I certainly don't believe that." He searched for a diplomatic conclusion. "The *New Haven Register* is better than it was, having gone from being a totally unambitious paper. They're trying to get the late sports in. . . . I maybe said that it looks to me like you're improving some."

I also contacted Tony Coyer, the *Times Herald*'s controller from 1982 until shortly after the sale to JRC in 1993, to ask about the losses Jelenic claimed in Norristown. As a consultant to the former corporate ownership, Coyer still had financial records from 1968 to 1993. He got back to me after reviewing them and said that in none of those fiscal years did the paper suffer a net loss in overall income or cash flow. Indeed, in the five years before the recession of 1991, the *Times Herald* averaged nearly $1.5 million a year in profits. When owner Peter Strassburger died in 1993, the paper's balance sheet had over $2.5 million in cash and equivalents.

There is no record, Coyer said, that Strassburger ever pumped money into the newspaper, as Jelenic claimed he had. "As an independent paper in a niche market, with stable circulation, no debt and plenty of cash, we were certainly not the picture of a desperate and dying franchise," Coyer said, adding, however, that he could "understand Mr. Jelenic's actions in Norristown as a businessman looking to quickly validate a $30 million investment."

T HE STAFF OF THE *Delaware County Daily Times,* in a Philadelphia suburb not far from Norristown, was braced for cutbacks after Journal Register purchased the paper in 1998 and fired four managers. (Within hours of the purchase, the managers' parking-space nameplates were on the floor of the front entrance. "People were flipping through them to see who got canned," said political reporter Adam Taylor.) After that, however, the only sign of a cutback in editorial was a reduction in newsroom copies of the paper.

And in Pottstown, following a Guild strike-authorization vote, the company surprised the union by agreeing to a thirty-day extension of the contract with retroactive pay increases. In Pawtucket, where the number of editorial clerks had been reduced from three to one, a second was hired, an arbitration settlement opened a position for a second photographer, and new computers were on their way.

At the *New Haven Register,* a second statehouse reporter was added, though what was once solely a bureau serving New Haven now files to the five JRC-owned Connecticut papers. Even the *Norristown Times Herald* has gotten a fresh coat of paint and a refurbished lobby.

And in January of 1999 JRC launched the Journal Register News Service with an eight-day package of education stories and graphics, titled "From the Ground Up." Two dozen reporters worked on the series, said Charles S. Pukanecz, vice president for news. In addition, individual papers were asked to do local sidebars.

The writing in the series was rocky, and in showcasing charter schools and other educational alternatives the reporters were more enthusiastic than critical. But the series nevertheless was an ambitious undertaking for the small chain, and jammed with information.

JOHN R. SPECK, publisher of the *Jacksonville Daily Progress,* an east Texas daily until recently owned by Donrey, twists his pen nervously, an anxious expression on his face. He's about to be grilled by his new bosses—Ralph Martin, founder and president of Community Newspaper Holdings Inc., and Kevin Kampman, regional vice president—now sitting across from him at the blond wood conference table.

As Martin flips through the pages of a *Daily Progress,* Kampman peppers Speck with questions. Who are the advertisers? Who is the advertising director? Is he strong? Where do the ad takers sit? Who gets the overflow calls? What are the volume numbers? When are they going to a 100 percent commission system? CNHI converts all its papers to commission-only sales.

"Let's skip the numbers for a minute," Martin interrupts, looking up from his reading. "What are you going to do to make your newspaper better next year?"

The question takes Speck by surprise—budget meetings with his old bosses from Donrey had been all about numbers. He looks at Martin blankly. "I don't think there's anything we can do to make it significantly better."

Martin is clearly taken aback. He says, "I've never had anybody tell me that."

Speck recovers enough to start talking about hiring another reporter and making less use of the wires. Martin starts punching numbers into his calculator, but he waits until just before leaving to answer—and warn— Speck: "You got your reporter. Make sure you use it. Because we're going to be watching."

Since its debut in 1997, CNHI has behaved like no other newspaper company. The speed with which it has swallowed up papers has caught not just its new publishers off guard but the entire industry. "I thought we were moving fast," says Liberty's Peter Nolan, "but they've blown us away."

Alabama-based CNHI owns 112 dailies with a circulation of over 1 million, plus 206 nondaily publications. It owns more than half the daily papers in Oklahoma, three of which are the smallest in the chain—only two thousand subscribers each. Its largest is the forty-four-thousand-circulation Johnstown paper in Pennsylvania.

At a time when most newspaper companies were paring editorial budgets, CNHI was taking some baby steps in the other direction. Martin (who has since resigned as CNHI's president) said he didn't have to squeeze newspapers for the returns demanded by Wall Street investors. Margins of 19 to 26 percent were sufficient to pay back loans totaling $1.1 billion from Retirement Systems of Alabama, or RSA, the pension source for every Alabama state employee from janitors to judges.

Martin is the son of a carpenter who labored in the West Virginia clay mines north of Wheeling. He got his start in newspapers as an ad salesman at the *Salem News,* a Thomson paper in Ohio. After nineteen years, he was running Thomson's entire eastern division. Then, in 1995, after flirting with the idea of starting his own newspaper company, Martin went to work for Park Communications as vice president of newspaper operations. Park owned 106 newspapers, twenty-two radio stations, and nine TV stations at the time.

He'd been there less than a year when Park was sold to Media General, parent of the *Richmond Times Dispatch,* the *Tampa Tribune,* and a number of smaller papers. When Martin learned that Media General was not interested in keeping all the Park papers, he dusted off his prospectus and started calling his contacts, including some he'd met through marketing junk bonds for Park. "Everybody we talked to—First Union, First Boston, lots of conventional banks, and even the people on Wall Street that I'd met through the Park offering—they all thought it was a great idea, they all thought they could finance a big part of it, and they all had people they could bring in from an equity standpoint."

That was the route taken by companies like Westward and Liberty. But it wasn't for Martin. "We were buying small papers that needed a lot of work and patience, so we didn't want to put ourselves on this ticking clock that says at this point in time we have to be ready for a public offering because that's the only way to take out this high debt." Martin ran into nothing but "dead ends" looking for alternative financing. He was beginning to wonder if he ought to start looking for a job, when an old Park colleague, Tom Lindley III, said he had a friend in high places.

That friend was David Bronner, head of the Alabama pension fund, whom Lindley had covered as capital bureau chief for the *Birmingham News*. Martin immediately went to see Bronner. It was not a hard sell. RSA, in fact, had provided the money when two businessmen, Donald Tomlin and Gary Knapp, first acquired Park Communications from the estate of media mogul Roy Park; in effect, it had loaned money for these papers once before.

To Bronner, putting money into stable, consistently profitable small-town newspapers was not only safe but rewarding. "When we got in," he told me in a telephone interview, "the bond market was providing lousy interest rates, 6 or 7 percent, and the stock market was living on jet fumes." In a good deal for both parties, RSA has made loans to CNHI with interest rates from 8.5 to 10 percent to finance all of CNHI's acquisitions. Three-quarters of the company's stock was owned in equal shares by Martin, Tom Lindley, and Jack Quick, another Park veteran. (After Martin's departure from the company, Lindley and Quick split this portion of the stock 50–50.) Publishers and general managers own the remaining 25 percent. As the company paid down its debt, Martin said, it would offer stock to lower-level employees. But Bronner rules on every deal, and CNHI would need his permission to go public.

CNHI's money man is a Minnesota transplant with a law degree and a Ph.D. in public policy—everybody calls him "Dr. Bronner"—who has boosted the assets of the pension fund from $500 million to $23 billion since taking over in 1973. Bronner is known for such unorthodox ventures as the $120 million, seven-course Robert Trent Jones Golf Trail across Alabama and a half dozen downtown Montgomery high-rises with distinctive green roofs. Although he wheels and deals as much as any master of the universe, Bronner said he earned only $240,000 a year. "He could go to Wall Street tomorrow and command a million dollars a year," said Lindley. "Some people like to be a small fish in a big pond. With Bronner I think it's more than that. I think Alabama suffered so many years, and he thinks that he can do things to really make that a better state."

One of those things was to order CNHI to move its headquarters from Kentucky, where it was first based, to Birmingham. Corporate headquarters mean a lot to a poor state like Alabama, Bronner said. "We want those people in the community making those sorts of salaries." Another was to compel CNHI papers to carry free advertising for the golf trail and other Alabama tourist attractions.

A few years back, when RSA tried to buy a Montgomery television station, a flood of articles raising First Amendment objections to government ownership of a media outlet forced Bronner to back off. In a recent transaction with Hollinger, CNHI acquired five small Alabama papers. As a lender, RSA was distanced from the purchase. Nevertheless, the *Huntsville Times*, owned by Newhouse, saw the potential for conflict of interest. Said a December 6 editorial, "When RSA owns outright or bankrolls the providers of news about Alabama government, the public can rightly wonder if it gets the independent coverage it deserves." Bronner said the CNHI papers were too small to have an impact. None is larger than the 7,500-circulation *Courier* in Athens. "They're little tiny things," Bronner said. "Who cares?"

When it comes to making money, Martin said the goal was to increase revenues, not cut costs. And to increase revenues, a paper must increase readership. "Without the readers, being a good old ad guy like I am, there's nothing to sell," he said. "If a reader says he doesn't want to spend 50 cents, it means he's not getting any value." One of CNHI's first hires was an in-house editorial consultant, Vickey Williams, who said she had visited some fifty-five properties to assist with redesigns, coach writers, and run seminars. In January of 1999 the company launched an Oklahoma news service, with a $125,000 yearly budget, a bureau chief and a capital correspondent. State stories are collected on a Web site and fed to more than fifty daily and weekly newspapers. An official said the company hoped to launch similar efforts in Indiana, Pennsylvania, Kentucky, Georgia, and Texas. He estimated that spending on editorial departments had increased in at least half the papers the company had owned for a year or longer.

In Lumberton, North Carolina, the seat of Robeson County, where gloomy economic clouds overhang the tobacco fields and textile plants, the future of the hometown paper, the thirteen-thousand-circulation *Robesonian*, has actually brightened. Editor Donnie Douglas said he had expanded the staff from thirteen to sixteen and boosted salaries 25 percent. Perhaps most significantly, he overran his overtime budget by $8,000 in 1998—"and nothing happened."

In Jacksonville, Texas, where the *Daily Progress*—circulation forty-six hundred—is housed in a former mortuary, editor Chris Fletcher and his staff of three full-time reporters published the paper's first election guide with interviews and endorsements, and investigated the death of a patient at a state mental institution. It was seen as a good sign there that CNHI management okayed $670 to copy police records. And when the *Marshall News Messenger* tried to hire the thirty-five-year-old Fletcher after the paper won several awards in 1998, CNHI matched the offer with a 25 percent pay increase. The townspeople are in a state of shock, said Fletcher. "People at our level don't expect us to be a real newspaper."

Across the river from Louisville, Kentucky, the *Evening News* in Jeffersonville, Indiana, circulation 10,300, was starting reporters at $265 a week when Tom Lindley returned to his hometown as publisher in 1995. He wanted to hire new people—nobody fancy, he said, just college graduates who "could read and write and interview." One journalism school dean told him, "We don't recommend people to your paper." Now starting salaries have risen to around $350 a week and the paper is acquiring a reputation as a training ground.

Lindley said that when Roy Park owned the *Evening News,* profit margins reached 40 percent, but the paper was starved for equipment. When Lindley arrived, the phone system could handle only six calls, and, until a new computer system was installed in circulation, "we couldn't tell you by name who 70 percent of our subscribers were." The *News* represented "everything that was bad and wrong with small-town newspapers," he said. "Take-take-take."

For all that may have gone right at CNHI, however, something went terribly wrong at a little paper in a corner of eastern Kentucky. The trouble began in the spring of 1998 when CNHI purchased the ninety-six hundred-circulation biweekly *Floyd County Times* in Prestonsburg and installed as publisher Ed Martin—one of Ralph Martin's four younger brothers who have worked for the company.

Two reporters at the time, Susan Allen and Chris McDavid, say that Martin took over the news operation even though he was not the editor and had told them his background was in circulation. According to the reporters, he relegated hard-hitting stories about the county's troubled schools to inside pages, promised raises to the entire staff and failed to deliver, threw employees into turmoil with plans that never materialized to take the paper daily, told them they could be prosecuted for repeating what was said inside the building, and used the paper to introduce odd money-raising schemes, such as a lifetime telephone reminder service.

Perhaps what most offended her, Allen says, was Martin's declaration that he preferred "happy" news. Located in the heart of Appalachia, amid long-depressed coal fields, Floyd County has a full complement of social and environmental ills. Deep mines and strip mines have scarred the land and polluted its rivers and creeks, and miners have paid the price in injuries and lung disease. Poverty in this hard-pressed county is compounded by political corruption. In a recent election, Allen says, four-fifths of all candidates running for county office had been charged with, or convicted of, crimes. Two were under federal indictment. Martin was pitching happy news, but Allen was thinking, "You're not in a happy place."

Even a visit from the chain's editorial consultant backfired. Allen says Vickey Williams told them the paper needed more upbeat features—perhaps a story on Viagra. "In Floyd County, men won't even talk about having sex with their wives, let alone that they're on Viagra," Allen says. Adds McDavid, "We tried to tell her Floyd County probably isn't like where you come from."

Shortly after the *Times* was purchased, its editor and publisher, Scott Perry, resigned to become publisher of a competing paper in Paintsville. His departure was followed several months later by the resignations of Allen and McDavid. By the time I arrived in Prestonsburg, even Ed Martin was on his way out.

Grudges here in eastern Kentucky span generations. A court official fearful of retribution from the paper "for the next 50 years" should he identify himself complained that he rarely sees a reporter in the courthouse now. A county worker who was forbidden by her supervisor to talk nevertheless volunteered that the police don't follow through on cases as much without the *Times* bird-dogging them. "The paper has changed dramatically," she said. And school-board member and environmental specialist Johnnie Ross, who is also an Episcopal priest, considered the shift to what he calls a "Happy Valley" format to have been "the biggest loss this county has had" in his lifetime. "It may be a little paper," he said, "but for most people it's the only news they read."

The *Floyd County Times* is housed in a modern, dove-gray building with a cylindrical tower and glass-block windows. I found Ed Martin in the publisher's office, surrounded by packing boxes. This was his last day with the company. Two ashtrays were filled with spent cigarettes, and the bright label of a box of Marlboros shone through his shirt pocket.

Martin acknowledged that the courthouse had been without a reporter since Allen and McDavid left the previous summer. He had nothing but praise for Allen—"a class act," he said—but he and she just didn't see eye to eye. "In the past nothing good about the community ever was reported." Now, he says, "Good and bad have the same weight." He conceded he was "not an editor. What I am is a person who reads newspapers."

There is a lesson here. A newspaper, even a little one that comes out only twice a week, is a powerful thing. Newspapers are not just another business. "It's on your doorstep every day," says broker Owen Van Essen with feeling. "If you've lived there in the community a long time, there's a good chance your name's been in the paper or your kid's. People read it, advertise in it. A newspaper can affect the standard of living and the livelihood in that community by the positions it takes." And to the extent that it fails to do its job, the community suffers.

Susan Allen now covers education for the *State Journal* in Frankfort, by most measures a step up. But she says she is having a hard time letting go of what happened back in Floyd County. "We poured our hearts into that place for eight years. We tried to make it such a good paper, to tell people what was going on. Some small-town papers are just horrible. This wasn't like that. Everybody respected and read the *Floyd County Times*."

*   *   *

A Frenzy of Selling

There are 1,483 daily papers nationwide, and they are changing hands at a dizzying pace. The Project on the State of the American Newspaper documented every sale between January 1994 and July 2000—719 transactions in all—which are presented in the following listings. In over one hundred cases, a newspaper changed hands two, three or even four times in that brief period (these are noted in the listings with an *). Circulation figures are daily, as of September 1999.

Paper	*Circulation*	*Buyer*	*Seller*
ALABAMA			
*[Athens] News Courier (1997)	7,549	Hollinger	Bryan
*[Athens] News Courier (1998)	7,549	CNHI	Hollinger
Cullman Times (1998)	10,195	CNHI	Hollinger
Dothan Eagle (2000)	34,974	Media General	Thomson
Enterprise Ledger (2000)	10,209	Media General	Thomson
Montgomery Advertiser (1995)	54,142	Gannett	Multimedia
Opelika-Auburn News (2000)	13,738	Media General	Thomson

Paper	Circulation	Buyer	Seller
ALASKA			
Kodiak Daily Mirror (1998)	2,912	MediaNews	D and N Freeman
ARIZONA			
Chandler Arizonan Tribune (1996)	9,550	Thomson	Cox
[Flagstaff] Arizona Daily Sun (1996)	12,508	Pulitzer	Scripps League
Gilbert Tribune (1996)	5,225	Thomson	Cox
*[Mesa] Tribune (1996)	98,978	Thomson	Cox
*[Mesa] Tribune (2000)	98,978	Freedom	Thomson
[Phoenix] Arizona Republic (2000)	433,296	Gannett	Central News.
Scottsdale Progress Tribune (1996)	98,978	Thomson	Cox
*[Sun City] Daily News-Sun (1997)	20,055	Thomson	Ottaway
*[Sun City] Daily News-Sun (2000)	20,055	Freedom	Thomson
Tempe Daily News Tribune (1996)	10,401	Thomson	Cox
*Yuma Daily Sun (1996)	15,717	Thomson	Cox
*Yuma Daily Sun (2000)	15,717	Freedom	Thomson
ARKANSAS			
[Arkadelphia] Daily Siftings Herald (1999)	2,996	Rupert Phillips	Donrey
*Benton Courier (1996)	7,746	Hollinger	Benton Courier
*Benton Courier (1999)	7,746	Horizon Publications	Hollinger
Blytheville Courier News (1994)	3,849	Rust	Hollinger
*[Fayetteville] Northwest Arkansas Times (1995)	13,929	Hollinger	Thomson
*[Fayetteville] Northwest Arkansas Times (1999)	13,929	Community Publishers	Hollinger
Harrison Daily Times (1998)	9,769	CNHI	Hollinger
[Helena] Daily World (1997)	3,074	Liberty	Hollinger
Newport Daily Independent (1997)	2,397	Hollinger	Liberty
Malvern Daily Record (1999)	5,160	Horizon Publications	Hollinger
[Mountain Home] Baxter Bulletin (1995)	11,136	Gannett	Multimedia
Stuttgart Daily Leader (1997)	3,337	Hollinger	Liberty
CALIFORNIA			
[Antioch] Ledger Dispatch (1995)	17,568	Knight Ridder	Lesher family
*[Banning] Record Gazette (1996)	2,147	Pulitzer	Scripps League
*[Banning] Record Gazette (1998)	2,147	Central CA Pub.	Pulitzer
[Barstow] Desert Dispatch (1995)	5,172	Freedom	Thomson
Chico Enterprise-Record (1999)	33,210	MediaNews	Donrey
[El Cajon] Daily Californian (1996)	7,140	USMedia	Kendell
[Escondido] North County Times (1995)	89,754	Howard Pub.	Tribune Co.

Paper	Circulation	Buyer	Seller
[Eureka] Times-Standard (1996)	20,002	MediaNews	Thomson
[Gilroy] Dispatch (1996)	5,810	USMedia	McClatchy
Hanford Sentinel (1996)	13,453	Pulitzer	Scripps League
*Hemet News (1999)	11,500	MediaNews	Donrey
*Hemet News (1999)	11,500	Belo	MediaNews
[Hollister] Free Lance (1996)	4,065	USMedia	McClatchy
Lompoc Record (1999)	7,768	MediaNews	Donrey
[Long Beach] Press-Telegram (1997)	105,710	MediaNews	Knight Ridder
[Los Angeles] Daily News (1997)	201,435	MediaNews	J.K. Cooke est.
Los Angeles Times (2000)	1,078,186	Tribune Co.	Times Mirror
Madera Tribune (1995)	8,700	USMedia	Lesher family
Merced Sun-Star (1995)	17,064	USMedia	Lesher family
Monterey County Herald (1997)	35,077	Knight Ridder	E.W. Scripps
Napa Valley Register (1996)	18,598	Pulitzer	Scripps League
[Ontario] Inland Valley Daily Bulletin (1999)	67,907	MediaNews	Donrey
[Pasadena] Star-News (1996)	40,575	MediaNews	Thomson
[Paso Robles] Daily Press (1995)	5,391	USMedia	Reddick family
[Pleasanton] Valley Times (1995)	44,354	Knight Ridder	Lesher family
[Red Bluff] Daily News (1999)	6,974	MediaNews	Donrey
Redlands Daily Facts (1999)	6,753	MediaNews	Donrey
[Richmond] West County Times (1995)	32,263	Knight Ridder	Lesher family
[Riverside] Press-Enterprise (1997)	165,043	A.H. Belo	Hays family
[San Bernardino] Sun (1999)	77,366	MediaNews	Gannett
San Francisco Chronicle (2000)	456,742	Hearst	Chronicle Pub.
San Francisco Examiner (2000)	107,129	Fang fam.	Hearst
San Gabriel Valley Tribune (1996)	56,440	MediaNews	Thomson
[San Luis Obispo] Telegram-Tribune (1997)	37,749	Knight Ridder	E.W. Scripps
San Mateo County Times (1996)	34,466	MediaNews	Amphlett
Santa Barbara News Press (2000)	44,869	Ampersand Holdings	New York Times
Santa Maria Times (1996)	19,490	Pulitzer	Scripps League
[Sonora] Union Democrat (1998)	11,775	Western	McGee family
*[Taft] Daily Midway Driller (1996)	3,896	Pulitzer	Scripps League
*[Taft] Daily Midway Driller (1997)	3,896	Hollinger	Pulitzer
*[Taft] Daily Midway Driller (1997)	3,896	Liberty	Hollinger
[Temecula] Californian (1995)	11,868	Howard	Tribune Co.
Turlock Journal (1996)	6,027	USMedia	Freedom

Paper	Circulation	Buyer	Seller
Ukiah Daily Journal (1999)	7,362	MediaNews	Donrey
Vallejo Times-Herald (1999)	20,456	MediaNews	Donrey
[Walnut Creek] Contra Costa Times (1995)	97,668	Knight Ridder	Lesher family
[Watsonville] Register-Pajaronian (1995)	8,065	News Media	E.W. Scripps
Whittier Daily News (1996)	19,056	MediaNews	Thomson
[Woodland] Daily Democrat (1999)	9,748	MediaNews	Donrey
[Yreka] Siskiyou Daily News (1997)	5,145	Liberty	Hollinger

COLORADO

Paper	Circulation	Buyer	Seller
Aspen Times (2000)	13,865	Swift Newspapers	Full Court Press
Boulder Daily Camera (1997)	33,041	E.W. Scripps	Knight Ridder
Craig Daily Press (1997)	3,400	WorldWest Ltd.	Yampa Valley News.
Fort Morgan Times (1996)	4,572	MediaNews	Hollinger
Glenwood Post (1994)	5,064	Morris	Stauffer
Lamar Daily News (1996)	2,680	MediaNews	Hollinger
Montrose Daily Press (1997)	6,774	Wick	Allen family
[Montrose] Morning Sun (1998)	8,400	Wick	DP News LLC
[Steamboat Springs] Steamboat Today (1994)	8,543	WorldWest Ltd.	J.K. Cooke
[Sterling] Journal-Advocate (1996)	5,442	MediaNews	Hollinger
Telluride Daily Planet (1999)	3,841	Amer. Cons. Media	DP News

CONNECTICUT

Paper	Circulation	Buyer	Seller
[Bridgeport] Connecticut Post (2000)	77,444	MediaNews	Thomson
Bristol Press (1994)	14,505	Journal Reg.	MediaNews
Greenwich Time (2000)	12,558	Tribune Co.	Times Mirror
Hartford Courant (2000)	207,511	Tribune Co.	Times Mirror
*Middletown Press (1995)	10,034	MediaNews	Eagle
*Middletown Press (1995)	10,034	Journal Reg.	MediaNews
Milford Citizen (1995)	6,442	Journal Reg.	Capital Cities/ABC
+ Naugatuck News (1999)	3,416	Maitland Pub.	Horizon Pub.
[Stamford] Advocate (2000)	28,379	Tribune Co.	Times Mirror

FLORIDA

Paper	Circulation	Buyer	Seller
*Boca Raton News (1997)	13,392	CNHI	Knight Ridder
*Boca Raton News (1999)	13,392	Michael Martin	CNHI
[Fort Pierce] Tribune (2000)	27,373	Scripps	Freedom
Jackson County Floridian (1999)	5,911	Media General	Thomson
Key West Citizen (2000)	9,935	Cooke Comm.	Thomson
[Leesburg] Daily Commercial (1995)	28,788	Better Built	New York Times
[New Smyrna Beach] Observer (1999)	4,000	Horizon Publications	Hollinger

Paper	Circulation	Buyer	Seller
Sanford Herald (1997)	3,737	Republic News	Haskell family
Vero Beach Press-Journal (1996)	31,950	E.W. Scripps	John Schumann Jr.
[Winter Haven] News Chief (1994)	10,104	Morris	Stauffer

GEORGIA

Paper	Circulation	Buyer	Seller
Americus Times-Recorder (2000)	6,962	CNHI	Thomson
[Carrollton] Times-Georgian (1995)	9,792	Paxton	Worrell
Cordele Dispatch (2000)	4,867	CNHI	Thomson
[Dalton] Daily Citizen-News (1998)	13,586	CNHI	Thomson
Douglas County Sentinel (1995)	7,844	Paxton	Worrell
Griffin Daily News (1997)	12,155	Paxton	Thomson
[Jonesboro] Clayton News/Daily (1997)	5,897	CNHI	Southern
[Milledgeville] Union-Recorder (1997)	7,831	CNHI	Knight Ridder
*[Moultrie] Observer (1995)	7,008	Gannett	Multimedia
*[Moultrie] Observer (1997)	7,008	Thomson	Gannett
*[Moultrie] Observer (2000)	7,008	CNHI	Thomson
Rockdale Citizen (1994)	10,404	Grimes	Gray
Thomasville Times-Enterprise (2000)	9,978	CNHI	Thomson
Tifton Gazette (2000)	8,635	CNHI	Thomson
Valdosta Daily Times (2000)	19,156	CNHI	Thomson
*[Warner Robins] Daily Sun (1994)	7,572	Tomlin, Knapp	Park Comm.
*[Warner Robins] Daily Sun (1996)	7,572	Media Gen.	Tomlin, Knapp
*[Warner Robins] Daily Sun (1997)	7,572	CNHI	Media Gen.
*[Warner Robins] Daily Sun (1997)	7,572	Knight Ridder	CNHI

HAWAII

Paper	Circulation	Buyer	Seller
[Lihue] Garden Island (1996)	8,312	Pulitzer	Scripps League
Maui News (2000)	17,024	Ogden	Cameron family

IDAHO

Paper	Circulation	Buyer	Seller
*[Burley] South Idaho Press (1994)	4,885	Tomlin, Knapp	Park Comm.
*[Burley] South Idaho Press (1996)	4,885	Media Gen.	Tomlin, Knapp
*[Burley] South Idaho Press (1997)	4,885	CNHI	Media Gen.
*[Burley] South Idaho Press (1998)	4,885	Liberty	CNHI
*Lewiston Morning Tribune (1997)	23,421	TCI	Kearns-Tribune
*Lewiston Morning Tribune (1998)	23,421	Al Alford Jr.	TCI
*Moscow-Pullman Daily News (1997)	5,903	TCI	Kearns-Tribune
*Moscow-Pullman Daily News (1998)	5,903	Al Alford Jr.	TCI

ILLINOIS

Paper	Circulation	Buyer	Seller
Alton Telegraph (2000)	27,885	Freedom Comm.	Journal Reg.

Paper	Circulation	Buyer	Seller
Belleville News-Democrat (1997)	52,762	Knight Ridder	Disney
Benton Evening News (1997)	3,318	Liberty	Hollinger
[Bloomington] Pantagraph (1999)	49,148	Pulitzer	Chronicle Pub.
[Canton] Daily Ledger (1997)	5,491	Liberty	Hollinger
Carmi Times (1997)	2,970	Liberty	Hollinger
[Chicago] Daily Southtown (1994)	50,853	Hollinger	Pulitzer
Chicago Sun-Times (1994)	468,170	Hollinger	Adler, Shaykin
[Danville] Commercial-News (1998)	18,086	CNHI	Gannett
[DeKalb] Daily Chronicle (1996)	10,616	Pulitzer	Scripps League
Du Quoin Evening Call (1997)	3,626	Liberty	Hollinger
*Effingham Daily News (1994)	13,148	Tomlin, Knapp	Park Comm.
*Effingham Daily News (1996)	13,148	Media Gen.	Tomlin, Knapp
*Effingham Daily News (1997)	13,148	CNHI	Media Gen.
*Effingham Daily News (1998)	13,148	Hollinger	CNHI
Eldorado Daily Journal (1997)	1,103	Liberty	Hollinger
[Flora] Daily Clay County Advocate-Press (1997)	3,860	Liberty	Hollinger
[Galesburg] Register-Mail (1996)	16,335	Copley	Journal Star
[Harrisburg] Daily Register (1997)	4,571	Liberty	Hollinger
Jacksonville Journal-Courier (1995)	15,166	Freedom	Thomson
[Kewanee] Star-Courier (1999)	5,872	Liberty	Lee Enterprises
*Macomb Journal (1994)	7,014	Tomlin, Knapp	Park Comm.
*Macomb Journal (1996)	7,014	Media Gen.	Tomlin, Knapp
*Macomb Journal (1997)	7,014	CNHI	Media Gen.
*Macomb Journal (1998)	7,014	Liberty	CNHI
Marion Daily Republican (1997)	4,358	Liberty	Hollinger
[Monmouth] Daily Review Atlas (1997)	3,159	Liberty	Hollinger
[Mount Vernon] Register-News (1996)	10,260	Hollinger	Thomson
Olney Daily Mail (1997)	4,330	Liberty	Hollinger
[Peoria] Journal Star (1996)	68,556	Copley	Journal Star
[Pontiac] Daily Leader (1997)	5,726	Liberty	Hollinger
[Shelbyville] Daily Union (1999)	4,313	Hollinger	Frazier family
[Sterling-Rock Falls] Daily Gazette (1995)	12,658	Shaw	Thomson
[Watseka] Iroquois Co.'s Times-Republic (1998)	2,593	Paxton	Nixon
[West Frankfort] Daily American (1997)	3,116	Liberty	Hollinger

INDIANA

[Anderson] Herald-Bulletin (2000)	30,446	CNHI	Thomson

Paper	Circulation	Buyer	Seller
Brazil Times (1998)	4,597	Paxton	Nixon
[Columbia City] Post & Mail (1999)	4,408	Horizon Pub.	Hollinger
Connersville News-Examiner (1998)	8,448	Paxton	Nixon
[Crawfordsville] Journal Review (1999)	10,493	PTS Comm.	Freedom
Decatur Daily Democrat (1999)	5,419	Horizon Pub.	Hollinger
[Frankfort] Times (1998)	7,215	Paxton	Nixon
[Gary] Post-Tribune (1997)	61,476	Hollinger	Knight Ridder
Goshen News (1999)	17,609	Gray Comm. Systems	News Printing
[Greencastle] Banner-Graphic (1999)	5,583	John Dille	Rust Comm.
*Greensburg Daily News (1996)	6,603	Thomson	Hollinger
*Greensburg Daily News (2000)	6,603	CNHI	Thomson
*[Hartford City] News-Times (1996)	2,105	Thomson	Hollinger
*[Hartford City] News-Times (1997)	2,105	Community Media	Thomson
Indianapolis Star (2000)	240,309	Gannett	Central News.
*[Jeffersonville] Evening News (1994)	10,147	Tomlin, Knapp	Park Comm.
*[Jeffersonville] Evening News (1996)	10,147	Media Gen.	Tomlin, Knapp
*[Jeffersonville] Evening News (1997)	10,147	CNHI	Media Gen.
Kokomo Tribune (2000)	23,716	CNHI	Thomson
*[Lebanon] Reporter (1999)	7,360	Thomson	Lebanon News.
*[Lebanon] Reporter (2000)	7,360	CNHI	Thomson
*Linton Daily Citizen (1997)	3,875	Thomson	Smith
*Linton Daily Citizen (2000)	3,875	CNHI	Thomson
[Logansport] Pharos-Tribune (2000)	12,563	CNHI	Thomson
[Martinsville] Daily Reporter (1998)	7,478	Schurz	Kendall fam.
[Michigan City] News Dispatch (1998)	13,621	Paxton	Nixon
Muncie Star Press (2000)	33,625	Gannett	Central News.
*[New Albany] Tribune (1995)	9,447	Hollinger	Thomson
*[New Albany] Tribune (1998)	9,447	CNHI	Hollinger
[New Castle] Courier-Times (1998)	10,538	Paxton	Nixon
[Noblesville/Fishers] Daily Ledger (2000)	11,056	Gannett	Central News.
Peru Tribune (1998)	7,143	Paxton	Nixon
*[Plymouth] Pilot-News (1994)	6,227	Tomlin, Knapp	Park Comm.
*[Plymouth] Pilot-News (1996)	6,227	Media Gen.	Tomlin, Knapp
*[Plymouth] Pilot-News (1997)	6,227	CNHI	Media Gen.
*Rushville Republican (1996)	3,921	Thomson	Hollinger
*Rushville Republican (2000)	3,921	CNHI	Thomson
Shelbyville News (1999)	10,734	Paxton	DePrez family
[Terre Haute] Tribune-Star (2000)	34,286	CNHI	Thomson

Paper	Circulation	Buyer	Seller
Vincennes Sun-Commercial (2000)	12,445	Gannett	Central
Wabash Plain Dealer (1998)	6,563	Paxton	Nixon
Washington Times-Herald (1998)	9,364	CNHI	Donrey
*[Winchester] News-Gazette (1994)	4,358	Tomlin, Knapp	Park Comm.
*[Winchester] News-Gazette (1996)	4,358	Media Gen.	Tomlin, Knapp

IOWA

Paper	Circulation	Buyer	Seller
[Ames] Tribune (1999)	10,123	Omaha World-Herald	Partnership Press
[Centerville] Daily Iowegian (1999)	2,990	CNHI	DLS
Charles City Press (1997)	2,814	Hollinger	Liberty
Cherokee County's Daily Times (1998)	2,389	CNHI	Edwards
Clinton Herald (1998)	13,735	CNHI	Donrey
[Council Bluffs] Daily Nonpareil (1997)	16,816	Thomson	MediaNews
Le Mars Daily Sentinel (1997)	3,409	Concord	USMedia
Oskaloosa Herald (1998)	4,293	CNHI	Donrey
Ottumwa Courier (1999)	17,867	Liberty	Lee Enterprises
*[Shenandoah] Evening Sentinel (1994)	2,443	Tomlin, Knapp	Park Comm.
*[Shenandoah] Evening Sentinel (1994)	2,443	G. Knowles	Tomlin, Knapp
[Shenandoah] Valley News Today (1998)	3,196	MediaNews	G. Knowles
[Spencer] Daily Reporter (1998)	4,098	CNHI	Edwards
[Storm Lake] Pilot Tribune (1998)	3,462	CNHI	Edwards

KANSAS

Paper	Circulation	Buyer	Seller
Arkansas City Traveler (1994)	4,886	Morris	Stauffer
*Atchison Daily Globe (1997)	4,307	Liberty	Hollinger
*Atchison Daily Globe (1999)	4,307	St. Joseph News-Press	Liberty
Augusta Daily Gazette (1997)	2,551	Liberty	Hollinger
*Coffeyville Journal (1997)	5,094	Murphy McGinnis	Hometown Comm.
*Coffeyville Journal (1998)	5,094	CNHI	Murphy McGinnis
Colby Free Press (1997)	2,098	Haynes Pub.	USMedia
[Derby] Daily Reporter (1997)	1,818	Liberty	Hollinger
Dodge City Daily Globe (1994)	9,700	Morris	Stauffer
El Dorado Times (1997)	3,950	Liberty	Hollinger
Goodland Daily News (1997)	1,690	Haynes Pub.	USMedia
Kansas City Kansan (1998)	11,346	Liberty	Inland
*Leavenworth Times (1995)	6,592	Hollinger	Thomson
*Leavenworth Times (1997)	6,592	Liberty	Hollinger
[Liberal] Southwest Daily Times (1999)	4,782	Lancaster Management	Southern News.
McPherson Sentinel (1997)	5,411	Liberty	Hollinger

Paper	Circulation	Buyer	Seller
Newton Kansan (1994)	7,757	Morris	Stauffer
*Olathe Daily News (1995)	6,722	Keltatim Pub.	Harris Ent.
*Olathe Daily News (2000)	6,722	Kansas City Star	Keltatim Pub.
[Pittsburg] Morning Sun (1994)	10,312	Morris	Stauffer
*Pratt Tribune (1997)	2,325	Murphy McGinniss	Hometown Comm.
*Pratt Tribune (1998)	2,325	CNHI	Murphy McGinniss
*Pratt Tribune (1999)	2,325	Liberty	CNHI
Topeka Capital-Journal (1994)	59,559	Morris	Stauffer
Wellington Daily News (1998)	3,170	Liberty	Mitchell fam.

KENTUCKY

Paper	Circulation	Buyer	Seller
*[Corbin] Times-Tribune (1995)	7,049	Hollinger	Thomson
*[Corbin] Times-Tribune (1998)	7,049	CNHI	Hollinger
Glasgow Daily Times (1998)	9,726	CNHI	Donrey
Harlan Daily Enterprise (1998)	7,000	CNHI	Hollinger
[Henderson] Gleaner (1997)	11,109	A.H. Belo	Dear family
[Madisonville] Messenger (1995)	9,276	Paxton	New York Times
[Middlesboro] Daily News (1998)	6,085	CNHI	Hollinger
[Owensboro] Messenger-Inquirer (1995)	31,764	A.H. Belo	Hager fam.
*Richmond Register (1995)	7,459	Hollinger	Thomson
*Richmond Register (1998)	7,459	CNHI	Hollinger
*[Somerset] Commonwealth-Journal (1994)	8,705	Tomlin, Knapp	Park Comm.
*[Somerset] Commonwealth-Journal (1996)	8,705	Media Gen.	Tomlin, Knapp
*[Somerset] Commonwealth-Journal (1998)	8,705	CNHI	Media Gen.

LOUISIANA

Paper	Circulation	Buyer	Seller
*Alexandria Daily Town Talk (1996)	36,951	Central	Smith, Harlin, Quinn
*Alexandria Daily Town Talk (2000)	36,952	Gannett	Central News.
*Bastrop Daily Enterprise (1999)	5,815	CNHI	Bastrop News.
*Bastrop Daily Enterprise (1999)	5,815	Liberty	CNHI
[Hammond] Daily Star (1998)	12,199	Paxton	Nixon
[Lafayette] Advertiser (2000)	44,283	Gannett	Thomson

MAINE

Paper	Circulation	Buyer	Seller
[Augusta] Kennebec-Journal (1998)	15,683	Seattle Times	Guy Gannett
*[Biddeford] Journal Tribune (1996)	9,973	Community	Alta Group News
*[Biddeford] Journal Tribune (1997)	9,973	Beacon Press	Community
Portland Press Herald (1998)	76,275	Seattle Times	Guy Gannett

Paper	Circulation	Buyer	Seller
[Waterville] Central Maine Morning Sentinel (1998)	20,728	Seattle Times	Guy Gannett

MARYLAND

Paper	Circulation	Buyer	Seller
[Salisbury] Daily Times (2000)	27,326	Gannett	Thomson
Cumberland Times-News (2000)	31,026	CNHI	Thomson
Baltimore Sun (2000)	314,819	Tribune Co.	Times Mirror

MASSACHUSETTS

Paper	Circulation	Buyer	Seller
[Brockton] Enterprise (1996)	42,687	News. Media	Enterprise
[Fitchburg] Sentinel & Enterprise (1997)	19,740	MediaNews	Thomson
Haverhill Gazette (1996)	8,562	Pultizer	Scripps League
[Lowell] Sun (1997)	51,594	MediaNews	Costello fam.
[Malden] Evening News-Mercury (1996)	11,392	D. Horgan	Stauffer
Milford Daily News (1996)	12,679	Community	Alta Group
North Adams Transcript (1996)	7,840	MediaNews	Hollinger
[Pittsfield] Berkshire Eagle (1995)	31,861	MediaNews	Eagle
[Quincy] Patriot Ledger (1997)	71,508	News. Media	G.W. Prescott
Salem Evening News (1994)	34,693	Ottaway	Dolan Media Co.
[Southbridge] News (1995)	5,080	Stonebridge Press	L. Ghiglione
Taunton Daily Gazette (1996)	14,142	Journal Reg.	Thomson
Worcester Telegram and Gazette (1999)	106,748	New York Times	Chronicle Pub.

MICHIGAN

Paper	Circulation	Buyer	Seller
[Adrian] Daily Telegram (1996)	16,159	Indep. Media	Thomson
[B. Harbor-St. Joseph] Herald-Palladium (1996)	29,677	Hollinger	Thomson
Cheboygan Daily Tribune (1997)	4,357	Liberty	Hollinger
*Coldwater Daily Reporter (1996)	5,711	Media General	Tomlin, Knapp
*Coldwater Daily Reporter (1997)	5,711	Indep. Media	Media General
*Coldwater Daily Reporter (2000)	5,711	Liberty	Indep. Media
Dowagiac Daily News (1999)	2,965	Boone Newspapers	Boone/ Narragansett
[Escanaba] Daily Press (1996)	10,573	Ogden	Thomson
Hillsdale Daily News (1994)	7,354	Morris	Stauffer
Holland Sentinel (1994)	20,166	Morris	Stauffer
[Houghton] Daily Mining Gazette (1996)	10,864	Ogden	Thomson
[Ionia] Sentinel-Standard (1997)	3,291	Liberty	Hollinger
[Iron Mountain] Daily News (1996)	9,904	Ogden	Thomson
[Marquette] Mining Journal (1996)	17,444	Ogden	Thomson
Monroe Evening News (1994)	22,325	ESOP	Gray fam.

Paper	Circulation	Buyer	Seller
[Mount Clemens] Macomb Daily (1997)	56,644	21st C. News	Indep. News.
Niles Daily Star (1999)	3,750	Boone Newspapers	Boone/ Narragansett
[Pontiac] Oakland Press (1997)	78,001	21st C. News	Disney
[Royal Oak] Daily Tribune (1997)	17,330	21st C. News	Indep. News.
[Sault Ste. Marie] Evening News (1997)	7,542	Liberty	Hollinger
*Sturgis Journal (1996)	7,267	Indep. Media	Hometown Comm.
*Sturgis Journal (2000)	7,267	Liberty	Indep. Media

MINNESOTA

Paper	Circulation	Buyer	Seller
*[Bemidji] Daily Pioneer (1994)	9,294	Tomlin, Knapp	Park Comm.
*[Bemidji] Daily Pioneer (1996)	9,294	Media Gen.	Tomlin, Knapp
*[Bemidji] Daily Pioneer (1997)	9,294	Forum	Media Gen.
Brainerd Daily Dispatch (1994)	13,665	Morris	Stauffer
Crookston Daily Times (1997)	3,745	Liberty	Hollinger
[Minneapolis] Star Tribune (1997)	336,510	McClatchy	Cowles Med.
*Stillwater Evening Gazette (1997)	3,743	Oordt, Dance	Hollinger
*Stillwater Evening Gazette (1998)	3,743	Minn. Sun Pub.	Oordt, Dance
[Worthington] Daily Globe (1995)	12,194	Forum	Thomson

MISSISSIPPI

Paper	Circulation	Buyer	Seller
[Corinth] Daily Corinthian (1995)	7,506	Paxton	New York Times
Laurel Leader-Call (1998)	7,725	CNHI	Hollinger
Picayune Item (1998)	6,470	CNHI	Donrey
Starkville Daily News (1999)	5,602	Horizon Publications	Hollinger
[West Point] Daily Times Leader (1999)	2,889	Horizon Publications	Hollinger

MISSOURI

Paper	Circulation	Buyer	Seller
Blue Springs Examiner (1994)	4,601	Morris	Stauffer
Boonville Daily News (1997)	2,741	Liberty	Hollinger
[Brookfield] Daily News-Bulletin (1997)	3,500	Liberty	Hollinger
[Camdenton] Lake Sun Leader (1997)	4,955	Liberty	Hollinger
Carthage Press (1997)	4,922	Liberty	Hollinger
[Chillicothe] Constitution-Tribune (1997)	3,647	Liberty	Hollinger
[Farmington] Daily Press Leader (1997)	5,131	Pulitzer	Hollinger
Fulton Sun (1995)	4,632	News Trib.	Stauffer
Hannibal Courier-Post (1994)	9,000	Morris	Stauffer
[Independence] Examiner (1994)	10,259	Morris	Stauffer
Kansas City Star (1997)	275,336	Knight Ridder	Disney

Paper	Circulation	Buyer	Seller
Kirksville Daily Express & News (1997)	5,393	Liberty	Hollinger
Macon Chronicle-Herald (1997)	2,363	Liberty	Hollinger
Marshall Democrat-News (1997)	3,705	Rust	USMedia
Maryville Daily Forum (1999)	3,291	Liberty	Fackelman News.
*Mexico Ledger (1995)	8,041	Hollinger	Thomson
*Mexico Ledger (1997)	8,041	Liberty	Hollinger
*Moberly Monitor-Index & Democrat (1998)	6,069	CNHI	Donrey
*Moberly Monitor-Index & Democrat (1999)	6,069	Liberty	CNHI
Neosho Daily News (1997)	4,710	Liberty	Hollinger
Nevada Daily Mail and Herald (1997)	2,855	Rust	USMedia
[Park Hills] Daily Journal (1996)	9,239	Pulitzer	Scripps League
Rolla Daily News (1997)	5,410	Liberty	Hollinger
*[Sikeston] Standard Democrat (1995)	6,725	Hollinger	Thomson
*[Sikeston] Standard Democrat (1996)	6,725	DAPublishing	Hollinger
[Waynesville] Daily Guide (1997)	1,888	Liberty	Hollinger

MONTANA
*[Ravalli] Hamilton Republic (1996)	5,268	Pulitzer	Scripps League
*[Ravalli] Hamilton Republic (1999)	5,268	Lee Enterprises	Pulitzer

NEBRASKA
*Beatrice Daily Sun (1998)	8,255	CNHI	Hollinger
*Beatrice Daily Sun (1999)	8,255	Liberty	CNHI
*Beatrice Daily Sun (1999)	8,255	Lee	Liberty
*Columbus Telegram (1998)	10,361	Indep. Media	Omaha Wld.-Her.
*Columbus Telegram (2000)	10,361	Lee Enterprises	Indep. Media
*Fremont Tribune (1996)	9,218	Indep. Media	Hometown Comm.
*Fremont Tribune (2000)	9,218	Lee Enterprises	Indep. Media
Grand Island Independent (1994)	24,192	Morris	Stauffer
McCook Daily Gazette (1997)	7,218	Rust	USMedia
*Nebraska City News-Press (1995)	2,458	Midwest Newspapers	Hollinger
*Nebraska City News-Press (1999)	2,458	Liberty	Midwest News.
North Platte Telegraph (1999)	13,761	Omaha World-Herald	Western Publishing
*Sidney Telegraph (1996)	2,603	MediaNews	Hollinger
*Sidney Telegraph (1996)	2,603	Western	MediaNews
[Scottsbluff] Star-Herald (1999)	15,939	Omaha World-Herald	Western Publishing

Paper	Circulation	Buyer	Seller
York News-Times (1994)	5,174	Morris	Stauffer

NEVADA

Paper	Circulation	Buyer	Seller
*Daily Sparks Tribune (1997)	6,098	TCI	Kearns-Tribune
*Daily Sparks Tribune (1998)	6,098	Al Alford, Jr.	TCI
Elko Daily Free Press (1999)	7,023	Liberty	Steninger family
[Winnemucca] Humboldt Sun (1998)	2,993	D. Singleton	Winnemucca Pub.

NEW HAMPSHIRE

Paper	Circulation	Buyer	Seller
[Claremont] Eagle Times (1997)	8,263	Harvey Hill	Dirk Ippin
Portsmouth Herald (1997)	14,674	Ottaway	Thomson

NEW JERSEY

Paper	Circulation	Buyer	Seller
Asbury Park Press (1997)	156,821	Gannett	N.J. Press
Bridgeton Evening News (1996)	9,047	MediaNews	Hollinger
Bridgeton News (2000)	9,238	Newhouse	MediaNews
[East Brunswick] Home News & Tribune (1997)	72,716	Gannett	N.J. Press
[Morristown] Daily Record (1998)	47,104	Gannett	Goodson
[Passaic] North Jersey Herald & News (1997)	45,941	MacroMedia	MediaNews
[Salem] Today's Sunbeam (2000)	10,801	Newhouse	MediaNews
[Toms River] Ocean County Observer (1998)	10,571	Gannett	Goodson
[Woodbridge] News Tribune (1995)	54,458	N.J. Press	Bergen Record
[Woodbury] Gloucester County Times (2000)	25,683	Newhouse	MediaNews

NEW MEXICO

Paper	Circulation	Buyer	Seller
Alamogordo Daily News (1998)	7,686	CNHI	Donrey
*Deming Headlight (1994)	3,352	WorldWest Ltd.	J.K. Cooke
*Deming Headlight (1999)	3,352	MediaNews	WorldWest Ltd.
[Farmingon] Daily Times (1998)	17,070	MediaNews	Eliot O'Brien
Portales News-Tribune (1997)	2,917	Freedom	Southern

NEW YORK

Paper	Circulation	Buyer	Seller
[Dunkirk-Fredonia] Evening Observer (1994)	13,315	Ogden	Williams fam.
*[Herkimer] Evening Telegram (1995)	6,271	Hollinger	Thomson
*[Herkimer] Evening Telegram (1997)	6,271	Liberty	Hollinger
[Hornell] Evening Tribune (1997)	6,846	Liberty	Hollinger
*[Hudson] Register-Star (1994)	6,900	Tomlin,Knapp	Park Comm.
*[Hudson] Register-Star (1996)	6,900	Media Gen.	Tomlin, Knapp

Paper	Circulation	Buyer	Seller
*[Hudson] Register-Star (1997)	6,900	Johnson	Media Gen.
[Kingston] Daily Freeman (1998)	22,110	Journal Reg.	Goodson
*[Little Falls] Evening Times (1996)	4,273	Community	Alta Group
*[Little Falls] Evening Times (1997)	4,273	Hollinger	Community
*[Little Falls] Evening Times (1997)	4,273	Liberty	Hollinger
*[Lockport] Union-Sun & Journal (1994)	16,265	Tomlin, Knapp	Park Comm.
*[Lockport] Union-Sun & Journal (1996)	16,265	Media Gen.	Tomlin, Knapp
*[Lockport] Union-Sun & Journal (1997)	16,265	CNHI	Media Gen.
*[Medina] Journal-Register (1996)	4,364	Media Gen.	Tomlin, Knapp
*[Medina] Journal-Register (1997)	4,364	CNHI	Media Gen.
Newsday (2000)	574,941	Tribune	Times Mirror
Niagara Gazette (1997)	25,160	CNHI	Gannett
[Norwich] Evening Sun (1994)	4,841	Snyder Comm.	Hollinger
*[Ogdensburg] Courier-Observer (1994)	6,712	Tomlin, Knapp	Park Comm.
*[Ogdensburg] Courier-Observer (1996)	6,712	Media Gen.	Tomlin, Knapp
*[Ogdensburg] Courier-Observer (1997)	6,712	Johnson	Media Gen.
*[Ogdensburg] Journal (1994)	5,182	Tomlin, Knapp	Park Comm.
*[Ogdensburg] Journal (1996)	5,182	Media Gen.	Tomlin, Knapp
*[Ogdensburg] Journal (1997)	5,182	Johnson	Media Gen.
Olean Times-Herald (1995)	17,370	Hollinger	Thomson
Oneida Daily Dispatch (1998)	7,581	Journal Reg.	Goodson
*[Oswego] Palladium-Times (1995)	8,645	Hollinger	Thomson
*[Oswego] Palladium-Times (1998)	8,645	CNHI	Hollinger
*[Oswego] Palladium-Times (1999)	8,645	Liberty	CNHI
[Saratoga Springs] Saratogian (1998)	11,147	Journal Reg.	Gannett
*Tonawanda News (1997)	10,722	Liberty	Hollinger
*Tonawanda News (1998)	10,722	CNHI	Liberty
Wellsville Daily Reporter (1997)	3,556	Liberty	Hollinger

NORTH CAROLINA

[Aberdeen] Citizen News-Record (1994)	2,242	Tomlin, Knapp	Park Comm.
Asheville Citizen Times (1995)	58,601	Gannett	Multimedia
*[Clinton] Sampson-Independent (1994)	8,629	Tomlin, Knapp	Park Comm.
*[Clinton] Sampson-Independent (1996)	8,629	Media Gen.	Tomlin, Knapp
*[Clinton] Sampson-Independent (1997)	8,629	CNHI	Media Gen.
*Concord Tribune (1994)	20,023	Tomlin, Knapp	Park Comm.
*Concord Tribune (1996)	20,023	Media Gen.	Tomlin, Knapp
*[Eden] Daily News (1994)	4,544	Tomlin, Knapp	Park Comm.
*[Eden] Daily News (1996)	4,544	Media Gen.	Tomlin, Knapp

Paper	Circulation	Buyer	Seller
[Elizabeth City] Daily Advance (1996)	11,583	Cox	Thomson
*[Elizabethtown] Bladen Journal (1994)	3,854	Tomlin, Knapp	Park Comm.
*[Elizabethtown] Bladen Journal (1997)	3,854	Media Gen.	Tomlin, Knapp
*[Elizabethtown] Bladen Journal (1997)	3,854	CNHI	Media Gen.
[Forest City] Daily Courier (1998)	11,937	Paxton	Paris, Blair
[Greenville] Daily Reflector (1995)	20,228	Cox	Whichard fam.
[Henderson] Daily Dispatch (1994)	8,508	Paxton	H.A. Dennis
Hickory Daily Record (1998)	19,402	Media Gen.	Millholland fam.
High Point Enterprise (1999)	29,741	Paxton Media	High Point Ent.
*[Kannapolis] Daily Independent (1994)	20,023	Tomlin, Knapp	Park Comm.
*[Kannapolis] Daily Independent (1996)	20,023	Media Gen.	Tomlin, Knapp
[Lenoir] News-Topic (1995)	10,121	Paxton	New York Times
*[Lumberton] Robesonian (1994)	13,449	Tomlin, Knapp	Park Comm.
*[Lumberton] Robesonian (1996)	13,449	Media Gen.	Tomlin, Knapp
*[Lumberton] Robesonian (1997)	13,449	CNHI	Media Gen.
*[Marion] McDowell News (1994)	4,420	Tomlin, Knapp	Park Comm.
*[Marion] McDowell News (1996)	4,420	Media Gen.	Tomlin, Knapp
[Monroe] Enquirer-Journal (1997)	11,722	Paxton	Thomson
*[Morganton] News Herald (1994)	11,625	Tomlin, Knapp	Park Comm.
*[Morganton] News Herald (1996)	11,625	Media Gen.	Tomlin, Knapp
[Newton] Observer-News-Enterprise (1999)	2,317	Horizon Publications	Hollinger
[Raleigh] News & Observer (1995)	159,156	McClatchy	Daniels fam.
Reidsville Review (1997)	6,260	Media Gen.	Southern
*[Rockingham] Richmond Co. Daily Journal (1994)	8,390	Tomlin, Knapp	Park Comm.
*[Rockingham] Richmond Co. Daily Journal (1996)	8,390	Media Gen.	Tomlin, Knapp
*[Rockingham] Richmond Co. Daily Journal (1997)	8,390	Community News.	Media Gen.
Rocky Mount Telegram (1996)	13,127	Cox	Thomson
Salisbury Post (1996)	24,895	Even. Post Pub.	Hurley fam.
Sanford Herald (1998)	12,699	Paxton	Horner fam.
Shelby Star (1997)	14,736	Freedom	Thomson
*Statesville Record & Landmark (1994)	15,408	Tomlin, Knapp	Park Comm.
*Statesville Record & Landmark (1996)	15,408	Media Gen.	Tomlin, Knapp
[Tarboro] Daily Southern (1998)	3,773	CNHI	Hollinger

NORTH DAKOTA

*Devils Lake Daily Journal (1994)	4,208	Tomlin, Knapp	Park Comm.
*Devils Lake Daily Journal (1996)	4,208	Media Gen.	Tomlin, Knapp

Paper	Circulation	Buyer	Seller
*Devils Lake Daily Journal (1997)	4,208	CNHI	Media Gen.
*Devils Lake Daily Journal (1998)	4,208	Liberty	CNHI
Dickinson Press (1995)	7,365	Forum	Thomson

OHIO

Paper	Circulation	Buyer	Seller
[Ashtabula] Star-Beacon (1998)	21,079	CNHI	Thomson
Athens Messenger (1997)	11,622	Brown Pub.	Bush fam.
*[Bucyrus] Telegraph-Forum (1995)	7,091	Thomson	D and N Freeman
*[Bucyrus] Telegraph-Forum (2000)	7,091	Gannett	Thomson
[Canton] Repository (2000)	62,885	Copley	Thomson
*Chillicothe Gazette (1998)	16,102	CNHI	Gannett
*Chillicothe Gazette (1998)	16,102	Thomson	CNHI
*Chillicothe Gazette (2000)	16,102	Gannett	Thomson
Coshocton Tribune (2000)	7,494	Gannett	Thomson
[East Liverpool] Review (1998)	10,014	Ogden	Thomson
[Fostonia] Review Times (1999)	4,662	Findlay Publishing	C. Pennington
*Gallipolis Daily Tribune (1995)	5,368	Gannett	Mulitmedia
*Gallipolis Daily Tribune (1998)	5,368	CNHI	Gannett
[Greenville] Daily Advocate (1998)	7,640	Brown Pub.	Thomson
[Hamilton] Journal News (2000)	24,501	Cox	Thomson
Lancaster Eagle-Gazette (2000)	15,623	Gannett	Thomson
[Lisbon] Morning Journal (1999)	13,560	Trinity US	Trinity PLC
[Mansfield] News Journal (2000)	34,154	Gannett	Thomson
Marion Star (2000)	15,654	Gannett	Thomson
[Massillon] Independent (1998)	15,034	Journal Reg.	Goodson
Middletown Journal (2000)	20,794	Cox	Thomson
[Newark] Advocate (2000)	21,764	Gannett	Thomson
Piqua Daily Call (1998)	7,551	Brown Pub.	Thomson
*[Pomeroy] Daily Sentinel (1995)	4,697	Gannett	Multimedia
*[Pomeroy] Daily Sentinel (1998)	4,697	CNHI	Gannett
Portsmouth Daily Times (1995)	15,311	Hollinger	Thomson
Salem News (1998)	8,157	Ogden	Thomson
[Steubenville] Herald-Star (1996)	16,715	Ogden	Thomson
[St. Mary's] Evening Leader (1999)	5,901	Horizon Publications	Hollinger
Troy Daily News (1998)	11,043	Pulitzer	TDN Pub.
Wapakoneta Daily News (1999)	4,928	Horizon Publications	Hollinger
[Warren] Tribune Chronicle (1998)	35,725	Ogden	Thomson
Xenia Daily Gazette (1998)	7,516	Brown Pub.	Thomson
[Zanesville] Times Recorder (2000)	21,274	Gannett	Thomson

Paper	Circulation	Buyer	Seller
OKLAHOMA			
*Ada Evening News (1995)	9,158	Hollinger	Thomson
*Ada Evening News (1998)	9,158	CNHI	Hollinger
Altus Times (1998)	4,749	CNHI	Donrey
[Ardmore] Daily Ardmoreite (1994)	11,319	Morris	Stauffer
Blackwell Journal-Tribune (1998)	2,641	CNHI	Donrey
Broken Arrow Daily Ledger (1994)	1,458	Retherford	Hollinger
Chickasha Daily Express (1998)	5,279	CNHI	Donrey
Claremore Daily Progress (1998)	6,414	CNHI	Donrey
Cushing Daily Citizen (1998)	3,246	CNHI	Reid family
*Duncan Banner (1997)	9,082	Hollinger	A.J. Hruby
*Duncan Banner (1998)	9,082	CNHI	Hollinger
Durant Daily Democrat (1998)	6,462	CNHI	Donrey
Edmond Sun (1999)	10,415	CNHI	Livermore
*Enid News & Eagle (1996)	20,258	Hollinger	Thomson
*Enid News & Eagle (1998)	20,258	CNHI	Hollinger
Grove Daily News (1998)	5,000	CNHI	Stipe
*Guthrie News Leader (1996)	2,830	Livermore	Donrey
*Guthrie News Leader (1999)	2,830	CNHI	Livermore
Guymon Daily Herald (1998)	3,082	CNHI	Donrey
Henryetta Daily Free-Lance (1998)	1,976	CNHI	Donrey
*Holdenville Daily News (1996)	2,500	Stipe	Pettis fam.
*Holdenville Daily News (1998)	2,500	CNHI	Stipe
*McAlester News-Capital & Democrat (1994)	11,502	Tomlin, Knapp	Park Comm.
*McAlester News-Capital & Democrat (1996)	11,502	Media Gen.	Tomlin, Knapp
*McAlester News-Capital & (1997)	11,502	CNHI	Media Gen.
Miami News-Record (2000)	5,396	Am. Cons. Media	Boone/ Narragansett
Norman Transcript (1998)	13,943	CNHI	Donrey
Okmulgee Daily Times (1998)	4,365	CNHI	Donrey
Pauls Valley Daily Democrat (1998)	2,777	CNHI	Donrey
Poteau News & Sun (1998)	3,354	CNHI	Murphy McGinniss
[Pryor] Daily Times (1998)	5,939	CNHI	Stipe
*Sapulpa Daily Herald (1994)	6,356	Tomlin, Knapp	Park Comm.
*Sapulpa Daily Herald (1996)	6,356	Media Gen.	Tomlin, Knapp
*Sapulpa Daily Herald (1997)	6,356	CNHI	Media Gen.

Paper	Circulation	Buyer	Seller
Shawnee News-Star (1994)	10,449	Morris	Stauffer
Stillwater News Press (1997)	9,767	CNHI	Bellatti fam.
Tahlequah Daily Press (1998)	6,005	CNHI	Stipe
Woodward News (1998)	5,263	CNHI	Hollinger

OREGON

Albany Democrat-Herald (1997)	19,746	Lee Ent.	Disney
[Ashland] Daily Tidings (1997)	4,885	Lee Ent.	Disney
[Coos Bay] World (1996)	14,709	Pulitzer	Scripps League
*The Dalles Daily Chronicle (1996)	4,957	Pulitzer	Scripps League
*The Dalles Daily Chronicle (1996)	4,957	Eagle	Pulitzer

PENNSYLVANIA

Allentown Morning Call (2000)	126,518	Tribune Co.	Times Mirror
Altoona Mirror (1998)	32,744	Ogden	Thomson
[Connellsville] Daily Courier (1997)	10,285	Trib.-Review	Thomson
*Corry Evening Journal (1997)	3,488	Liberty	Hollinger
*Corry Evening Journal (1999)	3,488	CNHI	Liberty
Delaware County Daily Times (1998)	50,746	Journal Reg.	Goodson
[Easton] Express-Times (1994)	48,911	MediaNews	Thomson
[Easton] Express-Times (2000)	48,911	Newhouse	MediaNews
[Hanover] Evening Sun (1996)	20,901	MediaNews	Thomson
*[Honesdale] Wayne Independent (1994)	4,267	Tomlin, Knapp	Park Comm.
*[Honesdale] Wayne Independent (1996)	4,267	Media Gen.	Tomlin, Knapp
*[Honesdale] Wayne Independent (1997)	4,267	Hollinger	Media Gen.
*[Honesdale] Wayne Independent (1997)	4,267	Liberty	Hollinger
*[Johnstown] Tribune-Democrat (1996)	44,075	Hollinger	MediaNews
*[Johnstown] Tribune-Democrat (1998)	44,075	CNHI	Hollinger
*Kane Republican (1997)	2,230	Liberty	Hollinger
*Kane Republican (1999)	2,230	CNHI	Liberty
[Kittanning] Leader Times (1997)	10,512	Trib.-Review	Thomson
Latrobe Bulletin (1999)	8,441	Biddle Publishing	Thomas Whiteman
[Lebanon] Daily News (1997)	20,465	MediaNews	Thomson
*Lewisburg Daily Journal (1994)	1,418	Tomlin, Knapp	Park Comm.
*Lewisburg Daily Journal (1996)	1,418	Media Gen.	Tomlin, Knapp
*Lewisburg Daily Journal (1997)	1,418	Hollinger	Media Gen.
*Lewisburg Daily Journal (1997)	1,418	Liberty	Hollinger
[Lock Haven] Express (1996)	9,548	Ogden	Thomson
*Meadville Tribune (1998)	16,089	Hollinger	Thomson
*Meadville Tribune (1998)	16,140	CNHI	Hollinger

Paper	Circulation	Buyer	Seller
*Milton Daily Standard (1994)	2,673	Tomlin, Knapp	Park Comm.
*Milton Daily Standard (1996)	2,673	Media Gen.	Tomlin, Knapp
*Milton Daily Standard (1997)	2,673	Hollinger	Media Gen.
*Milton Daily Standard (1997)	2,673	Liberty	Hollinger
[Monessen] Valley Independent (1997)	16,586	Trib.-Review	Thomson
[New Castle] News (1998)	18,954	CNHI	Thomson
[Pottstown] Mercury (1998)	26,099	Journal Reg.	Goodson
Pottsville Republic & Evening Herald (1995)	30,823	J.H. Zerbey	Goodson
*[Punxsutawney] Spirit (1997)	5,541	Liberty	Hollinger
*[Punxsutawney] Spirit (1999)	5,541	CNHI	Liberty
*Ridgway Record (1997)	3,112	Liberty	Hollinger
*Ridgway Record (1999)	3,112	CNHI	Liberty
[Sayre] Evening Times (1997)	6,631	Liberty	Hollinger
[Shamokin] News-Item (1995)	11,626	Scranton Times	Thomson
[Somerset] Daily American (1997)	13,778	Schurz	Somerset News
*[St. Marys] Daily Press (1997)	4,943	Liberty	Hollinger
*[St. Marys] Daily Press (1999)	5,128	CNHI	Liberty
[Tarentum] Valley News Dispatch (1997)	32,609	Trib.-Review	Gannett
*Titusville Herald (1997)	4,065	Liberty	Hollinger
*Titusville Herald (1999)	4,065	CNHI	Liberty
[Warrendale] North Hills News Record (1997)	15,775	Trib.-Review	Gannett
[Waynesboro] Record Herald (1997)	8,789	Liberty	Hollinger
[Wilkes-Barre] Times Leader (1997)	49,823	Knight Ridder	Disney

RHODE ISLAND

Providence Journal-Bulletin (1996)	166,888	A.H. Belo	Prov. Journal Co.
*[West Warwick] Kent County Daily Times (1994)	6,176	T. Holmberg	Comm. News of R.I.
*[West Warwick] Kent County Daily Times (1999)	6,176	Journal Reg.	T. Holmberg
Westerly Sun (1999)	10,794	Record-Journal Pub.	Utter family

SOUTH CAROLINA

Anderson Independent-Mail (1997)	39,634	E.W. Scripps	Harte-Hanks
Florence Morning News (1999)	33,944	Media General	Thomson
Greenville News (1995)	97,655	Gannett	Multimedia

SOUTH DAKOTA

Brookings Register (1999)	5,483	News Media Corp.	Omaha Wld.-Her.

Paper	Circulation	Buyer	Seller
Huron Plainsman (1999)	7,746	News Media Corp.	Omaha Wld.-Her.
[Mitchell] Daily Republic (1995)	11,866	Forum Comm.	Thomson
Yankton Daily Press & Dakotan (1994)	8,199	Morris	Stauffer

TENNESSEE

Paper	Circulation	Buyer	Seller
Chattanooga Free Press (1998)	69,082	Wehco Media	McDonald fam.
[Clarksville] Leaf Chronicle (1995)	20,784	Gannett	Multimedia
[Dyersburg] State Gazette (1995)	7,251	Paxton	New York Times
[Maryville-Alcoa] Daily Times (1994)	20,840	Horvitz	Persis
[Oak Ridge] Oak Ridger (1994)	8,218	Morris	Stauffer
[Sevierville] Mountain Press (1995)	8,927	Paxton	Worrell

TEXAS

Paper	Circulation	Buyer	Seller
Abilene Reporter-News (1997)	38,272	E.W. Scripps	Harte-Hanks
Alice Echo-News (2000)	4,014	Am. Cons. Media	Boone/ Narragansett
Athens Daily Review (1998)	6,060	CNHI	Donrey
*Big Spring Herald (1995)	5,686	Hollinger	Thomson
*Big Spring Herald (1998)	5,686	CNHI	Hollinger
[Bonham] Favorite (1998)	2,613	CNHI	Stipe
Borger News-Hearld (1998)	5,443	CNHI	Donrey
Brownwood Bulletin (2000)	8,452	Am. Cons. Media	Boone/ Narragansett
Cleburne Times-Review (1998)	7,447	CNHI	Donrey
[Conroe] Courier (1997)	11,371	Westwd. Comm. LLC	Westwd. Comm. Inc.
Corpus Christi Caller-Times (1997)	64,780	E.W. Scripps	Harte-Hanks
Corsicana Daily Sun (1998)	6,719	CNHI	Hollinger
*Del Rio News-Herald (1995)	5,616	Hollinger	Thomson
*Del Rio News-Herald (1998)	5,616	CNHI	Hollinger
Denton Record-Chronicle (1999)	15,954	A.H. Belo Cross	Patterson families
Ennis Daily News (1997)	3,862	Fackelman News	Genrty fam.
[Fort Worth] Star-Telegram (1997)	225,737	Knight Ridder	Disney
Gainesville Daily Register (1998)	6,263	CNHI	Donrey
Greenville Herald-Banner (1998)	8,881	CNHI	Hollinger
*Huntsville Item (1995)	5,567	Hollinger	Thomson
*Huntsville Item (1998)	5,567	CNHI	Hollinger
Jacksonville Daily Progess (1998)	4,662	CNHI	Donrey
Kerrville Daily Times (1995)	8,627	Southern News.	Thomson
Kilgore News Herald (1998)	4,022	CNHI	Donrey

Paper	Circulation	Buyer	Seller
*Marshall News Messenger (1995)	7,348	Hollinger	Thomson
*Marshall News Messenger (1996)	7,348	Cox	Hollinger
Mexia Daily News (1998)	2,478	CNHI	Hollinger
Orange Leader (1998)	8,631	CNHI	Hollinger
Palestine Herald-Press (1998)	8,980	CNHI	Patrick fam.
Pasadena Citizen (1997)	5,750	Westwd. Comm. LLC	Westwd. Comm. Inc.
*Plano Star Courier (1997)	8,312	E.W. Scripps	Harte-Hanks
*Plano Star-Courier (1998)	8,312	Lionheart	E.W. Scripps
Port Arthur News (1998)	19,462	CNHI	Hollinger
[San Angelo] Standard-Times (1997)	29,951	E.W. Scripps	Harte-Hanks
San Marcos Daily Record (1998)	6,045	CNHI	Hollinger
Stephenville Empire-Tribune (2000)	5,014	Am. Cons. Media	Boone/ Narragansett
Sweetwater Reporter (1998)	3,180	CNHI	Donrey
Waxahachie Daily Light (2000)	4,646	Am. Cons. Media	Boone/ Narragansett
Weatherford Democrat (1998)	6,140	CNHI	Donrey
Wichita Falls Times Record News (1997)	36,659	E.W. Scripps	Harte-Hanks

UTAH

Paper	Circulation	Buyer	Seller
[Provo] Daily Herald (1996)	29,357	Pulitzer	Scripps League
[St. George] Spectrum (2000)	20,292	Gannett	Thomson
*Salt Lake Tribune (1997)	135,018	TCI	Kearns-Tribune
*Salt Lake Tribune (1999)	135,018	AT&T	TCI

VERMONT

Paper	Circulation	Buyer	Seller
Bennington Banner (1995)	7,812	MediaNews	Eagle Pub.
Brattleboro Reformer (1995)	10,741	MediaNews	Eagle Pub.
*Newport Daily Express (1996)	3,911	Pulitzer	Scripps League
*Newport Daily Express (1997)	3,911	Hollinger	Pulitzer
*Newport Daily Express (1999)	3,911	Horizon Publications	Hollinger

VIRGINIA

Paper	Circulation	Buyer	Seller
[Bristol] Herald-Courier Virginia Tennessean (1997)	41,437	Media Gen.	Worrell
Danville Register & Bee (1996)	21,702	Media Gen.	S.J. Grant est.
[Fredericksburg] Free Lance-Star (1998)	43,343	J. Rowe III	C. Rowe
*Manassas Journal Messenger (1994)	7,107	Tomlin, Knapp	Park Comm.
*Manassas Journal Messenger (1996)	7,107	Media Gen.	Tomlin, Knapp
[Petersburg] Progress-Index (1996)	17,878	Scranton Times	Thomson

Paper	Circulation	Buyer	Seller
*[Pulaski] Southwest Times (1995)	6,138	New River News	Worrell
*[Pulaski] Southwest Times (1995)	6,138	Fackelman News	New River News
[Staunton] Daily News Leader (1995)	18,119	Gannett	Multimedia
*[Waynesboro] News-Virginian (1994)	8,102	Tomlin, Knapp	Park Comm.
*[Waynesboro] News-Virginian (1996)	8,102	Media Gen.	Tomlin, Knapp
[Woodbridge] Potomac News (1997)	26,145	Media Gen.	MediaNews

WASHINGTON

Paper	Circulation	Buyer	Seller
[Bellevue] Eastside Journal (1994)	26,927	Horvitz	Persis
[Ellensburg] Daily Record (1996)	5,418	Pioneer	McClatchy
[Kent] Valley Daily News (1994)	33,197	Horvitz	Persis
[Longview] Daily News (1999)	23,028	Howard fam.	Natt fam.
[Port Angeles] Peninsula Daily News (1994)	15,114	Horvitz	Persis

WEST VIRGINIA

Paper	Circulation	Buyer	Seller
[Beckley] Register-Herald (2000)	30,393	CNHI	Thomson
Bluefield Daily Telegraph (2000)	22,181	CNHI	Thomson
Charleston Daily Mail (1998)	34,730	MediaNews	Thomson
*[Fairmont] Times West Virginian (1998)	12,461	Hollinger	Thomson
*[Fairmont] Times West Virginian (1998)	12,461	CNHI	Hollinger
Logan Banner (1999)	9,574	CNHI	TLS
Mineral Daily News Tribune (1999)	4,859	Liberty	Tetrick/Layman
*Point Pleasant Register (1995)	5,277	Gannett	Multimedia
*Point Pleasant Register (1998)	5,277	CNHI	Gannett

WISCONSIN

Paper	Circulation	Buyer	Seller
[Appleton] Post-Crescent (2000)	56,218	Gannett	Thomson
Baraboo News Republic (2000)	3,539	Madison Newspapers	Ind. Media Group
Chippewa Herald (2000)	7,103	Lee Enterprises	Ind. Media Group
[Fond du Lac] Reporter (2000)	18,664	Gannett	Thomson
[Manitowoc] Herald Times Reporter (2000)	17,293	Gannett	Thomson
*Marshfield News-Herald (1996)	13,987	Thomson	Ogden
*Marshfield News-Herald (2000)	13,987	Gannett	Thomson
*Oshkosh Northwestern (1998)	23,511	Ogden	Heany, Schwalm
*Oshkosh Northwestern (1998)	23,511	Thomson	Ogden
*Oshkosh Northwestern (2000)	23,511	Gannett	Thomson
Portage Daily Register (2000)	4,665	Madison Newspapers	Ind. Media Group
[Rhinelander] Daily News (1996)	4,943	Pulitzer	Scripps League
Shawano Leader (2000)	6,133	Madison Newspapers	Ind. Media Group

Paper	Circulation	Buyer	Seller
Sheboygan Press (2000)	26,510	Gannett	Thomson
*Stevens Point Journal (1997)	13,856	Thomson	Leahy, Glennon
*Stevens Point Journal (2000)	13,856	Gannett	Thomson
Waukesha County Freeman (1997)	18,163	Conley	Thomson
[West Bend] Daily News (1997)	10,050	Conley	Thomson
[Wisconsin Rapids] Daily Tribune (2000)	13,292	Gannett	Thomson

+ *Naugatuck News* in Connecticut changed its name from the *Daily News* and began publishing twice weekly rather than daily when it was purchased by Maitland in September 1999.

3 | The End of Innocence

By Buzz Bissinger

OAK BROOK, ILLINOIS
0 MILES

I AM LISTENING to a man named Larry Randa in a tidy office in a tidy office building in a tidy office park in a tidy suburb west of Chicago. My initial impression of Larry Randa is that I like Larry Randa. He has a pleasant face without the distraction of sharp features, and one of those oval-twanged Midwestern accents that makes everything he says seem wholesome. To be honest, he strikes me as a bit of a milquetoast, a man who tells unfunny jokes at Chamber of Commerce lunches because he knows there is always a group at Table 6 who will laugh because they're all hard of hearing.

I realize this initial reaction to Larry Randa is not only superficial but firmly rooted in the hierarchy of journalism. My newspaper upbringing was in the world of the daily, the big metro daily, with newsrooms the size of football fields and reportorial specialists who decided to write every leap year and Pulitzer citations that cost more to frame than any Van Gogh. As for Larry Randa, he spent much of his life putting out a string of seventeen privately owned weeklies in the western suburbs of Chicago under the auspices of Life Newspapers.

They were sturdy enough products. The very local-ness of them was inescapably noble, in the way that a dog with a cast on one leg and hobbling around on the remaining three is inescapably noble. You couldn't help but admire the Life newspapers for their very perseverance in this age of slick packaging and celebrity. Dog bites man. Man bites dog. Or cat. Or perhaps fish. You probably would find it in one of the papers that were owned by the Randa and Kubik families. But the more I listen to Larry Randa, the more I detect something else about him—confidence, assurance, even a shade of conquering smugness.

When he looks at me with that sweet round face—for some reason, in this flat light it reminds me of a peach without juice—and says of the efforts of the *Chicago Tribune* to compete with products such as his, "The

Tribune has tried a lot of things against the suburbans, and all of them have failed," I chalk it up to requisite bravado from a man who, let's face it, has spent much of his life putting out the journalistic equivalent of Rodney Dangerfield.

Just like I chalked it up to bravado when Fran Zankowski, publisher of Connecticut's *Hartford Advocate* alternative weekly, said, "The only way these large dominant dailies can continue is through acquisition." Just like I chalked it up to bravado when Larry Fleischman, executive director of the Suburban Newspapers of America Association, said, "A lot of dailies are saying, shit, if you can't beat 'em, let's buy 'em."

But it all seems like a lot of self-protective bull and bluster. Until Larry Randa tells me the saga of Life Newspapers.

The Randas and the Kubiks had owned the Life papers since the 1930s. Business was good. Life was good. It only seemed a matter of time before Larry himself, who had started on the editorial side of the papers in the 1970s and belonged to the third generation of family ownership, would get a shot as publisher. "We were making a good living," he says. "We were all having fun."

Until the mania of acquisition in the weekly business, at record levels over the past three years, blew into the door of Life Newspapers. When their own company lawyer first approached the two families with a message of interest from a prospective buyer, their inclination was not to get too excited. They followed the industry, of course. They knew independently owned operations such as theirs were getting gobbled up by chains—some established, some that had risen out of the night with pension fund money and venture capital money. They knew how giddy a cold-eyed business entrepreneur could get at the idea of clustering a group of newspapers, particularly when the right consolidations and economies of scale could spike up an already remarkable profit margin of 20 percent even higher. Whatever you thought of the weeklies, there were plenty of them that had the potential to be mean profit hummers. But in nearly seventy years of operation the Randas and the Kubiks had been through such dances before, and their resolve had always been to set a price so high that no one would ever come close to matching it.

And according to Larry Randa, that was precisely the way they felt when they met with Ken Serota, president and chief executive officer of Liberty Group Publishing, in the fall of 1998. Liberty, a new player in the weekly game backed by leveraged buyout specialist Leonard Green, was looking for properties in the Chicago suburban market, particularly in areas that the other big player here, Pioneer Press, had not already conquered. That meant areas west of the city limits, and that meant Life.

"We laughed before the meeting," says Randa. "This is going to be a waste of our time. As in the past, no one's ever going to meet the price that we would take." More fundamentally, the owners shared a deep commitment to their papers as a local, homegrown product, as indigenous to the soil as a Jersey tomato. Try growing that product somewhere else and the results would be inevitable—the thick flesh of it would grow dry and mealy.

It wasn't something they were willing to casually give up. But after the meeting with the thirty-seven-year-old Serota, who prior to the invention of Liberty had been vice president of law and finance for the company that owned the *Chicago Sun-Times*, there wasn't laughter. Instead there was the realization that Serota had just named a price that was causing the Randa family and the Kubik family to wonder if their days as independent newspaper publishers might be over. At the very least, they had something to think about.

A short time later, they had even more to think about. Pioneer, always on the lookout for untapped suburban markets, just like every major newspaper chain in the country is on the lookout for untapped suburban markets, whether it's Minneapolis or Denver or Houston or Cleveland or Milwaukee, jumped into the fray with an offer that was even better than Liberty's.

Suddenly the families had a bidding war on their hands. A big bidding war. So they held their breath. According to Randa, they went back to Liberty with a price beyond anything they could have possibly imagined. They were in the heat of weekly fever, deliciously caught between two deep-pocket boys desperate to gain a strategic foothold in western Cook County and southeastern Du Page County. And then something miraculous happened to the Randa family and the Kubik family.

Liberty met their price.

Randa won't disclose how much was paid for Life Newspapers, which before the sale generated somewhere around $14 million in annual revenues and maintained a profit margin of roughly 15 percent. But when he talks about the purchase, he gets a certain look on his face, somewhat like a kid going to the circus for the first time and seeing all those elephants lined up on each other's backs. Based on filings with the Securities and Exchange Commission, Liberty paid roughly $28 million for the assets of Life, including its newspapers, equipment, and real estate.

"Was I shocked? Are you kidding?" he says. "It was probably 25 percent more than I thought anybody would ever offer."

As a result of the sale, Larry Randa, at fifty-one, is now the head of Liberty's Chicago suburban newspaper division. In that capacity he oversees fifty-two weekly and multiweekly newspapers covering seventy-five differ-ent communities, all of which were in the hands of four independent operations until Liberty bought them. In October 1998, Liberty purchased Press Publications. In January 1999 it bought the Life papers. In July it bought the Press-Republican newspapers. And in August it purchased Glen News Printing.

Randa talks with gusto about the war for readers in suburban Du Page County, with Liberty, Pioneer, and Copley Newspapers all fighting it out. He talks with delight about what a wonderful company Liberty is to work with—just as he talks, with slightly less gusto, about closing duplicative "weak sister" papers in Warrenville, Winfield, and Batavia, not to mention cutting seven part-time positions and eliminating ten more editorial jobs through attrition over the past several months. As for revenues, he acknowledges that Liberty is "tweaking" him a bit to push the numbers higher, but he says he is confident he can do it without compromising edi-torial quality.

Randa likes the clout that the Liberty suburban operation has. He likes to be able to brag to local and national advertisers of his 220,000 weekly circulation in the affluent suburbs of Chicago. He likes the fact that Liberty has a national sales office in New York, since, at last count, the company owned 147 weekly newspapers in seventeen states. He likes pulling out the color-coordinated map showing the power of Liberty's penetration in the Chicago suburban market, with its five zones in different colors and its multiple zone discounts (buy all five and get 30 percent off!). He has an eye on some Spanish-language publications, and like his competitors he is always looking to acquire other papers that fit into Liberty's suburban clus-tering pattern in Chicago (even though there are virtually none left that are independently owned). Like his brethren elsewhere, he sees the economic merit of taking all the papers that have been purchased and consolidating certain departments under one roof—circulation, classified, printing, and maybe even some editorial functions, such as sports and photography and lifestyle.

There is no reason to begrudge Larry Randa any of this. He is a news-paper businessman doing what he should be doing, working for a com-pany that got into business because of profit potential, not all the news that's fit to print. I understand why he and his dad and Jack Kubik sold Life Newspapers to Liberty—because they were literally handed an offer too good to pass up. I also understand his bullishness about the weekly newspaper market in America, since it is a view shared by virtually every-one you talk to—fellow owners of weekly chains, brokers who say prices for weeklies are at a record high, the owners of the big daily chains who are now leaping over themselves to get weeklies into their portfolios, be they suburbans, shoppers, or alternatives, particularly when they don't have to worry about the threat of antitrust action from the Justice Department.

For years the weeklies were the ugly little sisters of journalism, ridiculed by the arrogant and haughty metro dailies that thought they could conquer the suburbs with an endless androgynous wave of zoned editions. As it turned out, weekly publishers not only understood their markets far better than the metros ever did, but proved themselves to be damn good guerrillas in the journalistic war.

But as Larry Randa continues, I detect yet another attitude—not quite guilt at having sold out to a big and amorphous chain with a suite of offices that has all the charm of a mail-order house—but a tinge of regret that another independent operation fell like a leaf in the autumn wind.

"Nobody can have the commitment that a longtime family owner can have to the communities they serve," Randa says. And he is sincere enough, and honorable enough, to know that however you look at it, something has been surrendered by Liberty's acquisitions.

"By this consolidation," he says, "the newspaper industry has sadly lost a deep personal involvement on the part of the publishers of community newspapers. I can't do that, because I can't be in 75 communities at once."

I can't be in 75 communities at once.

As I leave the tidy office of Larry Randa and walk through the tidy hallway and out the tidy office building into the crisp air of the tidy office park, I find myself haunted by that comment. By the side of the building are eight newspaper boxes lined up in a row like well-behaved schoolchildren. They carry products that were once the sole domain of Life Newspapers and now operate under the massive cloak of Liberty—*Elmhurst Suburban Life, Villa Park Suburban Life.* I like the names of these papers, the simple sound of them like good vegetable soup that doesn't screw around with exotic ingredients. I like looking at their front pages, because they're so unadorned and down to earth. They aren't like dailies, because they were never supposed to be like dailies. They tell you what you want to know, sometimes artfully but most of the time not. I like the fact that they're as much a part of the fabric of the community they serve as the hardware store and the bakery and the mom-and-pop tailor (if of course any of them are still around). I like the innocence of them, and the gentleness of them, and yes, I don't mind saying it, the goofy sweetness of them, in a way that reminds us that not everything in life is a matter of modem speed and the Internet. They exude a familiarity and affection and connection that is becoming increasingly absent in American life.

But after talking to Larry Randa, I can't help but look at the papers in those newspaper boxes differently. It is psychological at this point, since Liberty's stewardship is still in relative gestation. But the idea of these papers in the ultimate authority of someone who doesn't live in the community in which they are published, and who has hundreds of other products to cultivate and look after and prod for more profits, stabs at me. Because even if these papers look the same as they were before the sale, they are no longer the same, and they never will be.

I have no doubt that Liberty, or any of the big-boy chains leaping over themselves to grab a piece of the weekly market, will put out a passable-enough product. On a certain level, perhaps they may well improve what is there with better printing and graphics, a slicker look, a sharper tone.

But as these chains take over and the independent voice further recedes, I can't help but wonder where the heart will come from that year after year has stitched the weekly into the soul and soil of America, a rhythmic reminder as old as the village square and the dappled oak of the place where we live and why that place, booming or bust, growing or dying, shiny or faded, is unlike any other.

It is a wrenching feeling, deeply embedded in the changes that have taken place in the American weekly over the past several years. And as I turn my back from those newspaper boxes and move toward my rental car in the tidy parking lot outside the tidy office building in the tidy office park in the tidy suburb, I realize there is only one way to come to grips with it.

Hit the road.

DIXON, ILLINOIS
100 MILES

It is somewhere around here, heading west across the flatland warp of Interstate 88 where topographical change is a stalk of corn that may actually be taller than the one next to it, that I come to a firm conclusion about these weekly boys so bullish about themselves.

They're right.

Interviews I did previous to getting into my car underscore all of this. And so do those gnarly and nasty things called the numbers. Taken together, they provide some basic fundamentals worth reminding myself of, particularly in the middle of the night in the pitch-black ribbon of

Highway 12 in South Dakota when I think I'm going to get attacked by a herd of buffalo, or get stopped again for speeding by some peach-fuzzed local cop who obviously has heart palpitations anytime he sees an actual car.

- Fundamental One: *Weeklies are smoking.*

Whereas circulation of daily papers continues to founder—in thirty years, the number of adults reading a daily paper has fallen nearly 20 percent —readership of the nation's weeklies shows growth and muscle. In 1965, according to the National Newspaper Association, there were 8,061 weekly newspapers in the United States, with a total circulation of 25 million. In 1998, there were 8,193 weeklies, with a total distribution (paid and free) of 74 million. In other words, the audience for weeklies has tripled over the past three decades.

And their revenues have been growing faster than those of daily papers. In 1999, the combined ad and circulation revenues for weeklies grew 8.7 percent, to $6.3 billion. Revenues for dailies grew 4.7 percent, to $56.7 billion.

- Fundamental Two: *Weeklies can set you free.*

If I was Larry Randa, I'd be dancing in the street outside my tidy office building, gulping champagne. The weekly market is hot, hotter than it has ever been, and Randa cashed out at the perfect time. According to brokers, weeklies are selling at all-time highs. On average, they are going for multiples of six to eight times earnings. But multiples of eight to ten are not unusual. (Dailies, by comparison, are fetching multiples of ten to fourteen.)

The only sector of the market that hasn't fared well are the itty-bitty weeklies in isolated towns with annual revenues of $300,000 or less. But if you're the owner of a group of suburban weeklies, the owner of a community weekly with revenues in the $1 million range, or even the owner of an alternative weekly in an urban market, you may well be sitting on a pile of cash you never thought possible.

From a business point of view, weeklies are perfect candidates for clustering, whereby an owner can achieve economies of scale by consolidating, under one roof, the various functions of several papers in the same geographic area.

- Fundamental Three: *Everybody wants weeklies.*

In 1997, according to an annual survey of nondaily newspaper sales by *Editor & Publisher,* there were 125 transactions involving more than four hundred papers and shoppers. With barely a whisper, such papers as the *Piggot Times* in Arkansas, the *Monument Tribune* in Colorado, the *Lewisboro Ledger* in Connecticut, the *Henry Herald* in Georgia, the *Zionsville Times-Sentinel* in Indiana, the *Fairbault County Register* in Minnesota, the *Yadkin Enterprise* in North Carolina, the *Antlers American* in Oklahoma, and the *Deer Park Progress* in Texas all became part of chains.

In 1998 the number of sales rose to 160, this time encompassing more than five hundred individual nameplates, with such papers as the *Gridley Herald* and the *Teutopolos Press* and the *Ascension Citizen* and the *Lone Peak Lookout* and the *Cleveland Post* and the *Minco Minstrel* all going to chains.

The *West Yellowstone News* became part of Big Sky Publishing, a subsidiary of Pioneer Newspapers, Inc. in Seattle, which owns eight dailies, four weeklies, nine shopper publications, one real estate guide, and several other niche publications. The *Wyoming State Journal*, a twice-a-week paper in Lander, Wyoming, was bought by the nearby daily, the *Riverton Ranger*, whereupon the *Journal* lost its name, its editor, its original look, and a chunk of its staff. The *Osseo Press* and seven other weeklies in Minnesota that were owned by Don and Carole Larson went to the creeping giant of Lionheart Newspapers, a Fort Worth-based company that in three years has amassed sixty-four weeklies in Kansas, Minnesota, and Texas.

- Fundamental Four: *If you can't beat 'em, buy 'em.*

Big-city chains, after years of turning up their noses at weeklies in their markets, or thinking they could effectively crunch them into dust, have now en masse discovered a different strategy:

Buy the feisty little bastards.

Among other reasons, such acquisitions allow the dailies to offer attractive combination deals to their advertisers. "It's just sound," says John T. Cribb, president of Bolitho-Cribb & Associates in Bozeman, Montana, of the buying trend. "All dailies are losing circulation and penetration. If you want those rich suburbs out there, the weeklies, and the free weekly groups, get you that penetration."

Perhaps the most active player here has been Times Mirror (which in 2000 became part of the Tribune Company). In 1997, the company, which owns the *Baltimore Sun*, bought the Patuxent chain of thirteen weeklies in the Baltimore suburbs. In 1999 Times Mirror, which also owns *Newsday*, bought Newport Media, a shopper group on Long Island with a total distribution of 1.9 million, for a price of well over $100 million. Shortly after that, Times Mirror set the journalism world on fire when it became the first major chain in the nation to buy an alternative weekly in one of its own markets. The company, which publishes the *Hartford Courant,* purchased the *Hartford Advocate* and four other free weekly sister publications.

Some other transactions that follow the same pattern:

Advance Publications, a subsidiary of the Newhouse empire that owns the *Plain Dealer,* bought the Sun newspaper chain in the Cleveland suburbs; Journal Communications, which owns the *Milwaukee Journal Sentinel,* bought another branch of the Sun newspapers in the Milwaukee suburbs; and Philadelphia Newspapers Inc., the Knight Ridder subsidiary that owns the *Inquirer* and *Daily News,* bought ProMedia Management, which published weeklies and shoppers in suburban Bucks and Montgomery Counties, and Consumer & Community News, which did the same just across the Delaware River in New Jersey.

Newhouse struck again in 1999 when it purchased a group of twelve weeklies in the suburbs of Grand Rapids, Michigan, from Badoud Communications. The company already owned the dominant daily in the region, the Grand Rapids Press. The purchase was a milestone, marking the twenty-fifth transaction in the country in which a daily with one hundred thousand or more circulation had acquired a group of suburban weeklies with combined circulation of one hundred thousand or more in the metro's own market.

But it didn't end there. In early 2000 Gannett purchased seven Iowa weeklies from Marengo Publishing and Poweshiek Publications, which were strategically located in the area between Gannett's two Iowa dailies, the *Des Moines Register* and the *Iowa City Press-Citizen.* MediaNews Group bought Nashoba Publications' six rural weeklies between Lowell and Fitchburg, cities where MediaNews also owns dailies. And Pulitzer Inc., owner of the *St. Louis Post-Dispatch,* outdid everybody by paying $165 million in cash to the Journal Register Company for a chain of thirty-eight weeklies blanketing the Greater St. Louis area.

Fifteen or twenty years ago, these transactions might have been blocked on the grounds of antitrust violations. But today's media environment is very different, and as media companies lobby Washington for greater freedom to consolidate, legal action by the Justice Department has become exceedingly rare.

For those in the industry, the litmus test of what kind of stance the Justice Department would ultimately take came when Advance purchased the Sun papers outside Cleveland. "The significance of the Sun papers is not to be understated," says Ted Biedron, executive vice president of the Pioneer Press chain in suburban Chicago. "The dailies own the weekly and no one said anything. We all held our breath and nothing happened."

- Fundamental Five: *If you're lucky enough to own an alternative weekly, all those years of blowing dope when you should have been working has turned out to be a stroke of business genius.*

The most virginal sector of the weekly market, the alternative, may also be the one most likely to explode off the charts, given the Times Mirror precedent with the *Hartford Advocate.* With the 1999 announcement that Stern Publishing was putting its seven alternative weeklies up for sale, including the venerable *Village Voice,* there was rampant speculation about who would buy them—an Internet company, for example, or maybe even the *New York Times,* looking to find young new readers. In the end, the *Voice* and its iconoclastic cohorts were snapped up by a new company whose investors included the money management firm of Weiss, Peck & Greer and a private equity fund associated with the Canadian Imperial Bank of Commerce.

The idea of a daily metro buying the alternative weekly in its market, *a la* Hartford, makes eminent sense to analysts and brokers, particularly since the alternative caters to a demographic market, the eighteen- to forty-five-year-old, that advertisers kill for. Some of their appeal to younger readers is inescapably due to the fact that many alternatives, for all their sophomoric smart-assedness and predictably contrarian slaps at the establishment, also practice journalism that is incisive, has an actual point of view, and is filled with the kind of edgy voices that young readers crave.

It is also clear that dope-smoking has made these guys good business-men, because, let's face it, most alternative weeklies in America aren't alter-native at all any more, but excuses for ads in between forty-four pages of club listings for Gen-X fashion plates who go to the Gap the next day and buy that jacket because, after all, isn't everybody in leather? According to the Association of Alternative Newsweeklies, the advertising revenues of these papers has doubled over a five-year period.

- Fundamental Six: *Even those weekly owners who believe in independ-ence may be finding themselves vulnerable.*

When you've worked all your life at a weekly, and you've made a good living in the last couple of years but still not a dazzling one, and someone comes along with a very nice cash offer that insures your retirement, it's hard to resist. Because the weekly business for an independent owner is still the weekly business—sixty- to seventy-hour work weeks, critical shortages of labor on both the production and editorial sides, the utilization of all sorts of entrepreneurial ingenuity to keep the cash flowing, fear of the next recession.

There is also another phenomenon driving weekly sales by family owners: No one in the next generation wants to run the things because the work is considered unglamorous, arduous, boring, plodding, and totally out of touch with the wave of new technology. Ten years ago, seeing this trend unfold, one weekly publisher in Washington state, Frank Garred of the *Port Townsend Jefferson County Leader,* brought in an editor he knew and trusted with the specific purpose of handing the reins of the paper over to him in order for it to remain independent and locally owned. "Why does a community desire to have its own medium?" asks Garred. "I kind of like the idea of the First Amendment. It's not owned by the press. It's owned by the public. Small-town newspapers have a niche: The only way they're going to be buried is by those of us who can't afford to be independent."

But the far-sighted planning of a publisher like Garred is rare. In many cases weekly owners, when they decide to sell, realize there is no one to sell to except a chain, particularly if they want cash up front.

As I head through the monotone night of Illinois into Iowa, I think about these fundamentals. I realize that I like the energy of the weekly newspaper business, the fact that there are still places out there where newspaper owners are fighting for readers tooth and nail. The weekly world can be vicious, nasty, petty, angry, and obnoxious. In other words quite glorious.

I have been told about Grayslake, a small suburb of about seventy-three hundred north of Chicago in which readers can choose among two paid weeklies, one free weekly delivered into the home, two different weekly shoppers, and two home-delivered weekly inserts. I have been told about Jackson, Wyoming, where there are no less than two paid weeklies and two free dailies serving a county of roughly fifteen thousand. And right below Jackson is Sublette County in Wyoming, a beautiful and bitter and basically empty moonscape where two weeklies are competing against each other like pissed-off cats.

But it's that last fundamental—the loss of independence—that I care about by far the most. Is there a way for a locally owned weekly to survive in this market? Can editorial product—good editorial product—make enough of a profit to resist the cash offers of the deep-pocket boys? Is distinctiveness—local homegrown distinctiveness, whether it's the bank or the funeral parlor or the weekly newspaper—of any value anymore? They go to the very tissue of what it means to be a community in American life, and it is why, in the silent ribbon of the night, I am headed for Mobridge.

MOBRIDGE, SOUTH DAKOTA
972 MILES

It is deadline day at the *Tribune,* and if this were a perfect world, or at least one that didn't seem hell-bent for chaos, Larry Atkinson would like nothing better than to edit this week's lead story without interruption.

Watching how Atkinson interacts—the way he says hello with the lilt of a minister on a pearly blue Sunday morning, his easy laughter in the face of code-red operational disintegration, the whole soft and avuncular body language—makes it clear that he is the opposite of a selfish man. Every week, at the used press that is as temperamental as an over-the-hill movie star who still thinks she has good legs, Atkinson prints not only 3,650 copies of the *Mobridge Tribune* but also the tiny weeklies that pop up in this northern band of the Dakota prairie like buried bottle caps. These runs are small, so small in some cases that there is as much waste in newsprint, just to get the press up and running, as there is actual product.

Atkinson is the first to admit that of all the ways to get rich in life, printing the *Faith Independent* and the *McLaughlin Messenger* and the *Selby Record* and the *Isabel Dakotan* will never be one of them. Ostensibly these papers are also competitors, and every time he tries to sell an ad for the *Tribune* in one of their communities, you can hear the grousing all the way to North Dakota. "Larry gets walked on by his customers" is the way his right-hand man, Leo Grosch, sees it, particularly when Grosch has to sweet-talk the ornery six-unit Goss Community into printing up 700 copies of the *Isabel Dakotan*. But Atkinson doesn't see these weeklies as competitors. He sees them as voices, voices in communities that otherwise would not have one, and because of that he has little interest in gouging for profit. "If I didn't print them, no one else would," says Atkinson, "and that town would lose its paper."

The forty-eight-year-old Atkinson runs his own paper on the same code of principles. He wants to make money like any businessman, and when times have been good, he has made money, enough to put his two oldest children through college and buy a boat (which he later had to sell). But the work goes deeper than that. The lithographic image of Ben Franklin at the printing press in Philadelphia does not dance in Larry

Atkinson's conscience as some merely sweet historical footnote. Nor is it any accident that when he thinks of what it means to be a democracy, he also thinks of the role of the printed word. "I'm here because I choose to be here," he says. "It is my community. Newspapers play a key role in molding communities into what we are. We are the voice of reason. We are the voice of questioning government." And if it means fewer dollars, if the profit margin isn't up there in the ozone, then that's what it means. "I make a lot of decisions based not on whether it's going to make me money, but on whether or not it serves the community."

It is a self-serving statement, but anyone in town who knows Larry Atkinson also knows that he means it. It may also explain at least part of his predicament and why his days as an independent publisher may be numbered, particularly when buyers are potentially looking for properties such as his, above that magic $1 million mark in annual revenues.

It is an area of conversation he would clearly like to avoid, but there are certain realities of the weekly newspaper business that Atkinson cannot avoid—the labor shortage, the constant push and pull of trying to find new sources of income from other products, the realization that a private buyer for the paper would be much less likely than a chain to have the up-front cash.

Keeping the *Tribune* locally owned has stretched him to the financial breaking point. He is leveraged in loans for about $1.3 million, and sometime last summer the primary holder of those loans, Norwest Bank, didn't mince words. "Larry, what are you going to do if a major piece of equipment goes out?" was the way the conversation went. As Atkinson fashioned a response, the banker for Norwest made it clear that another loan, from his bank at least, would not be an option. "You're going to have to come up with another solution, because I'm at the maximum I can give you."

THE LEAD STORY Larry Atkinson is editing broke late, tunneling into the newsroom from that greatest source of news in a small town, the Main Street rumor mill, blowing past the Brown Palace Apartments and Jerry and Mary's Appliances and the Good Neighbor Store and Anderson's Family Shoe Store and the Silver Dollar Lounge and the Scherr-Howe Arena where Bill Spiry once lit up the varnished parquet with 42 points.

The local hospital is going bankrupt. That's the talk.

Like all Main Street rumors, this particular one is an unbalanced cocktail of drama and truth, but there is a basis to it: Mobridge Regional Hospital, serving patients from a sixty-mile radius, has agreed to enter into an affiliation with a larger medical facility in Bismarck. It could be good news for Mobridge, if the result is better health care at lower cost, but any time a bigger fish decides to link up to a smaller one, there are other possible repercussions—loss of local control, potential loss of jobs, maybe even closure. The story has enormous ramifications for those who live in the area, and since the weekly newspaper is the only source of what the affiliation really means and what it doesn't mean, the wording can't be casual.

Atkinson is staring at the computer screen in his office, trying to edit the hospital story. Next to him is the reporter who wrote it, Eric Davis. Davis has been at the *Tribune* only four months, so Atkinson is gently probing him with basic questions. But virtually every time he asks Davis something, someone else casually walks in to ask Atkinson something. It creates a Beckett-like dialogue, in which Davis tries to answer Atkinson's question and Atkinson in turn responds to Davis's answer by answering a question from someone else who has suddenly appeared in the middle of the tiny office. At other moments people come in, offer brief bulletins on some aspect of the operation that either has gone haywire or is about to go haywire, then turn around and leave.

A couple of days earlier the hard-drive system on the computers had gone out, and since Mobridge is one of those places in America so remote that it's a hundred miles from every place you'd never dream of going to anyway unless you were threatened or hallucinatory, Atkinson has basically become the de facto computer technician for the Tribune. It took him two days to fix what was wrong, but some of the terminals are still crashing without rhyme or reason.

"Computers are dropping like flies," someone reports at one point, with the detachment of a war scout.

But Atkinson can't worry about it, at least not right now. He is still putting the finishing touches on Davis's story, and once he is done with that, he has the editorial to write. He already had one banged out, but the news of the hospital affiliation is too big to ignore without commentary. Atkinson's voice is needed, just as it has been needed on so many other issues that have affected this complicated community of thirty-eight hundred over the past fifteen years—the economy, racism, alcoholism, violence, the sad and seemingly irreparable fissures that exist between Mobridge and the Standing Rock Indian Reservation just across the Missouri River.

But now the phone repair guy is here, because there is annoying static in at least one of the outside lines, not to mention the sudden and mysterious absence of recorded music when a caller is put on hold. And even before the phone guy got here, there was the letter from Marlo Utter informing Atkinson that she was quitting her composing room job to take a position over in Corson County with the South Dakota State University extension service.

Given the critical shortage of labor at the *Tribune,* the shoes of Marlo Utter won't be easily filled, and her resignation comes right on the heels of the assistant pressman who quit. Grosch, who has the title of production manager and is Atkinson's perfect alter ego, has become so desperate for applicants that he is willing to take on just about anyone as long as they have a driver's license. It is an admittedly liberal hiring strategy, but it has its pitfalls anyway since, as Grosch somewhat forlornly notes, "Half the applicants don't have a driver's license." He did just manage to hire two guys he likes, but he has no idea how long they will last. He certainly isn't going to hold his breath, since the paper has been through five pressmen in five years.

It is Grosch who breaks the news to Atkinson that the phone repair guy is here, and it is Atkinson, still staring at the hospital story on the computer screen, who patiently tells Grosch to take the phone repair guy back to the cable boxes so he can get started. Grosch leaves, and Atkinson in turn continues to prod Davis on his story, because he understands him for precisely what he is—earnest, willing, and totally inexperienced.

The shortage of labor at the *Tribune,* a problem that weekly papers all over the country are being forced to confront, doesn't simply include people in production. About fifteen years ago, Atkinson had forty applicants to choose from when he advertised for the position of news editor at the *Tribune.* Roughly a year ago, when Travis Svihovec decided he wanted out of the weekly newspaper business, Atkinson placed advertisements in *Editor & Publisher,* the *Denver Post, Omaha World-Herald, Fargo Forum,* and Minneapolis's *Star-Tribune.* The net result was three applicants, one from the East Coast (How come the biggest wackos are always from the East Coast?) who told Atkinson of his determination to turn the *Tribune* into a national newspaper. Another wrote well but had floated around so many places that it made Atkinson nervous. That caused him to settle on Davis, who basically applied to the *Tribune* because his newlywed wife had roots in the community.

At the time, Davis was a student at Western Carolina University. He worked for the literary magazine, but when it came to journalism experience, the only thing he could point to was the *Cedar Cliff Echoes,* his high school paper. But Atkinson hired him anyway with the eventual hope of making him the paper's news editor. "I was very surprised," Davis admits. "I was just looking for something smaller. I was very surprised."

And Atkinson himself, as much as he likes Davis, also knows the whole thing is something of a crapshoot. "I had three applicants, two of which I never would have hired. The third, who had no experience, I did hire, because he was willing to try."

Atkinson wants to make sure that Davis has quoted people precisely in the hospital story. He questions Davis's use of the term "job engineering," since Atkinson knows it's one of those squirrelly corporate terms that can mean just about anything. He also wants Davis to pin down the precise date when the hospital board first told staffers what was in the works. The reporter doesn't know, but he's pretty confident he can find out quickly, since the wife of the paper's sports editor, Jay Davis, was at the meeting.

That kind of easy access has made life easier for Eric Davis in other ways. When he needs to find the mayor of Mobridge or the president of the Mobridge city council, he once again doesn't have to go very far—both of them work at the *Tribune*. The mayor, Darrell Gill, is an advertising sales rep with long experience, since he used to work for one of the local radio stations. And the head of the city council is Leo Grosch.

For Davis, this is a kind of journalistic godsend. "When I need a quote from one of 'em," he says, "they're right there."

For Grosch it's not so nice, since what's on the record and off the record inevitably becomes muddled. "I've gotten burned by talking in the office and having it in the paper," he admits, but it has also taught him a valuable lesson. "You just have to be careful around reporters," particularly, it seems, when they work around the corner from you.

Atkinson concedes the situation is less than ideal. In the past he had a policy prohibiting workers from holding public office. But Gill and Grosch are valuable employees who don't work on the editorial side, and in the difficult economic climate of the *Tribune* he can't afford to lose them. "Does it create a credibility problem? Yes it does," he says. "If I could wave a magic wand, I'd love to keep Darrell Gill and Leo Grosch and not have them as elected officials."

Grosch reappears in Atkinson's office to make sure he hasn't forgotten about the phone repair guy, since time costs money.

"You'll need to come back and talk to this guy."

"I'll be back in just a second."

"He's standing and waiting."

Atkinson gives Davis a final instruction on how to tighten the strands of the hospital story, then gets up from his chair and heads into the backshop to talk with the phone guy. Over the past eighteen months, this area has become a literal shop of horrors. The equipment is used, because Atkinson is a small weekly publisher. Because it is used, it breaks down, or it never quite works the way it should, and the cost of that has put a severe financial strain on him. It has become even more heightened by the fact that the Mobridge area, almost completely dependent on agriculture, is one of the few economically depressed places in the country. In 1997, the worst South Dakota winter in a century killed thousands of cattle. The following year, grain prices plummeted, and the little dollop of tourism there was in the area, because of the worldwide reputation for walleye fishing in Lake Oahe, dropped as well.

In the meantime, Atkinson decided he needed a better press both to print the paper in color and maybe make a little extra money doing some outside work. In a trade publication he saw an ad for one that belonged to the publisher of a black weekly newspaper in North Carolina. Atkinson bought it for $135,000, and according to various estimates figured he would have to spend around $100,000 to rebuild it. He swallowed and put that figure into the budget. But the cost of the rebuilding ballooned to $190,000. Then ad revenue started falling because of the economy, and Atkinson found himself facing negative cash flow.

To help with the cash situation, Atkinson has basically refinanced the operation through a series of different loans. Cash flow is positive again, and next year Atkinson hopes to do $1.5 million in revenue. Like many weekly publishers he has diversified to stay afloat—a vinyl sign business, a business trading in personalized coffee cups and pens and jackets (humming along at a quarter million dollars a year), the publication of several regional phone books.

But the situation is precarious, particularly after the bank told him there would be no more loans even if a piece of machinery went down and didn't come back up. There have been sleepless nights. There has been the stress and struggle of making bank payments. There is the awareness that there are thirty-one people who work for him and depend on him.

"It's probably why the *Tribune* has survived as long as it has," says Eryn DeFoort of Atkinson's efforts. "He could have really given up on it." But DeFoort, the special sections editor of the paper until she left in October, has also seen the toll it has taken on him, regardless of his stoic facade. She is well aware of the industry trend, how the chains are coming in and buying up papers like Atkinson's. She is also aware of the never-ending burden the publisher carries. "It's just not wondering if the industry will eat us up," she says. "It's wondering if the industry will eat up Larry."

ATKINSON STANDS in the corner of the backshop with the phone repair guy, who has fixed the mystery of the recorded music by pointing out to Atkinson, as gently as he possibly can, that there can be no recorded music if there is, as happens to be the case here, no tape in the tape recorder.

"That'll do it," says Atkinson.

"Yes sir," says the phone repair guy.

As for the static problem, the phone repair guy can't quite pinpoint it, but he is pretty sure that an open container of chemicals sitting in close proximity to the phone wires doesn't help.

"You got corrosive chemicals here and that'll eat away at these."

Atkinson nods. He chats for a few minutes with Jim Nelson, owner and publisher of the *Timber Lake Topic* in a town thirty-five miles to the west. They bemoan the fact that the nearest computer expert is very, very far away. Then Atkinson goes into Davis's office and reboots his computer, which has crashed. Then he goes back into his own office to work on the hospital editorial. Because of all the distractions, it takes him a bit of time to figure out where he left off. He has just gotten back into the rhythm of it when the receptionist comes in to ask if he wants to talk to a caller about an apartment that Atkinson rents out for extra income.

"Are you taking calls?"

"Just tell them to call back."

He finishes the editorial and goes back into the newsroom. Since Davis is still new he needs help with pagination, and Atkinson eagerly volunteers to do page 6. He returns to his office, where someone is using his computer because of another terminal crash, so he shifts back instead to Davis's office and begins the work of filling in an eighteen-inch hole with various briefs—a guilty plea to possession of heroin, the closing of Revheim Bay because of a high bacteria count, a correction, a three-column house ad.

As Atkinson toils, Davis is at a terminal in the newsroom working to close some other pages, another art he is still learning. When asked by DeFoort what stories he plans to use on a particular page, he says with Sad Sack weariness, "I have no clue."

DeFoort is only twenty-three, but she promptly gives Davis the best advice he will ever receive in his career, perhaps the best advice ever dispensed, on how to succeed in newsroom management:

"Eric, the art of being an editor is to bullshit your way through and say, 'I have a clue.'"

"What did you say?" asks Atkinson from the adjacent office.

She laughs. He laughs.

And somehow, despite the late break on the hospital story, despite the phone guy and the random computer crashes and the rewriting of the editorial and the mystery of the disappearing music on hold and the static in the line and the caller about the apartment, it all gets done.

"What I find is through all this confusion, I manage to get a paper out," says Atkinson. "I find that pretty amazing."

As for the product, it's pretty much the same as it has been since Larry Atkinson took over the *Tribune* in 1982—solid, exhaustive, not a rabble-rousing voice in the community but a voice willing to prod readers to face issues they may not want to face. It is a relationship made all the more complex by the fact that anyone who writes a story for the *Tribune* is pretty much guaranteed to have a personal relationship with those they are writing about—knows their kids, knows their golf handicap, knows whether that story of catching a walleye bigger than Shaquille O'Neal's shoe size is fact or fancy.

"The people you write about aren't these faceless names," says Atkinson. "I think it makes us better journalists. It makes us more accountable in what we write. I think we care a little bit more. We can write with more understanding, but that's a good check and balance to have in the industry."

But it doesn't mean that Atkinson shies away. Like the time he took the head of the school board, who also happened to be one of his closest friends, to task for advocating closed meetings. Or the special section, all locally produced, he put out to address the problem of alcohol and drugs in the community. Or the decision he made several years ago to reproduce in its entirety a poignant and horrifying story from the *Philadelphia Inquirer* that dealt with the monumental tragedy of alcoholism on the Standing Rock reservation. Or the letter to the editor he insisted on publishing that called him an "ignorant, small-town newspaper publisher" putting out a paper that encouraged racism and violence toward Native Americans.

In Atkinson's view, all this comes with the territory of being an independent weekly newspaper publisher, the same territory in which a reader calls and thanks him for that terrific picture of her daughter at homecoming, the same territory in which a reader calls and wants to know why in hell he didn't get his paper delivered, the same territory in which Hilda Jones has her shorts in a stitch because a reporter got her name confused with Hilda Smith.

As I watch Larry Atkinson, it is clear to me that he loves this profession in a way that, without getting too maudlin about it, is inspirational, a reminder of what it means to be a journalist, or at least what it used to mean before the Internet made all of us feel like we were counting down to a funeral. The work that he does is a part of his soul.

But he is not a saint. He is a man with a family to support. He is a businessman with a payroll to meet, and while the last year has had its sublime moments, it has also had moments where "it hasn't been fun." No fun struggling to make bank payments. No fun when the cash flow has gone red. No fun when the cost of repairing that bitchy press, even though the actual time in the shop was three hours, still came to $2,000 because Atkinson also had to pay the repairman's airfare, rental car, travel time, and parking in the airport lot. No fun when you advertise for seven months and realize that there is no one out there anymore who has any interest in doing what you have spent your life doing.

Over the past year Atkinson got calls from three brokers wondering if he might be interested in selling. They were calls he resisted, because he could pretty much predict what a lot of chains would do if they came in.

But the conversation with the bank, in which he was told there would be no more loans, jarred Atkinson to the bone, because it means there is no room for natural disaster in a business that is predicated on it. "I'm leveraged so much now that I can't make a mistake," he says. If the press needs a major repair, or the address labeler goes kaput, or the computer system fatally crashes, Atkinson knows he may be sunk. "I'm worried at this point. I'm worried about whether or not I'm going to be able to hold onto this business."

And it has created a harsh reality for him, one fraught with so many dimensions and questions of personal principle that it marks the only time he shuts the door to his office when he speaks to me.

"Prior to that discussion with the bank, I probably wouldn't have sold," he says. He pauses for just a second, knowing that the sentiment he is about to express is one that he never thought would occur to him.

"But after that discussion with the bank, I probably would sell."

The words linger in the cozy and cluttered office, swollen and sad and in their tiny way momentous, the specter of another independent weekly fluttering to the forest floor. Not right now. Maybe not even in the near future if the farming picks up and Atkinson can kick up the revenues to that $1.5 million goal. But sometime, because in the malling of America, weekly newspapers are just another tenant.

"Realistically," says Larry Atkinson, "I'm the last private owner of this paper."

Later that night, over steaks the size of meteorites at the Fireside, I watch Atkinson as he interacts with the other patrons. I see the mutual warmth, how Atkinson understands just how damn tough it is to make a living in Mobridge today, how the others exude a familiarity that comes with knowing that here is a man, a good man, who has become as important a fixture in their community as any preacher or teacher or politician. It is here, in these brief exchanges of how's the wife and how's the kids and good luck and God bless, that I understand why local ownership of the weekly newspaper is so indispensable. As I continue to watch, I try to think of what the community of Mobridge would be like without Larry Atkinson as the publisher of the *Tribune,* putting out that reliable product week in and week out, year in and year out.

And I can't.

I just can't.

Two days later, when I cross the bridge over the Missouri that separates Mobridge from the Standing Rock reservation and head further west, it is still something I am thinking about. The prairie of South Dakota is a flood of burnished gold in the crystal morning, shimmering and magnificent and breathless. There isn't another car in sight, and as the ribbon of highway carves its way to what must be eternity, I feel I may be in the only place left in America as close in spirit to the last century as to this one.

I can hear the hoofbeats of the buffalo tamping over the floor of the golden grass before they were slaughtered for sport. I can see men and women in the sun of the early morning fitting together hard beams of wood. Somewhere out there in that prairie, the holder of all secrets and dreams and disappointments, I can hear the sound of a fiddle at a barnyard dance, just as I can hear the coughing breaths of a farmer who is dying before he should. Mile flows into mile and reflection into reverie, until I pull into the town of Faith, population 542, to get some gas. I look around as I fill up, getting a fix on the Wrangler Cafe and the Bogue & Bogue law offices and the blue of the Faith water tower. I walk inside to pay, and I also pick up a copy of the *Faith Independent.*

I read about the death of Grace Lenk at the age of sixty-three, and how Aldene Carmichael, while visiting her daughter Judy, did something she hadn't done in years and picked wild grapes so she could make jelly. I see that Cori Lee Collins is getting married to Joshua Wade Mackaben—their parents have taken out an ad inviting everyone to the wedding. I learn that Ace Gallagher, an aide to South Dakota senator Tom Daschle, has been in town, and I read a lead paragraph that the *New York Times* would never have the guts to print:

That's right. Ace is a female. I have no idea if she is a "fast-draw" or a poker player, but what I do know is that she has a lot of information. . . .

As I read the *Faith Independent,* I realize that for all my romanticized perception of awesome isolation, there is a community here, a spirited and proud one woven together by its newspaper. And then I remember that this is one of the little weeklies that Larry Atkinson prints up each week at tiny profit, and I also remember what he said.

"If I didn't print them, no one else would, and that town would lose its paper."

Would a chain, if it were to buy Atkinson's operation, share a similar philosophy?

As I place the *Faith Independent* on the back seat and turn toward Wyoming, I know that of all the questions I have posed to myself on this trip, this is the one most effortless to answer.

Jackson, Wyoming
1,693 Miles

It was earlier in my travels, during a stop in Sheldon, Iowa, to see the operation of the *N'West Iowa Review,* that I heard publisher Peter Wagner offer the theory that the plethora of buy-ups by the deep-pocket boys was actually a good thing for the weekly newspaper business.

It didn't make much initial sense to me, given that Wagner's newspaper, arguably the best community weekly in the country, crafted with a blend of color and photos and columns that most good metro dailies don't come close to, is a testament to the very act of being able to do something without some obsequious memo to the corporate office.

The Wagner theory made even less sense when he told me he had resisted the overtures of three different media companies within the past year dying to have the *N'West Iowa Review* among their holdings. After all, if the chains are good for the weekly newspaper business, then why not sign on the dotted line like so many others?

The first two overtures, expressed through panting brokers, were easy to ignore, he had told me. But the third one, up in that stratosphere of multiples times earnings, made Peter Wagner slightly woozy, in the same way that it made Larry Randa slightly woozy.

"The first two I said no to," says the fifty-nine-year-old Wagner, who whirls around the office with such determined speed he makes the Energizer Bunny look like a shut-in. "The third I said to myself, 'Maybe there's something they know that I don't know.'"

The company, which is involved in a variety of different products besides the newspaper, was doing about $3 million in revenues. Wagner won't disclose the amount of that third offer, except to say that it was so "incredible" that he turned to his wife and son and daughter-in-law to see if it was something that in all good conscience could be refused.

They said it was up to him. So he thought about it. Thought about that first year when he decided to publish on Sunday and just about every minister was ready to boot him out of town because that was the Lord's day, not some newspaper's. Thought about how the initial subscription base was three—that's three paying customers—and how revenues had once been just $360,000. Thought about how, despite flirtations with bankruptcy, he had always believed that the best way to long-term profitability was through quality and community commitment. Thought about how an outside bean counter would come in, take one look at his editorial payroll and start constructing the gallows. And he realized he couldn't accept that third offer, unless, as he put it, "I could sell it and move to Timbuktu and never see a copy."

And yet, here is Wagner saying that the entrance of the big companies into the weekly business is a good thing. He seems to be arguing with himself, a contrarian view for the sake of attention, until I figure out what he is getting at. A fancier of bow ties, Wagner is too nice to phrase it this way, but what he is basically suggesting is the natural tendency of the big, whenever they try to subsume the small, to screw up everything.

As Wagner sees it, the major holders of weeklies, by the very act of coming into a market and stripping the existing papers of their distinctiveness, or merging one paper with another, or closing a paper completely, create an opportunity for someone else to seize readers starving for something that has some actual stake in their community besides profit margin. Newspaper startups are always risky, of course, but the cost of getting a weekly going, especially given today's technology, is considerably more manageable than it once was. And in recent years there have been some nice success stories: *Main Line Life,* which took on both the *Main Line Times* and the *Suburban & Wayne Times* in the Philadelphia suburbs and now outpaces both of them in the number of ads; the *Stranger* alternative weekly in Seattle, now considered a far more hip and fresher voice than the *Seattle Weekly* and with the ad lineage to prove it; the *Sublette County Journal* in western Wyoming, which has been an absolute stinger in the butt of the far more established *Pinedale Roundup* and just took away that sweetest of all mother's milk—the weekly grocery insert.

In a sense that's exactly what Wagner did in 1972 when he started the *N'West Iowa Review,* capitalizing on a perceived vacuum in the market and an abiding faith that readers, unlike cows, will not simply graze at whatever is beneath their feet but will know the difference between what is home-grown and some biogenetic ripoff. With time and patience and persever-ance, Wagner saw it happen at the *N'West Iowa Review.* The subscription base is up to fifty-five hundred. Ads come in sweet bucketfuls, and so do awards. The paper has won the National Newspaper Association's "Best of the Best" honor the past three years in the medium-size weekly category, and it has been named Iowa Newspaper of the Year eleven times. In other words, quality does have a place in the weekly marketplace, and as Wagner peeks over his shoulder and sees what is happening slightly to the east of him, he can't help but wonder if the same thing may happen there.

At the end of 1998, Community Newspaper Holdings Inc., a company that didn't even exist four years ago and now owns more U.S. newspapers than anyone except Gannett, thanks to its backing from Alabama's state pension fund, moved into the northwest Iowa market. The company purchased a package of six weeklies and three dailies from Edwards Publications. Since then, all the weeklies, in such towns as Alta, Aurelia, and Sioux Rapids, have been closed and merged into other products. Three were combined into a single new weekly called the *Dickinson County News.* The other three were merged with daily papers in the area. In addition, one of the dailies CNHI purchased, the *Storm Lake Pilot Tribune,* has been pared back from a five-day-a-week publication to three days. "These are small communities with small circulations," says Kevin Kampman, senior vice president and chief operating officer for CNHI's western papers. "They were very, very small, and we didn't think we could serve the read-ers." What readers are getting now, says Kampman, is "a more complete package."

That may be so, even if it's a package that has to be shared with some-one else. From Wagner's vantage point, what CNHI has done is put this market in flux, and he believes the closures and mergers could ultimately create new opportunities for enterprising, locally based publishers. "This is the best time that has existed for honest to God hometown community papers since World War II," he says bullishly.

Driving through Wyoming, I took some small measure of solace in what Wagner said, particularly since his own homegrown product is such exquisite proof that profitability and quality, far from being the principals in endlessly bitter and acrimonious divorce proceedings, can in fact snuggle up and share a bed and get along pretty well. Over the past several years there has been more than 10 percent annual growth at the *N'West Iowa Review* and its other properties. Despite declining population in the area, circulation of the weekly is going up. "We're reinvesting each week to continue those volumes that we're doing today," says Wagner.

An admirable philosophy with ample reward. Still, I couldn't help but wonder: Could Peter Wagner be perceived as a workable model for the weekly newspaper business? Or in a world of 20 percent margins on a bad hair day and 30 percent on a good one by snips and cuts, was he just some anomaly? After watching the noble struggle of Larry Atkinson in Mobridge, I wasn't so sure.

And then I pulled into Jackson.

I want to like Mike Sellett.
I *do* like Mike Sellett.
But I hate Mike Sellett.

Hate him out of jealousy. Hate him because there he is across the desk from me, smart and satisfied and successful, the realization of the dream all we journalists have fancied at a given point in our careers to get out of the mental ward of the city desk and away from all those editors who insist on hovering around you on deadline like fruit flies (is there any stupider question in life than "Are you finished yet?") and go buy a little weekly in some part of the country that is so beautiful there is no point in trying to describe it. Which of course is exactly what Mike Sellett did when he ended up in Jackson, a relentlessly charming resort town at the foot of the Grand Tetons. Which of course is why, for a little bit at least, he deserves to be hated, even if he did once play a round of golf with President Clinton and nail him by seven strokes with a seventy-eight.

In 1972 Sellett left Chicago, where he was a regular contributor to the *Chicago Tribune*'s Sunday magazine, and became managing editor of the *Jackson Hole News*. In a way, the situation seemed too fairy-tale to be true, and in fact it was, since the *News* was a startup competing against the established *Jackson Hole Guide*.

"I wasn't walking into Bumfuck, Idaho," says Sellett. "This was already a competitive town."

But the founders of the paper, Ralph Gill and Virginia Huidekoper, had a vision of creating a product that was rich and deep and graphically breathtaking. True to Peter Wagner's philosophy, they saw a crack in the market and they went for it. A year later, in 1973, when running the paper began to take up far more time than they had bargained for, they turned to Sellett and asked him if he would like to buy it. He found the suggestion quite tantalizing, and also quite amazing since he had no money. But since

Gill and Huidekoper believed he would continue the mission of the *Jackson Hole News,* they agreed to carry a note for roughly 90 percent of the $100,000 purchase price.

But it was still a lot of money, and as Sellett mulled over what to do he called Mike Howard, whose family knew a little about the newspaper business since they were the Howards of Scripps Howard. Howard, himself a year away from becoming editor of the *Rocky Mountain News* in Denver, wrote Sellett a lengthy letter back saying that his accountants, after taking a look at the financials, had come to the firm conclusion that the *News* would never be able to compete effectively against the *Guide.* Its pockets were simply too deep. "I don't know why I persisted after that," says Sellett. "I suppose that I had no place to go."

Nearly three decades later, the fifty-year-old Sellett still owns the *Jackson Hole News.* According to unofficial figures, he can boast of a circulation lead over the *Guide,* about 7,100 to 5,100. Over time, Sellett also began to see value in another Wagner principle: Make quality the cornerstone of your product and they will come.

Or as Sellett himself put it, "What I had to learn for survival was, How do you turn editorial excellence into dollars?"

Of course, on the business side of the equation, Sellett had the serendipitous fortune to be in an area that was rich and exclusive when he bought the paper, and twenty-six years later has only become more rich and more exclusive. Each week the paper is chock full with color real estate ads in which a three-bedroom, three-bath TERRIFIC OPPORTUNITY adjacent to Grand Teton National Park at the Jackson Hole Mountain Resort can be yours for $2.45 million. Not grand enough for all those IPO earnings? Then try the UNMATCHED VIEWS AND PRIVACY of 117 acres at the top of the north end of East Gros Ventre Butte for $4.95 million.

The editorial-excellence part of the equation was established through a series of hires over the years that any paper in the country would envy: chief layout artist Cammie Pyle, who graduated from Radcliffe and worked at the *Atlantic Monthly* before having enough sense to chuck it all to become a ski bum; Richard Murphy, the paper's first chief of photography, who was at the helm in 1984 when the National Press Photographers Association cited the *News* for best use of photographs by any paper in the country; Garth Dowling, who guided the photo department when it won the Wyoming Press Association's overall award for photographic excellence in 1993 and 1994 and 1995.

Today the news side is in the hands of forty-seven-year-old editor Angus MacLean Thuermer Jr., a soft-spoken and slightly laconic and very windburnt Yale graduate who speaks a kind of mountain-climber patois that reveals itself in such keep-on-trucking whispers as "I always wanted to be a photographer. Fuck this word shit. Way too complicated."

There is something inscrutable about him, probably due to the fact that his father, after a stint as a foreign correspondent in the late 1930s when Europe was exploding, quit and joined the OSS. But Angus Thuermer knows how to get what he wants. Twenty-one years ago, when he was trying to land a job at the *News,* he sweet-talked Sellett's golden retriever onto the porch, put a sign around his neck that said "Hire Angus or Else," signed it "The Phantom" and then sent the dog to find his owner. And on each Tuesday night when it's deadline, Thuermer stares at his computer with a look that is far more intense than dissolute. He coaxes the staff gently, and it bothers him that there wasn't enough time to get an interview with the guy from Seattle who got mauled by the grizzly in Yellowstone. Because news is news. "A good grizzly mauling, if you get the victim, goes on the top of Page 1 automatic. That's kind of a rule of thumb around here."

Acutely aware of how easy it is for a weekly to fall into the malaise of meat-grinder laziness, Thuermer derives inspiration from the front page mockup of an imaginary paper called the *Bugle-Beacon* that has been posted on the newsroom bulletin board. It carries the following headlines:

BORING STUFF DEBATED AT DULL MEETING
SOMETHING CRASHES, BURNS OR BLOWS UP
SOME OLD POLITICIAN RETIRES OR DIES
ANOTHER PROJECT WILL COST LOTS & LOTS OF DOLLARS
HEY! THEY'RE DOING THAT WACKY THING OVER THERE

On a given week, it isn't unusual to find a fifty-inch, in-depth piece in the *Jackson Hole News* on some aspect of life in Teton County, whether it's an investigative story on a local developer who kept trying to develop despite a string of bankruptcies, a story on the scarcity of affordable housing in the region or a series on the future of the national park system. But this is a community newspaper, and when the community doesn't like something it tends to stampede. "People here are sensitive," is the way a photographer at the paper, Jim Evans, gently puts it. "It's a very sensitive town."

The issue of what properly belongs in the paper and what does not came to a boiling point last Christmas season. Some twenty-five hundred students from California were in Jackson for their usual winter-break sojourn, and chief photographer John Brecher, as talented a young shooter as you will find in this country, set out to take a picture that would capture it all. But he didn't want the usual saccharine fluff shot. "I thought this year, well shit, maybe there's something else I can photograph."

Brecher ended up in a hotel room where fifteen teenage girls were partying at high velocity. With their permission, he shot a picture of several of them that captured the rite of adolescent passage in all its essence—the sexuality of the girls with their tight midriff shirts, the way one of them held a lollipop with one hand and guzzled down a can of beer with the other. It was a spectacular picture. Thuermer published it without consulting Sellett, and then all hell broke loose. Members of the community felt that the very prettiness of the picture glorified teenage drinking, and so did Sellett, who would not have run it had he known about it.

To a certain degree, Brecher wondered if Sellett's attitude reflects a basic reluctance "to put [the *News*] in the firing line." But after thirty years, Sellett has come to realize that community reaction is intertwined into every story. For better or worse, richer or poorer, readers view a weekly as something that belongs to them.

Several months after the picture episode, a student at Jackson Hole High School was arrested when police found a suspected explosive in his pack. Given that the shootings at Columbine High School in suburban Denver had occurred only two days earlier, the *News* decided to put out a special edition—not to inflame the community but to inform it. Included in the four-page package was a heated session of the Teton County School District Board, in which a parent claimed that members of the school's speech club were part of what she described as the "trenchcoat church."

The special edition came out Friday. By six that night, Sellett had already gotten a call from an outraged reader. On Saturday, Sellett went to a meeting with speech club students and their parents at the famed Wort Hotel in Jackson. He tried to explain why the paper had a right to print what had been said at the school board meeting since it was a matter of public record, but for most of the three hours he listened as kids he knew, and parents he knew, vented and expressed their devastation and sometimes cried.

"It was such a vivid reminder for me . . . that this community is small and we know these people," says Sellett. And although it was difficult, it was also a welcome reminder of the role that a weekly plays in a community, and the role that a publisher with local roots plays within it. "The difference in small towns is that people end up in the publisher's office. They just walk up the back stairs, sit in that chair and call me an asshole."

I wondered how other weekly publishers around the country might feel about such interaction with the community, but in the current climate of buy and swap and consolidate, I figured they had other things on their minds.

In a corner of the Jackson newsroom there is a bookcase crammed with weekly papers from all over the region. During the two days I was there, in between interviews and trying to get Thuermer to say two complete sentences in a row, I rummaged through it, and what I found only confirmed the seismic shifts that are taking place in the weekly business. "Either you chain up or you get big or you die," was the way Ted Biedron, the executive vice president of Pioneer Press, had put it to me before I hit the road, and the reality of that statement was only underscored by that helter-skelter bookcase.

There was the *Steamboat Pilot,* which used to belong to Jack Kent Cooke, late owner of the Washington Redskins, but was now held by a company from Lawrence, Kansas, called WorldWest LLC. There was the *Aspen Times,* which was looking for new investors. There was the *West Yellowstone News,* which was bought by Big Sky Publishing. There was the *Wyoming State Journal* in Lander, which was bought by the daily in Riverton. There was the *Hungry Horse Tribune* and the *Whitefish Pilot* in Montana, which were bought by Lee Enterprises out of Davenport, Iowa, in 1999, and now not only ran identical commentary page columns (in the *Hungry Horse Tribune* G. George Ostrom is identified as a columnist for the *Tribune;* in the *Whitefish Pilot* he's identified as a columnist for the *Pilot*), but on at least one occasion had an identical editorial, as if to suggest that the two communities are fundamentally identical.

The trend suggested by that bookcase does not go unnoticed by Mike Sellett. At a certain point in his life he will sell out, because everyone sells out, but he is determined, just like the owners who sold to him were determined, to find the right buyer.

"If I sell, I don't want to sell to a chain," he says. "I would take less money from a buyer who lived here and worked here than from someone who showed up with an armored truck and then made [the *News*] part of some homogenized chain."

Sellett's statement gave me a surge of hope. But the results of that bookcase sampling were ominous at best. When I walked back to the hotel that night, I swore I saw pinstripe boys for Liberty and CNHI and Dean Singleton riding around town in their armored trucks. And the next day, when I left Jackson for good and headed for the coast, I figured I had only one final shot of salvation left—the alternative weekly market.

SAN FRANCISCO
3,155 MILES

If you're going to end a trip like this, it seems to me there is no better way to do it than with bluster, iconoclasm, outrage, and a promise to fight to the last drop of blood even when you know you're probably screwed.

I had come to San Francisco to see Bruce Brugmann of the *San Francisco Bay Guardian* and the dean of alternative weekly publishers. He did not disappoint, nor did the ambiance of the office on Hampshire Street—a little fish tank at the corner of the reception desk; old *Guardian* promotional posters spouting such slogans as "Protecting your right to fight City Hall" and "Protecting your right to sunbathe naked;" a man walking around in what appeared to be a mumu that had once been worn by Mama Cass; an executive editor with a streak of gray hair not all the way to his derriere, but impressively close.

In other words everything an alternative weekly should be—unorthodox, unrestrained, mad as hell, and worried that the very mission of such papers in America, "to print the news and raise hell" as the motto on the *Guardian* masthead puts it, is being tamped into mush.

In person, Brugmann looked more like a book editor than a flame-thrower. He is tall, with a close-cropped white beard, and he was wearing suspenders and black wingtips. He is originally from Iowa, which isn't his fault but has resulted in that maddening Midwest combination of talking all the time and taking a very, very, very long time to do it, as if each word has its own planting season. For some reason, he reminded me a bit of Burl Ives after a weight-loss program.

But Brugmann is no idle commentator. For nearly thirty-five years, he has been in the face of just about every mayor and bloated politician and fatcat utility in San Francisco. It's no accident that the following statement from the current mayor, Willie Brown, hangs on his office door: "I'd recommend first you don't read the *Guardian*. Because there's absolutely nothing accurate on any page of that particular newspaper." It's no accident that when he talked to me about the two daily papers in town, the *San Francisco Chronicle* and the *San Francisco Examiner,* he called them "conservative papers in the last stages of arterial sclerosis."

And it certainly is no accident that legal bills for various public records–access suits lay on the desk of his wife, Jean Dibble, the associate publisher. There was one for $25,472, and another one for $828, and when Dibble, who handles the business side of the *Guardian*, picked them up and looked through them, she could only sigh. But for her husband, these suits, and the costs of filing them, form the sweet music of what makes an alternative weekly an alternative weekly, beholden to nothing and no one with the sole exception of that masthead motto.

"We can sue," says Brugmann. "We can threaten. We can make statements. If you can't sue the bastards, you condemn the bastards."

That kind of hellfire contempt extends beyond politicians to include the city's daily papers—to poke at them and prod at them and constantly challenge their potential monopoly on the news. Which is why Brugmann could only shake his head in dismay when the *Hartford Courant,* owned by Times Mirror (which has since been bought by Tribune Company), bought the alternative weekly in Hartford. Brugmann says the very image of the same corporate parent owning these two products sickened him. He railed against the sale in print and hoped that the Justice Department would block it because of antitrust violations that, in Brugmann's estimation, were blatant and obvious. But the Justice Department didn't see it that way. The sale whistled through, and Brugmann now sees it as a barometer of things to come in the alternative weekly business. "Times Mirror is leading the way," he says. "These are just toxic viruses that are being set loose."

From a business standpoint, the *Courant's* purchase of the *Hartford Advocate* was a no-brainer. For years, metro dailies have tried to woo young readers, and for years they have failed. In the meantime, the sleepy little alternatives seized on the eighteen-to-forty-five-year-old market with a vengeance. Readership increased, particularly when publishers stopped playing air guitar to "Stairway to Heaven," found corporate religion and realized that the most effective way to get an alternative weekly into the hands of those young and hip readers was to give it away. As readership increased, so did advertising lineage, and if you go to any major city today you're bound to find at least one alternative weekly as thick as a phone book, and maybe two.

The dailies, of course, could only sit back and shed self-pitying tears at the loss of another sector of the market. Until April 1999, when the *Courant* basically said to hell with it and figured out that the only effective way to compete with the alternative weekly in Hartford was to buy it, along with four sister publications in Connecticut, Massachusetts, and New York. For a huge corporation like Times Mirror, the amount of that purchase, about $18 million, was the equivalent of petty cash. But from an editorial standpoint, it created a nightmare.

When Janet Reynolds, editor of the *Advocate,* first heard the news of the sale, she literally started screaming "No! No! Not the *Courant!* No!" Five months later, sitting in the offices of the *Advocate* in downtown Hartford, she was still feeling the effects of what had taken place. "With the exception of being sold to the Journal Register Co., which is the evil empire, this is the worst thing that could have happened," she says.

In 1999, at the annual convention of the Association of Alternative Newsweeklies in Memphis, a motion was made to revoke the *Advocate*'s membership because it could no longer be considered independent. But Reynolds cautioned her fellow brethren not to get too righteous, given the likelihood that other metro dailies might imitate the Times Mirror purchase in their own markets. What she actually told them was, "The cancer is in the bloodstream." She asked that the *Advocate* get a grace period, and the motion was tabled.

When the sale was consummated, Reynolds told *Courant* executives that she would publicly scream bloody murder at the slightest show of editorial influence on the *Advocate*. She hasn't done that, because in her view there has been no editorial influence. As a result, her initial revulsion has given way to a wary cautiousness that maybe, just maybe, this bizarre pairing of longtime enemies can somehow work. "I feel as good as I can about it," she says, "given that I basically think it's a bad idea. . . . Would I apply to the alternative weekly that is owned by Times Mirror? I don't think so."

Because even if there has been no editorial interference, there is still the power of perception, the fact that some readers will never again see the *Advocate* as an independent voice but as the *Courant Junior*.

But she is still there, and so is Fran Zankowski, who was recently made publisher of the entire five-publication operation under the umbrella of a separate company called New Mass Media. Zankowski is convinced that there can be a firewall between his operation and that of the *Courant*. His company is completely separate, to the degree that his employees are not even eligible for the Times Mirror health plan. He does go over to the offices of the *Courant* once a week to meet with executives, but so far at least the extent of their involvement has been to standardize financial reporting and insist on budgeting in April instead of September. In other words, the talk is almost purely about business and making sure that the *Advocate* papers, whatever the hell they do, just keep on doing it. "In a static market, it was a way [for the *Courant*] to grow," says Zankowski. "The other reason was, we were profitable. They were looking to gain market share at a pretty reasonable risk."

As for poking and prodding the *Courant*, the *Advocate* received a laurel from *Columbia Journalism Review* for disclosing that the city of Hartford has lost more than $2 million in revenues by allowing companies, in particular the *Courant*, to rent municipal land for parking lots at rates well below the market.

When I reported to Bruce Brugmann these various views from the *Advocate* front line—that autonomy is still intact—he gave a kind of pitying smile. And then the smile ceased, and a moody cloud creased over him, as if what Reynolds and Zankowski were saying wasn't simply self-delusional but the journalistic equivalent of spitting in his face.

"I sure as hell wouldn't want them working for me."

At first I thought it was just another Brugmann line of bluster, said for the verbal pugilism of being a left-of-center tough guy in wingtips and suspenders. But then I detected something else: a genuine sense of hurt, maybe even fear, that all he has worked for as a journalist, all he believes in when it comes to maintaining independence, is about to come crashing down.

"I've spent my entire life doing this," he says. "I'll be goddamned if I'll sell to . . . any of these chains. I've put too much into it."

I found myself rooting for him when he said that any self-respecting newspaper should have two public-access suits and two libel suits pending at all times. I found myself rooting for him when he said of the Times Mirror purchase, "It's sad there's no antitrust. It's sad there is not more opposition." I found myself rooting for him when he said, "The people who wrote the First Amendment were not writing it for Gannett and Knight Ridder and for the big boys to get bigger."

But after 3,155 miles on the road in search of the American weekly, I also realized that rooting for someone, however it soothes the troubled soul, is just a momentary respite. Along the path of interstates and farm roads and mountain curves, I had encountered all sorts of delights—honor, feistiness, locally grown products that were stunning. But my head was also crammed with terms that I had never encountered before: clustering, consolidation, contiguous markets, chaining up, economic synergies, volume discount pricing, economies of scale.

As a journalist, I appreciate the newfound knowledge of those terms, because I had learned something. But as a journalist, I could hear the tap-tap-tap of another nail in the coffin, as if the words, and the reporting, and the quotes, the stuffing that makes a weekly paper a weekly paper, were about to become little more than tinsel and blinking lights in the corporate Christmas tree of new profits and new markets. The voices of independence are still out there in the American weekly, out there in the fields of Iowa, out there in the prairie of South Dakota, out there in the mountains of Wyoming, out there in the sexual sizzle of San Francisco. I found inspiration and solace in the men and women who put out these weekly papers, who believe in their communities and love them and give back to them because they live in them. They are as close to the First Amendment as you can get, its most dedicated protectors and practitioners. But for all their nobility, my heart also tells me they are nothing more than the last survivors.

4 | Newspaper Monopoly

By Jack Bass

THE NEWSPAPER CHAIN is trying to figure out if it makes sense to add a certain forty-thousand-circulation daily to its portfolio. Decision time is fast approaching, so the CEO spreads before him all the pertinent documents to be studied—cash-flow models, market analyses, payroll and circulation breakouts, broker recommendations, highway maps.

Highway maps?

Absolutely—in some ways maybe the most crucial papers in the stack, truth be told. That's because where newspaper companies once were quick to gobble up most any property that came available—call it growth for growth's sake—today they have come to embrace the real estate agent's mantra of "location, location, location."

On a scale never before seen or imagined, newspaper chains are concentrating their holdings into tight geographic groups. Stimulated by new opportunities for cutting costs and building revenues, and encouraged by tax laws and changing trends in retail advertising, such established companies as Knight Ridder, Cox, Media General, Gannett, Donrey, and MediaNews are swapping properties like baseball cards, unloading papers that don't fit their geographic strategies and acquiring ones that do.

Thomson Newspapers coined a fancy name for a complex of papers in close proximity—"strategic marketing groups." Cox speaks of "regional groups," while MediaNews and other companies use the more generic term "clusters." Whatever you call them, they have transformed the landscape of newspaper ownership in America and fundamentally changed the way the industry does business.

The Project on the State of the American Newspaper has identified 125 major regional concentrations, involving more than four hundred papers—or well over a fourth of the nation's dailies. By the time you read this, the numbers will be even higher.

The ultimate cost-cutting prize is to have two or more papers share the same printing plant. But even when this isn't possible, nearby papers may share overhead costs such as accounting, they may pool their regional sports coverage or their state and regional political coverage, and (although this is rare) they may even share a centralized copy desk. "The closer you are, the more you can share," explains Brian Cooper, senior vice president of Cox Newspapers.

Geographic concentration allows more enticing deals to large retail advertisers. With one buy order, one ad sheet and one bill, a Sears, a Circuit City, or a big regional bank can place ads in any combination of papers it wants within the group. For advertising agencies, which increasingly make buy decisions for the major retailers in regional malls, the combined circulation of a newspaper cluster, purchased on a cost-per-thousand basis, makes more sense than buying space in bits and pieces from competing papers with overlapping circulation areas.

But while the economic advantages of clustering become more obvious every day, the implications for readers and for journalism are less clear.

After Cox acquired it in 1995 and integrated it into a three-paper group, the *Greenville Daily Reflector* in North Carolina got a new printing plant, updated its computer system, and began getting Washington coverage of its congressional delegation for the first time.

When MediaNews bought the thirty-five-thousand circulation *San Mateo County Times* in 1996 to add to its other holdings in the San Francisco area, it reinvigorated an afternoon paper that was losing money and lacked the resources to adequately cover local pro sports teams. Three years later the *Times* was showing a profit, running nearly twice as many pages as before, and covering local news well enough to hold its ground against the *San Francisco Chronicle* to the north and the *San Jose Mercury News* to the south.

On the other hand, after MediaNews bought Long Beach's *Press-Telegram* from Knight Ridder in 1997, it slashed newsroom salaries, damaging morale and prompting more than half the members of a seasoned and respected staff to leave. Knight Ridder did a similar thing with the *Monterey County Herald,* which it acquired in 1997 in an exchange of California and Colorado papers with Scripps Howard. The new owner cut staff in Monterey, refused to recognize the existing Newspaper Guild contract, crushed morale, and alienated many people in the community.

An obvious drawback to geographical concentration is that it reduces competition and the diversity of journalistic voices. In twenty-two states, one company already controls 20 percent or more of the daily newspapers. For example, Media General owns one-third of all the dailies in Virginia. Lee Enterprises owns nearly half of Montana's daily papers—five out of eleven. More than half of Oklahoma's dailies belong to a single company,

CNHI. And two companies, Gannett and Donrey, together own two-thirds of the dailies in Hawaii.

Journal Register owns five of Connecticut's eighteen daily papers; they cooperate in both newsgathering and business operations. The Tribune Company owns three other Connecticut papers, which share some editorial functions. These two chains account for more than half of all the local papers sold in Connecticut each day.

Between them, Gannett and Newhouse own thirteen of New Jersey's nineteen daily papers. These two companies account for nearly three-fourths of the circulation of all New Jersey–based dailies. They also provide twenty-five of the forty newspaper reporters who cover state government on a full-time basis.

Concentration of ownership is nothing new, but in recent years it has become pervasive. Daily newspapers changed hands 713 times in the United States between January 1994 and August 2000, and in almost every case the result was a stronger concentration of ownership within a state or region. The idea of building clusters was what prompted most of those transactions in the first place.

Some major players have taken advantage of the seller's market to pare their holdings to more manageable levels. In the late 1990s, Thomson reduced its U.S. daily newspaper holdings from more than 150 to just 49. "The problem with the 150-odd newspapers was rather like a biblical farmer scattering his seed on the land," Stuart Garner, Thomson's chief executive officer, told the *Milwaukee Journal Sentinel*. "There was no logic in where the newspapers were located." After the sell-off, there was a logic. Forty-five of Thomson's 49 remaining U.S. papers were in specific clusters —three in southeastern Indiana, eight in central Wisconsin, and so on.

Then, in 2000, Thomson turned around and unloaded all its U.S. papers to companies that integrated them into even larger clusters. Gannett, for example, bought Thomson's eight Wisconsin dailies (plus six weeklies) to add to the two daily papers it already owned there, creating a local monopoly across twelve adjacent counties. Gannett also bought six Thomson papers in Ohio (plus four weeklies) to add to the four Ohio dailies it already owned. CNHI bought six Thomson dailies in Georgia and eight in Indiana; it already owned four dailies in each of those states. CNHI and Gannett together now account for about 40 percent of Indiana's daily circulation.

"Newspaper companies are going to have to find more and more creative ways to keep their companies growing," says Dean Singleton, CEO of MediaNews and one of the industry's leading practitioners of clustering.

"Eliminating duplication is one of those things that help do that. This is not a growth industry."

David Lord, president of Pioneer Newspapers in Seattle, agrees. "Overall, there is an industry recognition that we have to do it. Logically, it makes sense."

Imagine a huge game of Monopoly, with all the players trading properties. Everyone knows that Boardwalk and Park Place are worth more if you own them both, which means a player who owns one will pay a premium to get the other. It's the same with newspapers. Consider a 1998 deal between Thomson and Ogden, a subsidiary of Nutting Newspapers. Thomson traded away four dailies in Ohio and Pennsylvania with a combined circulation of ninety thousand to get a single paper in Wisconsin, the *Oshkosh Northwestern*, with a circulation of just twenty-five thousand. The reason Oshkosh was so important to Thomson was that the company already owned the four other dailies that ring the Lake Winnebago area. Ogden co-owner Robert Nutting hadn't planned to sell the *Northwestern*, according to a member of the family that originally owned it. "The story we heard," the family member, Thomas H. Schwalm, told a Milwaukee reporter, "was that Thomson kept throwing newspapers at Ogden until he couldn't say no."

Or try following this transaction without a scorecard. In 1996, three companies—Thomson, Cox, and Hollinger—executed an elaborate three-way swap involving fifteen daily papers in seven states. Thomson picked up Cox's six newspapers in Arizona: the *Yuma Daily Sun* on the California border and five suburban dailies along Phoenix's long eastern flank—the *Chandler Arizonan-Tribune, Gilbert Tribune, Mesa Tribune, Scottsdale Progress Tribune,* and *Tempe Daily News-Tribune.* Subsequently Thomson merged all five of the Phoenix-area papers into the Mesa-based *Tribune,* with zoned editions for each community. (A year later Thomson would augment its Phoenix cluster by acquiring, from Ottaway Newspapers, the *Daily News-Sun* in Sun City.) Cox, meanwhile, got from Thomson two North Carolina papers—Elizabeth City's *Daily Advance* and the *Rocky Mount Telegram*—to go with the nearby *Greenville Daily Reflector,* which it had bought from an independent owner. Simultaneously, Cox got from Hollinger the *Marshall News Messenger* in East Texas, where it already owned three dailies, one of them less than twenty miles from Marshall. Cox said it also received cash and "other considerations."

Hollinger sent Thomson a weekly and a cluster of three small dailies—the *Greensburg Daily News,* the *News-Times* in Hartford City, and the *Rushville Republican*—in the southeastern corner of Indiana. The dailies had a combined circulation of not quite thirteen thousand. In return, Hollinger got three dailies from Thomson—the *Enid News and Eagle* in Oklahoma, the *Register-News* in Mount Vernon, Illinois, and the *Herald-Palladium* in Benton Harbor-St. Joseph, Michigan. (The Enid paper was subsequently resold, to CNHI, bolstering that company's concentration in Oklahoma.)

As a result of this complex trade, both Thomson and Cox were able to concentrate their holdings. Hollinger did not, but the three stand-alone newspapers it received had a combined circulation of sixty-seven thousand, while the four papers it gave up totaled only about twenty-one thousand —suggesting how much more highly valued papers may become when they can be sold into a geographical group or cluster.

Such groups need not be limited by state lines. Knight Ridder owns the largest newspapers in each of the Carolinas, the *Charlotte Observer* (244,000 daily circulation) in North Carolina and *The State* (120,000 circulation) in Columbia, South Carolina, as well as the fast-growing *Sun News* of Myrtle Beach (45,000 circulation) on the South Carolina coast. Peter Ridder, publisher of the *Observer* and the younger brother of Knight Ridder's chairman and CEO, Tony Ridder, says the distances between these papers "prohibit clustering in the traditional sense." It's 90 miles south from Charlotte to Columbia, 140 miles east from Columbia to Myrtle Beach, and almost 200 miles northwest from Myrtle Beach to Charlotte.

Still, since coming to the *Observer* in 1997, Ridder has pushed for greater sharing and "partnership" among the three newspapers. The Observer has joined in the sharing of content—especially sports—that had been going on for some time between Columbia and Myrtle Beach. Because Myrtle Beach is a golfing mecca, the *Sun News* files golf coverage to all three newspapers. It gets coverage of Clemson and University of South Carolina football from *The State* and racing news from Charlotte, a NASCAR hub. A Carolinas.com Web site lets users click on any of the three papers.

After Ridder's arrival, Columbia and Charlotte started sharing South Carolina government and political news. And the *Observer*'s Columbia bureau was cut from two reporters to one.

Traditionally, the *Observer*'s reputation in South Carolina has been one of aggressive enterprise in covering state government and politics. *The State* currently runs stories generated by the *Observer*'s one-man shop in Columbia. A veteran journalism watcher there told me the arrangement has reduced competitiveness. If the *Observer* was covering a story at the statehouse, he said, *The State* wouldn't assign one of its reporters, who might see a different angle.

So far, the *Observer* hasn't developed any significant joint advertising arrangements with its South Carolina partners, but it is exploring ways to do that, especially something related to golfing in Myrtle Beach. Since all these papers circulate in the Myrtle Beach area, "We're in a lively three-way competition," said Paula Ellis, publisher of the *Sun News*. She added, "We cooperate when everyone agrees it's to the advantage of all." Said Ridder, "I can see more and more synergies between the three Carolina newspapers. I am certain that will happen."

Synergy notwithstanding, the proliferation of geographic concentration all across America raises hard questions for journalism:

- As time goes by, will there be fewer competing journalistic voices in a given state or region? One already sees this happening in Connecticut, Virginia, New Jersey, Wisconsin, Indiana, Montana, and elsewhere.

- What happens to clusters when they mature? Since the trend is so new, it's impossible to say with any certainty. In and around Westchester County, just north of New York City, Gannett for years operated one of the nation's tightest and most conspicuous clusters. But in 1998 it merged those ten separate nameplates into a single suburban paper, the *Journal News*. Now readers get late sports results, a bigger newshole and other editorial improvements that efficient consolidation can offer. Yet, with Westchester County's scores of incorporated municipalities and independent school districts, many readers mourn the diminishment of local news and the vanishing of a newspaper masthead that was overtly "theirs." Strong, independent weeklies are thriving there.

  Out in California, meanwhile, the Contra Costa papers that Knight Ridder bought in 1995 from the family of Dean Lesher still publish as separate entities through the week. But the chain consolidated what were five separate Sunday papers into a single muscular edition that circulates nearly 200,000 copies.

- Will the fatter profits generated by the new geographic strategies mean more money for journalistic improvements, or will newsrooms languish even while earnings rise, as so often happened in the 1990s? Singleton speaks optimistically on this point, despite his reputation as a newsroom cost-cutter. "The revenue implications are more important than cost-cutting," he argues, "because selling advertising jointly not only helps your revenue base, it increases your newshole. If you sell a page of department store advertising that you didn't have before, you get a page of news you didn't have before. One of the beauties of clustering is that it takes papers standing on the brink and makes them very healthy."

- Will there be less journalistic competition? It depends. In the Bay Area, Knight Ridder's *San Jose Mercury News* and its Contra Costa papers go head-to-head against the complex of papers owned by MediaNews, and both those groups compete vigorously against the area's dominant metro, the *San Francisco Chronicle.*

This new order, though, raises another concern. As a few newspaper companies ring big cities with their coordinated groups of small to medium-size papers, will major metros lose the fight for suburban readers and advertisers? Will this further isolate suburbs from their central cities, and further deprive suburbanites of an understanding of big-city problems? It's easy to imagine this happening in places like Philadelphia and Los Angeles. But for now, it's an open question.

Nowhere is the question more pressing than in the affluent communities east of San Francisco Bay, where you can find one of the nation's most sophisticated clusters coolly humming along, twenty-four hours a day, seven days a week.

I T'S ALMOST 8 P.M., and Nancy Conway, executive editor of the five Alameda Group dailies, drops by the "news center" for a final checkup before heading home. In a large second-floor room that approaches the size of a basketball court, dozens of copy editors, grouped in units of three to six, sit at their terminals. They're doing the usual things—polishing copy, writing headlines and captions, laying out pages. But not for one newspaper—for five. Simultaneously.

The news center, in the upscale, aptly named Alameda County town of Pleasanton, is a unique place. Some seventy people work here, many of them processing copy and photos for newspapers in communities thirty miles apart. The staff is young, and most don't live in those communities, don't work there, and seldom visit.

Centralizing the copy desk and composing room functions of five different papers is designed to promote efficiency and save money for their owner, MediaNews. From that standpoint it appears to work well. Still, watching the dispatch with which these people do their jobs, in almost assembly-line fashion, it's easy to conclude that something important may be lost in the process.

An editor of one of the outlying newspapers admits as much to me. "It's harder to do a good job," he says, when your paper's editing team "is not sitting next to you. There's a communication that's so intimate, especially when you're on deadline. . . . It's hard for copy editors in a different location to have a sense of the community and a feel for the newspaper."

There is little time to fret about it, though. The copy streams in steadily, not only from the five scattered newsrooms but also from a regional staff that produces news, business, and entertainment stories for all the papers within the cluster—the *Oakland Tribune,* the *Tri-Valley Herald* in Pleasanton, the *Daily Review* in Hayward, the *Argus* in Fremont, and the *Times* in San Mateo. The operation is so complex that Conway says it took her a year to fully grasp it. She has tried to decentralize as much of the operation as possible. But due in part to the mechanized atmosphere and the limited opportunity for collegiality, turnover is high. "There's an open position most of the time," she acknowledges.

On the other hand, without the kinds of innovations MediaNews imposed, a couple of the papers in the Alameda cluster might now be losing money instead of making it. They might even be gone.

With its centralized control and coordination, the news center is part of what makes Alameda County one of the country's most thoroughgoing examples of newspaper clustering. It is the brainchild of William Dean Singleton, who has popularized several of today's hot newspaper trends. He engaged, for example, in one of the first tax-free trades of daily newspapers—an exchange with Harte-Hanks in the mid-'80s. Such exchanges were common in real estate back then. Now they're common among newspapers as well.

It was also Singleton who popularized the word "clustering" as it applies to newspapers. As a broader business term, clustering refers to the geographic concentration of interconnected companies and institutions within a field. Silicon Valley is a cluster in this sense—a nexus of enterprises, all engaged in high technology, cooperating and competing simultaneously. For Singleton, however, the term means the combining of operations for newspapers in close proximity to one another—usually in the same or adjacent counties.

Singleton developed his version of the idea sixteen years ago—not in California but in southern New Jersey, where he and a partner bought the *Gloucester County Times* in Woodbury and *Today's Sunbeam* in Salem, an adjacent county seat. (They have since sold these papers to the Newhouse chain.) "Clustering seemed the right thing to do," Singleton says. "The papers are 28 miles apart. They had many of the same advertisers. It did not make sense to have two operations."

It occurred to him that both papers could be printed in a single plant, with a single composing room, and that one accounting department would suffice for both. Besides the cost-cutting, their combined circulation made the papers more attractive to department stores and other regional advertisers, who could get a combined, discounted, "one buy, one bill" rate.

Singleton doesn't claim he invented this kind of clustering, but he says he wasn't aware of any other papers that were doing it when he started. A boyish-faced man of medium height, Singleton, forty-seven, met with me at the unpretentious MediaNews headquarters in Denver, where the *Denver Post* is its flagship paper. Dressed in slacks and a long-sleeve pullover shirt, he looked like a relaxed suburban real estate broker who enjoys desserts.

Singleton explained how, in clustering the two New Jersey papers, he and his business partner and mentor, Richard Scudder, hit upon the formula that would help propel MediaNews into the big time. Today it is the country's seventh-largest newspaper company, based on daily circulation; it is fourth largest in terms of the number of daily papers owned, forty-seven.

In New Jersey, Singleton says, he found out the hard way—from subscriber complaints—that readers can be passionately parochial about editorial content. Though Salem and Gloucester counties are side by side, he says, "we learned early that [they] are very different. Readers in one county went through the roof if stories about the other county ran in their paper." He came to believe that highly localized news was the key to attracting and holding an audience advertisers would want to reach.

In 1985, MediaNews purchased three family-owned East Bay papers— the *Daily Review,* the *Argus,* and the *Tri-Valley Herald*—all in fast-growing Alameda County. Over the next decade, the deathbed resurrection of the *Oakland Tribune* and the purchase of the money-losing *San Mateo County Times* south of San Francisco added 100,000 more in circulation to the Alameda Newspaper Group, or ANG.

"San Mateo was a family-owned newspaper that could not have remained viable if standing alone," Singleton says. "It was squeezed between San Francisco to the north and San Jose to the south. It had lost major advertising and was deteriorating. It had all the overhead of a single newspaper of 37,000. They couldn't cover the Giants and 49ers on the road. It was losing money when they decided to sell it. We made a lot of overhead go away. We were able to put in a lot of regional and national advertising, opening up the newshole. Suddenly a paper running 24 to 28 pages is now running 40 to 48."

For the year ending March 31, 1999, ANG's newspapers were the only ones in the Bay Area to show circulation gains.

The *Oakland Tribune* publishes three zoned editions daily, each with a section of local news. There's an Oakland cityside edition, one for the upscale East Bay Hills, and a third for the city of Alameda, which was already there when MediaNews acquired the paper in 1992. The paper's overall daily circulation is sixty-eight thousand.

"After doing some initial flushing out of circulation in certain areas, the Tribune's circulation has remained steady," says ANG president Scott McKibben.

But Singleton wasn't done shaking up the state's newspaper landscape. In 1999, in a boldly innovative stroke, MediaNews cut a deal to take over a majority stake in nine Donrey papers in California. Most of these are in the southern part of the state. But in the Bay Area's hotly contested newspaper wars, the merger allowed ANG to leapfrog Knight Ridder's Contra Costa group to acquire the *Vallejo Times-Herald,* with its twenty-thousand circulation. This gave Singleton a foothold in the North Bay, at the base of Solano and Napa Counties and not far from Sonoma and Marin Counties —all unclustered areas with single-owner newspapers.

McKibben moved to California in 1996 to run ANG. Along the way he has raised editorial salaries—with reporters starting at $525 a week minimum and averaging a bit over $700—and ended a decade of newsroom rancor by overseeing an agreement for a Newspaper Guild contract that covers newsroom employees at the five core papers.

And as much as it pained him, he won points from his editors in 1998 by acceding to a majority vote of the editorial board to endorse Democrats Barbara Boxer and Gray Davis for senator and governor. A self-described Midwestern Republican ideologue, McKibben notes that as group president he had the authority to dictate political endorsements. "I told them vehemently how much I disagreed with them," he recalls, "but they convinced me that their position was built on good, sound logic and on fact and not on emotion, and the only reasons we differed were on philosophical background. So I let the editorial board go with who they wanted for governor and U.S. senator here. I am now in a part of the country that is basically Democratic, although out where I live in the suburbs is 57 percent registered Republican. I opened the paper here on two consecutive days and I was sick to my stomach."

ANG's combined one-buy, one-bill circulation of 236,000 attracts national advertisers and major retailers. Roughly 35 percent of all display advertising runs in all the papers, McKibben says.

The readers of all ANG's papers get staff coverage, at home and on the road, of the Oakland Athletics and the San Francisco Giants in the summer and the Oakland Raiders and San Francisco 49ers in the fall—coverage that none of the papers could afford alone. The top reporter's salary, $58,000, goes to a sports columnist.

Nancy Conway directs the overall news operation, but each paper has its own editor and reporters to cover local news. Although editorials are written for the group, local editors decide whether to run them or substitute their own on local issues.

In 1997, when welfare reform was a major issue, Conway assigned a five-person team that worked five months on a comprehensive, five-day package of stories and photographs that focused on Alameda County. Across the bay, the San Mateo paper published a different version that was localized for its area. The series won the 1998 Casey Medal for Meritorious Journalism from the Casey Journalism Center for Children and Families at the University of Maryland. It also won the 1997 California State University at Sacramento print journalism award for excellence in reporting on California state government and politics.

A Sacramento-based reporter files state government news for all of ANG's papers. Conway keeps a rapid response team on alert seven days a week for big breaking stories. The regional news staff covers growth and transportation issues and other stories of common interest to all Bay Area readers. After a major storm, a single story may run page one in all the papers, but each will have localized color photos and perhaps local sidebars. "We'll get the story and tailor it to our readers," says editor Ernie Hines of the *Tri-Valley Herald.*

During my visit, a story on a major Bay Area traffic study got heavy front-page play. The four Alameda-oriented papers focused on how the Sunol Grade, a notorious climb of Interstate 680 in the southern portion of the county, was becoming the Bay Area's worst commuter nightmare. The San Mateo paper, however, emphasized increased congestion on the cross-bay San Mateo Bridge.

Page 2 of each paper is devoted to Bay Area news, which reader surveys show is second in interest to more localized news. Regional, state, and national-international stories fill up the A section. Local news, sports, editorials, and letters to the editor may differ in the papers that have zoned editions. On a random day's look at all five of the ANG core papers, the two Tri-Valley editions carried a lengthy local editorial endorsing a $150 million school bond issue affecting both circulation areas, but the editorial did not run in the zoned *San Ramon Valley Herald* that serves a separate school system.

The local section for each newspaper is staff-written, with the editor determining story placement by phone or e-mail with his designated news editor at the news center. The center is in the same building as the *Tri-Valley Herald*, which works well for Hines; his news editor can simply walk downstairs to confer on story play or quietly discuss a personnel problem. News editors for the outlying papers—the farthest of which, San Mateo, is forty miles away—are less fortunate; they make do as best they can by phone. Because the papers serve suburban commuters who travel clogged highways, McKibben says the goal for home delivery is 5 A.M. for readers with longer commutes, and 5:30 elsewhere.

San Mateo editor Terry Winckler says one of the great advantages of clustering for small papers "is pooling resources when it makes sense. You metro-ize those things in common—major tragedies and crime news; the earthquake; major grass and wildfires; bigger-picture stories, such as Yosemite, that everybody relates to [and] that you couldn't get by leaving each newspaper totally autonomous. We've learned to select those news and information areas that all can use to combine our resources."

Early on, ANG made some of the same mistakes in San Mateo that Singleton's New Jersey papers had made in regard to what is, and isn't, "local." ANG's natural East Bay sports bent drew huge complaints from Peninsula readers in San Mateo. "Focus groups showed that San Mateo fans loved the Giants and 49ers, but loathed the A's and Raiders," Singleton recalls. "We were catching hell because we were emphasizing East Bay sports. We learned the hard way in San Mateo that it was a separate county."

MediaNews has been just as aggressive in Southern California as it has in the Bay area. Here again, starting from scratch, Singleton cobbled together a major presence in just a few years. The process began in 1996, when MediaNews acquired a cluster of three papers from Thomson—Pasadena's *Star-News*, the *San Gabriel Valley Tribune*, and the *Whittier Daily News*. The price was $110 million.

A year later MediaNews picked up the *Los Angeles Daily News*, a paper with a 200,000 circulation in the San Fernando Valley, from the estate of the late Washington Redskins owner Jack Kent Cooke, at an announced price of $130 million. Cooke had paid $176 million for the paper a decade earlier. Beyond that, Cooke had spent another $76 million to move the paper from Van Nuys to a new plant in Woodland Hills, and for a modern printing facility in nearby Valencia designed with extra press capacity.

About the same time, MediaNews added the *Press-Telegram* in Long Beach, a troubled paper that Knight Ridder was trying to unload. Although marginally profitable, the paper was printing on letterpress units nearly half a century old, and Knight Ridder was facing the prospect of having to lay out tens of millions of dollars to replace them. Singleton got the paper as an "asset sale"—a device for reducing taxes—for $38 million.

Thus, for a total of $278 million, MediaNews wound up with a cluster of five newspapers with roughly 425,000 total circulation in Los Angeles County, ringing the home turf of the formidable *Los Angeles Times.* Their combined operations function as the Los Angeles Newspaper Group, or LANG.

Then came the Donrey deal. Singleton originally approached Donrey's owners, the Stephens family of Little Rock, Arkansas, about buying the company's California papers outright. They weren't interested. "They didn't want cash," he says. "They didn't need cash. It would have meant substantial taxes for them. They liked California, its growth. We showed them how their newspapers and ours together created a lot more crucial mass. We arranged a partnership share with a lot of the newspapers we owned. It gives them a piece of a growing company instead of cash. We would have preferred to pay cash."

Under the deal, Singleton became a two-thirds owner of the partnership. His contribution included all five papers in his Bay Area cluster, plus the Pasadena, San Gabriel, and Whittier papers from the L.A. cluster, plus twenty-three weeklies with a combined circulation of 125,000. Donrey brought the *Vallejo Times-Herald,* expanding the Bay Area cluster. And in Southern California, it contributed the 68,000-circulation *Inland Valley Daily Bulletin* in Ontario, extending LANG's reach into a demographically desirable area to the south, crossing into San Bernardino County.

Although most of the other Donrey papers lie farther out from Los Angeles, they still fit into Singleton's long-term thinking. That strategy came into sharper focus in 1999 when Singleton acquired, from Gannett, the seventy-thousand-circulation *San Bernardino Sun.* With the *Daily Bulletin* in Ontario controlling the western half of San Bernardino County and the *Sun* covering the rest, Singleton dominates a lucrative market that is expected to double in the next twenty years. "It was the icing on the cake for our Los Angeles strategy," he says.

The deal with Gannett pushed circulation in California to over 900,000 for dailies operated by Singleton. As a stand-alone newspaper, the *Sun* was getting competition from a San Bernardino edition of A.H. Belo's Riverside-based *Press-Enterprise*. It also faced growth plans there by the *Los Angeles Times,* one of whose executives saw the *Sun* as "struggling." As part of Singleton's domain, it stands to get a share of any national or regional advertising LANG sells.

For the *Sun,* Gannett received 12 percent ownership and a seat on the seven-member California Newspapers Partnership board, with MediaNews and Donrey sharing the remaining ownership on a two-thirds, one-third basis.

Following the Gannett and Donrey deals, there was speculation that Singleton would expand even more in California. When I asked him about that, he declined to comment. He did say that in Southern California the immediate future would be a time "of digesting, of weaving them all together."

But in digestion there is sometimes heartburn. And in Southern California, the biggest dose has been at the *Press-Telegram.*

An asset sale means the purchase is treated as if the buyer were purchasing the hard assets and starting the business all over again. In a $100 million deal, for example, the buyer may acquire $10 million in fixed assets, such as buildings, land and equipment. The other $90 million may be in intangible assets, mostly goodwill, which can be amortized over forty years. Furthermore, in an asset sale the existing labor contracts aren't binding on the new owner unless they contain "successor" language. If a union is already in place and 51 percent of its members are rehired, the union has to be recognized, but negotiation of a new contract starts from scratch. That's what happened in Long Beach with the local unit of the Newspaper Guild. Singleton cut the salaries of most editorial employees by more than 20 percent, to roughly the level of the Guild contract at the larger *Daily News.* A typical reporter with five or more years of experience saw a drop in pay from $851 a week to $673—or from $44,252 to $34,996 a year. Senior editors and top local columnists were retained with no cut in pay.

Singleton argues that the new pay levels are fair. "If you've got a newspaper over here with a wage scale that is X and one next door that is Y, and you cluster, you've got problems. So when you're buying assets in a cluster you make changes you don't make if you're buying somewhere else. . . . The salary level at Long Beach was way, way high for a 100,000 daily, just way overpaid for a paper their size."

To add to the bitterness at Long Beach, MediaNews laid off a large number of noneditorial employees—the first cuts coming just eight days before Christmas of 1997. According to the Newspaper Guild, some two hundred jobs were eventually lost among mailers, pressmen, truck drivers, janitors, customer-service workers, and distributors. "None in the newsroom were dismissed," Singleton says, "but Long Beach was dramatically overstaffed in other areas. It was a very fat operation under Knight Ridder. Too many people in the composing room, accounting and the pressroom."

Just over a year later, half the existing newsroom staff—57 out of 110, according to one journalist who actually counted the noses—had left the paper.

Russ Parsons, a food columnist for the *L.A. Times* and a Long Beach resident who has long depended on the *Press-Telegram* for local news, says, "When Singleton took over, the theory was that it was going to become a local paper. But in reality the *Press-Telegram* provided fine local coverage before. Many things now remain uncovered, often because of green young reporters who don't know the community and don't have the memory or the contacts. They have a reduced staff."

"That's hogwash," counters *Press-Telegram* executive editor Rich Archbold. "I've been here for 20 years. Our managing editor has been here for 30. Our local columnists all stayed. The institutional memory—I've got it and other editors have it." As for the size of the staff, Archbold says, "We haven't lost any positions, but we've been prudent in not filling all positions when they became open—to help us with expense budgeting. We have 104 positions."

It was Singleton himself who met the Long Beach workforce to deliver that Yuletide news about pay cuts and layoffs. He also invited any employee who wanted to talk to him personally to do so. Several took him up.

"'I went to his office," one reporter recalls. "I said, 'Dean, I need more money.' He said, 'Maybe we can cut the difference. It's up to the managers; we give them a budget.'

"The managing editor told me he didn't have any money. That's what negotiating one-on-one got me. I went back to talk to Dean in a few months. He said he would get back to me, and he never did.

"Singleton was amiable. He was approachable. He gets some points from me on that." The reporter laughs. "I talked to the Big Cheese, and all I got was holes."

Singleton says it's part of an editor's job "to take the budget he has and use it to get the job done. Salaries should be based on local supply and demand. A reporter in a small town will get less than a reporter in a city because it costs less to live. We set profit goals based on what we had to pay to buy the newspaper."

While the idea of lower cost of living in small towns may be true generally, editors at some of Singleton's Bay Area papers acknowledge that most of their reporters can't afford to live in the suburban communities where their papers operate. Cost of living in the Bay Area is among the highest in the country. "What I see," one editor warns, "is that the pool of people coming in as reporters is shallower and smaller than it's ever been, and it's getting more so."

Singleton says the editorial payroll at his papers averages "between 10 and 10.5 percent of revenue"—slightly higher, he says, than the industry as a whole. But he adds, "We as an industry have underpaid. Raising pay scales is part of our long-term strategy. We recognize that when you pay for quality, you get quality."

In Los Angeles, Singleton retained the top editors at all the papers in his LANG group. Dorothy Reinhold is vice president and executive editor for the three-paper San Gabriel Valley group, which has a combined circulation of about 120,000 and operates as a subcluster within the larger group. "It's much better to be bought by somebody who wants you than to sit on a shelf waiting for someone to buy you," she says. "Dean bought us on purpose. He had a plan for us. He stitched us together and made a quilt of us. And the quilt will get larger. It's working."

The LANG editors seem happy with the freedom they have under Singleton—and with improved resources. These include a $5.5 million upgrade of newsroom computer systems. For the *Press-Telegram*, now printed in the *Daily News* plant, the new offset presses have vastly improved its use of color.

Although they operate primarily within Los Angeles County, the LANG papers serve different markets. The San Gabriel group—with separate papers for Whittier, Pasadena, and the rest of the San Gabriel Valley—has thirty-one municipalities within its circulation area. Long Beach covers twenty municipalities, and Archbold says that where they compete head-on the *Press-Telegram* outsells the *L.A. Times* by more than two to one. The *Daily News* concentrates on the San Fernando Valley. Besides its main edition and a Los Angeles version for street sales, there are four-page local wraps for zoned editions for Santa Clarita, Simi Valley, Conejo Valley, and Antelope Valley, as well as a combined Glendale and Burbank edition. LANG also publishes a free, seventy-thousand-circulation Spanish-language weekly.

The *Daily News'* one-person state capital bureau in Sacramento was expanded to a two-person bureau for LANG, which produced a Sunday column and briefs tailored to each of LANG's three circulation areas. A third person, the Alameda group's Sacramento reporter, shares office space and information with the two LANG reporters. MediaNews also announced plans for a six-person Washington bureau, to include two California reporters, one from the north and one from the south.

Another addition is a Sunday travel section for all the LANG papers. Reinhold recalls that when she went to work for her paper five years ago there was talk of adding a travel section. Staffers got excited about it and developed a prototype, "but it never went anywhere because we were told they couldn't get the numbers. Working with a larger group, we're giving our readers a freestanding travel section."

Unlike his Alameda Group counterpart, who accepted the vote of his editors on major political endorsements, LANG president Ike Massey made the decision to endorse Republican candidates for governor and senator.

Asked about Guild issues, LANG editors agree that it is a question for Massey to answer. He doesn't equivocate. "Certainly we would rather not have the Guild," he said. Neither the San Gabriel nor the Donrey papers have Guild units.

The Guild unit at the *Daily News* signed a three-year contract in 1999, which included a 3 percent raise for the first year and 2 percent for the next two, created a merit pay pool, raised the mileage reimbursement, and improved some other benefits. A contract was also eventually signed with the *Guide* at Long Beach, where the company had denied sick leave to editorial employees during negotiations, adding to the rancor in the newsroom. "I was sick for a week, with fever and a terrible cough," one reporter told me, "but I went to work every day because I didn't want to deprive my family of vacation time."

When I visited the *Daily News*, I found the reporters less happy than the editors. They complained that expenses for news coverage were being picked at as never before.

The spacious newsroom is housed in a building converted from a manufacturing facility for electronic parts. It has long corridors, solid walls and not a single window. Editor Dave Butler was working on a design to break out an exterior wall and add a long window. It would cost $7,500. In the *Daily News* building's executive offices, Massey occupied an airy space with windows opening onto the sunny Southern California landscape. He had worked as a manager for Singleton much of his career. Asked about the newsroom window, Massey said, "It's not a high priority."

In 1998, however, he contributed $60,000 in company funds to a San Fernando Valley organization seeking to have the valley secede from Los Angeles County. It was the largest single donation to that group and a gesture that drew widespread criticism and upset many of his own reporters. The *Daily News* Guild unit sent Massey a letter complaining that the paper's contribution "jeopardized its credibility."

When I spoke to him months later, Massey was unrepentant. "We make editorial endorsements all the time," he said. "Does that mean we can't cover elections?" And the Guild's rebuke? "Self-serving bullshit," he said.

Unsurprisingly, the *L.A. Times* was one of those that kicked Massey around for his largess. MediaNews' consolidated ring around Los Angeles has given the West's preeminent paper plenty to think about, and it's clear the LANG editors relish this newly stoked sense of competition. But that didn't keep Singleton from consorting with the opposition when he saw an opportunity for mutual benefit. In 1998 MediaNews and the *Times* entered a joint venture to provide total market coverage for preprint advertisers. The fifty-fifty joint venture, called the California Independent Postal System, is a door-to-door delivery system. The way it works, Massey explains, is that LANG and the *Times* provide computer tapes of their subscribers to a third party for merging and purging. The preprints then are distributed as inserts to all subscribers of both papers, and CIPS makes deliveries to the nonsubscribers. Massey says the joint effort shows that the two companies, despite being fiercely competitive, still "can do things together that our customers want."

Adds Singleton, "Every preprint advertiser will tell you this is what they've been wanting for years. What we're doing allows advertisers to print fewer copies because they don't have overlap. I've never seen it done before."

He professes to be unconcerned about reports in trade publications of a Justice Department investigation. "If somebody complains, the Justice Department is required to look at it," he says. "We have very savvy lawyers, as does Times Mirror. We both have been in this business long enough to know what you can and can't do."

To him, the joint venture reflects his belief that newspapers get stronger if they can work with each other to increase profits without compromising areas of competition. It's no different, he believes, than a Knight Ridder paper printing a national edition of the *New York Times*. It's just business.

L EST YOU GET the impression that clustering is only a high-stakes game played in sunny metro markets, consider the case of the *Oshkosh Northwestern* in east central Wisconsin.

In June 1998, the staff of the twenty-four-thousand-circulation daily was stunned to learn that the paper had just been acquired by Thomson Newspapers. They were stunned not only because it was Thomson, but because the paper had been sold only two months before.

That April, the paper's family owners had sold the *Northwestern* to West Virginia–based Ogden Newspapers. Now Ogden was flipping it again. In the fog of the announcement, one reporter recalls hearing Thomson executive Paul Seveska tell the staff, "I know you've heard a lot of bad things about Thomson, but things have changed. Have an open mind."

To get the *Northwestern,* Thomson traded away four papers in Ohio and Pennsylvania whose combined circulation was more than triple that of Oshkosh. The company was willing to give so much because the *Northwestern* completed Thomson's cluster of dailies around Lake Winnebago. In a three-hour drive you could hit all five towns in this cluster —up the Fox River Valley from Oshkosh to Appleton, and then around the lake to Manitowoc, Sheboygan, and Fond du Lac. These five papers around Lake Winnebago had a combined daily circulation of 143,000 when I visited them in 1999, and three smaller Thomson papers seventy miles away—in Marshfield, Stevens Point, and Wisconsin Rapids—added another 43,000.

A little over a year after my visit, and shortly before this book went to press, Thomson sold all eight of these papers to Gannett, which already owned two other dailies nearby, in Green Bay and Wausau. The sale created for Gannett an even larger cluster than Thomson had had. (It also made Gannett the fourth owner of the Oshkosh Northwestern in just over two years—an extraordinary rate of turnover even in these turbulent times.) What follows is a description of the operations of the Thomson cluster shortly before the papers were sold.

By joining what Thomson called its Winnebago Strategic Marketing Group, the *Oshkosh Northwestern* got access to a reporter in Madison, the state capital, and another in Washington. Business reporters no longer had to limit quotes in news stories to those who advertised in the paper, as had been the policy in the past. On the other hand, Thomson cut the reporting staff, and those reporters who remained soon understood that they were expected to stretch out their reporting without the expectation of a raise or overtime pay.

The five papers' close proximity allowed savings from shared overhead, pressrooms, and other operations. Advertisers could purchase the papers in any combination. Furthermore, these papers lacked the competitive pressures that MediaNews faced in California. The small cities of central Wisconsin were not like California communities, where people are as likely as not to be from somewhere else. ANG's Scott McKibben, who had worked in Oshkosh, said the Wisconsin cities differ from one another more than those in the Bay Area do. "There's a world of difference between Appleton and Manitowoc," he said.

One thing these cities did have in common was a strong allegiance to the Green Bay Packers. The Thomson group capitalized on this with tabloid specials before and after every Packers game—sixteen weekends during football season. The 1998 package included a column by the team's head coach. The Packer specials, produced by a sportswriting team, were a big hit with fans and a good revenue source, with each paper selling local ads and deciding how much of the copy to use. The tab might run sixteen pages in one paper and only eight in another.

Thomson CEO Stuart Garner contended that his company had the most sophisticated clustering operation of them all. Unlike Singleton—who has enhanced competition in parts of California, mostly by clustering properties that had dim prospects on their own—Garner had a strategy of unite-and-conquer. Primarily, he sought to dominate smaller markets where Thomson already had a presence and where competition was minimal.

The advertising operation for Thomson's Wisconsin groups went a step beyond what Singleton was doing in California. One sales unit functioned as an in-house ad agency to seek out regional advertisers. For a Broadway play like *Showboat* coming to Milwaukee's Performing Arts Center, for example, prospecting might begin more than a year ahead of time. A buy for the central Wisconsin market might even include papers outside the chain, such as Gannett's *Wausau Daily Herald*. Thomson charged a 15 percent agency commission to non-Thomson participants.

As it had elsewhere, Thomson introduced advertisements on the front pages of the Wisconsin papers. Putting ads on the front page is a practice many American journalists and critics deplore, but Thomson was a pioneer in violating the taboo. (Gannett and others have recently followed Thomson's lead.) Certainly the practice didn't bother Garner; the papers in his native England run front-page ads all the time. He said the ads drew a significant amount of revenue, and he turned away the suggestion that they might undercut a paper's credibility.

The smallest of the Thomson papers in the Lake Winnebago area was the *Herald Times Reporter* in Manitowoc, with a circulation of seventeen-thousand. Editor Gerald Guy told me the paper also published a thirty-seven-thousand-circulation shopper for Manitowoc County that gave advertisers total market coverage and published features and "whatever anybody sends in." The shopper, with its own full-time editor, was sufficiently popular that the distributors called on patrons once a year for voluntary $10 subscription payments—and more than a quarter of them paid it.

A tall, large-boned man who used to be a college football player, Guy said he liked to train young reporters and copy editors and have them move on after a couple of years. "With new people, you get new ideas," he said. While I sat in his office, a cohort in Appleton called about a young copy editor working for Guy. Guy explained that she was a quick learner, had mastered the editing software and was ready to move up to the eighty-thousand-circulation *Post Crescent*. The phone call sealed the transfer, which included a pay raise. Another call to Sheboygan involved talk about a higher-paying job for a reporter who had done well.

But as with MediaNews in Southern California, newsroom pay and labor relations were thorny issues for the Wisconsin cluster. The 1997 merger of the Guild and the much larger Communications Workers of America indirectly linked the unions representing editorial employees in Sheboygan, a Guild shop, and Appleton, which had been affiliated with CWA since the mid-1980s.

The pay and benefits at these two papers outstripped those at Thomson's other Wisconsin papers, where the newsrooms had no union. In 1999, a reporter at Sheboygan with five or more years' experience earned a Guild contract minimum of $717 a week, or $37,284 a year. But at the *Oshkosh Northwestern,* whose circulation is almost identical to that of Sheboygan, an editorial staffer told me that no reporter earned as much as $28,000, which is the starting nine-month salary for an Oshkosh public school teacher.

The head of Sheboygan's unit, Dave Gallianetti, said contract negotiations were much more difficult after Thomson took over. He said he thought the company's "ultimate goal is to get rid of the union." But, Gallianetti added, the company did keep its "hands off the editorial product."

And in Appleton, I found a staff proud of its statewide reputation for quality. "We have a good working relationship with our editor and publisher," said John Lee of the Guild/CWA local. "I think there's a relationship between quality and the union. It adds stability, with staff continuity committed to this newspaper and this community."

CLUSTERING HAS EVEN found its way to the tobacco-growing region of eastern North Carolina. In and around Greenville—by far the least urban part of the state—economic development has come late. For 114

years, the local paper, the *Greenville Daily Reflector,* was owned and operated by its founding family, the Whichards. But in 1996, they decided it was
time to sell. Recalls Jordan (Jordy) Whichard III, "The family wanted to
find a buyer who produced good newspapers, who had resources and
could provide good long-term opportunities for our employees, and who
had exhibited good stewardship in communities where it owned newspapers." They settled on Cox, a private company whose flagship paper is
the *Atlanta Journal and Constitution.*

After the sale to Cox, Whichard agreed to stay on as publisher of the
twenty-thousand-circulation morning daily and a companion group of
weeklies. His newspapering apprenticeship had begun at age fourteen
and had touched on virtually every job, from stuffing inserts to writing
editorials.

Whichard's duties quickly expanded, as Cox acquired two nearby
dailies from Thomson—the fourteen-thousand-circulation *Rocky Mount
Telegram* in an adjoining county and the twelve-thousand-circulation
Daily Advance in Elizabeth City, roughly one hundred miles in the direction of the Outer Banks.

The transition has gone "better than we expected, as well as we could
have hoped," he says. "Cox not only has not interfered in the core group of
newspapers and how we operated them, but has contributed significant
financial support to secure acquisitions and to centralize and update our
computer systems."

A new printing plant opened in 1999 on the outskirts of Greenville.
Besides providing a new home for the *Daily Reflector,* the new facility
prints the *Reflector,* the *Rocky Mount Telegram,* and several of Cox's weeklies. The Elizabeth City paper continues to use its own printing plant.

"I'm not sure there's a true model yet for newspaper clustering,"
Whichard says. "You can translate that concept into a wide array of operation initiatives that meet particular strengths and cultures of the companies. I'm sure we do it a lot different from Dean Singleton in California."

There is no universal copy desk here, and the newspapers run no common sections. Except for accounts payable, each newspaper operates its
own local business as well as its own editorial offices. But all operate from
a central computer system housed in Greenville, using high-speed telephone lines. The editors meet monthly at rotating locations and alert one
another if their staffs are covering a story of regional interest. The sports
editors work informally to coordinate and share their coverage of East
Carolina University, the pride of Greenville, and Atlantic Coast Conference
teams.

The three North Carolina newspapers and four others in east Texas form what Cox calls "regional groups." They are the only such groups among the company's fifteen daily newspapers.

What is unique about Cox is its areawide computer network, CoxNet, which links all the newspapers together with a common technology and software. It grew out of coverage of the 1996 Olympics in Atlanta. A team of more than three hundred reporters, editors, and photographers from all the Cox papers assembled in Atlanta to publish a separate newspaper covering the Olympics. The *Daily Reflector* used material from this operation to provide special coverage that included a package for advertisers.

The personal relationships and technology ties established that summer evolved into CoxNet, a daily internal wire service that provides the various papers with such material as a food page developed by the *Journal and Constitution*.

Greenville's executive editor, Al Clark, says, "It allows us to use material from other papers regularly. We use a steady stream of material—food pages, for example, and health page material and commentary/insight for Sunday readers. At our staff levels, we're not able to create this material, and it frees up time for our local folks to work on local stories."

CoxNet also transmits editorials from its larger papers, which local editors may use if they wish. "We don't run editorials from other Cox newspapers," Clark says. "We run local editorials on local issues seven days a week. I'm concerned about some other papers that say it's too much trouble, or they don't want to stand the heat. There's a great big silence out there when the local newspaper isn't doing it."

Clark is enthusiastic about having access to a reporter in Washington, who was hired to provide stories exclusively for the chain's smaller papers. "It's adding something we never had," Clark says. "It's the first time we've had someone who can go directly to our congressman's office and get reaction on national issues." Clark and Whichard say they hope to develop similar local coverage from the state capital in Raleigh.

Cox has provided no influx of cash for the editorial side, Clark says, "but it's made things available to me, such as the *Washington Post* and *New York Times* news services, that we didn't have before. We find them valuable. There's no difference in how we approach community journalism, but there's people we can call on for advice and assistance. The Cox purchase has been positive from the sense of more resources."

In addition to transmitting news and features and a food or book page with a modular design that allows space for local advertising, CoxNet also produces spec ads, created by the twenty-eight-person graphic design staff of the Atlanta newspapers. An example might be an ad for an optometrist, which could be sold by a salesperson at any Cox paper. "A reader looks at the whole paper," says Arnold Rosenfeld, Cox's vice president for news, "and a side effect of better-looking advertising is that it makes the whole paper look better."

WHY HASN'T THE GROWTH of newspaper clusters—especially in huge monopoly-like concentrations—drawn the attention of the Justice Department? Why wasn't it an antitrust issue, for example, when Gannett ended up owning every daily paper in a dozen adjacent counties of Wisconsin?

Although the Justice Department rarely challenges the regional consolidation of newspapers under a common owner, it does take a look at almost every deal. And this in itself has a deterrent effect, some antitrust lawyers maintain.

In the early 1970s, newspapers engaged in what were called "midnight mergers." One paper in a city would buy another, and Justice wouldn't know about it until the deal was done. To prevent that, Congress passed the Hart-Scott-Rodino Act, which requires automatic review of almost all daily newspaper sales before they become final. "Justice is not giving a green light to consolidation," says Alan L. Marx, a former Justice Department section chief responsible for newspaper antitrust matters. Today he advises newspaper companies on mergers and acquisitions. "Private counsel will tell their clients, 'This deal has real problems; do you want to go along?'"

Still, some observers wonder how much deterrence there is. The issue, according to Marx, turns on whether competition is preserved within a market. Take Thomson's 1998 purchase of the Oshkosh paper, which gave it a five-paper monopoly around Lake Winnebago. Marx says those papers were contiguous but their markets and circulation areas had little overlap. In such a case, he says, "the antitrust laws are not going to cover it."

When Justice talks about competition, it usually emphasizes competition for advertising business, because it's more difficult to ascertain "facts" about news. "When I was at Justice," Marx says, "the theory we always had [was] that if you find commercial competition for advertisers, you get the preservation of editorial competition. Preserving editorial voices was an important consideration, but under antitrust law the only question was whether there was competition" within a market.

Lee Enterprises owns five of Montana's eleven daily papers. But even though its Helena bureau dominates the coverage of state government, this doesn't raise antitrust issues. Its papers—in Helena, Butte, Billings, Missoula, and Hamilton—have little commercial overlap.

"Justice asks a lot of questions about editorial competition," says Marx, "but has yet to see how to use the answers." The issue involves both First Amendment considerations and political sensitivity. "It would have bothered me a lot to figure out how to use differences in editorial content in deciding what kind of actions we bring."

In 1997, when MediaNews sold the *North Jersey Herald & News* to Macromedia, owner of the nearby *Record* in Bergen County, the sale was held up for eight months while Justice tried to establish that both papers would continue to operate separately and that their markets didn't overlap significantly. Charles W. Gibney, a *Record* executive who was closely involved in the investigation, says the government expressed concerns about whether "an independent voice would be leaving the community." Still, Justice's nineteen-page request for documents, which filled about three hundred banker boxes, focused primarily on the sale's impact on advertisers. Although the two papers continue to operate separately, they have consolidated their accounting, press and composing room operations, and they cross-sell advertising. The *Record*, with a daily circulation of 141,000, remains a regional newspaper, while the *Herald*, with only 43,000 circulation, remains highly local.

The fact that Justice is investigating a pending deal often means little. Usually, Marx says, it means "that some staff lawyer got authority to ask for more information on a deal. Any complaint almost automatically results in an investigation."

A little-heralded 1995 case from Northwest Arkansas, however, forced the resale of a daily paper to its original owner, with the result that newspaper competition was preserved. The Justice Department did not initiate this case, but it intervened in a lawsuit brought by private litigants.

Thomson had sold the *Northwest Arkansas Times*, in Fayetteville, to the Stephens family, whose Donrey Newspapers already owned the *Morning News* in Springdale. These two small cities adjoin each other in Washington County. The Springdale paper also competed with a smaller paper, the *Daily Record*, in adjacent Benton County.

In voiding the sale, U.S. District Judge H. Franklin Waters cited a 1953 U.S. Supreme Court opinion saying that for antitrust purposes daily newspapers have two markets: one for readers and one for advertisers. He noted that by owning both the Fayetteville and Springdale papers, the Stephens family would control 84 percent of the circulation and 88 percent of the newspaper ad revenue in the two-county market. This, he concluded, would deter the *Times* and *Morning News* from vigorous competition.

Craig Conrath, the Justice section chief who participated in the case, says Waters's interpretation of market forces "is still the way we look at transactions today." The department, he says, doesn't want "to bring a case . . . where the evidence is weak."

After the sale was reversed, Thomson sold the Fayetteville paper to Hollinger. The *Morning News* in Springdale responded by beefing up its coverage, expanding to a five-person news bureau in Fayetteville and an eight-person bureau in Rogers, the largest community in Benton County. A three-person bureau in Little Rock provides a flow of news from the state capital to Springdale and Donrey's two other papers in the state.

Jim Morriss, the *Morning News'* executive editor, said the paper also expanded its copy desk and sports coverage. "We're very strong on political and legislative coverage," he said. "We have improved the quality of our newspaper."

As a result, Washington and Benton counties became one of the most competitive daily newspaper markets in the country. Maybe the case of Northwest Arkansas was unique, with little impact on the industry as a whole, but it does seem to suggest that preserving editorial competition can improve newspaper quality and provide for a better-informed citizenry.

✶   ✶   ✶

Togetherness, Newspaper-Style

In one of the hottest trends of recent years, efficiency-conscious newspaper owners have succeeded in their efforts to concentrate, or "cluster," their properties in close proximity. Listed here is a state-by-state breakdown of major clusters around the nation, involving more than four hundred—that is, well over one-fourth—of the nation's daily papers. These groupings comprise papers under common ownership that are within roughly 100 miles of one another and have a daily circulation of at least ten thousand.

ALABAMA	*Circ.*
New York Times	
Tuscaloosa News	37,407
Times Daily (Florence)	32,408
Gadsden Times	25,693

Newhouse

Birmingham News	152,007
Mobile Register	94,674
Huntsville Times	59,077
Times-Picayune (New Orleans, LA)	273,076
Mississippi Press (Pascagoula, MS)	20,180

Media General

Dothan Eagle	34,974
Enterprise Ledger	10,209
Opelika-Auburn News	13,738

ARIZONA _Circ._

Freedom

Tribune (Mesa)	98,978
Daily News-Sun (Sun City)	20,055
Yuma Daily Sun	15,717

ARKANSAS _Circ._

Wehco

Arkansas Democrat-Gazette (Little Rock)	175,145
Sentinel-Record (Hot Springs)	17,252
El Dorado News-Times	10,114
Texarkana (TX) Gazette	31,511

Donrey

Southwest Times Record (Fort Smith)	41,658
Morning News (Springdale)	35,364
Pine Bluff Commercial	18,300

CALIFORNIA _Circ._

Knight Ridder

San Jose Mercury News	285,848
Monterey County Herald	35,077
Contra Costa Times (Walnut Creek)	97,668
Valley Times (Pleasanton)	44,354
West County Times (Richmond)	32,263
Ledger Dispatch (Antioch)	17,568
Telegram-Tribune (San Luis Obispo)	37,749

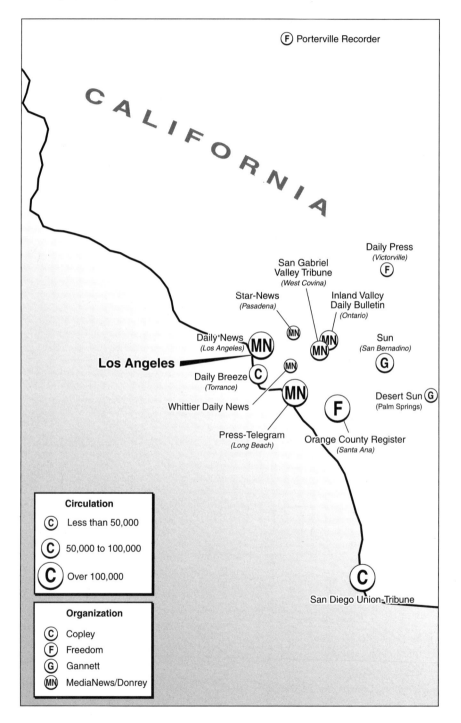

Porterville Recorder (F)

C A L I F O R N I A

Daily Press
(Victorville)
(F)

San Gabriel
Valley Tribune
(West Covina)

Star-News
(Pasadena)

Inland Valley
Daily Bulletin
(Ontario)

Sun
(San Bernadino)
(G)

Daily News
(Los Angeles) (MN)

(MN)

(MN)
(MN)

Los Angeles ▶

Daily Breeze
(Torrance) (C)

(MN)

(MN)

(F)

Desert Sun (G)
(Palm Springs)

Whittier Daily News

Press-Telegram
(Long Beach)

Orange County Register
(Santa Ana)

(C)

San Diego Union-Tribune

Circulation
(C) Less than 50,000
(C) 50,000 to 100,000
(C) Over 100,000

Organization
(C) Copley
(F) Freedom
(G) Gannett
(MN) MediaNews/Donrey

Gannett

Northern California

Visalia Times-Delta	22,860
Californian (Salinas)	19,409
Marin Independent Journal (Novato)	39,494

Southern California

Sun (San Bernardino)	77,366
Desert Sun (Palm Springs)	46,109

MediaNews/Donrey*

Northern California

Oakland Tribune	68,293
Tri-Valley Herald (Pleasanton)	43,187
Daily Review (Hayward)	38,218
Argus (Fremont)	31,438
San Mateo County Times	34,438
Times-Standard (Eureka)	20,002
Chico Enterprise-Record	33,210
Vallejo Times-Herald	20,456

Southern California

Daily News (Los Angeles)	201,435
Press-Telegram (Long Beach)	105,710
Inland Valley Daily Bulletin (Ontario)	67,907
San Gabriel Valley Tribune (West Covina)	56,440
Star-News (Pasadena)	40,575
Whittier Daily News	19,056
Sun (San Bernardino)	77,366

* Merged California operations in early 1999.

McClatchy

Sacramento Bee	291,007
Fresno Bee	156,466
Modesto Bee	84,287

McNaughton

Daily Republic (Fairfield)	19,879
Mountain Democrat (Placerville)	12,767

Pulitzer

Hanford Sentinel	13,453
Santa Maria Times	19,490

Copley

San Diego Union-Tribune	376,604
Daily Breeze (Torrance)	84,681

Freedom

Orange County Register (Santa Ana)	358,754
Porterville Recorder	10,312
Daily Press (Victorville)	27,899

COLORADO   *Circ.*

Scripps Howard

Denver Rocky Mountain News	396,114
Daily Camera (Boulder)	33,041

Lehman

Daily Times-Call (Longmont)	20,970
Loveland Daily Reporter-Herald	16,903

CONNECTICUT/RHODE ISLAND   *Circ.*

Journal Register

New Haven Register	100,030
Herald (New Britain)	21,172
Bristol Press	14,505
Register Citizen (Torrington)	11,352
Middletown Press	10,034
Call (Woonsocket, RI)	16,199
Times (Pawtucket, RI)	15,021

Tribune

Hartford Courant	207,511
Stamford Advocate	28,379
Greenwich Time	12,558

FLORIDA   *Circ.*

New York Times

Sarasota Herald-Tribune	107,168
Gainesville Sun	52,509
Ledger (Lakeland)	76,037
Palatka Daily News	11,882
Ocala Star-Banner	50,432

Scripps Howard

Naples Daily News	51,620
Press-Journal (Vero Beach)	31,950
Stuart News	36,811
Tribune (Fort Pierce)	27,373

Media General

Tampa Tribune	224,972
Highlands Today (Sebring)	16,609
Hernando Today (Brooksville)	13,813

Morris

Florida Times-Union (Jacksonville)	173,867
St. Augustine Record	14,546

Freedom

News Herald (Panama City)	33,276
NW Fla. Daily News (Fort Walton Beach)	37,539

GEORGIA *Circ.*

Gray

Rockdale Citizen (Conyers)	10,478
Gwinnett Daily Post (Lawrenceville)	60,721
Albany Herald	29,454

Knight Ridder

Macon Telegraph	67,124
Columbus Ledger-Enquirer	47,763

Morris

Augusta Chronicle	72,772
Savannah Morning News	61,118
Athens Daily News/Banner-Herald	26,479

HAWAII *Circ.*

Donrey

Hawaii Tribune-Herald (Hilo)	19,117
West Hawaii Today (Kailua-Kona)	10,509

Gannett

Honolulu Advertiser	101,948
Honolulu Star-Bulletin	64,979

IDAHO

Circ.

Pioneer

Idaho State Journal (Pocatello)	17,624
Herald Journal (Logan, UT)	15,012

ILLINOIS

Circ.

Hollinger

Chicago area

Chicago Sun-Times	468,170
Daily Southtown (Chicago)	50,853
Post-Tribune (Gary, IN)	61,476
Herald-Palladium (Benton Harbor, MI)	29,677

Downstate

Register-News (Mount Vernon)	10,260
Effingham Daily News	13,148

Small

Dispatch (Moline)	27,488
Daily Journal (Kankakee)	26,651
Rock Island Argus	12,743
Daily Times (Ottawa)	11,826

Shaw

Northwest Herald (Crystal Lake)	33,450
Kane County Chronicle (Geneva)	13,014
Daily Gazette (Sterling)	12,658

Copley

Journal Star (Peoria)	68,556
State Journal-Register (Springfield)	61,217
Register-Mail (Galesburg)	16,335
Herald-News (Joliet)	35,906
Beacon-News (Aurora)	28,389
News Sun (Waukegan)	22,576
Courier-News (Elgin)	17,278

Howard

Mattoon Journal-Gazette	11,652
Pekin Daily Times	14,637

INDIANA   *Circ.*

CNHI
Tribune-Star (Terre Haute)	34,286
Herald Bulletin (Anderson)	30,446
Kokomo Tribune	23,716
Pharos-Tribune (Logansport)	12,563
Evening News (Jeffersonville)	10,147

Gannett
Indianapolis Star	240,309
Star Press (Muncie)	33,625
Vincennes Sun-Commercial	12,445
Daily Ledger (Noblesville/Fishers)	11,056
Chronicle-Tribune (Marion)	20,175
Palladium-Item (Richmond)	19,574
Journal and Courier (Lafayette)	37,300

Schurz
Herald-Times (Bloomington)	28,091
Times-Mail (Bedford)	13,863

Home News
Daily Journal (Franklin)	17,872
Republic (Columbus)	22,409

IOWA   *Circ.*

Gannett
Des Moines Register	158,537
Iowa City Press-Citizen	15,245

Nutting
Times-Republican (Marshalltown)	10,519
Messenger (Fort Dodge)	18,659

Lee
Quad-City Times (Davenport)	51,967
Globe-Gazette (Mason City)	19,681

KANSAS   *Circ.*

Harris
Hutchinson News	36,165

Salina Journal	30,848
Hays Daily News	12,590
Garden City Telegram	10,393

Morris

Topeka Capital-Journal	59,559
Morning Sun (Pittsburg)	10,312
Examiner (Independence, MO)	10,259

KENTUCKY   *Circ.*

Belo

Owensboro Messenger-Inquirer	31,764
Gleaner (Henderson)	11,109

LOUISIANA   *Circ.*

New York Times

Courier (Houma)	19,753
Daily Comet (Thibodaux)	12,060
Daily World (Opelousas)	12,169

Gannett

Times (Shreveport)	73,023
News-Star (Monroe)	36,711
Alexandria Daily Town Talk	36,951
Advertiser (Lafayette)	44,283

MAINE   *Circ.*

Seattle Times

Portland Press Herald	76,275
Central Maine Morning Sentinel (Waterville)	20,728
Kennebec Journal (Augusta)	15,683

MARYLAND   *Circ.*

Whitcom

Star-Democrat (Easton)	16,140
Cecil Whig (Elkton)	13,374

MASSACHUSETTS   *Circ.*

MediaNews

Sun (Lowell)	51,594

Berkshire Eagle (Pittsfield)	31,861
Sentinel & Enterprise (Fitchburg)	19,740
Brattleboro (VT) Reformer	10,741
Connecticut Post (Bridgeport, CN)	77,444

Journal Register

Herald News (Fall River)	26,210
Taunton Daily Gazette	14,142

Newspaper Media

Patriot Ledger (Quincy)	71,508
Enterprise (Brockton)	42,687

Community Newspaper

Metrowest Daily News (Framingham)	59,570
Milford Daily News	12,679

Dow Jones

Cape Cod Times (Hyannis)	53,392
Standard Times (New Bedford)	37,876
Salem Evening News	34,693
Daily News of Newburyport	13,866
Gloucester Times	11,977

New York Times

Boston Globe	462,850
Worcester Telegram and Gazette	106,748

MICHIGAN	*Circ.*

Newhouse

Grand Rapids Press	141,643
Flint Journal	91,940
Kalamazoo Gazette	59,154
Ann Arbor News	57,315
Saginaw News	50,041
Muskegon Chronicle	47,918
Bay City Times	37,480
Jackson Citizen Patriot	35,936

Gannett

Detroit News	232,434
Lansing State Journal	69,602
Times Herald (Port Huron)	31,303
Battle Creek Enquirer	25,741

21st Century

Macomb Daily (Mount Clemens)	56,644
Daily Tribune (Royal Oak)	17,330
Oakland Press (Pontiac)	78,001

Nutting

Mining Journal (Marquette)	17,444
Daily Mining Gazette (Houghton)	10,864
Daily Press (Escanaba)	10,573

MINNESOTA   *Circ.*

Knight Ridder

St. Paul Pioneer Press	204,430
Duluth News-Tribune	51,999

Forum

West Central Tribune (Willmar)	17,106
Daily Globe (Worthington)	12,194

MISSISSIPPI   *Circ.*

Gannett

Clarion-Ledger (Jackson)	101,632
Hattiesburg American	22,574

MISSOURI   *Circ.*

Rust

Southeast Missourian (Cape Girardeau)	15,737
Daily American Republic (Poplar Bluff)	13,107

MONTANA   *Circ.*

Lee

Billings Gazette	47,800
Missoulian	31,739
Montana Standard (Butte)	14,720
Helena Independent Record	13,206

NEBRASKA   *Circ.*

Omaha World-Herald

Omaha World-Herald	222,688
North Platte Telegraph	13,761

Star-Herald (Scottsbluff)	15,939
Kearney Hub	12,615

NEW HAMPSHIRE/VERMONT   *Circ.*

Newspapers of New England

Concord Monitor	21,310
Valley News (White River Junction, VT)	17,618

NEW JERSEY   *Circ.*

Newhouse

Star-Ledger (Newark)	407,129
Times (Trenton)	79,415
Jersey Journal (Jersey City)	45,808
Gloucester Co. Times (Woodbury)	25,683
Today's Sunbeam (Salem)	10,801
Express-Times (Easton, PA)	48,911
Staten Island (NY) Advance	66,861

Gannett

Asbury Park Press	159,705
Home News Tribune (E. Brunswick)	72,716
Daily Record (Morristown)	47,104
Ocean County Observer (Toms River)	10,571
Courier-Post (Camden)	83,789
Courier-News (Bridgewater)	42,210
Daily Journal (Vineland)	17,456

Macromedia

Record (Hackensack)	141,006
North Jersey Herald & News (Passaic)	45,941

NEW YORK   *Circ.*

Gannett

Rochester Democrat and Chronicle	174,800
Press & Sun-Bulletin (Binghamton)	62,380
Observer-Dispatch (Utica)	48,630
Journal News (Westchester Co.)	144,916
Poughkeepsie Journal	41,291
Star-Gazette (Elmira)	30,303
Ithaca Journal	18,905

Nutting

Evening Observer (Dunkirk)	13,315
Post-Journal (Jamestown)	23,073

CNHI

Niagara Gazette	25,160
Union-Sun & Journal (Lockport)	16,265
Tonawanda News	10,722

Johnson

Watertown Daily Times	35,615
Daily News (Batavia)	15,592

Journal Register

Record (Troy)	23,668
Daily Freeman (Kingston)	22,110
Saratogian	11,147

Dow Jones

Wall Street Journal	1,752,693
Times Herald-Record (Middletown)	81,906
Daily Star (Oneonta)	19,312
Pocono Record (Stroudsburg, PA)	21,021

NORTH CAROLINA   *Circ.*

Cox

Daily Reflector (Greenville)	20,228
Rocky Mount Telegram	13,127
Daily Advance (Elizabeth City)	11,583

Media General

Winston-Salem Journal	89,482
Independent Tribune (Concord)	20,023
Hickory Daily Record	19,402
Statesville Record & Landmark	13,980
News Herald (Morganton)	11,625
Florence (SC) Morning News	33,944
Danville (VA) Register & Bee	21,702

Freedom

Gaston Gazette	34,894
Times-News (Burlington)	27,088

Daily News (Jacksonville)	21,537
Shelby Star	14,736
Sun Journal (New Bern)	15,177
Free Press (Kinston)	12,063

Paxton

Sanford Herald	12,699
Enquirer-Journal (Monroe)	11,722
Daily Courier (Forest City)	11,937
High Point Enterprise	29,741
News-Topic (Lenoir)	10,121

New York Times

Morning Star (Wilmington)	56,537
Times-News (Hendersonville)	20,468
Dispatch (Lexington)	13,338

Knight Ridder

Charlotte Observer	243,990
The State (Columbia, SC)	118,298

OHIO   *Circ.*

Gannett

Cincinnati Enquirer	195,744
Repository (Canton)	62,885
News Journal (Mansfield)	34,154
Advocate (Newark)	21,764
Times Recorder (Zanesville)	21,274
Lancaster Eagle-Gazette	15,623
Chillicothe Gazette	16,102
News-Messenger (Fremont)	13,983
Marietta Times	13,137
Marion Star	15,654

Nutting

Tribune Chronicle (Warren)	35,725
Times Leader (Martins Ferry)	19,020
Advertiser-Tribune (Tiffin)	10,745
Review (East Liverpool)	10,014
Herald-Star (Steubenville)	16,715

Flint Journal

Oakland Press
(Pontiac)

Bay City Times

Muskegon
Chronicle
Saginaw News
Lansing State
Journal
Times Herald
(Port Huron)

Grand Rapids
Press
Macomb Daily
(Mount Clemens)
Daily Tribune *(Royal Oak)*

Battle Creek Enquirer
Detroit

Kalamazoo Gazette
Detroit
News
Cleveland

Chronicle-Telegram *(Elyria)*
News-Herald *(Willoughby)*
Record-Courier *(Kent-Ravenna)*
Tribune Chronicle *(Warren)*

Ann Arbor News

Jackson Citizen Patriot
News-Messenger
(Fremont)
Morning Journal
(Lorain)
Alliance Review
Repository *(Canton)*

Crescent-News
(Defiance)
Review *(East Liverpool)*
Independent *(Massillon)*
Herald-Star *(Steubenville)*

Advertiser-Tribune
(Tiffin)
Marion Star
Times Leader *(Martins Ferr*
Times Reporter *(New Philadelphia)*

Medina County Gazette
(Medina)
Daily Record *(Wooster)*

Ashland Times-Gazette
OHIO

Columbus
Daily Jeffersonian *(Cambridge)*
Times Recorder *(Zanesville)*

News Journal
(Mansfield)
Advocate
(Newark)

Springfield News-Sun
Marietta Times

Dayton Daily News
Lancaster
Eagle-Gazette

Middletown Journal
Journal News
(Hamilton)
Cincinnati
Enquirer
Chillicothe
Gazette

Circulation

C	Less than 50,000
C	50,000 to 100,000
C	Over 100,000

Organization

CX	Cox
D	Dix
G	Gannett
JR	Journal Register
L	Lorain
N	Newhouse
NU	Nutting
21	21st Century

Journal Register

News-Herald (Willoughby)	50,823
Morning Journal (Lorain)	35,850
Times Reporter (New Philadelphia)	24,118
Independent (Massillon)	15,034

Dix

Ashland Times-Gazette	12,185
Alliance Review	12,507
Daily Jeffersonian (Cambridge)	12,659
Crescent-News (Defiance)	16,568
Daily Record (Wooster)	23,111
Record-Courier (Kent-Ravenna)	19,406

Cox

Dayton Daily News	140,891
Middletown Journal	20,794
Journal-News (Hamilton)	24,501
Springfield News-Sun	32,864

Lorain

Chronicle-Telegram (Elyria)	29,542
Medina County Gazette (Medina)	15,356

OKLAHOMA   *Circ.*

CNHI

Enid News & Eagle	20,258
Norman Transcript	13,943
McAlester News-Capital & Democrat	11,502
Edmond Sun	10,415

Morris

Daily Ardmoreite	11,319
Shawnee News-Star	10,449

OREGON   *Circ.*

Lee

Albany Democrat-Herald	19,746
Corvallis Gazette-Times	12,598

PENNSYLVANIA	*Circ.*
Calkins	
Philadelphia area	
Bucks Co. Courier Times (Levittown)	66,510
Intelligencer/Record (Doylestown)	44,257
Burlington Co. Times (Willingboro, NJ)	39,074
Pittsburgh area	
Beaver Co. Times	42,917
Herald-Standard (Uniontown)	28,817
Journal Register	
Daily Local News (West Chester)	33,127
Mercury (Pottstown)	26,099
Times Herald (Norristown)	21,515
Delaware Co. Daily Times (Primos)	50,373
Trentonian (Trenton, NJ)	53,177
Tribune-Review	
Tribune-Review (Greensburg)	83,801
Valley News Dispatch (Tarentum)	32,609
Valley Independent (Monessen)	16,586
North Hills News Record	18,172
Leader Times (Kittanning)	10,512
Daily Courier (Connellsville)	10,285
Nutting	
Altoona Mirror	32,744
Williamsport Sun-Gazette	30,190
Sentinel (Carlisle)	15,498
MediaNews	
York Dispatch	40,335
Evening Sun (Hanover)	20,901
Knight Ridder	
Philadelphia Daily News	162,434
Philadelphia Inquirer	399,339
Times Leader (Wilkes-Barre)	49,823
Centre Daily Times (State College)	24,657

Times Publishing

Erie Daily Times/Morning News	32,244
Warren Times-Observer	11,533

Times-Shamrock

News-Item (Shamokin)	11,626
Scranton Times/Tribune	33,037

SOUTH CAROLINA   *Circ.*

McClatchy

Herald (Rock Hill)	30,546
Island Packet (Hilton Head)	15,098
Beaufort Gazette	11,469

Evening Post

Aiken Standard	13,839
Post and Courier (Charleston)	105,296

TENNESSEE   *Circ.*

Gannett

Tennessean (Nashville)	187,618
Jackson Sun	39,269
Leaf-Chronicle (Clarksville)	20,784

Cleveland

Cleveland Daily Banner	15,370
Herald-Citizen (Cookeville)	11,161

TEXAS   *Circ.*

Scripps Howard

Corpus Christi Caller-Times	64,780
Abilene Reporter-News	38,272
Wichita Falls Times Record News	36,659
Standard-Times (San Angelo)	29,951

Cox

Austin American-Statesman	184,825
Waco Tribune-Herald	40,660
Longview News-Journal	29,277
Lufkin Daily News	14,206

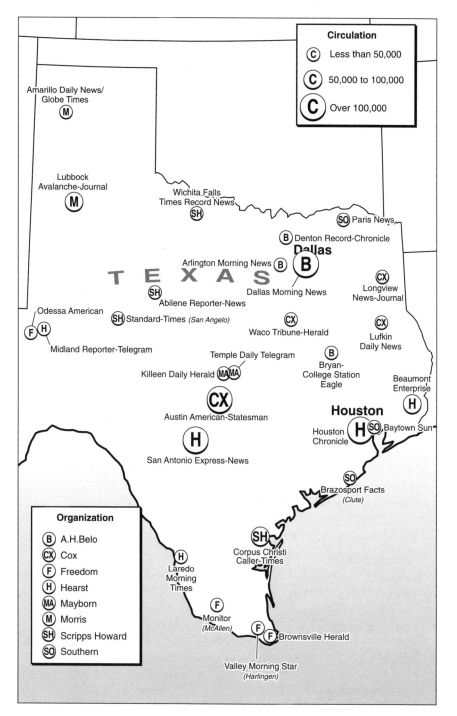

Circulation

C Less than 50,000

C 50,000 to 100,000

C Over 100,000

Amarillo Daily News/
Globe Times
M

Lubbock
Avalanche-Journal
M

Wichita Falls
Times Record News
SH

SO Paris News

B Denton Record-Chronicle

Dallas
B

Arlington Morning News B B

T E X A S

Dallas Morning News

CX
Longview
News-Journal

SH
Abilene Reporter-News

Odessa American

SH Standard-Times (San Angelo)

CX
Waco Tribune-Herald

CX
Lufkin
Daily News

F H
Midland Reporter-Telegram

Temple Daily Telegram
Killeen Daily Herald MA MA

B
Bryan-
College Station
Eagle

Beaumont
Enterprise
H

CX
Austin American-Statesman

Houston

H SO Baytown Sun
Houston
Chronicle

H
San Antonio Express-News

SO
Brazosport Facts
(Clute)

Organization

B A.H.Belo
CX Cox
F Freedom
H Hearst
MA Mayborn
M Morris
SH Scripps Howard
SO Southern

H
Laredo
Morning
Times

SH
Corpus Christi
Caller-Times

F
Monitor
(McAllen)

F F Brownsville Herald

Valley Morning Star
(Harlingen)

Mayborn

Temple Daily Telegram	22,159
Killeen Daily Herald	17,773

Belo

Dallas Morning News	490,249
Arlington Morning News	32,795
Bryan-College Station Eagle	23,493
Denton Record-Chronicle	15,954

Hearst

Houston Chronicle	542,414
San Antonio Express-News	219,837
Beaumont Enterprise	57,823
Laredo Morning Times	20,925
Midland Reporter-Telegram	19,330

Southern

Brazosport Facts (Clute)	16,727
Paris News	10,266
Baytown Sun	10,368

Freedom

Monitor (McAllen)	37,279
Odessa American	26,155
Valley Morning Star (Harlingen)	23,503
Brownsville Herald	16,632

Morris

Lubbock Avalanche-Journal	58,952
Amarillo Daily News/Globe Times	43,938

VIRGINIA

Circ.

Media General

Richmond Times-Dispatch	199,814
News & Advance (Lynchburg)	37,502
Daily Progress (Charlottesville)	31,296
Potomac News (Woodbridge)	20,078

Byrd

Daily News-Record (Harrisonburg)	32,103
Winchester Star	21,050

Journal Newspapers

Montgomery Journal (Rockville, MD)	29,952
Prince George's Journal (Lanham, MD)	28,369
Fairfax Journal (Fairfax)	50,448

WASHINGTON   *Circ.*

Seattle Times

Seattle Times	219,698
Walla Walla Union-Bulletin	14,538
Yakima Herald-Republic	39,192

Horvitz

Eastside Journal (Bellevue)	26,927
South County Journal (Kent)	23,160
Peninsula Daily News (Port Angeles)	15,114

WEST VIRGINIA   *Circ.*

Nutting

Wheeling News-Register/Intelligencer	20,979
Inter-Mountain (Elkins)	10,636
Journal (Martinsburg)	18,801
Parkersburg News/Sentinel	20,765

CNHI

Register-Herald (Beckley)	30,393
Bluefield Daily Telegraph	22,181

WISCONSIN   *Circ.*

Gannett

Post-Crescent (Appleton)	56,218
Sheboygan Press	26,510
Oshkosh Northwestern	23,511
Reporter (Fond du Lac)	18,664
Herald Times Reporter (Manitowoc)	17,293
Marshfield News-Herald	13,987
Green Bay Press-Gazette	59,339
Wausau Daily Herald	23,108
Daily Tribune (Wisconsin Rapids)	13,292
Stevens Point Journal	13,856

Lee

Wisconsin State Journal (Madison)	87,492
Journal Times (Racine)	30,861
La Crosse Tribune	31,445
Winona (MN) Daily News	11,880

5

Journalists suffered throughout much of the 1990s as publishers and CEOs downsized news staffs, shrunk the space for news, squeezed newsroom budgets, and held down the wages of working journalists to push their companies' profits (and their own compensation) higher. Industry surveys showed staff morale sinking at papers throughout the country. Newsroom turnover was the highest it had been within living memory. A veteran copy editor at the Chicago Sun-Times, Margaret Maples, calculated that 92 editorial employees (from a staff of 225) had left the paper in three and a half years. She posted a memo on the bulletin board complaining that "we're all doing more work to maintain the quality of the Sun-Times. We're joking less, gossiping less, spending less time on office friendships. . . . Some of us are desperately treading water. We see it in managers who are in over their heads. These individuals are swamped. They lose the power to laugh. Their jobs eat them alive."

Understandably, many journalists have come to view their corporate employers as distant and even hostile figures—greedy, unethical, and traitorous to the cause of good journalism.

Caught in the middle—in a no-man's-land between the underpaid reporter who worries about the news report and the seven-figure-income CEO who worries about the annual report—stands the senior editor. Most senior editors come from reporting backgrounds themselves, but in today's environment their loyalties may be painfully torn between the values of their newsroom colleagues, with whom most of them can sympathize, and the demands of their bosses, to whom they owe their jobs and yearly bonuses.

Editor Inc.

By Geneva Overholser

1. TROUBLEMAKERS

Gil Thelen found himself in that rock-and-a-hard-place sort of situation not uncommon these days in the profession of newspaper editing.

He'd been executive editor of the *State* in Columbia, South Carolina, for five years, and for three years before that he'd held the same title at its sister paper over in Myrtle Beach, the *Sun News*. So Thelen knew something about South Carolina, and he had some firm ideas on how his newspaper ought to be run. Problem was, a new publisher had come in from another Knight Ridder paper, in Gary, Indiana. Fred Mott had firm ideas, too—different firm ideas.

"We were trying to refocus the paper from statewide to increasingly zoned local coverage," Thelen recalls. "And the publisher and I really had a significant and profound disagreement on this point." Both men, of course, were trying to build the *State*'s readership and revenues, but Thelen felt increasing pressure to steer an editorial course for his paper that he didn't believe in.

In the middle of this dispute came Thelen's job review. Mott suggested that Thelen might work on his outlook. As the editor remembers it, the publisher said that while "it is appropriate for a reporter or college professor to struggle over this tension between journalism values and business imperatives . . . it is not appropriate for an executive editor."

Thelen was abashed. He knew as well as anyone how the ground rules for editors had been shifting, but this was the first time they had been put to him quite so explicitly. "I told him that I respectfully disagreed, and I felt that tension was central to the editor's job," Thelen recalls. "And if that was his position—and clearly it was—then I'd choose to leave.

"So I did."

Thelen recounts this story from a glass-walled office in the *Tampa Tribune* newsroom, where he has just become the executive editor. He landed here after a few months' consulting stint with his old company; on this late-June morning he has been in the newsroom only ten days. His wife, in fact, is still up in South Carolina, overseeing the transplanting of her day lilies. Thelen is still dealing with his own case of root-shock. He seems a man both bruised and blessed.

Having to leave so unexpectedly the job he'd hoped would be his last— he was nearing sixty, with two little kids—was tough. But Thelen feels lucky to be here. The *Tribune,* Media General's largest newspaper, is in a punishing war with the *St. Petersburg Times* for the hearts and minds of Tampa Bay readers. There is no shortage of pressure. But Thelen, an intense, animated man, is eager for the challenge. And he speaks enthusiastically about his new publisher, Reid Ashe, who himself had left a Knight Ridder paper, the *Wichita Eagle,* to come to Tampa.

"You have to work for a publisher who understands and is willing to live with the tension, rather than to try to deny the tension exists, or turn the editor into the vice president of marketing," Thelen says with a conviction reinforced by his experience in Columbia.

"I worry very much that we're losing some of our very best people before their time."

2. EVOLUTIONARY SPECIES

Once upon a time an editor was the paramount figure at a newspaper. In an age when most papers were independent and family-owned, he was often the editor and publisher (not for nothing was the industry's trade magazine so named). He cared about the cash register, yes, but he hired the people to watch it for him. He (needless to say, back then it was virtually always a he) reigned like a prince—sometimes benevolent, sometimes imperious, almost always autonomous.

But over the years, with the decline in newspaper readership, the emergence of the publicly owned newspaper company and the concomitant ascent of the business side, the editor's role has evolved. Dramatically. The importance of the position—in the newsroom, in the company, in the community—has diminished. Editors are still pivotal figures at their newspapers, of course, but increasingly they are team players, replaceable faces in a management constellation. Princes they are not.

This evolution of roles over the last couple of decades has not been easy for editors. I experienced something of it myself, as editor of the *Des Moines Register* from 1988 to 1995. Along with other editors, I dealt with the swelling business-side demands and the encroaching influence of other departments. I heard the low grumblings and caught the glancing asides at corporate gatherings. Once or twice, along with some other editors, I raised my voice in righteous indignation. And I saw the backlash, as a pull-up-your-socks, tough-it-out attitude emerged among still other editors.

Along this bumpy way some editors quit. Many stayed on, making a quiet if uneasy peace with the new order; to continue to argue about marketing or corporatization seemed pointless, even destructive. And more than a few editors came to believe that much of what had happened was necessary, even overdue. To them, a desire to keep the newsroom aloof was both arrogant and misguided. "The world has changed," says Julia Wallace, who edits the *Statesman Journal* in Salem, Oregon, a Gannett paper. "I think there was a time when editors said, you know, 'Eat your peas. We know what's best for you. Leave me alone and let me do my job.' The reality of today's world is that everyone wants a piece of what we're doing. . . . You've got to be pretty open to that or it's going to drive you crazy."

Most editors would agree that the job today means being all things to all people. Editors are more itinerant than ever, but pressed to find better ways to understand their communities. They are better paid than ever, but largely because of bonus arrangements that link their compensation to company profit and circulation goals. They agonize more than ever over what good journalism is, but get less and less time to do it. They try to be sensitive managers of their employees—well, many do—but to headquarters these same employees are mere "full-time equivalents." The editor's world is circumscribed by corporate news evaluation procedures, byzantine personnel requirements, and elaborate budgeting processes. Declining readership compels editors to be marketers. Corporatization compels them to be entrepreneurs.

Most of the foregoing litany boils down to money. America became obsessed with business, and newspapers did, too. John Carroll, long-time editor of the Baltimore Sun and now the editor of the *Los Angeles Times*, sees the larger changes when he looks back, past his four-decade newspaper career, to his alma mater, Haverford College. "Business is ascendant in this society to a degree it has not been in my lifetime," he says. "The best and the brightest from my college are all becoming investment bankers. When I went there, I'd never heard the term 'investment banker.' People all wanted to be journalists or doctors or college professors. But now—a lot of publishers and CEOs want an editor who talks about leveraging assets."

To be fair, one reason editors' jobs have changed is that newspapers have confronted a series of economic challenges over recent years, with pressure to keep profits high even as costs have risen and advertisers and readers have turned elsewhere. "The business people to some extent felt they had to take firmer charge and do something," says Carroll. "And they weren't without reason there."

The changes did not come unheralded. I vividly remember how, more than a decade ago, Mike Fancher, then the bold new executive editor of the *Seattle Times*, told every editor who would listen that the best defense was a good offense. He preached that we in editorial owed it to ourselves to gain a better understanding of the business side. All the energy in the industry—and control of resources—was clearly moving in that direction, he said. It would serve little use to sit around, wringing our hands over the corporatization of the news. Savvy editors had to act, not react.

I also remember the thanks he got—being cast by many colleagues as the embodiment of that evil specter, the MBA editor.

Since then this merry-go-round profession has spirited away many an editor, but Mike Fancher is still contentedly running the *Times*. And now we know that he was on to something. The trends he warned about—the loss of power and editorial autonomy, increasing business pressure, the threat to journalistic values—they're conventional wisdom now. Indeed, plenty of editors would agree with the cautionary assessment of wily Harold Evans, who now runs Mort Zuckerman's publications, including the *New York Daily News:* "The challenge of the American newspaper is not to stay in business, it is to stay in journalism."

3. CORPORATE CREATURES

It's a sticky summer night in Tampa. At a comfortable, long-established Italian place called Donatello's, I'm having dinner with Gene Patterson, one of the few living newspaper people with a cult following. (For example, Bill Ketter, former president of the American Society of Newspaper Editors, will tell you, "I'm in the Gene Patterson School.") A man of electric energy, the seventy-five-year-old Patterson has a jaw that calls to mind Billy Graham and a laserlike gaze that seizes attention. He's spinning out stories from his brilliant career, which he capped by running the *St. Pete Times.* The best yarn concerns publishing legends John S. Knight, who built the Knight chain, and Nelson Poynter, who then owned the St. Pete paper.

"Jack saw Nelson at a Gridiron dinner in Washington," Patterson tells me. "They were in the men's room, standing at the urinals beside each other. And Jack leaned down to Nelson, who was a diminutive guy, and he said, 'I've got an announcement coming up next week and I wonder what you think of it.' Nelson said, 'Well, what is that?' And Jack said, 'I'm taking Knight Newspapers public. Whaddya think about that, Nelson?' And quick as a shot Nelson replied, 'Jack, I think it'll be just fine—as long as you're alive.'"

Patterson pours us another glass of Chianti. "Nelson loved to quote that little conversation. He was vastly amused by it. Knight was not amused. But the fact is, what would Jack Knight think today?"

Good question. Of 1,483 dailies in the United States, only about 280 remain independently owned. In 1940 there were some 1,300.

Corporatization didn't rock editors' lives suddenly. It began with cost-cutting campaigns in the '70s and '80s, then gathered speed as computers gave bean-counters new clout to pressure newshole and payroll. As readership fell and bottom lines flattened out (or worse), corporate headquarters in distant cities stepped up their memos and publishers turned up the heat. Bit by bit the editor's autonomy was eroded: from the overall budget to the newshole, from personnel policies to new sections, from job tenure to the shape and size of stories. Stress fractures appeared everywhere along the traditional wall between business and editorial.

In reporting this story I talked to fifty current and former editors, and their views were augmented by a detailed questionnaire sent to editors around the country by the Project on the State of the American Newspaper. What I found most striking was how many editors volunteered candid, on-the-record concerns about public ownership of newspapers. It's almost a new article of faith: Investors demand quarter-to-quarter profit increases. When the local economy does not promote or permit growth, profits have to be squeezed up by cost-cutting. In so doing, the journalism is diminished. Thus can public ownership undermine the basic newspaper imperative—public trust.

Of course, you don't hear that everywhere—not, for instance, in the office of one-time editor Jay Harris, who is now publisher of the *San Jose Mercury News*. Harris has seen the dynamics of newspapering from every vantage point. He was a reporter for Gannett News Service, executive editor at the *Philadelphia Daily News*, and an assistant to Knight Ridder CEO Tony Ridder in Miami. Since 1994 he has occupied the publisher's suite in the capital of Silicon Valley.

In his grand office, once Ridder's, with classical music playing softly in the background, I tell Harris the Patterson story about Knight and Poynter. He sees nothing portentous about it: "Jack Knight was pretty strong on the point that good business and good journalism are not only not in opposition to one another, but, indeed they require each other to exist over a long time."

Harris is among those who believe public ownership has uplifted papers, providing new resources, stronger journalism—and one thing more. He speaks pointedly as an African-American publisher to a female former editor: "I am sure that were it not for what we talk about as corporatization of newspapers that I would not be here to be interviewed—and there's at least a fair chance you would not be here interviewing me."

Harris is frankly tired of the nostalgia of purity. He well recalls his early newspaper days, conjuring for me an image of one of his first managing editors. "He sat there in a white shirt and smoked all night and he was the god of the newsroom," Harris says. "As far as I could tell, that was all he did. He may have been 'pure' in the narrow sense of it. But I would not want to have that person running this newsroom today."

Maxwell King also ran a big Knight Ridder shop, the *Philadelphia Inquirer*. But King stepped down in 1998, after seven pressure-packed years as the top editor. Like Harris, King recalls earlier jobs, in a different time.

"I remember when I worked in Louisville [at the *Courier-Journal*], I knew a guy on the business side and I asked him what the profit margin was. And he said two-and-a-half percent was their margin before taxes. Well, of course, the Binghams did lose the paper. So it's silly to be glib and say, 'Oh, why can't it all be like that?' On the other hand, it is a reflection of the fact that they weren't focused on profits, they were focused on what the paper meant to the community."

As we visit, King is still on his ten-month "sabbatical," as he calls it. In the *Inquirer*'s West Chester bureau, a transformed movie theater near the handsome small-town courthouse, he is wearing jeans; his shirt sleeves are rolled up. We meet here because it's close to his farm, where he's been reading, clearing fence lines, building stone walls, and relaxing. But on this topic, he is not relaxed. He's passionate.

"I think the . . . paradigm of the family-owned newspaper, where the family lived in town, cared about the local issues, cared about the community —certainly it led to some evils, you know, Colonel McCormick storming around the *Chicago Tribune* telling them what to say about things," he says. "But it also led to a newspaper that was far more responsive to the needs of the local community than to the financial needs."

This is not green-eyeshade nostalgia. And King wants that known: "What I am not saying and what I feel some people misunderstand me to be saying—and what I hear from so many people in newsrooms around the country is, 'It's just those greedy bastards who run the companies. And if they really cared about journalism instead of caring so much about profits, everything would be okay.' . . . I think that is such a shockingly simple-minded view of what's going on in our business. And it pisses me off because it's not what I'm saying."

What he's talking about is the pressure built into the situation and built up over so many quarters, so many budgets, so many balance sheets. "For efficiency, efficiency, efficiency. . . ." King is saying. "To drive costs down, drive market share up, all in the interest of serving the shareholder. . . ."

4. Money Makers

In 1985, the year I left the *Des Moines Register*'s editorial-page staff for a Nieman Fellowship, the company (then owned by the Cowles family) made a profit before taxes of just under $6 million. Gannett bought the paper that year for $165 million. Within a year the newspaper had raised its profits to $11 million, then $17 million the next year. By the time I returned as editor, in 1988, the *Register*'s earnings had reached $20.5 million. I heard Douglas McCorkindale, then Gannett's chief financial officer, tell a gathering of editors that year, "People thought we paid too much for Des Moines, but [the margins] are right on track."

Newspaper profits are the envy of the business world. In 1999, the operating profit margin for newspapers, as a sector, was 22 percent, says industry analyst John Morton. (That's double the figure for U.S. industry at large.) Margins ranged from 29.2 percent at the Tribune Company to 17.9 percent for the Washington Post Company. The largest newspaper company, Gannett, had a pre-tax margin of 24.6 percent, according to Morton.

Newspaper stocks operate under the "theory of elevated expectations—that's certainly there, and it certainly has an impact," he explains. Much of this profitability in recent years, Morton goes on, was achieved through fairly severe cost cutting, including layoffs of staff, trimming of news space, and various forms of downsizing—"all of which raise questions from some constituencies about whether corporate management had become too focused on profitability at the expense of journalistic quality."

It's not that editors don't understand the necessity for making a profit. But with the kind of margins newspapers are used to, asserting a need for solvency is a bit like having a 350-pound man tell you he needs his ice cream sundae.

The man most responsible for the particular pattern of profit pressures on American newspapers is Al Neuharth, former Gannett CEO, who retired as chairman of the Freedom Forum in 1996 and lives in Cocoa Beach, Florida. He stays busy these days contributing a regular column to his best-known creation, *USA Today,* and tending the growing, multiracial brood of kids he and his wife have adopted. Over two decades Neuharth built the nation's largest newspaper company by demonstrating to analysts that a large newspaper chain could overcome the downward drafts of the business cycle and deliver reliable profit increases. Every single quarter.

I ask Neuharth how he feels being blamed for this "terrible chain around your neck," as one critic put it. Neuharth is pleased to respond: "Well, the fact is that at Gannett we *did* have 86 uninterrupted quarters of earnings gains. The degree of those earnings gains varied a good bit from time to time, but we simply said that there are two objectives for a media company. One is to produce products and the other is to produce profits, and it was my feeling then—and I'm even more convinced now—that nearly all of the editors and publishers that I know could set similar goals for themselves without in any way compromising their news judgment or news product—and probably enhancing it."

Neuharth goes on with cheerful confidence. "I realize there are a good many who would differ with me, but it's my feeling that if you charge what a product is worth . . . and if you're willing to invest the proper amount of that income in the product itself, that you can indeed change or improve newspapers and at the same time enhance the bottom line. I believe that in the majority of the 60-something papers we acquired while I was around, the Gannett ownership enhanced the professionalism of the news product."

Whatever one thinks of Gannett newspapers' journalism, everyone can agree that Neuharth was positively fearless when it came to charging customers what he believed the market would bear—and thought his papers warranted. He boosted Gannett profits with an aggressive pricing strategy, which, to the horror of many a circulation director, was sometimes employed even during recessions. Neuharth continues to point to this as the best way for papers to fulfill their dual profit and public service commitments. Publishers like the *Washington Post*'s Donald Graham, he says, are "afraid to charge what their paper is worth."

So call San Jose's Jay Harris a neo-Neuharthian. He says the *Mercury News* tried to fight the California recession of the late 1980s and early 1990s with aggressive cost-cutting. It didn't work. In December 1993, Harris became publisher. "When I got here we began to shift the focus over to growing revenue," he says. "So now there is at the heart of our mission at the *Mercury News* a goal of providing sufficient revenue each year to do four things: invest in employees; do new product development; improve quality; and, number four, do all of that after we have met our obligations to Knight Ridder shareholders. And what I think is happening in some other places is that the company is only growing enough to do the fourth of those four things, and not leaving enough money for investment."

However the company sets priorities, the business demands wear on editors. "The journalism tends to get crowded out by administration and marketing issues," says Sig Gissler, editor of the *Milwaukee Journal* until early 1993, and now teaching at the Columbia Graduate School of Journalism. "The first time you have to take a hundred thousand out of payroll, it's kind of a fascinating exercise. The fifth time you have to do it, it's lost its allure. That becomes a drain. You come in and start killing the nearest snake."

John Carroll says editors once got away with saying, "This is my newsroom, get the hell out of here—no, I won't cut my budget." But as financial pressures increased and revenues grew scarce, he says, that had to change. "That's not the song I was singing back then, but that happens to be the truth, with the benefit of hindsight. And I think in that process a lot of editors were really beaten down. They lost a sense that all things were possible and they started . . . just showing up for work. They were demoralized. And some of them just never got back up off the canvas."

The most demoralizing problem stemmed from financial expectations that many editors considered unrealistic. Traditionally, newspaper people have taken up and down cycles for granted. Investors don't. "That's been a really pernicious notion: that profits in what is a cyclical business have to go up every quarter," says Carroll, a former editor of Knight Ridder's *Lexington Herald-Leader.* "I'll tell you, I can remember when Knight Ridder got a down quarter, but Gannett was marching steadily upward. Analysts killed 'em. I could see they were going to do all they could to avoid having that happen again.

"I don't know any way out of it," he goes on. "But I think newspapers might be better long-term investments if they didn't try to have an up quarter every time. When revenues fall off, as they do cyclically, newspapers scramble to cut costs—it might be your bridge column or your horse-racing agate—but you add them all up and it hurts your paper a whole lot."

Editors feel the squeeze not only in figuring out how to do more with less, but in explaining the rationale to staffs and readers. Several years ago, newsprint prices shot up and newsrooms were forced to cut news columns and features. How many editors told readers that the cuts would allow the newspaper company to keep its operating profit at 21 percent rather than see it drop to 19 or 20? What other business covered on the news pages would be let off that hook?

Says Carroll, "I think that in chain operations in which the shareholder interests are conspicuously put first—sometimes really to the exclusion of public service and journalistic values—a fundamental shift occurred in the role of the editor vis-a-vis the corporate and business side."

A few days after my interviews with King and Carroll, Knight Ridder reported its second-quarter results: Profits soared 107 percent to $127 million. Then more Knight Ridder news: Things look bad at the *Miami Herald;* staffing cuts are said to be "inevitable" in order for the paper to reach a 22 percent profit margin over the next three years. Days later Miami's publisher, David Lawrence, one of the most relentlessly optimistic figures in the business, resigns.

5. Marketers

Walk into any sizable newsroom in the country, ask where you can find the editor, and chances are good the answer will be: in the marketing committee. It's the place today where key decisions affecting newsrooms are made—how to boost circulation, how to create new sections, how to structure zoned coverage, how to define the paper's target audience. Editors spend long hours plotting strategy with their counterparts from advertising, marketing, and circulation, and they are being pushed to turn news coverage toward the most profitable territory: the interests of women, younger readers, suburbanites, and the affluent.

Bob Ingle, former executive editor of the *San Jose Mercury News* and now Knight Ridder's president for new media, says marketing committees merely institutionalized what was always part of the editor's job. "The best editors are marketers," he says. "You know, that's what I tried to do when I was editor—get the bloody staff to listen to the audience. I wanted them to say about me, 'He's a terrific marketer.' Goddamn, that's what we do."

Editors adept in the marketing committee say they have won support from other departments that previously would have been difficult, or impossible, to obtain. Jerry Ceppos, Ingle's successor in San Jose, is a believer. "I want to be in on those decisions," he says. "And I want to build a case saying, 'Here's why we need more resources for business coverage.' Even when I was making a pitch for additional resources for business staff a couple of years ago—which we got in a big way—somebody said, 'You know what you're actually doing is marketing.' And I said, 'No, I'm not. What I'm doing is journalism.' At some point they intersect." Then, grinning broadly, Ceppos adds, "I guess that's a terrible thing to say."

Yet as newspaper marketing strategies grew more sophisticated—the audience increasingly analyzed, sliced, and diced—many editors got nervous about emerging conflicts between the needs of a modern newspaper and the needs of the community. Does the notion of continually targeting specific reader preferences—or perceived preferences—set us on the wrong road?

"Back in the early '80s, when I became editor, I think we thought about news as being the hard news, breaking news," says Dave Zweifel of the *Capital Times* in Madison, Wisconsin. "It's really changed today as we look at the audience or potential audience. Some of the journalists' instincts don't necessarily hold true today. I find myself torn between what I feel is the more traditional approach—Damn it, this is news you ought to have and it's really important to you, it's gonna mean something to your pocketbook or to your kids' future—torn between that and something like a story on modern women and day care."

There's no confusion about the reasons behind the marketing push. After years of assuming that Americans would continue their daily reading habits, papers began to suffer a steady decline in readership. Today some fear that the next generation, weaned on the Internet, will not even want newspapers. Beyond that, aggressive marketers for broadcast and other media started using sophisticated research and marketing techniques to lure away traditional print advertisers. Even classified ads, the bedrock of newspaper revenue, are under pressure from online competitors.

Max King notes that the *Inquirer* did extensive research in the '70s and '80s "because our life was on the line. There's no question that a lot of newspaper companies put too much emphasis on market research. But if you're conducting market research and the newsroom's using it and the decisions are being made by editors who are better informed by market research, I don't see it as a huge problem. Nobody ever tried to take our decisions away. They wanted results, but they didn't specify what the [methods] should be."

But editors may find the front lines of marketing being drawn increasingly in treacherous terrain. Does the editor beef up coverage of crime in a bid for circulation and downplay the reality that serious crime is actually declining in the community? Does the editor shift coverage from inner-city problems to suburban soccer leagues because that's where the affluent live and, in any case, the circulation director has removed the vendor boxes downtown and the ad director reports no business?

Gregory Favre, vice president for news at McClatchy and former editor of the *Sacramento Bee,* voiced this precise concern when he told a recent forum sponsored by the Committee of Concerned Journalists, "I see a trend emerging in our business of seeking out only those readers in the areas that our advertisers, and too many of our executives in this business, believe to be 'the best areas of our communities.' Someday, if we continue to do that, we will be without good, strong newspapers representing the wholeness of our community. . . . We will be without newspapers that will give voice to all segments of our communities so that we can learn from each other, so that we can listen to each other, so that we can grow together and learn from our differences."

6. Number Crunchers

I still have a November 1994 memo from the newsroom administrator, the fellow who did our basic newsroom budget calculations at the *Des Moines Register.* It reads: "There are times when our budget is finalized that I feel like I've taken out its heart and soul. This time I took out a lot of other giblets as well. The 1995 budget is not just tight, it squeaks."

The budget process for that year had begun with a memo from Gary Watson, Gannett newspaper division president, saying:

"1995 will be a difficult year because of the increases in newsprint pricing. Thus, you and your team must plan accordingly. Often, we see comments such as these in the Publisher's Letter: 'Without the increase in newsprint prices, NIBT (net income before taxes) would be up X percent....' Don't allow yourself or your team to be lulled into some false sense of reality by thinking you can plan for 1995 as if the newsprint price increase didn't exist. Newsprint prices will be going up, and we still have the responsibility to produce a return for our shareholders."

The controller of the *Register*, Susan Smith, put it more candidly: "Despite the significant increase in newsprint cost in 1995, we are expected to grow our bottom line over 1994."

Thus, having already removed heart, soul, and giblets, we cut some more—another $63,000 in newsroom spending. Very shortly thereafter, by January, we learned that during the months we were engaged in these hope-withering negotiations, Gannett earnings were up 22 percent over the previous year's fourth quarter.

The *Register*'s plan for 1995, the year newsprint prices were soaring, was for a 23.4 percent profit margin before taxes—compared to the previous year's 21-plus percent with low newsprint prices. I don't know if they made it. I had happily departed the world of advertising shortfalls, newsprint price increases, and contingency plans. Just before I left, Watson had sent another memo, describing yet another challenge ahead: Interest rates were rising, he noted; expense controls required an especially watchful eye.

Now consider another of Gene Patterson's anecdotes:

"Jack Knight loved to quote his Washington bureau chief, Ed Lahey, an old, tough Washington reporter. He was talking to Lahey one night and Lahey said, 'You know sum'n, Knight? You're a publisher and I'm a reporter and there's only one thing I expect of you.' Jack asked, 'What's that, Ed?' And he said, 'I just want you to stay solvent.' You see, staying solvent is kind of a complex undertaking in the newsroom. But Ed Lahey just left all that to Jack: You stay solvent and I'll cover the news."

These days "solvency" starts at home, in the newsroom. For many editors, the brave new world of budget controls came to be symbolized by an innocent-sounding acronym, the FTE. The FTE, which stands for full-time equivalent, is a bean-counter's dream. Whereas editors once used to keep track of old-fashioned human beings—reporters, photographers, copy editors, librarians, clerks—and their individual salaries, the FTE is a formula that encompasses all the hours it takes to put out a paper: the employee hours, yes, but often overtime worked and, in some companies, stringer contributions, correspondents' hours, and the like. Thus, a paper may have 100 newsroom employees, but 120 newsroom FTEs.

FTE accounting, common in other businesses, began showing up at newspaper companies in the '70s, and by now some variation is employed at most major chains. Because the FTE formula flattens the highs and lows of a department's salaries into an average figure, because FTEs don't take vacations or get sick, and because they are computer friendly, this accounting technique enabled companies to track actual costs much more rigorously —on a month-to-month, week-to-week, even day-to-day basis.

Used more aggressively, however, FTE accounting sharply limits the flexibility editors traditionally have had to juggle positions while staying in the budget—that is, it's another outside restriction on newsroom management. If you've got a huge story to cover one week and you sail past your FTE allotment to do it, you may have to suck up the difference next week by eliminating overtime or forgoing certain stories you otherwise would cover.

Or consider this example: In many large companies FTEs have a first cousin called "dark time," known elsewhere as "churn." These terms refer to the fact that in a newsroom of any size, over the course of the year X number of hours will go unfilled because of temporary job vacancies. It's the editor's job to manage that churn. But he can get cuffed no matter which way he goes. If there's too little churn, he'll exceed his FTE budget and get a pounding. If there's too much churn, he'll run under his FTE budget and invite someone from corporate HQ to say: Well, if you don't really need all those resources, we'll take them away next year. And often they do.

FTEs are used throughout the paper, not just in the newsroom, and their manipulation can reach almost comic proportions. Robert O'Sullivan, now vice president for circulation at the *Record* in Bergen County, New Jersey, recalls the days of very tight FTEs a decade ago when he was with the *Philadelphia Inquirer*. "What I remember about how Knight Ridder did those calculations was that if you had independent truckers doing your trucking, they converted that into FTEs," he says. In fact, at one point the *Inquirer* shipped some fifteen hundred newspapers a day by bus, which was cheaper and faster than mail. But because buses counted as truck-driver hours, and thus as FTEs, the paper started mailing them instead, which was slower and more expensive, and drove away readers. Thus did FTEs exercise their power.

The fact is that most editors I spoke with don't consider FTEs a particular nuisance today, at least at their own papers. But at franchises under financial pressure, vast amounts of time and energy can go into FTE reporting and management. In Philadelphia, for example, Max King found the FTE count too important to leave to anyone else. "If I was over on FTEs at all, that was a big concern," he says. "By the same token, I didn't want to be under on FTEs because then I was wasting a resource."

King says it used to be that he'd have time to check the records when corporate officials called about his FTE count. Then, as computer linkages became more sophisticated, the nature of the calls changed. Knight Ridder already knew what was happening. "They'd ask, 'Why are you running 2 or 3 percent over on X category?' They knew where we were and often they knew that we hadn't looked it up. And then you thought, 'Oh God, I should have known that,' and then you thought, 'Do I have to know? Is that what I should be doing, parsing these numbers at 9 o'clock in the morning instead of trying to figure out what the stories are?'"

Our checks with corporate offices show wide variation in the degree of specificity required in reporting FTEs. But as King described, the most detailed use is generally identified with Knight Ridder. "Let's cut to the chase here," says Gil Thelen. "Someone once said, in corporate, [Knight Ridder CEO] Tony Ridder knows whenever an FTE moves in this whole company. Clearly, FTEs are an important issue to Tony. And what's an important issue to the CEO becomes an important issue to everybody else in the company. So yes, there is a lot more focus put on FTEs."

Replies Jay Harris, who worked with Ridder in Miami for five years, "That's bullshit. I mean, if somebody chooses to call Tony and tell him every little thing they do, that's their business. [At San Jose] I make changes all the time. I have an overall obligation for a budget. I deal with it."

Regardless, FTEs were—are—part of a wave of business initiatives that impose control on editorial. The ultimate in this sort of thing, now abandoned, occurred at the *Winston-Salem Journal.* Consultants there developed a system dictating the amount of time and space various stories should require: "An A1 story should be six inches or less. A reporter should use a press release and/or one or two 'cooperative sources.' He or she should take 0.9 hours to do each story and should be able to produce 40 of these in a week."

Ostensibly such initiatives as FTE accounting are intended to improve overall efficiency. But because of the time involved, they have the practical effect of changing the shape of the editor's job. In making these reporting requirements, corporate officers are insisting that editors spend much more of their time on personnel and budgetary management, much less on the news.

The impact was obvious in the informal survey the Project on the State of the American Newspaper conducted to help assess how editors' roles have evolved. Questionnaires about job satisfaction and compensation were sent to two hundred top editors around the country, representing papers of every size and ownership; seventy-seven responded. One question asked how much of the typical workday involves "budgeting, business or marketing matters, and non-news administration." Fourteen percent of the editors said they spent more than half their time on matters other than news; another 35 percent said between one-third and one-half their time. In other words, half the editors were spending a third or more of their day on matters other than journalism. Even more striking, almost 90 percent said this percentage had risen in the last five years—risen "somewhat" for 58 percent, "dramatically" for 30 percent.

For a different perspective on this subject I ring up an old friend, George Gill, longtime editor and then publisher of the *Courier-Journal* in Louisville, now retired and living in nearby Peewee Valley. He says today's reality of an editor poring over newsprint usage and FTE spreadsheets is an inevitable result of public newspaper ownership.

"I don't know how you can avoid that," he says. "When you look ownership in the eye every day and it's local, and you've worked for them forever, you can argue and probably win the day. But now—what is it?—86 percent are owned by corporations. It is a fact of the marketplace that profitability drives everything. It's too bad, but I don't know what you can do about it. And in the meantime," says Gill, neatly signaling the interview to a close, "I've gotta go cut five acres of grass."

Having been privy to something of the complex transition Gill made, from the gentle hands of the Bingham family to the corporate dictates of Gannett, I tease him now about being exceptionally diplomatic.

"Well, my dear, that comes with age," he replies. "It comes with age and a good pension check."

7. PRAGMATISTS

There are days Wayne Poston feels like he's been at it forever. Enthusiastic at times, discouraged at others, the veteran editor of Florida's *Bradenton Herald* has been determined not to be bothered by the growing number of business demands from his corporate seers at Knight Ridder.

FTEs? Just numbers—punch 'em into a computer.

Newshole? Knows it better than anyone in the building.

Circulation? Get the paper in the door, he'll make it stick.

Even so, Poston spends—at most, he says—30 percent of his time on journalism. The job of being an editor "is just a lot harder than it used to be. Corporations are cyclical, and we're at a high point of publisher influence. There are a lot of people who think anybody can do content. And it's not gonna work."

These days, however, Poston is sanguine. Come January and his 55th birthday, he's going to retire.

"I have a good mind, and I want to be able to use it," he says, adding, "I'll sleep like a baby."

8. NOUVEAUX RICHES

People don't like to talk about their salaries, and editors are no exception. Still, editor pay is so much higher today that, as Poynter Institute president and former *Philadelphia Inquirer* executive editor Jim Naughton told me, "it ought to be the product of embarrassment. If I were the top official of the local public utility company, we'd be writing about it."

The story would go like this:

Fueled in large measure by incentive bonuses, editors' compensation for decades has been rising much faster than wages in the overall economy, and much faster than the paychecks of their newsroom colleagues. Over a ten-year period, editors' total compensation has shot up 50 percent, to an average $106,124, according to a 1998 survey by the Inland Press Association. By comparison, consumer prices during the same period went up 38 percent.

What's interesting is that among the 314 editors who reported their compensation, base wages rose roughly at the same rate as inflation. But incentive pay shot up 70 percent to an average $16,500 per editor.

The big beneficiaries are editors at larger newspapers. According to the survey, total compensation for editors in the 250,000 to 500,000 circulation category topped $250,000 in 1998, up 77 percent over a decade. Bonuses doubled over ten years, reaching an average $56,470. By contrast, incentive pay went up only 25 percent for editors in the 75,000 to 100,000 category.

While the mode of payment—various incentive packages, most tied to profitability—has varied in recent years, the trend toward rapidly increasing editor salaries has been building for a long time. Compensation packages have skyrocketed over the last thirty years, growing at more than twice the rate of inflation and considerably faster than wages in the newsroom. Take, for example, editors in the 100,000 to 250,000 circulation category, again looking at Inland data. In 1968, the average editor was making $17,500 a year; today's editors in the same circulation category average a little more than $157,000, a nearly 900 percent increase. Consumer prices during the same time went up about 470 percent.

Why has this occurred and what is the impact—besides a lot of editors with tax problems? An obvious answer would be that American publishers have concluded that editors need to be paid as top executives so that, even though they're not direct revenue-producers, they don't have to take a back seat to advertising directors and circulation directors (who are really bringing in the big bucks). Still, there is some unease with this situation, and L.A.'s John Carroll is among the uneasy.

"One thing that's crossed my mind more than once," he says, "is that I never expected to make this kind of money when I came into the business as a reporter on $75 a week. It's my job to think up stories and pass judgment on stories that reflect things that are important to the people of this community. And I can't really say that my problems are the same problems as the people in this community. You know, I don't really have any financial problems, which puts me in a very privileged situation. So I think just in terms of the things that weigh on one's mind, they are not those of the common man."

The MBO, or management by objective, was envisioned in the early 1950s by management guru Peter F. Drucker. The idea was this: By setting goals and attaching rewards to their achievement, a company can get the most out of its managers and coordinate their efforts at the same time. Editors generally work with others in the newsroom to draft the coming year's editorial plans, which are presented to the publisher and ultimately redrawn as the editor's personal goals. At performance review time, the publisher decides to what degree the goals have been achieved.

The vast majority of top editors now have MBOs, though there are exceptions: Newhouse editors, for example, still receive straight salaries, no portion of which is tied to corporate performance. Of the editors responding to the Project's questionnaire, 71 percent said their company employs MBOs. Of those, 60 percent said MBOs were limited to the top editor and managing editor. Those who do have MBOs can thank them for a goodly proportion of their compensation—half the editors responding said they get 20 to 50 percent of their pay from MBOs. And the majority of these editors said that more than half their bonus is tied to their paper's financial performance.

Some corporate types react to queries on this matter as if they're being asked to expose national security secrets. In calling a dozen human resources and public affairs offices to inquire about the use of MBOs, we got a few answers like this (at Donrey): "I can't discuss that; we are very private." Or (at Hollinger): "I'm not the person to ask and I don't know who would be!"

Indeed, editor bonuses are one of the newsroom's enduring mysteries. Most everyone in journalism knows about MBOs, but unless you've ever had one, chances are you've never seen one. (See the sample MBO at the end of this chapter.) No doubt that's one reason why these same rank-and-file are a tad cynical about them: Are their bosses manacled, for better or worse, to corporate goals?

Jim Naughton contends that the MBO has become an "insidious process" that makes editors "unduly conscious or even subconscious of their own potential gain at the risk of something that they might otherwise want to do in the newsgathering process.

"I don't think people sit there and pull out their MBO charts and say, in October, 'How many things do I need to kill to make a bigger bonus?' But I do think the existence of that process in a newsroom setting, where historically we have prided ourselves on being separate from profit-makers, has changed the perception among editors. And it has spread throughout the newsroom, to department heads, which may be draining their enthusiasm to bust the budget when they oughta by God bust the budget because the news is important." (About 40 percent of editors who responded to our questionnaire said their newspapers also awarded MBOs to assistant managing editors, or department heads, or both.)

Some editors agree that increased linkage of MBOs to financial performance is raising doubts in the newsroom about their own motivations: Would the editor have bucked this hiring freeze a little harder if his year-end $10,000 bonus wasn't at stake? What an unsettling appearance problem —especially if the staff sees the boss as being increasingly scarce, more often in business-side meetings than the daily news huddle.

Deborah Howell, who now runs the Washington bureau for Newhouse, was executive editor of Knight Ridder's *St. Paul Pioneer Press* and recalls with some anguish the pressures. "I sometimes felt that I was doing things for MBOs and not for the right reasons," she says. "And I wasn't the only one. It's not just the bonus that can multiply the distance between editors and their newsrooms. It's also the fact that editors aren't providing nearly the same level of pay increases for their staffs."

The Inland survey again is instructive. Thirty years ago, city editors in the 100,000 to 250,000 circulation category made $11,500 a year; their editors earned about 50 percent more. But if those overworked city editors thought that pay gap was too big, think how they feel today. City editors' average salaries are up to $61,750, but their editors are making two-and-a-half times as much.

"Newspaper editors make a *lot* more money than they used to," Howell says. "I've heard editors say they've been amazed at what they've made— tons of money. Does it make them more careful about holding onto their jobs? The golden handcuffs? The velvet coffin? It's making it more difficult for editors to fight back. Because of stock options and bonuses, your family's security is tied to your staying in the job. I walked away from tons of stock options."

In the end, she says, profit-based MBOs create doubts about integrity. "Editors are often looked on as sellouts," says Howell. "And that's one thing an editor does not ever want to be."

There are those, of course, who say the picture of an editor being bought off, or selling out to live the good life, is either flat wrong or at least vastly overdrawn. Indeed, some newsroom executives point out that at a paper where MBOs are the rule, if the editor declined one he would be at a disadvantage dealing with his business-side counterparts: They could complain that he had nothing at stake when strategic decisions needed to be made, leaving him with less leverage than ever.

Other editors say it's about time they were decently paid. "I cannot complain about how my company has treated me," says Dave Zweifel in Madison. "I think through the years as the job has become perhaps a little more complicated and tougher, the company has recognized that." Zweifel's paper, locally owned, pays him a bonus based in part on circulation and profit performance.

And then there are those few who see MBOs and high pay as but a ball and chain.

Irene Nolan is the former managing editor of Louisville's *Courier-Journal*. After several years adjusting to the contrasting ownership styles of the Binghams and Gannett, Nolan quit in 1991. She lives now in a considerably more blissful setting along an inlet on North Carolina's Outer Banks, and from time to time has contemplated why more people weren't leaving high-profile editing jobs about which they complained bitterly. "They make a lot of money, and of course the higher-up editors are getting stock options," Nolan says, "and I think that's why they stay."

"Plus," at Gannett, "they get rings."

9. COMPROMISERS

Of all the changes editors cite, perhaps the most affecting is loss of editorial autonomy. This comes in many forms, from the desire of other departments to get their clutches into content to the corporate controls on every dime and every minute that go into news gathering.

Consider, for example, Gannett's News 2000, a complex corporate prescription for working out each newspaper's content goals in accord with detailed formulas. The aim was to have each paper do a better job of representing a community's interests, getting minority voices into the paper, involving readers, reflecting First Amendment values, etc. The degree of the News 2000 impact on Gannett editors varied enormously—depending primarily on the publisher, and how seriously he or she took the program. When Ron Thornburg was editor of the *Free Press* in Burlington, Vermont, that turned out to be very seriously indeed.

In a 1994 deposition in the case of a reporter who was fired and then sued the company, Thornburg acknowledged that his publisher had called him in and "suggested that I either be transferred or put on a Performance Improvement Plan," and that one of the reasons was that the publisher "felt that the newspaper's News 2000 score needs to be higher." Thornburg described the paper's scores as average, but said the publisher "wants the paper to be above average." Thornburg resigned after his meeting with the boss.

The 1991 unveiling of this elaborate recipe for better newspapering was quite the event at Gannett, bringing together publishers, editors, and managing editors. Irene Nolan was still managing editor at the *Courier-Journal* when News 2000 came down. As you might expect from a woman who raised a couple of kids mostly alone even as she rose through the editing ranks of a major paper, Nolan wastes no time. She calls things exactly as she sees them, with sometimes sardonic wit.

"Remember that I told you it was the end of journalism as we knew it?" she recalls for me. "You all were trying to put a nice light on it. For me, it was the final straw. Although Gannett kept saying it doesn't take away local autonomy, the idea of filling in all those sheets and sending in all those papers and being judged by editors who know nothing of your community, know nothing about your paper's history! It was formulas.

"The whole time I was managing editor of the *Courier,* the readers' satisfaction levels and the circulation were good. And the paper kept flunking News 2000 all the time. You know, it didn't satisfy Gannett or their committee of editors, but it satisfied the community."

Nolan also recalls the time she was running for the ASNE board and had composed for the organization's magazine a short summary of what her goals would be. She wrote of the need for editors to do all they could to continue to put out a good newspaper even as they met a tight budget.

It sparked quite a response, she says, from Gannett vice president for news Phil Currie, who wrote to Nolan's boss, David Hawpe, then the *Courier-Journal's* editor.

"Currie practically demanded my ouster. And David gingerly went to bat for me. He didn't let them get me. But it was kind of like—you didn't even feel like you could speak freely. I do believe editors cannot spend totally freely, and they have to have some fiscal responsibility. But on the other hand, feeling like, if you say something that will offend the corporate bosses they will want your head on a platter, is not exactly something that encourages bold editorship."

Sometimes, albeit rarely, editorial undercutting is brutally direct. Witness the *Chicago Sun-Times'* acknowledgment in 1998 that it tilts news coverage in favor of advertisers. Nigel Wade, the editor, told the *Washington Post* that, on a story about fashion trends, for example, "You don't send a reporter to a store that routinely refuses to support us with their advertising. On the fashion page, you don't choose a gown from a store that refuses to do business with us."

The pressure is usually more subtle. Corporate makes its expectations clear to the publisher, the publisher gets his management team together, the team draws up a list of goals, then everyone agrees . . . and everything is affected—who spends time doing what, what goes into the newspaper, how it's displayed. This leaves room for fewer calls from the gut, fewer last-minute judgments. Consultants and retreats and goal-sharing and performance reviews come together to drive the newspaper.

Bill Woo, former editor of Pulitzer's flagship, the *St. Louis Post-Dispatch,* was a traditionalist in an organization whose higher-ups wanted change. After years of worsening difficulty, he left in 1996 and was replaced by Cole Campbell, one of the least traditional of today's newsroom managers.

Woo, who had been at the paper for thirty-four years, now teaches journalism at Stanford. He retains his elegant, almost Old World manner, but his views are arrestingly frank. One of his areas of research at Stanford is the theory of organizational accidents. "Looking at Bhopal or Three Mile Island or the crash of ValuJet—the view of these accidents as arising out of certain organizational and business environments, with certain elements in common, such as the normalization of deviance, the progressive relaxation of professional standards," he explains.

Woo proceeds to draw parallels in the newsroom. "The expectations of the editor have been removed from the daily news role. One of the things that's expected of editors now is that editors are to be managers. Now look at this paradox: At a time when the emphasis on management has never been higher—it's unprecedented—all around, the landscape is littered with disasters of journalism. We find that people are making things up to put into the paper. You find in the Clinton/Lewinsky thing a kind of systematic meltdown of fact-checking, sourcing, reliance on rumors, hearsay and so forth. You look at papers such as the *Cincinnati Enquirer* having to walk away sort of wholesale from a big project—which the *San Jose Mercury News* had to do a couple of years ago."

The industry has lost the sort of editor who would make a decision on the spot, he says, the fast thinker and hard charger who brought to the job a view of the news, a view of the world, that gave him a context for making decisions: "Let's do it." "I like it." "Never!" "I hate it."

Woo believes that if the model of the maverick editor—Woo calls it the "non-team player"—is destined to die out, perhaps we should figure out the things about it that were good for the paper and recreate those qualities today in different structures. Because, he says, "I'm not sure that the way we're going now is the way to do it. One bright person makes better decisions than one bright person in a room with eight dull people."

The *Post-Dispatch* under Campbell has become a very different place, one where he has said the emphasis is on "building the capacity of the newsroom to be innovative and problem-solving." An editor there describes it this way: "Process is an enormous focus for us—and particularly for Cole. There was a moment months ago when he said, 'The next day's paper doesn't matter.' His point was that we must create the proper processes, the proper organization. And if you get sidetracked thinking about what goes into the next day's paper, you'll be handicapped. We're in the midst of something called mountaineering school—the AMEs and above, which is now a rather large group of people. It's leadership and management training—and figuring whether we're suited to what level of function."

The training is based on management guru Stephen Covey's four quadrants: urgent and important; important but not urgent; urgent but not important; not urgent and not important. "Basically, Cole has been pushing the top layer of editors—11 of them—to shift toward quadrant-two-type activities: important but not urgent. Basically we're not making decisions about what goes in that next day's paper, or even that week's papers, but setting up processes so that good decisions will be made."

But processes have a nasty way of draining energy, not to mention pleasure, from newspapering. "A lot of editors feel they are slowly taking the paper down," says Deborah Howell. "It's so different working for a private company. [In public companies, the executives] are looking at editors and saying, 'We want someone who'll get along and not be a troublemaker. If you are viewed as a troublemaker. . . .'" Howell ends her thought with a sigh.

10. LIONS

John Carroll smiles wistfully. He is recalling Knight Ridder meetings of two decades ago when editors mingled with the corporate brass. "Coming into those sessions, the top corporate people knew that nobody was gonna give them an inch," he says. "That they were gonna get questions that were barbed, that were sarcastic, that were hilarious, that were irreverent. And it was done in a good spirit. There was no viciousness about it. But there was a total outspokenness and self-confidence on the part of these big-paper editors who thought they had to bow to no man. The spirit there was that although the corporate officers got the biggest salaries, the editors were the heart of the company. They were lions. They really were."

Al Neuharth, a bona fide lion himself, professes no such sense of loss. "I think that's one of the benefits of what we've seen happen," he says. "I know a lot of those swaggering, quick-decision, tough-guy editors. And more often than not they made the wrong decision, and they edited the newspaper for themselves rather than for the general public. They were more responsible for the demise of their newspapers than anybody in the business office."

11. ITINERANTS

So the life of a newspaper editor today is a mixed blessing. The pay is better and the opportunities for advancement richer. But the job has become more complex and frustrating, the days longer, the autonomy constricted. And the moving van comes along with increasing frequency. Today's editors have more education, stronger management skills and a better understanding of the market. And they call on these richly, because the odds are they don't know their communities very well. With the overwhelming majority of newspapers owned by large chains, the editor who works his or her way up through the ranks and then stays on for a longer tenure is the rare editor indeed.

Of those replying to the Project's survey, the average tenure as editor was just above five years. Almost four in ten said they'd been at the top job for two years or less. Companies large and small are moving editors around. And in other cases, editors are simply opting out.

Sig Gissler, the former Milwaukee editor, calls it the "revolving-door phenomenon" and notes a benefit in some cases "because it brings a fresh set of eyes to the newspaper. But I think over the long haul it has hurt us because too many editors lack this organic sense of connection with the community. To go into a community and really understand what's going on takes a number of years and a sort of soaking in the environment."

Ken Paulson, who now heads the Freedom Forum First Amendment Center in Nashville, was editor at three Gannett newspapers during my less-than-seven-year tenure as editor at the *Des Moines Register*. He believes he more than made up for his short stays in Wisconsin, Florida, and New York with spark and good instincts. "I was an editor who never spent more than four years in a single place," says Paulson. "The downside, of course, is that you don't develop the deepest possible understanding of your community in just four years. The upside is that in those four years you bring a certain energy and commitment . . . and are determined to make a difference in the time you are there."

One of the men responsible for moving Paulson, Al Neuharth, contends that when Gannett found an editor who truly wanted to remain in a community, "to my recollection we never moved anyone who had that feeling. The vast majority of our people felt they were in a farm system where they could work their way up—and they wanted to."

Keith Moyer, another editor who was at three Gannett newspapers during my tenure in Des Moines, remembers the situation differently. "I think that in Gannett, you turned down one chance for a transfer and you might get a second opportunity, but you rarely got a third. If they wanted you to move and you didn't, there were times, I think, when people were ultimately sort of rousted out and sent on their way."

Moyer, now publisher at McClatchy's *Fresno Bee,* says that within Gannett, it was a "constant gripe that the publishers and editors were never in town long enough and the company didn't seem to care. Belo, McClatchy and others work to strike that balance and try to put good people in the right places and let them stay awhile and do their jobs. And I think that serves the community well."

That longer tenure is better for the readers is the same conclusion Sandy Rowe reached when she decided to remain editor of Portland's *Oregonian* rather than be drawn to the publisher's suite. "I really don't expect or want to run another newsroom," says Rowe. "The fact that editors move around has a huge impact. . . . I really believe that I can make the greatest difference in the newsroom only if I'm willing to stay in that newsroom for a significant amount of time. What we're doing here can't be done in two years, three years, four years."

Rowe, who came to the Newhouse paper five years ago, says readers aren't stupid—they know the paper's ownership isn't local, they see editors come and go. "They think, 'That person is not one of us,'" she says. "I was astounded coming here, being a child of the South, how different the place was—and I frequently felt I was editing by Braille, that I was literally blind to the nuances here. I wanted nothing more than for the *Oregonian* to be much more of the Northwest and of Oregon, and for it to feel and smell and look like Oregon. But that's been very difficult to achieve because I'm from somewhere else, and I can't imagine doing that every couple of years and being locally competent. [That's] a very important quality."

12. ADVOCATES

In 1995 Carl Sessions Stepp, a University of Maryland journalism professor, wrote about how the business demands on editors had sucked much of the fun out of newspapering. Several heated responses were published in ASNE's own journal, the *American Editor,* and Arnold Garson, then editor of the *Sun* in San Bernardino, California, was among the irritated. "I am growing weary of whining editors," he wrote. Will Corbin of Newport News, Virginia's *Daily Press* had even less patience: "We can sit around wringing our hands and wailing over the demise of newspapers. We can bitch about bean counters and Wall Street and budget cuts. We can whine about the flagging commitment in American newspapers to quality journalism. Or we can get over it."

If "getting over it" is the only alternative, you can understand the anger at those who can't or won't. But my conversations plainly reveal that today many editors see options beyond complaint or resignation. They speak forcefully about creating a dialogue with media bigwigs about the dangers of over-commercialization and the values of journalism. Yes, these editors say, they understand that business and market imperatives come with the job. But in turn they want their bosses to understand that there are some things editors must not accept if newspapers, and indeed a democratic society, are to flourish.

"I think the ball is in the editors' court," says Max King. "We have to be clear and articulate and strong-voiced about what our values are and what we stand for and why that should be accorded importance in the company. We must realize that we have a fine and noble profession, and we must fight for it."

King is among those who believe that editors must become advocates. "My thesis is that the people who run these big corporations . . . go to the top jobs because they're very sharp, and very responsive—particularly responsive to the shareholders, which is their job," he says. "However, I think that if the editors and other staff members in newsrooms were more vocal and clear about what their mission is, and spoke to that instead of just bitching about it, that they'd be responsive to us. We need to make the damned case as journalists, saying it's important in and of itself."

So are editors really ready to talk turkey with their bosses? Perhaps. In 1997 ASNE gathered an impressive group of editors and other newspaper leaders to launch a project on credibility—what has happened to it, what could restore readers' faith. At first when anything "corporate" surfaced in the discussion, many editors were clearly gun-shy: Please, no whining. Yet the company-induced financial and organizational realities of an editor's everyday life kept coming up. Finally, the group agreed to add companies' failure to invest in their products to its list of concerns—gingerly couching it in the publishers' own language.

Editors, the conclusion read, "must find ways to better articulate the franchise value of newspapers to those on the business side—how a paper is indispensable to a community which in turn translates into corporate value. Think tank members agreed that a group of editors should come together to help frame and spur and carry forward the economic issues conversation. And they strongly urged that editors approach such discussions with the business side of newspapers in the context that everyone at the table seeks good journalism."

Are the bosses listening? The early signs are not exactly inspiring. Fact is, corporate executives have generally avoided this subject. But an instructive source of their thinking is a Poynter Institute booklet titled "The View from the Top: Conversations with 14 people who will be running journalism organizations into the 21st Century."

In it, Marty Linksy of Harvard's Kennedy School of Government interviewed these media moguls, then wrote up their responses. One of the first and most significant things Linsky noticed was that when he asked the corporate leaders to describe themselves, they generally didn't reply in journalistic terms. "One of the clearest ways to gauge the differences in vision between the newsroom and the corporate suite is the extent to which the bosses see themselves as corporate managers rather than journalist managers," he wrote, "the extent to which they identify with CEOs of widget companies more than with Pulitzer Prize-winning reporters."

Gannett CEO John Curley told Linsky that the lives of some reporters and editors "changed from laissez faire, where you had people sitting around in newsrooms, going to the movies in the afternoon, and now they're required to perform at a different level. . . . The journalism issues have flared because a couple of people bitched about their inability to go where the hell they wanted to go, whenever they wanted to, and not be accountable."

As Linsky concluded, "Whatever else one can say about Curley's attitude, it is not likely to make his reporters and editors want to talk through these issues with him."

The same problem is evident even a couple of levels down. Trying to set up an interview with Phil Currie, Gannett's vice president for news, I made numerous phone calls. I assured his assistants that I was not asking about the *Cincinnati Enquirer*'s problems (the Chiquita debacle was just unfolding). Finally I sent a fax outlining the issues I hoped to discuss.

After weeks of this, Currie's secretary replied, "Phil actually responded to me. He said to tell you that he's sorry, but he's really not interested in having the discussion you are seeking."

This lack of dialogue is precisely what Burl Osborne and his colleagues at the *Dallas Morning News* and, more broadly, at A.H. Belo Corp., have sought to avoid. "The best way to deal with those concerns," Osborne says, "is to have a very clear understanding at the highest level of the organization about what its qualitative and journalistic goals are, in addition to what its financial goals are—an understanding at the board level and with the CEO and anyone else involved in important decision-making. There must be a common understanding of what the institution's objectives are."

Osborne says Belo's "rules of the road" include treating each other "with respect and candor—with emphasis on the candor," he says, chuckling.

Candor has been in short supply in most newspaper companies, a fact that surely contributes to the difficulty of establishing good relationships among executives, publishers, editors, and newsroom staff.

Says Sandy Rowe, "You have to be able to look news people—skeptical, even sometimes cynical, reporters—in the eye and tell them the truth and have it be believable. And a lot of editors haven't been able to do that because they're so conflicted with the level of profits or with the business principles or anything else—and so the newsrooms understandably don't come along."

One of the most powerful and overlooked factors in this evolving process will be the view of the public. Ponder this from a recent Freedom Forum survey of how Americans use and view the news: "Special interests are pulling strings in newsrooms, most Americans believe. They think profit motives, politicians, media owners, big business and advertisers influence the way news is reported and presented."

As Columbia professor Jim Carey sees it, finding a way to reaffirm journalistic values may be crucial to survival. "The press as understood by the courts is the only commercial enterprise that is singled out within the

Constitution for distinct treatment. There are no clauses on automobiles or natural resources or commodities or anything else. The courts have over the course of the last 50 years regularly supported the press in case after case." But that could change, he believes, if newspapers are so focused on profits that "the public comes to the conclusion that freedom of the press means simply freedom to make money."

So you must balance the marketing pressures that may lead to a thinning of seriousness, an overabundance of sensationalism, with the newspaper's fundamental role in nourishing a democracy. You must balance the growing fragmentation of markets—the economic reality of needing to appeal to narrower and narrower segments—with the journalistic goal of serving as many readers as possible. You must square a business that, on the one hand, stands for ferreting out difficult truths and, on the other, hides unpalatable facts from its own newsroom, eschews difficult discussions up and down the line and keeps its own business from the public. But how?

Once, this dilemma was confronted by a single forceful person—say, a man like Jack Knight who, for all his power, valued most of all being editor. For years thereafter, there were editors who inspired others to think of them as lions. But then the story Knight told Poynter at the Gridiron dinner became a business reality. Today, Knight's beloved paper in Akron is but one small piece of a huge corporate machine in which editors struggle to show how willing they are to understand the business side—but too often, it seems, fail to win more than lip service from the business side about the importance of journalism.

Staying solvent, it turns out, is not just the publisher's concern. But if the editor must take on that responsibility, it's all the more crucial for publishers and owners to understand—to take deep into their hearts and minds—the other side of the equation: Newspapers are not just another business. As Yale law professor Stephen Carter, discussing his recent book *Civility* with a Washington audience, put it, "The problem in America today is not that we have a market economy. The problem is, we have let that market economy and its values dominate too much of our lives."

Isn't that the dilemma of journalism? Not that we have corporate ownership. Not that we are businesses and have to be commercially viable. But that we have let economic realities and market values dominate too much of our newspapers'—and our journalists'—lives. The question is whether today's editors, bred in a different era, chosen by publishers with an eye on different traits, rewarded for corporate successes and shaped by managerial procedures, have the taste, the talent, the time, or—with economic difficulties again on the horizon—the latitude for the battle.

13. OPTIMISTS

Kay Fanning, former editor of the *Christian Science Monitor* and before that of the *Anchorage Daily News,* has seen more newspapering than most of us ever will. Now retired (though still writing) in Boston, Fanning surveys the dilemma of the modern editor and remains hopeful. Why? "I'm a believer in the pendulum theory—I think things swing one way and then another," she tells me. "We happen to be in a phase where corporate and business interests are everything. I have a great hope we will have a swing back toward caring about people."

A continent away, the "MBA editor" whose views sparked so much distress a decade ago is bullish, too. "Things have unfolded pretty much as I expected they might," says the *Seattle Times'* executive editor, Mike Fancher. "The opportunity for editors to participate is as great as ever. The fortunate thing is that it's not too late."

*   *   *

Here are extensive excerpts from a recent MBO for a senior editor at a Knight Ridder newspaper. These goals accounted for just over a third of the editor's bonus; the rest hinged on that paper meeting its financial targets.

1. Leadership—10 points (out of 100 for the entire MBO)
The dozen top leaders in the newsroom, including myself, will work to shift the focus of the newsroom from itself to its readership, to develop the relevance of the paper to its readers, and to build the paper's essentiality in the community while sustaining its commitment to excellence....

In reorienting the newsroom to the community, we will educate the staff—from middle management through the ranks of reporters, photographers, copy editors, news editors and artists—to appreciate the value of understanding and responding to the needs of readers.

As part of this effort, I will work with department editors and the supervisor of the support staff to drastically improve telephone-answering capabilities in the main office and in the bureaus by July 1. Failure to get through our switchboard and interlocking voicemail is a cause of major frustration to our readers.

2. Readership/Partnering with Circulation—25 points
a. We will ensure that each news-gathering department of the newsroom, with the involvement of its staff, develops a readership plan.... This plan will serve as a guide, not a rigid road map. It will outline the goals of

the department and describe how the department will focus on immediacy and explanatory journalism to achieve those goals. . . .

b. We must reverse the losses in circulation that threaten our value to advertisers and the significance of our voice in this community. To help achieve this, we will undertake a newsroom-wide effort to collaborate with the circulation division to build the readership of the daily and Sunday paper. We will establish a series of forums—daily news meetings, weekly production meetings, staff interactions, leadership conferences—that will build collaboration and understanding at all levels of both organizations. We also will educate the newsroom staff on circulation matters. To that end, we will form a group of a dozen staffers who will learn about circulation and readership first-hand: riding trucks, talking with people who run sales outlets, watching the paper being printed . . . and spending a day with Customer Service. . . .

c. We will accept as our own a company objective of beating substantially the circulation goals established by the circulation division and approved by the publisher.

d. We will reaffirm our commitment to public-service journalism by publishing a significant number of aggressive, distinguished enterprise projects. In each month of the year, there will be high-level enterprise journalism that spins directly off the news and relates directly to the needs and interests of the readers. . . . There will be at least a dozen multi-story public-service projects in either the news pages or the editorial/commentary pages.

3. Editor-Staff Relations—15 points

I will assume a leadership role in bringing about a culture change in editor-staff relations in the newsroom. . . . We will foster a culture in which editors are much more forthright in their appraisal of staffers' work, and are more persistent in seeking to improve the work of the few who fail to meet our standards. Also, we will continue to improve a culture in which we freely share information, ideas and responsibility for decision-making, as well as accountability for the results of our work. . . .

4. Communication with Advertising and Production—7 points

a. To help [the paper] achieve its goal of increasing advertising revenue through shifts from competitors' share of the market, we will foster a relationship with the advertising division that results in a constant exchange of information on matters of mutual concern. These include special sections produced by the newsroom that might result in additional advertising; the opportunity to sell advertising adjacent to regular news features; and flexibility on our part, when appropriate, on the placement of advertising on pages with news content. . . .

b. To reduce production costs, we will cooperate with the production division to [complete pagination]. We also will work with production to achieve a high level of compliance throughout the year with deadlines for composing room closes.

5. Instructions for Staff—6 points

I will refine and improve the basic instructions that staff members need to do their jobs, including revised guidelines on style, typography and policy, and ensuring that up-to-date electronic versions are available by September 1. . . .

6. First Amendment Duties—5 points

I will become the newsroom's point person on First Amendment and legal issues. Specifically, I will:

- Work with our attorneys in deciding whether to take legal action to ensure that the staff has access to meetings and information involving the public's right to know.
- Read stories that might have libel ramifications, and make sure the attorneys review these stories before publication.
- Work with the attorneys to respond to libel suits and threats of libel suits.

7. Diversity—5 points

a. In a year in which our hiring opportunities are expected to be severely limited, we nevertheless will show an improvement in the following:

- Percentage of minorities and women in journalist jobs.
- Percentage of minorities and women in "all supervisors" category.

b. In whatever hiring is done, we will meet [the paper's] pluralism goals.

c. Minorities and women will be represented in career-development activities at least to the extent of their proportion of the staff. . . .

8. Budget—10 points

We will meet general budget obligations by:

a. Staying within the [annual] news budget—that is, spending no more for the news/editorial operation than has been earmarked for [the year], and as modified and revised.

b. Operating at or below the approved newshole budget for the year.

c. Operating at or below budgeted FTE levels in the newsroom for the year.

d. Planning for [next year's budget] and making adjustments to [this year's] spending plan based on anticipated operating requirements next year. . . .

6

The conflict between commerce and journalism is apparent even in the languages the two sides speak. Where journalists think of their readers as citizens, many of the corporate executives who manage newspaper companies consider them customers. Journalists speak with some pride of the thing they produce as "the newspaper," while the corporate people call it "the product," a term devoid of First Amendment overtones.

The philosophical differences implied here are not small. American journalism's ultimate purpose, as conceived by Jefferson, Franklin, and Paine, is to arm self-governing citizens with the truth. While this ideal isn't executed to perfection in every newsroom, it is at least present in the minds of reporters and editors, and it is part of what attracts people to journalism as a career.

By contrast, the corporate voice—as commonly expressed through advertising, lobbying, and public relations—does not aspire to balance, fairness, or edification of the public; it is, in its essence, one-sided and promotional. Every man and woman who ever worked in a newsroom has been barraged by the special pleadings of corporate "flacks," as reporters often call them, and knows how questionable their claims can be. Journalism, in fact, gives its most coveted awards to reporters who expose the lies and coverups of some of these people.

In other words, distrust runs high. Journalists try to maintain a wall between the work they do and the influences of the marketplace, insisting for instance that advertising and news be clearly distinguishable and that the news be free of hidden influences. Mindful of the past damage done to public trust by William Randolph Hearst and others who used their papers as propaganda machines, good journalists try to protect against the charge that their reporting is slanted to favor advertisers, to promote their own agendas, or "just to sell newspapers." The credibility of our greatest papers rests on their success in this.

In 1995, one of those great papers, the Los Angeles Times, *came under the control of an executive with no journalistic background and a minimal appreciation of newsroom ethics. Journalists deplored his highly-publicized efforts to "break down the wall" between the* Times' *news and business operations, but many newspaper business executives across the country applauded. "Brilliant. That's what newspapers have to do," the* Houston Chronicle's *vice president of advertising, Dwight Brown, told the* Columbia Journalism Review. *Paul Seveska, a marketing executive with Thomson Newspapers, agreed and said that Thomson too was introducing "the marketing process directly into the editorial department."*

In the autumn of 1999, the Times *suffered a conflict-of-interest scandal that brought shame to the paper and a grassroots uprising in the newsroom.*

Down and Out in L.A.

By William Prochnau

FOR KATHRYN DOWNING, publisher of the *Los Angeles Times,* life appears to have been a string of almost unbroken successes. But on November 3, 1999, as she sat in the corporate sterility of her glass-walled office atop the Times Mirror Building in downtown L.A., all that seemed to be unraveling.

For more than a week Downing had taken a frightful emotional beating. Two days in a row she had been required to stand before her reporters and editors and admit a blunder so colossal that it proved, in her own words, that she lacked a "fundamental" understanding of the culture and ethics of the huge newspaper she directed.

Now it was late afternoon, a Wednesday. The early dusk of fall began to darken the skylights above her after yet another day of misery. A man who had once held Downing's job, a man so legendary no one could ever replace him, a man who was described in this building in the same terms as Greek gods, had humbled her beyond the breaking point. In a letter that had just been read aloud to her newsroom three stories below, he had called her mistake "unbelievably stupid and unprofessional." He said her employees had been "abused and misused" and the integrity, quality, and honor of their newspaper undermined.

Down the corporate hallway, Downing's boss, a man of now endless controversy, had decided to remain silent. But Kathryn Downing had been bruised enough that this last abasement had pushed her emotions to the limit. On a plain sheet of white paper she hastily committed two sentences of response.

To be sure, Downing had not suffered more than the great newspaper she headed. Once primed to challenge the *New York Times* as the best paper in the land, the *Los Angeles Times* for a decade had suffered humiliation after humiliation—personal, psychological, professional. The paper's careening fortunes had triggered boardroom intrigues and emotional confrontations that most *Times* staffers, to this day, are unaware ever occurred. And yet for all that, the *Times* remained a testing ground for a revolutionary scheme that kept all eyes on it and, if successful, might still make it the newspaper of the new century.

The revolution may have begun to falter, but suddenly this seismic event, known as the Staples Affair, threatened to bring it all down.

Kathryn Downing sent the two sentences downstairs to the Metro desk. That would prove another mistake; the words were so harsh that her own editors took it on themselves to protect her, editing their publisher.

The words and the turmoil became something of a coda to a decade the proud *Los Angeles Times* would like to forget.

THERE CAME A DAY ten years ago when so many Angelenos had fled north that Seattle finally burst its seams, its freeways becoming a gridlocked caricature of the Santa Monica, the Pasadena, and the Santa Ana. "Don't Californicate Us," the bumper stickers read. But it was too late. It was as if Southern Californians had finally given up on the golden dream and Los Angeles was about to fall on such hard times that the only fair thing would be to give back all that stolen water.

In pinpointing the date, historians are not without resources. At their fingertips are the endless sheets of the *Los Angeles Times,* a paper that had become as big, rich, and sprawling as the area it served. It is difficult to restrain the superlatives about the *Times.* Its mother company, the $3.5 billion Times Mirror Co., owned good papers "back East," including one that had invaded Manhattan. The *Times* itself circulated to homes in an area as large as Ohio. It printed enough words each morning to fill the New Testament. For more than two decades it had gorged itself on more advertising than any paper in the country, becoming so voluptuous that wonderful stories were spawned about the delivery boy who sued the paper for causing his hernia, the subscriber who claimed the Sunday behemoth flattened his chihuahua.

The *Times* had become more, too. By late 1989 it had finally earned the respect it deserved and spent a mother lode to attain. *Adweek,* the bible of the advertising industry, called it the second best paper in the country.

Even the most high-hat of those Easterners had trouble ranking it lower than third. The man who had propelled it to these heights from the depths of mediocrity—lower than simple mediocrity—wrote to a colleague, "We're going to push the *NYT* off its perch." That man, Otis Chandler, was the most unlikely person—a tall, blond California sun-child, a surfer who could take the coast's best curls, a former shot-putter who came within inches of the world record, a car racer, a big-game hunter. He had created a great newspaper in the most unthinkable manner in the business—making money by lavishing it on quality, all the while outflanking the most dysfunctional family in American publishing, his own. Jack Nelson, a Southerner who took reporting to a fine art, ran Chandler's expanding Washington bureau. "I was in tall cotton," he says, recalling the days when he had the backing to hire the best reporters and chase the best stories he could find. In American journalism the making of the *Los Angeles Times* was one of the stories of the century.

On the eve of the 1990s the *Times* still acted its robust self. Circulation peaked at 1,225,189 daily and 1,514,096 Sunday, making it the largest in the country. *Washington Journalism Review* called it the "Newspaper to Watch for the '90s." It was that, all right.

In the final months of 1989 Joan Didion hung out around Times Mirror Square, preparing a story for the *New Yorker.* If anyone can spot a bad turn coming, it is Didion. A native Californian, her moods can be as forlorn as the howling Santa Ana winds that build over her hometown of Sacramento. Didion can smell gloom in a flower shop.

So the rest of us might look back now and see the inevitable in the story that business writer Stuart Silverstein wrote November 25, 1989, about the bleak Thanksgiving weekend for local retailers: "'Tis the season to shop, but it's off to a slow start." Or we'd spot it in the piece four days later by real estate writers Tom Furlong and Michael Flagg—"Prices drop, sales slow"—with its eye-blinking news that home prices had declined almost 20 percent in forever affluent Orange County.

Or we would flutter back through three weeks and a few thousand pages of newsprint and nod sagely at foreign correspondent Bill Tuohy's story from Berlin on November 10: "Wall has 'no more meaning.'" When that last great symbol of the Cold War—the Berlin Wall—came crashing down, with it collapsed forty years of a weapons economy that had nurtured Southern California's seemingly endless boom almost as surely as that first water siphoned off from the Owens Valley two hundred miles to the north early in the century. The Chandler forebears got rich quietly buying up San Fernando dry land before the deal was announced and selling it after the *Times* trumpeted that the desert now would bloom. It did, as did Los Angeles and the Chandler fortune.

As 1989 ended, the money still gushed at the *Times*. At one point the paper not only had fourteen reporters and photographers stationed throughout the crumbling Soviet empire, but it also began publishing a Moscow edition, eight pages faxed in daily. Nothing was too big for the *L.A. Times*. Not even hubris. The paper spent money like it was going out of style. It was.

Didion picked up on that and more. Not only was the bottom falling unseen out of the California boom, the superglorious era of Otis was ending, too. People had begun to wonder, she wrote, if "having the number one newspaper in the country was a luxury the Chandlers, and the city, could still afford."

Chandler had stepped down as publisher a decade earlier, worn out by the family fights and his own internal struggle to be so many different people. "I was wearing out at an early age," he said later. Late in 1989 he also quit as chief executive officer of Times Mirror for the relative quietude of a seat on the board of directors. A family putsch, some said, payback time for the "bad Chandlers" against the "good Chandler." Others said Otis, then only sixty-one, had too many curls still to catch. He would never be an easy man to fathom. The paper had a new editor and a new publisher, the second since Chandler, both top newsmen but both imports from the East. They brought with them ambitious ideas and a redesigned format. But what they really brought was more fearsome: Change.

Bill Boyarsky, city editor of the *Times,* was hired almost broke off an Associated Press picket line thirty years ago. He landed in the middle of a world in which the boss chewed you out for not flying first class. Boyarsky is a rare bird from his era in American newspapering, being neither too cynical nor too romantic about the game. He can love without creating a haze. Now sixty-five, he has had a hell of a ride. "I always thought the good old days were too good," Boyarsky says. "It was great. It was incredible. I always knew it would end."

At the annual Christmas party in 1989 no one is quite sure why David Laventhol, the new publisher, gave the traditional toast such an unusual twist. Maybe it was simply the wistfulness in the air. No one in that room could imagine what the decade of the '90s held for the *L.A. Times*. It had been a good year, Laventhol said, and it had. Then with glass still raised he added: But he was glad it was over.

If you look now at the charts that economists and social scientists use to mix numbers and paint a downturn, L.A.'s line moves upward in zigzags until a day or two shy of that Christmas. Then it drops like a rock. The Cold War bust, they called it. The country suffered a little glitch. But for Southern California it was not just another recession. It was a punch in the gut.

With all the calories that had larded up the *Times* for a century, it took most of a year for reality to sink in. During the Persian Gulf War in early 1991 the paper sent in dozens of reporters and photographers, more than any other paper, and set up a fourteen-editor war desk. *Time* magazine called theirs the best coverage of the conflict. But the drumbeat had already begun. First came a hiring freeze. In the first seven months of 1991, 177 full-timers from throughout the paper left. Seventeen were replaced. It wasn't enough. In August the paper offered rich buyouts, sometimes as much as two years' pay, to staffers over fifty-five. Three hundred accepted, among them some of the best Otis Chandler had assembled.

For the paper, it was a cut of fat, meat, and bone. In rapid order, but not without blood spattering behind closed doors, the paper ditched its P.M. edition—an eight-page wraparound for home-bound commuters. Then it ceased costly home delivery in the Central Valley and east into Arizona and Nevada. Last to go was the expensive San Diego edition, fifty-thousand copies, and with it the dream of dominating all of Southern California.

They call it "ego" circulation—circulation that costs more than it brings in. It is expensive to deliver and, as the circulation director at the time, Jack Klunder, puts it, "a Los Angeles grocery store doesn't need to advertise tomatoes in Fresno." But the circulation is not valueless. It had a value to national advertisers and in power, reputation, even a reporter's ability to report. Ego had always been worth money to the *Times*.

Klunder fought like hell. Jeffrey S. Klein, a marketing executive and one of the morning-line favorites to become publisher some day, argued the cuts were "a huge error," according to Klunder. So did Shelby Coffey III, the editor.

"Now this economy was grim, almost a depression," Klunder says. "We looked at everything. Some cuts you can get back when the economy turns. Not these. I said this is going to blow up in our face and they didn't think that would happen. But it sure did."

Klunder remembers that *Times* executives would look at a cut and say "this is going to cost us 50,000 in six months." Then the numbers would come in later "and we'd say, 'Whoops.' Finally we got down to that magic million mark. I was going nuts." By the end of the decade intentionally dumping a couple hundred thousand circulation would become one of the great ironies in the travails of the *Times*.

Most of the focus on the *L.A. Times* story has been on the newsroom—outside reporters writing about other reporters. But on the business side, chaos reigned. It was about to get much worse—so bad that Klunder finally quit. "It became panic," he says. "The place became impossible. I was third generation at the *Times*. My grandmother worked there. But I began to question whether the paper had lost its fastball." Klunder quit in 1996. There have been three circulation directors since him. Execs shuffled jobs and came and went dizzily in other departments as well. At the height of the confusion in early 1999 one executive arrived, became a vice president and left—all in a period of six weeks. Sardonic *Times* reporters began calling them "the Flying Wallendas."

By the early '90s Times Mirror profit margins fell into single digits. Those are not dangerously low numbers in all American industries. But the "dying newspaper business" is whistling its way to the graveyard. The industry expects, and often gets, margins of 20, even 30, percent and more. In Los Angeles the margins and the circulation numbers, which bottomed out in 1995 at 1,012,189—down almost a quarter million in five years and the lowest in twenty-four years—became catalytic events and brought the somnolent Chandler family briefly out of their country clubs.

Watered down through the generations, the Chandlers are now split into four wings—the Otis wing and three right wings that still mutter about stories about gays and the Jews who run Hollywood and the Eastern media, usually in more pointed language. Until recently it was impossible to overestimate the impact the Chandlers, and the merged descendents of *Times* founder Harrison Gray Otis, had on the development of Los Angeles and Southern California. "It would take in the East a combination of the Rockefellers and the Sulzbergers to match their power and influence," David Halberstam wrote in *The Powers That Be*. The city's Dorothy Chandler Pavilion, for instance, familiar to millions of Academy Award viewers, is named for Otis's mother. The family simply ran the place—the politics, the business, the growth and the creation of wealth, stashing a goodly portion of the latter in their own pockets first. Among American publishing families they remain the wealthiest in the business with a collective fortune well over $3 billion.

All this was built on what was, quite simply, a rag. *Time* magazine called it one of America's ten worst newspapers in 1957. It had been that way for all its seventy-five years—when Otis Chandler's great-grandfather came west in 1882 to a town of five thousand souls and bought into a failing, four-page sheet for $1,000 down. Through some still unforgotten family elbowing by his father and mother, Otis got the paper in 1960. At first the publishing world snickered at the overgrown California boy. By 1964, *Time* rated the reborn paper one of the ten best—and it was up from there.

Then, as now, the other Chandlers viewed Otis as totally aberrational. To this day, beyond making certain they maintain control and milk the dollars, they seem to take no interest in the newspaper at all. They almost never talk to the lowly press. Their few friends who will talk guardedly stare back in disbelief when asked if they have ever seen a Chandler drop any loose change into a *Times* sidewalk rack. They are on this earth to take money out of the newspaper, not put it back in.

A ND SO IT WAS that they hired Mark H. Willes. Willes was a business-man, and apparently a good one, with all the qualities that go with that—hard-headed, totally self-certain, quick with decisions. He never looked back, his eyes riveted instead on the bottom line. He came out of the Cheerios division of General Mills, a business heavy on marketing and hard-sell. "It's the kind of business that when you get in trouble with the numbers, you add sugar and come out with a multimillion-dollar ad campaign that says 'New and Improved,'" one of the highest-ranking Flying Wallendas tells me, no sourness intended.

No historical evidence exists that Willes had ever been inside a newspaper building before he walked through the portals at Second and Spring on May 1, 1995, establishing himself in the sixth-floor corner office of the chairman and CEO of Times Mirror. Willes had spent the previous eighteen years in powerful positions in Minneapolis. He had arrived as president of the regional Federal Reserve Bank, staying there three years before moving on to General Mills, where he would become vice chairman. But he operated at such a low profile that even some well-connected executives in the Twin Cities had never heard of him.

Visitors to Willes's office aerie invariably described the long window wall and his sweeping view of the city and the sunburnt San Gabriel Mountains. But another striking vision was the Los Angeles Civic Center just across the street. When Willes first arrived, the O.J. Simpson trial was going full swing in the courtroom at his feet and Marcia Clark was well into the prosecution case. Willes would sit there and watch her witnesses emerge into the usual pressing mob of reporters.

"My first thought was, 'Why don't they just leave them alone?'" Willes recalls. "Then I thought, 'Wait a second, half those people are mine. Go get 'em!'"

Willes could be beguiling. And when he went wooing, he wooed the reporters and editors the most. After more than four years of cutting, squeezing, and, to the high chieftains of journalistic theology, unmitigated heresy—"I'll use a bazooka, if necessary" to blast away the longstanding walls between the news and business sides, he famously decreed—the most unreported part of the Mark Willes saga was that by early 1999 he had more support in the third-floor newsroom than he did in any other department.

On a scale of one to ten, any newsroom's morale probably tops out at about a high five. Caustic black humor is the order of the day. No one at the *Times* can fire off a black one-liner faster than Tim Rutten, a forty-nine-year-old city desk hand (and husband of celebrity defense lawyer Leslie Abramson). A sample: "Not since the battle of the Somme have troops been so badly led as they have been led here in the past 10 years." But, like many of his colleagues, he did not want to be the lumberjack, the steelworker, the fisherman of the twenty-first century. Willes played to that fear. He was going to grow the Times, grow the industry, and plow some of the wealth back into the product, which is what Willes called news. These were words that even the most skeptical and hard-nosed journalist wanted to believe. "Now we have someone whose life every day has been a Darwinian struggle for shelf space," Rutten said. "Maybe we're there, too. If he can bring his marketing skills in to save this newspaper, it will be a blessing to the whole industry."

Willes's real admirers, of course, were the Chandler family. In his years at the *Times* he made them at least three, perhaps four times richer than they were when they hired him. It was enough to make even Otis feel warm and fuzzy for a while. Willes didn't do so badly for himself, either. His total direct compensation in 1998, according to the *Wall Street Journal,* was $13.3 million, which included $9.9 million in unexercised stock options. In addition, he already owned or had the rights to 490,715 shares of Times Mirror stock.

It is extremely difficult to get a handle on Willes. He was born in Salt Lake City, son of a banker. But he headed east to Columbia University in New York, where he earned a Ph.D. in economics. He went on to teach briefly at the Wharton School, discovering a professorial bent that still emerges occasionally, before moving to Philadelphia's Federal Reserve Bank. He is married with five children. His wife, Laura, is rarely seen in public and Willes refuses to talk about his personal life—perhaps, but doubtfully, an unrecognized contradiction in a man who sent out legions each day in search of such detail in others. He is a Mormon, nephew of the president of the Mormon Church, Gordon B. Hinkley. But he acknowledged, in a one-word answer so brittle it threatened to crack before it reached me, that he did not put in the youthful missionary stint encouraged by his church. Some said he was making up for that at the *Times*. His style could be passionately evangelical. He talked in terms of grand, even grandiose, missions—saving Los Angeles by pulling the fractured city back together through the newspaper, saving the newspaper business from its hopelessly outdated self. He could make a spellbinding speech. He could cry in public. Some say on cue. This is, after all, the city of the silver screen.

People who talked to him regularly—even those who left the paper by the dozen, in angry despair—tended to like him personally. However, many also said that the more they saw of him the less they understood him. "Mark is one charismatic cookie," said a former high executive who met with Willes daily. "The question you have to resolve is the difference between the public man and the private man. No one has been able to do that. He has few friends and nobody knows who they are."

Speculative insights did pop up along the way. His entry in *Who's Who* was typically stark in detail until, in a departure from the norm, he added a personal credo at the end, set apart in italic type:

> *My success is based on adherence to principles I learned in the home, which is the most basic and important organizational unit in the world. Three of those principles stand out in my mind: Be just, honest and moral—do things not only because they are required, but because they are right. Have mercy— care enough about others to be fair and kind. Be humble—you can get more done effectively with the help of others than you can do on your own.*

Tips also occasionally popped up in what was clearly his second favorite paper, the *Wall Street Journal.* "You only get one chance to make a first impression," he once told it.

Willes did that, all right, and with a nouveau capitalist's élan. He had hardly hung his hat before he presided over the closing of the long-suffering *Baltimore Evening Sun,* not much of a surprise. But the next one caromed off every wall in the newspaper community. Ten weeks into the job, Willes shut down the money-losing but journalistically acclaimed New York edition of *Newsday.* The Long Island survivors didn't come out of their depression over losing the Big Town for more than a year. Willes was not afraid to take his medicine, agreeing to meet two days later with one of the firebrands he had just landed on the bricks. Sydney Schanberg, a *Newsday* columnist and survivor of both the Khmer Rouge and the B-52 carpet bombings in Cambodia, thought the closure "a corporate homicide." Willes opened their one-on-one meeting by saying, "Would it surprise you to know that I have a romantic feeling about newspapers?" Replied Schanberg, "Yes, it would." A week later the CEO pink-slipped 150 at Times Mirror's surviving morning paper in Baltimore, the *Sun*. The next day it would be the *Times'* turn.

July 25, 1995. Black Friday, they called it. The toll was 750 this time, 150 in the newsroom, and they were not buyouts. Willes also closed the Washington edition (it was reopened several months later after strong pressure), the World section, an experimental Spanish-language insert called Nuestro Tiempo and six other sections or zoned editions.

By then, Laventhol was no longer publisher. A victim of Parkinson's disease, he weakened steadily in front of his troops for six months in 1993. Finally he told them privately, "This is a 16-hour-a-day job and I can't even do eight." (Subsequent advances in drug therapy helped him greatly, and he now is publisher of *Columbia Journalism Review*.) Richard T. Schlosberg III, a lithe veteran of newspapers and Vietnam, where he flew fighters, had become the paper's third publisher in four years.

Shelby Coffey remained and his fate was in some ways tougher to endure than Laventhol's. Coffey is an unusual man, with different ways. Even before he arrived in Los Angeles, he was known for quoting Greek philosophers and calling struggling reporters at home at night to read them Russian poetry for inspiration. But he was an editor of unquestioned quality. A veteran of the *Washington Post,* he ran the Style section during its finest hour and was the last to fall in the Dance of the Long Knives to replace the newspaper's legendary editor, Ben Bradlee. Coffey first met Otis Chandler lifting weights in a Washington health club. Chandler wanted to hire him on the spot. Out of courtesy he went to Bradlee, who replied, "Keep your fucking hands off him." When Coffey did arrive at the big, rich *L.A. Times,* in 1986, he came brimming with ideas. He ran into a new poverty and retrenchment instead. His quirks became liabilities, then the butt of bitter jokes. A yuppie doorknob to Hollywood glitz, they called him; "the Hologram."

One of Coffey's reporters spotted him the night before Black Friday and had never seen a man look so gray, like a sinking battleship. But Coffey remained stoic and circumspect when he stood before the newsroom with the news. Boyarsky remembered being irritated by the cool manner. Later, when he became city editor, he regretted his feeling. "People really don't want to hear the boss whine," he said. "A whiner can't help them. I can understand why Coffey never told us his dreams had been shattered."

Then, on that day, the cops came in—"I guess they were afraid of people going postal," Boyarsky says—and employees began getting called into offices all over the building and tears flowed and hugs were hugged and CNN recorded the departures at the main entrance, and the *Times* has never quite been the same place since.

In the courthouse below Mark Willes's office, Marcia Clark had just rested the state's case against O.J., and Johnnie Cochran had begun for the defense. Willes had been in town less than ninety days and he had made his first impression, reflected by the headlines and dark nicknames in other publications: DEMOLITION MAN ... CEREAL KILLER ... THE MURDER OF NEW YORK NEWSDAY ... THE AMAZING RISE OF CAPTAIN CRUNCH ... THE VISIGOTH ... SNAP, CRACKLE, POP ... ULTRA SLIMFEST IN L.A ... THE SHRINKING L.A. TIMES.

Willes later would complain mightily in a speech to the American Society of Newspaper Editors and elsewhere about the brutality of his welcome to the corps. "Some of it's been kind of mean," he said to the *New York Times*. But there was a telling footnote to his first ninety days. That first move in Baltimore, closing the *Evening Sun,* had been planned for months and even announced in the Baltimore papers before he was hired.

You only get one chance to make a first impression. Willes wanted credit—no greater proof, perhaps, of the degree to which we all live in parallel worlds. A general's triumph is a mother's atrocity. The words "fiduciary responsibility" were heard often around the *Times* in the next few years. The stockholders were pleased, the Chandlers ecstatic. Wall Street reacted, as the *Washington Post* put it, "with a big wet kiss," Times Mirror stock rapidly doubling and climbing from there.

Willes was convinced that journalists were completely naive about the need to create money to survive. But the real question, crucial to both the country's newspapers and the country, if you believe the dogma journalists have been taught, was beyond that. The question was: How much money? If other industries can survive on 10 or 12 percent margins, do newspapers really need 20? Thirty? More?

Willes added many new terms to the language of newspapering. One of his favorites: "Outside the box." The phrase was common in business and a rationale for his existence in Times Mirror Square. It took for granted that the newspaper industry was so hidebound, so hogtied with ancient liturgy, even self-delusion and a fair share of sanctimony, that only someone who was "outside the box" could see inside with enough clarity to fix it. It would be foolish to discard that thought out of hand. But it is equally foolish to discard the thought that someone "outside the box" of Wall Street might be required to resolve the profit issue that is bedeviling American newspapers. Parallel worlds.

By the summer of 1995 the Mark Willes story had barely started. In the next four years he would cut again and then again. He would trumpet radical changes that he never was able to make work—the walls between the newsroom and the business side of the *Times* withstood the bazooka assault. He would make promises that seemed as ephemeral as the seaside mist in Santa Monica—pledges to "grow" the *Times* through circulation gains of 500,000, then 1 million, foundered. He would astound almost everyone by naming himself publisher in what bordered on a coup d'etat. He would astound them even more by quitting as publisher after only two years and naming a protege, also with no newspaper experience. In less than six months the protege, Kathryn Downing, the fifth publisher of the *Los Angeles Times* in ten years, would be scrambling to survive after a series of small "outside the box" missteps and one huge one. Newsroom morale had plummeted lower than at any time in the newspaper's dreadful decade—so far down that Otis Chandler, at seventy-one, concerned about "my friends" and his place in history, would surf back briefly out of the Pacific sunset. (There is an oft-told story about a former city editor, Noel Greenwood, who got so tired of hearing that "this wouldn't happen under Otis" that he finally declared to the troops, "Otis has gone surfing and he's not coming back.")

For those who were worried about the state of the American newspaper as the new millennium began, all eyes were on Los Angeles. An intelligent being outside all the boxes might look in and say: Why would a troubled institution experiment with the most radical surgery on one of its finest specimens? But, virtually on his own, Willes had decided that the *Times* would be the canary in the coal mine.

In 1999, four years into the experiment, the canary coughed.

THERE WAS NO QUESTION about how to begin the conversation. So, although we had never met, I said, "Good morning, Otis."

This was California and the only other real option was "Shoulders," the honorific his staff gave him in note of the breadth of his launch pad in the shot-put days. Those days, while long gone, were not as distant as they would be for most seventy-one-year-olds. Otis Chandler presented a powerful presence, and it was still easy to see him as a young man forty years ago in the regal Biltmore accepting his publisher's crown with an L.A. "Wow!"

We were at the Vintage Auto Museum in Oxnard, sixty miles and a light year or two up the coast from the power avenues of Los Angeles, and the owner greeted me in his workday clothes—khaki Hemingway shorts, shortsleeve shirt open at the neck, well-trafficked running shoes worn California style, which is no socks. The setting was unusual—one that paid homage to almost everything that had intrigued this complex and often perplexing man—everything but a newspaper, which was nowhere in sight. Our hands shook over the poised hulk of a Bengal tiger, standing guard with unseeing eyes inside the door.

In the glass-walled conference room stood two other guards, a ten-foot polar bear Chandler bagged near Kotzebue in northwest Alaska and a ten-foot brown taken in the southeast part of that state. Both stood full height, teeth bared, the polar with his arms up on offense. It is the way Chandler likes them—coming at him. He had been on his way hunting when I talked to him on the phone in August. "Well, I'll see you then, 10 A.M. on September 16, if a bear doesn't eat me." It was not all bravado or manly joke. Chandler goes out after these beasts heavily odds-on. But they can get through. If not, what would be the point? Nine years earlier a musk ox got to him in northern Canada, mauled him badly, ripped his arm out of its socket. There is a famous picture of the muscular young publisher in swim trunks holding his first wife, Missy, over his head like a barbell. He was still built like a ramrod. But he no longer could lift anything of consequence over his head. It deterred him not at all.

The full glass wall behind him displayed an array of his other trophies, perhaps fifty polished vintage automobiles—Cadillacs from the '30s, Duesenbergs, twelve-cylinder Lincolns, twelve-cylinder Packards, Pierce Arrows. Above on a balcony sit the outriders of his 150 motorcycles—Harleys, Kawasakis, Indians. In New Zealand five years ago, at about the time Willes was hired, one of the Kawasakis had taken him down, too. Almost killed him. Recovered, he bought an identical bike.

Of all the crucial players in the story on the plight of the *Los Angeles Times,* I thought Chandler the least likely to talk. He had done, as he pointed out, his fifty years at the paper—as a Chandler, and that familial obligation alone seemed a demand no mortal could understand. In a town that busied itself creating folk figures, being a folk figure came naturally to him. I had dinner the next night with a prominent movie director. There were a dozen things I wanted to talk about; all he wanted to talk about was my meeting with Otis Chandler. Chandler always had other yearnings, two of them on display so vividly here. Everyone has at least one tale about the tugs and pulls inside this man: He had been meeting in the Times Mirror boardroom when an aide walked in and handed him a note. Otis read it, crumpled it up and dropped it in a wastebasket. Then he rose without a word and strode forcefully from the room. After the meeting, a concerned executive retrieved the crumpled note. "Surf's up," it said.

Until our September 1999 meeting, Chandler had not spoken publicly about the *Times* for three years and, in his mind, he had been burned in that session, an interview with *Vanity Fair*. He disillusioned his idolizing newspaper friends by endorsing Mark Willes's early moves ("I just can't believe it is Otis," said one). He also angered his relatives, who now effectively controlled the paper and had boxed him out. He called one of his board-member cousins "not very bright" and quoted the acknowledged powerhouse of the antediluvian family forces, Warren "Spud" Williamson, as a bigoted annoyance who repeatedly asked him questions like, "Oh, God, Otis, do we have to see another damn story about gays?" Chandler claimed later that his words had been spoken off the record and maybe juiced up a bit for publication. But most of his friends rolled their eyes at his complaint—the reporter was of first rank—and figured that Chandler had finally said what he thought only to regret it later. Whatever, the episode sent him on silent running after that.

So I came to see him after brushing up on Duesenbergs and Kawasakis. I couldn't have misread him more. "OK," he said quickly, interrupting my small talk. "All this is well and good, but we should get on with it." Then he simply launched. Chandler was pent up and damned mad.

"The paper is very disappointing to me today. It is not moving forward. It is moving backward in some areas. The exodus of top-flight reporters is very, very disturbing. There are some 18 or 20 who have gone to the *New York Times* alone. And I know how hard it was for me to attract and paint a vision for people to come and join the paper in the '60s, how difficult it was to talk the Robert Donovans, the Ed Guthmans, the Jim Murrays. There are no new top reporters that we have attracted from other media, we do not have the reputation we did have of being one of the top papers in the country, second only to the *New York Times*. And once you lose that reputation, you put the paper in neutral. That's the word now. We're in neutral. The common phrase I hear now is: 'Otis, it's just another job. I just put in my hours and go home.' There is no leadership, no excitement, no future.

"So I'm very concerned about the *Times*. It is not in free fall. But morale is way down."

Briefly, I recalled a conversation with one of the *Times'* top young reporters as he spoke of the "terrible dilemma" of the paper's elite corps, the reporters still there who could work on any paper in the country but didn't want to leave: "We ask ourselves, 'What is the Times going to be like in 10 years? Is it a worthy place to be?'"

"You keep in touch?" I asked Otis.

"Yeah, I keep in touch. They come up here. They look on me as kind of the Godfather or something."

And they did. "Your name comes up in almost every interview," I told him. "Sometimes wistfully, sometimes lonesomely. . . ." I didn't add that sometimes it came up almost angrily, as if he had deserted them. Not so much in body; the body ages. In spirit. For the silence. But he knew that.

"Yeah, those are the right words," he said, arching his eyebrows and frowning ever so slightly. "Some people are bitter. Some people don't understand why I don't come back and fix things. . . ."

He stared at the big brown for a moment, no empathy there, and a flash of anger betrayed what he had been trying to cover with level tones. He began talking directly about Mark Willes. "He was going to reinvent the wheel. He has had some unique ideas"—the words growled—"but none of them have worked. They're going to double the circulation of the daily *Times,* which is an interesting comment because not only is it impossible to do unless you spend hundreds of millions of dollars to buy circulation [but] that kind of circulation will just quickly disappear. It's insulting to me and the previous publishers and marketing executives, implying that we didn't try to increase circulation as fast as we could prudently do it. If I had come in 1960 and said, 'Well, I've now finished the seven-year training program my father put me on and I therefore have all the ultimate wisdom about how to run this newspaper and I'm just going to double the circulation . . . .'" He chuckled. "If it were as easy as he thinks, he would have inherited a two- or two-and-a-half million circulation. It's an astounding comment coming from a man that just started in the business. But that's his style. I've come to understand that he has these unbelievable goals that he sets but can't be achieved. It's just dreaminess. It's in la-la land.

"I don't know where that takes him, but it certainly is embarrassing to me to have these announcements by Mark because I get these calls from my publisher friends and they say, 'Otis, what is going on there? We can't believe what is coming out of that organization. How do you feel about it? Why don't you do something about it? Why don't you go back in?'"

But Otis couldn't go back in now. Except in spirit. "He's not the Chandler in charge anymore," his old editor, Bill Thomas, had said a few days earlier.

Chandler's cousins had been like fire ants in his britches for the past forty years. Some think it was their constant nipping, not the lure of his exotic outside interests, that drove him slowly into his unusual exile and put at risk the grand castle he built. The family was watered down by second cousins and shirttails now, but it was wealthier than ever and only a kind of silent ineptness prevented it from wielding more power than it did in Los Angeles. And that remarkable right-wingism. Stories of Chandler racism, extremism, and narrowness are legend. Two obscure cousins went unusually and aggressively public in *Forbes* and the *New York Times* not long after Willes was hired and shortly before Otis's *Vanity Fair* interview. Cousin Jeff Chandler of San Diego complained that he was tired of hearing that "as long as dividends were flowing [the family] was just a bunch of rich people clipping coupons." Cousin Corinne Werdel of Bakersfield left no room for doubt in her message about the paper Otis had left them: "We have the inmates running the asylum. They're so far out in left field." Neither was a board member, but they savored the sea change they foresaw in Willes. Jeff Chandler railed about "the gays" again, complaining about a photo in the *Times* of two boys helping each other adjust their cummerbunds at a gay high school prom. He added, ominously to those who had spent lifetimes bringing the *Times* into the bigs, that the family feelings had been "made known to Willes—that we simply weren't going to tolerate this stuff anymore."

That, in the beginning, was the overriding fear about Willes in the newsroom of the *Times*. That the bad Chandlers had brought him in with marching orders that went beyond making money. When nothing seemed to happen, Jeff's words were written off as more prattling from the Chandler right. But, in classic film-town fashion, there was a back story to that, one that few *Times* executives even knew. A very private meeting did occur in Willes's office shortly after he was hired, with implicit demands from owners to hireling.

Otis sat silently and watched Willes perform. He had been impressed during their pre-hiring interview and, still a board member at the time, he had gone along enthusiastically. Willes had seemed like the right man to take Times Mirror and get it rolling again. "That's why we hired him," Chandler says. "Not to fix the *L.A. Times* because the *L.A. Times* didn't need fixing. It was one of the great newspapers in the country." The recession had come, the recession would go—and the *Times* would roll on. Those were always Otis Chandler's thoughts. Nothing could bring down the paper he had molded.

The national economy was already on a terrific romp. (Unknown to both of them, Southern California's collapse had bottomed out, too; on those charts the economists drew later, the line halted its downward plunge just before Willes was hired. By the time he completed his Sherman-like first ninety days, it was headed sharply up again. Just as Laventhol and

Coffey had borne the curse of the economic forces of the early '90s, Willes bore their blessing in the late '90s.)

The meeting in his old office impressed Chandler even more. His cousins played to the old theme: Take us back to the arch-conservative *Times* of the '40s and '50s. They were sick of reading about poor people and brown people, about people they had never met and never would. They wanted to read about their Los Angeles again. It was a Los Angeles gone, hiding in increasingly isolated rich ghettoes and colorized films. But that was what they wanted. And it was their newspaper.

Like Chandler, Willes also is a remarkable man to sit across a table from. He wears large metal-rimmed glasses—designer fish lenses—and his eyes rarely leave you. They brim with empathy and interest. He listens, usually waits for you to pause before he talks. He is on your side. So he sat and listened, gathered them in, played them perfectly, finessed them. Well, I'm new here. I don't know the place. I've barely talked to the editorial people and, you know, we can't avoid reality. He went on that way, parrying them, until they finished. And nothing ever happened.

Willes may have turned the *Times* back in size and scope and, increasingly, in reputation. But he had not turned the politics of the place. Kenneth Reich, a former political reporter and a veteran of thirty-four years, remembered a conversation in 1998 just after the paper endorsed Gray Davis, the first Democrat it had ever backed for governor. "I thought this paper was turning to the right again," someone had said. Willes was simple and direct, a businessman not an ideologue. "If the *Times* wants to grow circulation," he said, "it will have to move where the Californians are, and the Californians are shading left."

So Otis Chandler had been impressed by Willes in his maiden test. Happy with it. The news operation is the soul of a newspaper and the classy behemoth that Otis had created took some deep whacks. But its basic integrity had remained intact. Chandler soon grew uneasy about the rigidity and painfulness of the personnel cutbacks—the *Times*, for all its idiosyncrasies, had always prided itself as a "family" operation in the sense that it took care of its own. But Otis Chandler knew there was fat to be trimmed after thirty-five years of growth. And it wasn't just his cousins' personal fortunes that were multiplying. Willes made the Chandlers a billion dollars before he had been there a year.

But it was Willes's decision in 1997 to become publisher of the *Times*, as well as CEO of Times Mirror, that turned Otis's uneasiness into antagonism. Chandler was not the only one unhappy with this. At least two and perhaps as many as four members of the Times Mirror board thought the move at least unwise—and one would issue a muted but public warning. No one in the history of the company had held both jobs before.

But for Chandler it was more than that. He saw it almost as a coup. He also saw it as personal and, he thought, intentionally handled in an offensive way. The change occurred September 12, 1997, when Richard Schlosberg quit suddenly and, it would seem, surprisingly. Willes said later he had no one in the organization ready to move in, and he thought he had to act fast. Chandler, who was hunting bear in the Aleutians at the time, thought not that fast. When Chandler returned, his secretary reported just a single phone call from Willes. He had left no message, only the note that he had called. The blood started running then, and a month later it would spill onto the boardroom floor. Willes hadn't called the man who built the modern *Times* since.

"He has no interest in the past," Chandler said. A roadster gleamed behind him. "He is out to prove that the old way of doing things at the *Times* is no longer valid. He has not called me once. He has not called Bill [Thomas] once."

"He hasn't called you once?"

"Well, when he first became CEO he called me when he was about to drop the New York edition of *Newsday*. He's just not interested in the past."

At 6 feet 2 inches, Chandler was twenty or thirty pounds lighter than in his muscle-man publisher's days. His face had become a picture of crags and gorges that mapped out his new life, not his past life. He was not a bitter man. He contained too much self-certainty to have room left for bitterness. His eyes, Nordic blue, flashed and then twinkled. He did not forget a slight. But anger was not a sustainable part of his life. He let it bounce in and out.

"It never crossed my mind that Mark should disappear. I just wish he had moved more carefully and more prudently, because it could have saved us some of the public embarrassment."

He remembered his first conversation with Willes. He told him how romantic the work would be, how heady.

"I told him he was going to be sought out by business leaders and political leaders and minority leaders, the community in all its facets, the mayor and special-interest groups, and the president of the United States, he should get to know the president of the United States, and the majority and the minority leaders. . . ."

He paused with a wisp of a smile that said he never had any doubt why Mark Willes wanted to be publisher. It was so much fun.

"Mark came in as CEO of Times Mirror and I think he just became infatuated with the *Times*. I think it just swept over him. Living in Los

Angeles and having people come up to him and saying, 'Boy that was a great story you had' or 'Why didn't you do this better?' I think he became intrigued with this, and he came out with these ideas, and I think he is an impatient person, somewhat like I am, and so he became publisher."

At that point, in Chandler's view, the entire Willes program faltered. Recovery at both Times Mirror and the *Times* slowed. At the corporate level, most of the "growth" came from the sale of properties, such as its textbook and technical publishing divisions. "He's been dismantling the diversified company that I helped build and my father started. You look at all those announcements every day and it's just 'sell.'" Even in a record market, Times Mirror's stock price slowed from its early surge.

At the *Times* itself, meanwhile, chaos reigned. The irony is that this tumult was on the business side of the paper, not the editorial side. Longtime marketing and advertising and circulation executives quit by the dozen, unable to make sense of the mainstays of the Willes program —immense, racehorse circulation growth in the heart of a rapidly changing metropolis, and a breakfast-cereal marketing organization of "mini-publishers" connecting the news and business side of each "niche" of the paper—straight news, sports news, living news, business news; Cheerios, Frosted Cheerios, Honey Nut Cheerios, Multi-Grain Cheerios Plus. By June 1999, the end of Willes's nearly two-year reign as publisher, six of the eight "mini-publishers" had left and not been replaced. Circulation was going down. And in the inner regions of the tattered business departments at Times Mirror Square, the survivors had a favorite saying: "The emperor is wearing no clothes."

Chandler was almost as stunned by Willes's departure as publisher as by his arrival. As we talked, he struggled for the first time, editing his words, trying to describe the latest Willes team. The appointment of Kathryn Downing as publisher, another person "outside the box," left Chandler flummoxed. He referred to her once as "that woman," then checked himself.

"And now we have Kathryn Downing. Kathryn is a bright, attractive and proven executive, but she has absolutely no newspaper experience. She's a blank face to everyone."

He groped. We were talking three months after Downing became publisher.

"The morale is still down, and people want to leave, and they call me."

Business people mostly or both? I asked.

"It's business and editorial people, all the marketing people, the production people. They just so dislike her."

Downing had a modern approach to corporate morale. She got groups of her employees together and smiled and talked about dead wood and performing at 110 percent at all times and bell curves, emphasis on the bottom of the curve.

A relatively new editor was on board, too. Michael Parks ascended in the fall of 1997 when Coffey quit suddenly, but not unexpectedly, soon after Willes became publisher. Parks, a Pulitzer Prize winner, had strong news credentials. But he was an unusual choice nevertheless. He was only partly "inside the box." He had spent almost all his career as a foreign correspondent, had never lived in the complicated city he now surveyed. He clearly would not have been Chandler's choice.

"He had been a very fine foreign correspondent," Chandler said, "but he had never been an editor of any kind, to suddenly hand him the *L.A. Times.* . . ."

And then I was thanking him and leaving, heading back toward Los Angeles, taking the beach route because I was a tourist, past the great rock outcroppings, the incredible new-moon curve of Malibu, along the hills with the puny attempts to stop their certain slide into the Pacific, up the palm-tree-lined incline to Santa Monica and Wilshire and back through the city.

More than one hundred people from all areas of the newspaper and from without were interviewed for this story, some as many as five times. After awhile nothing became too surprising—except the totality of it, that a great institution, a great American newspaper, could be kept roiling in disarray so long. A decade, with no end in sight. In the city of the future. The city that the *Times,* always boosterish (but most newspapers are) calls the New York of the twenty-first century. The city that will take in the new immigrants and assimilate them, that will be the open door to the new Asia instead of the old Europe. It is simply not possible to imagine anything like this happening at the *New York Times* or the *Washington Post.* Max and Abe can go at it and feed the headlines of the *New York Post* for a few days—but a decade?

This is earthquake country, and seven weeks after I left Otis in Oxnard, Times Mirror Square was rocked with the biggest shaker yet—the event that would be called the Staples Affair. To the general public, the details bordered on inside baseball. But if you happened to be inside baseball, where all the players in this drama were, it rang simple: This was a spitter.

LOS ANGELES: The modern towers of the Mitsubishi Bank and the Bank of Korea elbow the Bank of America and Wells Fargo for a panorama of gray-green palms amid the low-slung stucco sprawl of a dusty subtropical megalopolis stretching as far as the eye will carry. Or until the eye hits brown desert mountains or ocean or loses focus in the haze. One passes from neighborhood to neighborhood named Little Salvador or Koreatown or Little Honduras or Hmongtown.

I'd made the trip downtown to the Times Mirror Building a dozen times now, but had yet to make it to the sixth floor. The executive branch—Willes, Downing, and Parks—had been stiffing me from the beginning. Too busy, not interested, we've had enough ink, we're in the middle of a redesign, come back later when we've had a chance to finish the job we've started. Willes had been at one helm or both for more than four years and I'd come too soon? Their reasons were so limp I almost felt embarrassed for them. Parks had agreed to a lunch interview during September, then felt compelled to call me back and cancel after Willes and Downing turned me down. "What could I say to you?" he asked. "Whatever you asked, I would have to say 'no comment.'" This was a July 1999 phone conversation, three months before Staples.

"They are in their defensive crouch," an executive with one of their Eastern papers told me. David Shaw, the *Times'* Pulitzer Prize–winning media correspondent, thought the rejection was wrongheaded and said he'd told his bosses as much. But, never at a loss for an interesting take on a situation, he stated the devil's-advocate obvious from the heights of the executive suite.

"I can understand the feeling they might have that they have nothing to say at this stage," Shaw observed. "If a reporter comes in to talk to Willes now the reporter is going to say, 'Well, OK, you told me you were going to increase circulation by half a million and Kathryn says a million and basically it's gone down. And you put in all these general managers and almost all of them have quit. Promised all of these new revenue streams and none of them are there.'"

Shaw did indeed make it sound unpleasant. But they made their millions sending out hirelings to ask the same questions of others. Finally, the key *Times* executives relented. The interviews lay a few days ahead.

Meanwhile, the time waiting had not been wasted. The chaos of the Willes years had been so great that the arroyos were littered with former *Times* employees, enough vice presidents alone to get up a sandlot ball game with short and long relievers. More than a dozen executives who once graced the masthead had talked, most asking not to be identified so they could continue to earn a living in Los Angeles. And many other interesting folk, too.

One of the latter was Eric Malnic, sixty-two, gray, balding and lithe as a cat. Too old to chase fire engines, he chased airplanes instead. Malnic did crashes—from Lockerbie to Peggy's Cove. In the elite corps of reporters occupying that particular specialty, he was considered one of the best. He had been at the *Times* since 1957, longer than anyone in the newsroom.

Malnic took me out the art deco lobby of the Times Mirror Building, turned left and then down Broadway, a street that had changed far more than the *Times* in the past forty years. Broadway was now all open-air shops, blaring trumpet music and hawkers, a transplant virtually in toto from south of the border. Malnic loved the street; change didn't bother him. A man on the sidewalk was handing out flyers and he started to offer one, then pulled it back, not just its Spanish but its culture presumed to be wasted on gringos.

We looked at each other, the same thought passing: How does the Times sell 500,000 or a million more newspapers against those odds?

The *Times* itself, after sifting through computer data on white flight, had reported that Los Angeles County was turning Latino at a rate of one percentile a year and that Hispanics likely would become a majority sometime in the first decade of the next century. But the polyglot was more remarkable than that. In one ten-square-block area of the city, 140 languages and dialects were spoken.

A few days earlier I walked the cops beat in Santa Monica with Gina Piccolo. Technically, Piccolo did not work for the *L.A. Times,* although her bylines appeared regularly within its covers. She got her paychecks from a subsidiary called Times Community News, which published fifteen—going on forty to fifty, according to Publisher Downing—local news packets called *Our Times.*

The paycheck was a bone of contention almost everywhere except among the bean counters. Piccolo, thirty, an English major with eight years' experience, was paid about $450 a week—less than half what a comparable job would pay in the main office. She left Georgia last year for a shot at the "big time," liked her job but was so embarrassed about her salary that she refused to tell her parents or her friends how much she made.

The *Our Times* idea was part of an attempt to "grow" circulation by giving readers what focus groups said they really wanted—local news. Whether the dependence on endless focus groups produces more hocus than focus stood to get one of its cleanest tests in this experiment. *Our Times* was going so local—PTA sessions, police blotters, and Little League scores—that Parks described the content of his paper as foreign news, national news, local news, and local-local.

Santa Monica was the largest of the *Our Times* productions and not quite what Kathryn Downing had envisioned. In the local cop shop, the Pacific Division headquarters of the L.A.P.D., Piccolo found no reports of stolen lawn mowers. Her front-line news decisions centered on where to cut off the reports on activities of local gangs—the Venice Shoreline Crips and the Culver City Boys. The gangs were so organized that Culver City had recently sent an emissary to the police station to protest the insistence on calling them "boys." They wanted to be known as the Culver City Gang.

In an effort to jam them up, a judge had recently issued a restraining order to stop gang members from talking to each other. The police used mug shots to ID them. "It's kind of silly," said Piccolo, thumbing through the reports. "They all wear identical black clothes and now they've just added ski masks. See, here's a typical one."

She was about halfway through three inches of reports. Two Culver City Boys, one with a pit bull, were spotted ten feet apart. The officer reported that he saw them make eye contact. That was enough. He served them with notice that they had violated the injunction. "Talk to my lawyer," said the fifteen-year-old as he accepted the complaint, turned his back, and walked away.

This was not the Los Angeles the controlling Chandlers wanted to recapture. They were like the Miami Cubans who wanted to return to the lost dream of Havana. Los Angeles was no longer a Cary Grant movie. It was a Robert Altman movie. It was the modern American megalopolis. And it's one devil of a tough place to peddle a newspaper under any circumstances.

"I think you have to take into account that Southern California is the most difficult market in the country," said David Shaw. "The geographic spread is greater. The sense of identity more fragmented. Orange County. Ventura County. Riverside County. People who don't speak the English language are the predominant ethnic majority. All that. It's scary and it's one of the reasons that I was not quick to cast Willes as the devil."

The *Los Angeles Times* was being delivered to about one in five homes in its circulation area, a drastically low figure, the lowest of any major newspaper in the country except the *New York Times*, which had made a command decision, so far very successful, to go national. *Newsday,* for example, was delivered to half the homes in its area, the *Washington Post* to almost half. Shaw and others believed that solving this Southern California Rubik's Cube was the most fateful of all of Times Mirror's challenges.

So fateful that Shaw was willing to give Willes the "apparition" of goals of 500,000 or 1 million if he needed it to jar people's thinking to new levels.

Keating Rhoads, a former senior vice president for operations and technology, was blunt about it. "A lot of people seized on these numbers as evidence of insanity," he said. "But Willes is saying, 'For crying out loud, quit trying to figure out how to get from 1,000,050 to 1,000,051. It causes you to continue thinking about the teeny things you get into every day. Think big. Think globally. Let's get excited about the power and the mission of the *Los Angeles Times.*'"

IF YOU HAD TO pick a day when tumult turned to chaos, it would be October 9, 1997. On that day Shelby Coffey commanded the headlines and most of the buzz by resigning as editor, giving way to Michael Parks. But outside the glare of that news, so many dramas played out in the Times Mirror Building that day, affecting the newspaper in such extraordinary ways, that years later even people in the middle of it still couldn't believe that it had all happened in a matter of hours.

Coffey's resignation came almost exactly one month after Richard Schlosberg had quit as publisher with the same abruptness. The departures gave rise to widespread speculation that the two men had been elbowed out. And to a large degree, intentionally or unintentionally—for Willes is complex enough for it to be either or even both—the speculation almost surely was true. It is quite possible he wanted neither man to leave but elbowed them anyway until they could take it no longer.

Neither Schlosberg nor Coffey has said a definitive word about it since—although Coffey, inimitably, offered me an enigmatic yarn from Andre Malraux. During World War II, Malraux and a priest had been sent out in the forest one night with orders to dynamite a German convoy at dawn, an almost certain suicide mission. At first light Malraux turned to the priest and said, "You've heard a lot of confessions in your life, Father. What have you gathered from all that?" "Two things," the priest replied. "One, there are far more unhappy people in the world than we think. And, two, there are no grownups."

The tension between Schlosberg and Willes had been slow to start but then became obvious to all around. "They both had smiles on their face," says the former circulation chief, Jack Klunder. "But they seemed to be grinding their teeth at the same time. You could tell not all was well in the Land of Oz." A former senior vice president, who would not speak for attribution, says, "Mark started doing the publisher's job. He humiliated Dick."

For Schlosberg, it became intolerable; for Willes, it was a golden opportunity. Jack Nelson says Schlosberg told him immediately after he quit that Willes's first response was, "I want to be publisher."

"You have to understand two things," one of the now many former publishers of the *Times* told me. "First, the *Times* drives Times Mirror. It's the flagship and it has to drive revenues. Once Mark had done the cutting and tinkering in the rest of the corporation, what was left? Second, being publisher of the *Times* simply is more fun than being CEO of Times Mirror. Mark acknowledged that right up front."

Whatever, Willes took the job. And once again he went with his credo: You only get one chance to make a first impression.

Up to that time he had spoken about circulation in relatively conventional terms. We can raise it 5 percent, he said. If we raise it 5 percent, we can raise it 10 percent; if we can raise it 10 percent, we can raise it 20 percent. But less than two weeks into the new job, he dropped his first revolutionary bomblet on a *Times* middle-management group: It was, he said, the newspaper's "civic responsibility" to increase circulation by 500,000.

Beyond that, Willes had scheduled October 9 as the day for the real nuke, the mainstay in his manifesto. He would deploy the organizational structure for his assault on the church-state wall—the shot that would reverberate through the sanctum sanctorum of the newspaper world like abortion in the Vatican. Breaching the wall was the linchpin in his belief that, through branding and modern marketing and a proper understanding of the Madison Avenue world of niches and silos, newspapers could be sold the way anything could be sold. Two years earlier he had carried this belief to the extreme: Latinos had taken to Cheerios as a brand-name favorite, he told the *Wall Street Journal,* and he saw no reason why they couldn't flock to the *Los Angeles Times* brand in the same way.

By coincidence, the Times Mirror board of directors had scheduled its regular executive session that same morning. It would be followed by a farewell lunch for Schlosberg. Both events, one shrouded in the usual corporate secrecy and the other open and emotional, would take place just strides apart on the sixth floor. The board meeting would be the first since Willes had, with a bare telephone quorum, made himself publisher, the first since Otis Chandler's bear hunt in the Aleutians. It also would be Chandler's last. He was about to reach the mandatory retirement age of seventy, a rule that later would be overlooked for Spud Williamson, the new Chandler family powerhouse. Four other board members were retiring with Otis. Willes, who had a majority before, would have a lock afterward.

Emotions ran the gamut downstairs in the newsroom at the news of Coffey's resignation. But behind the closed doors on the sixth floor, they immediately ran quick, hot, and heavy—perhaps hotter than ever in the paper's 125-year history. There are seventeen members of the board of directors, but only about ten attend executive meetings. Otis was livid, by far the angriest. "It's simply not what we hired you for," he told Willes. He said it several times. John E. Bryson, CEO of Edison International, was calmer. But his position was clear. He didn't think it was a good idea for Willes to be his own boss. He carefully suggested that Willes should step down as publisher immediately. Donald R. Beall, the retired chairman of Rockwell International, seemed to agree. Willes was shaken but adamant. He had gathered a quorum of the board when he gave himself the job, and he had one now. "I like the job," he said. "I'm going to continue." C. Michael Armstrong, about to leave the board because of his duties as CEO-designate of AT&T, was smiling and conciliatory, attempting to mediate. But his views were clear, too, as would be shown later. Not a single member of the other side of the family spoke.

(Later, Willes acknowledged the basic description of the meeting but added, "I'll give you that with quite a different perspective. The board was just doing its job." He said the contention was not over whether he should be publisher. "When I appointed myself, there was some general concern about whether I should try or can I do two jobs at one time." He said that he told the board members that since the *Times* was the biggest part of his job as CEO of Times Mirror, he didn't see why not.)

Meanwhile, the meeting dragged on and on, well past the starting time of the farewell lunch. Elsewhere on the sixth floor, Schlosberg and other executives fidgeted. The executive suite is largely a collection of glass offices facing in on an atrium—and each other—and the executive dining room, known as the Picasso Room until Willes removed the Picassos, where the lunch was to be held. The boardroom and Willes's office are closed off with the windows looking out over the city. With everyone outside the board-room able to see virtually everyone else, eyebrows began rising. The lunch went a half hour, then an hour late, a notable event in itself in an institution where being five minutes tardy for a meeting was cause for speculation. The place ran on time.

"I think it was clear to everyone there that blood was running," says one masthead executive still with the *Times*. "It was awkward."

Another top executive, since departed, remembers just how awkward. "Things were already confused enough, with Shelby suddenly out the door and a major reorganization announcement coming. . . . Then they finally came out and Mark was ashen."

The board went back behind closed doors after the lunch and wrapped up the contentiousness quickly with the first word out of the other side of the Chandler family. Their lawyer, William Stinehart Jr., rose. "I speak for the family," he said pointedly, "and the family like this move." Hostility hung in the air as Stinehart continued for a few moments. But it was over. There are no coups in a boardroom. Coups take place in the hallway. And, from the beginning, Willes had all the votes he needed and soon would have more.

As the board meeting finally ended, the newspaper's public relations department churned out the press release that announced Lenin's arrival in Moscow:

> "LOS ANGELES, October 9, 1997—The *Los Angeles Times* has initiated a top-level reorganization that will focus its business functions, such as advertising and marketing, around the sections of the paper in order to help the *Times* grow and connect more effectively with readers."

Jeffrey S. Klein, senior vice president for marketing, would become general manager of news, with five new "general managers" under him. (Willes and his lieutenants had toyed with calling them "mini-publishers" earlier but discarded the title as too controversial.) Janis Heaphy, senior vice president for advertising, would take a new twenty-eight-word senior vice president's title and oversee three other general managers, including one for a new section that would "broaden the paper's appeal to women." Titles and functions changed for three other masthead executives, the Wallendas soaring high and wide.

Meanwhile, the press release noted a sister release about an "editorial reorganization at the *Times.*"

Michael Parks, moving up from managing editor, was as corporately reassuring as Willes. "Our high journalistic standards and the integrity of everyone involved in publishing this paper allow us to discuss section planning issues with people on the business side without compromising our editorial judgment." Parks had found out about his promotion the night before. So had four new managing editors named to replace him.

Leo Wolinsky, who was to become the new managing editor for news, remembers being called to a meeting in Coffey's office. He sank deep into a leather couch across from Coffey and Parks before realizing he was the only other person there. Rumors had been flying, but "I was completely shocked," Wolinsky says. "I must have looked like I was drooling. My mouth fell open, catching flies. I felt numb. I didn't say a word. It was scary. It wasn't like there was a training period. Shelby was leaving. I didn't really want the job. It is a terribly annoying job. Actually, I got kind of angry about it later. I went home pissed off."

Almost everyone went home in some high state of emotion that night. Later, as I reconstructed that day, it became clear that no one had a full sense of its extraordinary drama, so personal and commanding had its individual events been.

Mark Hinkley Willes had been publisher for twenty-eight days.

THERE WAS A FOOTNOTE to the events of October 9. Six months later, in the spring of 1998, Times Mirror gave a farewell party to the five departing members of the board—Dave Laventhol; Mike Armstrong; Harold M. Williams, chairman of the J. Paul Getty Trust; Robert F. Erburu, the powerful CEO of Times Mirror before Willes; and Otis Chandler.

Mary E. Junck, president of Times Mirror's Eastern newspapers, introduced the main speaker, Armstrong, who had tried to be so conciliatory in that brutal board meeting. He looked out at several hundred members of management and their spouses and expressed surprise. He thought, he said, he would be addressing members of the board and had prepared his speech for them. But he'd give it anyway. According to various people there, Armstrong then proceeded to critique the performance of the board he was leaving. He warned that the new board should use "due diligence" in watching over the affairs of Times Mirror. Using careful but clear language, he restated his earlier position given in private: It was unwise for the CEO of the corporation to also be the publisher of its largest entity. The CEO's job is to keep an eye on the publisher.

"It got the room quiet in a hurry," says Mark Sande, a nineteen-year *Times* man excited about his new job as a spearholder in the revolution, the sports general manager. "Nobody got up and said, 'Hear! Hear!'" Just sober applause, then silence. "I recorded it as a most interesting moment in the life of the corporation. A theatrical moment. An uncharacteristically honest one."

All eyes in the room, another *Times* executive says, were trained on Mark Willes. He sat through it clench-jawed. But life is never quite what it seems. As usual, there were plots among the subplots at the battered *L.A. Times*. No more than a handful in the room knew this irony:

Three months earlier Willes had offered the publisher's job to Mary Junck. She turned him down for personal reasons, just as she had nine months earlier while Schlosberg still held the job. Now head of Lee Enterprises, a medium-size newspaper chain based in Davenport, Iowa, Junck would make no comment. Willes, though caught by surprise, confirmed to me that he had made the offers.

Why Junck passed up the chance to be the first woman publisher of what then was the largest metropolitan newspaper in the country is anybody's guess. But others in the Eastern organization of Times Mirror thrived on their "splendid isolation." After his first death-dealing foray through the "colonies," Willes had mostly left the *Baltimore Sun, Newsday,* and other Eastern papers—the company also owns the *Hartford Courant, Greenwich Time,* and *Stamford Advocate* in Connecticut and Allentown's *Morning Call* in Pennsylvania—to themselves. The Eastern papers had no general managers and no hyperbolic circulation goals. They maintained themselves and actually outperformed the chaotic *Times* in most regards. Analysts began to note that *Newsday* and the *Sun* were carrying the Times Mirror newspaper division. The journalism they performed was considered among the best in the country.

Newsday, as if it had a score to settle after the humiliation of losing New York, won more Pulitzers than the *Times* in the '90s. It had less than half the newsroom staff. The *Sun* turned out some stunning news coups. In one memorable example, the newspaper's highly regarded editor, John Carroll, sent two reporters to the Sudan to prove claims, denied by the Sudanese government, that slaves were still bought and sold in that African country. To do it, his reporters bought two slaves.

Carol Stogsdill, a former *Times* senior editor who walked out the same day as Coffey, remembers that the Easterners often caught early planes home from meetings in L.A., ostensibly because of the three-hour time loss flying back. But Stogsdill, Chicago-born, recalls a high Eastern executive asking her one day, "How can you stand it in L.A.? They are all here."

There was another major subplot working that March night. Otis Chandler was furious. He had been told about the party only hours earlier, and he had thought, with terribly mixed feelings, OK, here comes the gold watch—or, as was the case at the *Times,* a replica of the paper's silver eagle emblem. He thought back to what he had done at the retirement of significant old codgers—a private lunch in the executive dining room and then an arm-around walk through the building to say goodbye to old friends. That's what Otis wanted.

"Instead, I walked in and there are 400 people there and we are a footnote to a management meeting," he said. And while the memory may be warped by the hurt of it all, his recollection of the speech bidding him farewell is: Otis is here and Otis is a wonderful hunter and he's a good surfer and he's leaving the board. "They wrote me off as a jock," he said. Chandler, who had been wrestling internally with his sense of obligations to family, newspaper, and self for the past twenty years, remembered thinking, "OK, I'm out of here. This is the current culture of this man and I'm glad I'm not around."

In the audience these subplots went almost unnoticed. But Armstrong's speech sank in with all, Otis's departure with almost all, and the continuing tumult with most.

This is the way one attendee, a top-ranking executive who had given his life and, he thought, his future to the *Times,* remembers his feelings: "The whole night was melancholy. People were confused and down and it clearly was the end of an era—maybe their era—and the beginning of another— probably someone else's."

Willes's new crew surely did not understand what Otis Chandler, perhaps the legend of him more than the man, meant inside this building— as would become so painfully clear when Kathryn Downing fired off her angry response to him a year and a half later. Her words would show a greater misunderstanding of that than of newspapering.

John Arthur, another of the new managing editors and speaking in a totally different context, tried to explain the phenomenon: "Otis is Zeus."

But by that time, just six months into Mark Willes's foray into publishing, his revolution, too, already was foundering. He had, in many ways, started before he was ready. So chaotic were the beginnings that his new and revolutionary general managers had neither staffs nor desks for the first six months.

Still, publishers watched Willes with fascination—and surely some sullen hope. If he were a new-age California messiah, with an unseen path to double-digit profits and hot-market stock prices, he would have no trouble gaining a substantial following. Publishers are a fretful bunch, and many would follow Willes into a new future as readily as the industry's old owners had stampeded into the gold rush of Wall Street.

Meanwhile, Willes's troops, while smart and mostly supportive of his goals, just couldn't deal with the chaos and the alien nature of it all. "You cannot understand," one of them tells me, "what those huge circulation goals did down at the grunt level. They are scratching, clawing, for 20, 30, 50 subscriptions at a time. You throw that number at them and they were instant failures. Tell them to get 100 and they might get them and they would be instant successes. Morale plummeted."

At the higher levels Willes was unyielding with his executives. He came up with so many new ideas so often that middle management began asking, "What is the strategy du jour?" They didn't know what he wanted that day, but they felt he would be on something else the next anyway.

One former executive says that beyond the general chaos, a more fundamental problem was happening, "what psychologists call cognitive dissonance—doing something that is not in line with your head." He remembers two incidents that finally persuaded him that he couldn't stay.

One was a circulation study, done in Willes's first months as publisher. It lay the paper's actual subscriber base against Los Angeles demographics and the qualities of likely newspaper readers: people who speak English, earn $30,000 or more, and have some college education. It turned out that the *Times,* the paper with a meager overall penetration in the low 20s, already reached 60 percent of this more select audience. Further study showed that virtually all those in the other 40 percent had tried the *Times* at some point and decided they didn't want it.

"It was extremely distressing," the executive says. "We all concluded that gaining 500,000, which had never been done before by anyone, was a pretty crazy, Herculean task. Then we took it in to Mark. He looked at it and said, 'This is going to be easier than I thought.' We walked out as if we were in la-la land."

Some time later, close to the first anniversary of his regime as publisher, Willes called together the top executives of Times Mirror for a summit meeting in the Century Plaza Hotel. Electronic voting keys for instant tabulation nestled at every exec's side. The devices allowed votes on a scale of one to five. Willes then announced an array of financial goals and asked his troops to assess the likelihood of attaining them. The tabulator immediately announced results that were dominated by threes. Willes became visibly angry.

"How can we grow if the leadership doesn't think we can grow?" he demanded. "I've studied generals and we're gonna take that hill. I don't know how. But we're gonna. Strong leaders set a goal and don't waver from it." In the hallway afterward the grumbling among the troops was louder than usual. There is another kind of general who figures out a strategy for taking the hill. Do we have to just charge? Can we go around the flank and up the back? A lot fewer people in the battalion would die.

In late 1998 Willes laid off another 850 *Times* employees, although only a handful came from the newsroom, minimizing the publicity. By that time, Willes's plans and his reputation for wizardry were badly wounded. The business-executive exodus had far outpaced the more publicized departure of top reporters to the *New York Times* and other papers. One of the first to go was Janis Heaphy, who had been given responsibility for almost half the new general managers in the original October 9, 1997, reorganization. She quit two months later—angry, her friends say, albeit for a very nice job: publisher of the *Sacramento Bee.* Her departure left the controversial assault on the church-state wall collapsing before the squad leaders could direct the attack. Her general managers were divvied up between Klein and another vice president. But soon it was clear that the pressure was affecting Klein. Around the office they began calling him "Sick Bay." By the end of 1998 he too had quit. Mary Junck left the company two months later. Of the eight general managers who would lead the revolution, six were gone, or soon would be.

At about that time Doyle McManus, chief of the *Times'* highly regarded Washington bureau, decided he should at least meet his general manager. He called Los Angeles and was told the man had left. "I felt deprived," McManus says. "Here we had had a revolution in journalism and I missed it."

Indeed, it became one of the great ironies of Willes's failed church-state revolution that, despite all the ink, the newsroom for the most part took the whole affair with a few yelps followed by yawns. It was on the business side, particularly in advertising, that Willes couldn't get any cooperation. "Can you imagine an ad man who wants even the hint out there that he can reach the newsroom?" asks one. "My God, every time he sold an ad he'd get hustled for a story on page one."

"There was so much turf stuff going on," says Kelly Ann Sole, who was the one star of the general manager system. Sole, a forty-one-year-old total believer, set the standard at the *Times* by working closely with business editor Bill Sing. The result was more advertising, more pages, and more staff—although there were some newsroom grumbles about whether the quality of business coverage had gone up or down, and whether the success was transferable to other sections.

"In the final analysis," Sole says, "if the execution of brand management is not successful at the *Times*, it doesn't mean that it's not the right idea at the right time for this industry. It's dead right. It's what newspapers have to do to survive."

For her part, Sole has since moved on to become director of Western region sales for NBC's cable networks.

Meanwhile, one other general manager also hung on. Mark Sande was putting the finishing touches on his deal of a lifetime—a multimillion-dollar profit-sharing agreement with the new Los Angeles sports arena, the Staples Center. "It seemed like such a great idea," he says. "It just seemed like a terrific opportunity. There was no secret regarding the deal or the profit-sharing. Mark said this is a good deal. Kathryn said this is a good deal." He remembers the signing ceremony well. It was December 17, 1998.

"There was a sense of occasion about it. At the Staples Center office, overlooking the building site. Mark and Kathryn were there. Half a dozen

Times senior vice presidents. [Timothy J.] Lelweke, the arena's executive vice president, was there. And some of his senior vice presidents. Mark said a few words. Tim said a few words."

Downing, as *Times* president and CEO, signed the contract for the paper. That night, Sande recalls, a group of them went down to watch the Los Angeles Kings' hockey game.

On May 17, 1999, *New York Times* media writer Felicity Barringer captured the story of Willes's eighteen-month reign as publisher. The headline on the story read, "The difficulty in being earnest: Efforts to reinvent the *Los Angeles Times* falter."

But an accompanying piece of artwork told the story better. The *Times* ran copies of two *Los Angeles Times* mastheads, one from September of 1997 and the other from May of 1999. The earlier mast had the executives who had left in eighteen months crossed out in red. The later one had those who had arrived marked in yellow. The 1997 mast had twelve executives gone, eleven remaining. The 1999 masthead had twenty-one new executives and eleven holdovers, most of them in new jobs.

By most any count, it had not been a good season. In the one measurable year of Willes's stewardship, reported in March of 1999, circulation had grown by a mere seventeen thousand. But almost immediately it was falling off rapidly, causing a tremendous scramble within the building to shore things up. Ad revenues had fallen $20 million below forecast in 1998, leading to a 3 percent cut in the paper's newshole for 1999. The Times Mirror stock price had moped more than leapt, hovering in the 50s. This led to a revival of an old line at the *Times:* "Never get between the Chandlers and their money."

Seventeen days after Barringer's article, Mark Willes retreated. He gave the publisher's job to Kathryn Downing.

IT IS OCTOBER NOW, a time when Los Angeles is almost what it used to be, the smog blown out, the temperature in the shirtsleeve low 80s, actually nippy at the beach. It has been a cool summer, La Niña's summer.

The interviews with the *L.A. Times* triad have been delayed and juggled so long they are almost anticlimactic. I am staying at the regal old Biltmore, a place of velvet and scrollwork and Persian rugs and an era long gone, where forty years ago Otis said "Wow!" but which now is stranded in a downtown that turns hostile at 7 P.M. But it is daytime, a fifteen-minute walk to Times Mirror Square, and I hoof it.

As I walk I wonder if they realize that they have delayed this too long and that a delay wasn't in their interest if it wasn't in mine. Journalism is not always a fair game but it is their game, too. So the interviews now are more pro forma than informative. There are far more mandatories than Willes could logically expect. What's this about offering the job to Mary Junck? Twice? What about the meeting over the secret circulation study? And Otis.

The walk turns left on Broadway past the very same man who started to hand Eric Malnic and me a leaflet, then withdrew it. He repeats himself. And the trumpets blare amid the amplified sales pitches, and the sidewalk is as jammed with as much humanity as any in New York. I recall something Malnic told me. This short stretch of Latino Los Angeles, five or six blocks of *bienvenido!*, does more dollar volume per day than Rodeo Drive. At two-bits a sale, he added. The new, reduced price of the *L.A. Times*—a circulation stimulant.

I am five minutes late as I am escorted into Willes's office by Martha Goldstein, corporate public relations officer, another VP, who is also my minder. She takes notes as I tape.

Immediately, I like the man. I've been told—warned by some—that I might. He puts a person at ease, even a late person, which I know irritates him. He's a minute manager, I'm a minute waster, the difference in the events that formed our lives. He introduces me to his view—the browned San Gabriels, the white buildings out of which people struggle to run this city. He tells the O.J. Simpson story, a good story for him, and then he signals with a glance at his watch.

He immediately blunts personal questions. Just a dead end. "I've chosen not to go down that road because I don't think it's useful and productive from the organization's point of view." He gives me instead a *Who's Who* recitation of his life, a bone here that maybe he wanted to be a banker when he was ten years old because his father was a banker and "I couldn't think of anything better than being like my father."

And then he is through to the present and he says, "I ended up in absolutely the best job I've ever had by far, which is in the newspaper business. I love it."

Q: And you loved being publisher.
A: I loved being publisher. Best job I ever had.
Q: Why did you stop being publisher?
A: Because I wasn't hired to be publisher. I was hired to be CEO.
Q: You gained a sense of that as you went along, that there was a difficulty. . . .
A: Well, you can't, I mean you really can't do two full-time jobs.

Q: Excuse me, but I guess what I'm asking you is, you did it for awhile. Why did you go into it? Or did you discover afterwards that you couldn't do it?

A: No. No. No. It was absolutely clear when I put myself in that I couldn't do two jobs. But you can't tell the organization you're a lame duck the day you start.

Q: All right.

A: And so you go on with everybody thinking you're going to be there forever. But the plan always was, as soon as I felt comfortable that the fundamental changes were under way, and that we had an organization that could reinvent this thing and make it work, that I would step back. What I didn't honestly fully appreciate, I knew I would find the job interesting and exciting and fun, but I didn't honestly expect to fall in love with it.

Q: Yes.

A: And I did.

Q: What part—

A: The whole part.

Q:—did you like best?

A: The whole thing.

I'm entranced, both with the passion of his words, but also with the fleeting feeling I'm in one of those Woody Allen movies with the split screen, man on one side, wife on the other, and they are talking about the same life in different perspectives.

The interview racehorses from issue to issue, no real news, none expected. No looking back on the *Newsday* decision. Was he elbowing Schlosberg and Coffey? "I had no sense of that at the time." Does it surprise you that some people are afraid of you? Pause. "No, it doesn't surprise me." Do you still think you are going to gain 500,000 circulation in a reasonable length of time? "Sure."

The bristling comes occasionally. I say it bothers some news people to hear the branding language, to hear someone calling the *L.A. Times* a "brand" on radio and television. Why do you continue to use the language when it puts them off?

"It's the future language of this business." Period. Snap, crackle and pop. Willes leans slightly forward, certain.

"The problem is the following: If you assume that everything newspapers were doing was right and wonderful and good, then all of this concern about terminology and new ways of doing things is totally misplaced and I should be thrown out on my ear. But our newspapers are declining. Now, why do I talk about brand? Because if we don't brand, if we don't give the value of the brand, we become increasingly marginalized. You don't just inch down forever. You have what science calls the 'tipping point.' You go like this"—his hands nosedive—"and all of a sudden, boom, you've fallen; you're gone. And I happen to believe in newspapers and I'm not going to let that happen on my watch."

Time is running out and I bring up Otis, that Otis is angry and disappointed in Willes and that he says that Willes hasn't called him since he became publisher. "Is that so, and if so, why?" I ask him.

"I haven't called him." The words come immediately and they crackle again. Then he pauses ever so briefly, as if searching for repartee, finds it, and adds almost with a lilt, "I had the impression Otis wanted to retire. And I wanted to respect that decision."

"Simply that?" I ask.

And Willes adds that he thinks the world of Otis and Otis has had enormous impact on this newspaper. And we really are almost out of time. He points to one of his favorite books, Intel chairman Andrew Grove's *Only the Paranoid Survive,* and concludes, "Well, you know, if you are sitting comfortable and quietly thinking all is well in the world, the world's going to take your head off."

Kathryn Downing is next. She is pleasant and artful and says almost nothing. She clearly has been forewarned that the Otis question is coming and is ready.

"Otis Chandler was pretty blunt when I talked to him," I say. "He really didn't like what is going on. He thought you were a poor choice and said so on the record. He wasn't too thrilled with Michael, either. I think I should give you the opportunity, obviously, to respond to that."

"I have tremendous respect and admiration for Otis," she replies, smiling. "And that's all I want to say."

Later, I will think she should have been taking notes.

Downing, forty-six, has been publisher for four months and everyone in the building is curious about her. She is immensely private, more so than Willes. A native of Portland, Oregon, where her parents owned a landmark eatery called the Pancake Corner, she graduated from Lewis and Clark University, then took a law degree at Stanford. After two years practicing law in Sacramento, she moved into business and rose rapidly, joining the Times Mirror legal publishing division in 1995. Willes named her president and CEO of the *Times,* her first newspaper job, in the summer of 1998. Along the way she met and married Gerald Flake, a former executive of Thomson Newspapers. She has three stepchildren and six stepgrandchildren.

That is more than she is going to tell me. "What I don't want to do is talk that much about my family," she says.

For Downing the leap into this glass-walled office as publisher of one of America's major news institutions in one of America's major cities has been monumental. "I think it is an incredible responsibility. And there is a lot to learn about Los Angeles and the newspaper. But I've also been here for 16 months now so it is getting a bit easier." It is a Wednesday. On Sunday the largest edition of the *Los Angeles Times Magazine* will land on doorsteps with the rest of the paper. The cover is a mauve-toned photo of the Staples Center. "Taking Center Stage," says the cover headline.

We talk about circulation. The paper is going through the Perils of Pauline now on that issue, desperately trying to keep circulation on at least a gradual rise while continuing the talk about gaining a million. A lot of people find it difficult to believe that the Times can achieve that, I say.

When she first became president and CEO, Downing says, she consulted with Michael Parks about the numbers. "I asked him what he thought about a half million. And he says, well, that isn't enough. We had to double it."

It is difficult to get anyone to spell out how they will do this. "Is there any way to see some of the data?" I ask. "It's not data we share publicly," Downing responds. "Give me a hint," I ask.

Two samples Downing dwells on are the *Our Times* local-locals and a program, begun last August, to stuff the *Times* inside *La Opinion,* a ninety-thousand-circulation Spanish-language paper half-owned by Times Mirror. Both are high cost and high risk. *La Opinion* sold for 25 cents before the stuffing. Now the price is 35 cents. The *Times* is being sold for a dime to people who prefer the Spanish language. The Audit Bureau of Circulations has been leery of the idea and would not count all the gains in the most recent reporting period. Times circulation drifted down to 1,078,186.

Downing seems truly perplexed that critics even raise the issue of the circulation goals. "What I don't understand is what the issue is. Every journalist wants more people to read their story. If we don't grow in circulation, if circulation continues to decline, who will our readers be? Where is this going?"

Sitting here, we seem to be back in the parallel worlds. "I don't think anybody has argued that this is an undesirable thing," I say. "I think the critics don't know how you are going to get there."

"Let me give you an analogy," she counters. "I would wager that when [Michael] Dell decided to sell computers the way he sells them, the folks at IBM thought he was nuts. But he's built a wonderful business that went contrary to IBM. I think we can grow this paper."

At times, it seems more like a religion than a plan.

Parks is next. He is waiting for me in his newsroom office rather than his corporate office.

For three people who apparently think so much alike, their personalities could not be more different. If Willes is cool, collected, and quick, and Downing is cordial, cautious, and occasionally vague, Parks is all smiles and effervescence—the opposite of the classic, laconic, big-city newspaper editor. He is Mr. Enthusiasm.

Even as I bring up Otis's more muted criticism of him, he cuts me off before the words are completely out. If he were to come back as publisher, I begin, he would "evaluate Michael Parks to see if he's grown enough to continue as editor—"

"Absolutely," Parks breaks in. "Yeah. I would say that's one of the chief responsibilities of the publisher."

Parks, fifty-six, landed in his job suddenly and with limited experience as an editor, a corporate infighter, or even an Angeleno. He spent the bulk of his career overseas as a foreign correspondent. Nevertheless, he was highly regarded as a journalist, and he has been viewed in the newsroom as a counterbalance to the newspaper rookies above him.

Still, Parks is every bit the Willes convert.

"Let's look at circulation because it's the subject of so much controversy, not over the wish but over the means," I say. "Willes came in and people scoffed when he said 500,000. Now you and Kathryn are both saying a million. Do you have a time schedule for that?"

"No I don't. Let me tell you how I got to where I was. Mark said, 'Let's grow a half million.' Many people told him that was impossible. I went in and I said, 'Mark, I've got a problem with your half million.' He said, 'Oh, not you too.' 'I've got a different problem, I think. That gets us into 42, 44 percent of the households in Southern California. We have a paper that I believe everybody needs. We have a paper that seeks to create the basis of understanding across Southern California. It's a huge area divided into many different communities. But the only institution, the only thing that can create common understanding is the *Los Angeles Times*. We need to be in well over half the households. We need to have 2 million circulation to do that. That's what I think our goal should be.'"

"Now, the means?"

"Now, the means," Parks repeats. "I turn to my colleagues on the business side and say, 'How do we do that?'" End of explanation, and I think, whew, Parks started all this with a wish.

"Yours is almost a social goal."

"It is," Parks says. "It's very aspirational. It's very aspirational. But it's, you know, it's what I believe a newspaper should be to its community."

A S THEY GOT TO KNOW their new publisher in June of 1999, the reporters found Downing to be pleasant, personal, engaging if a little out of sync with them. She scheduled a meet-and-greet for 9 A.M. the first day after the Fourth of July weekend. Five reporters showed up. Leo Wolinsky later described it as a "cultural mishap"—the new boss not quite on the circadian rhythms of a morning newspaper.

There also was an appreciation for her candor, but by fall the journalists were becoming uneasy with her message. The meet-and-greets had evolved into conversations that sounded ominous.

Downing reportedly said she was concerned that people weren't performing well enough, that at any institution with eleven hundred professionals, at least 10 percent would not pull their own weight. Words like dead wood and bell curves came up. She sounded to many like she was reading from a textbook on modern management. Until everyone was pulling 110 percent, she said, there would be no additional help for the newsroom. Nonperformers needed to improve or find jobs somewhere else. She also said she had read about the "velvet coffin"—the legendary term coined for the cushy days of an era that had ended ten years ago. Long before Downing's arrival at the Times in 1998, a sour newsroom joke had begun calling the old velvet coffin a pine box.

The stir came as the 2000 budget was being prepared, fueling rumors of more cuts. Bill Boyarsky, the city editor, tried to calm things down. He told the staff no one would lose his or her job but there would be a hiring freeze. Parks, who had good-naturedly lamented how time-consuming it had been for him to break in two novice publishers, now sighed to the same friend, "If you apply the bell curve to Nobel laureates, you will get a bottom 10 percent, too. But they still are Nobel laureates."

Then suddenly, all these jitters became background to a blunder of such monumental proportions that it validated every old fear about the church-state wall. It convulsed the newsroom in an uproar that dwarfed anything in the tumultuous decade that had consumed the *Los Angeles Times,* and it raised questions about the very integrity of the paper's editorial independence.

The *Los Angeles Times Magazine* issue of October 10 was highly unusual —164 pages containing a record $2 million worth of advertising. It was dedicated entirely to the opening of the Staples Center, the arena intended to become the centerpiece of a downtown renovation. The *Times* is one of ten "founding partners" of the arena, an arrangement that provides the paper with a skybox and the right to advertise around the facility. For these privileges, the *Times* pays the Staples Center $3 million a year. The payments contain three components: cash, free or discounted advertising, and profits from "joint revenue opportunities." Those opportunities, as outlined in the contract, called for a special section of the newspaper or a commemorative yearbook to be distributed at the Staples Center.

The fatal moment that led to scandal came with the decision to place the joint project in the Sunday magazine. That decision was made in the spring of 1999. Willes was still publisher.

The opening of the arena, home to the city's professional basketball and hockey teams, was big enough to warrant major coverage on its own merits. Sports editor Bill Dwyre and executive sports editor Rick Jaffe began planning a special section even before the deal was signed. But where would such a section go? The business logic was compelling—a huge section in the Sunday paper would dry up ads for the already thin magazine. It should become the magazine.

The thought horrified the magazine's editor, Alice Short. Knowing nothing about the profit-sharing, she felt the subject was just too puffy. She didn't want it. Neither did managing editors John Lindsay, who oversaw the magazine, and John Arthur, who oversaw sports. They argued against it through most of the winter. By spring, they had lost—and disaster became almost unstoppable.

In late September the magazine was shipped off to the printer in Reno, Nevada. That's when Short received her first clue that something was seriously wrong. Someone from accounting was on the phone, wanting man-hour totals put in by the reporters so that the paper could figure its expenses into the division of profits.

Over in sports, Rick Jaffe got the same request. He walked into Dwyre's office.

"You're not going to believe this, but we have shared revenue with the Staples Center," Dwyre recalls Jaffe saying. "We both pry ourselves off the ceiling and I go in to see John Arthur and say, 'Are you aware of this?' He looked pretty amazed."

Not long after, Dwyre bumped into Parks. From their conversation, Dwyre drew the conclusion that Parks already knew. It was still three weeks before the magazine came out.

"There was a fairly long time in the life of a daily newspaper between the discovery and when it appeared," says Short. "So the big question is:

Should we have put something in the newspaper that explained the business relationship?"

"I was trying to communicate to [Parks] how bothered I was by this," Dwyre says. "I remember the last thing I said was, 'I hope nobody finds out about this.'"

There are few secrets in a newsroom. Word leaked out to Rick Barrs, who writes a scrappy, often over-the-top column known as The Finger in the alternative weekly *New Times*. Barrs reported the basic details of the profit-sharing in his usual provocative language. The Finger's self-appointed mission is to needle the *Times* and it rarely disappoints. So not many paid attention when the story broke October 21. That changed when the *New York Times* weighed in with its own piece on Tuesday, October 26, followed by the *Wall Street Journal* the next day. In the *Journal*, the *Times'* advertising director, John McKeon, defended the Staples deal with disastrously ill-chosen words. Why can't "a promotional vehicle like the *L.A. Times*" do a profit-sharing deal, he asked? It was like dropping a match in a tinderbox.

At that morning's news meeting, Parks began by blaming the "Eastern media" for banging the *Times* again. His editors moaned. Parks quickly backed off, saying, "This confirmed all the suspicions that the critics of this general manager system have conveyed."

Parks said he learned of the profit sharing at a management meeting after the magazine went to the printer but before it was published. He also tried to get Downing off the hook, blaming a general manager, obviously Sande, who had since left the paper. (Sande says he left before the crucial question of using the magazine was settled.)

Metro editor Roxane Arnold expressed horror at McKeon's words. Parks can get "very Jesuitical," friends say. Now he did, beginning, "Well, we are a promotional vehicle, we have ads that promote products, we promote ourselves. . . ."

Bill Boyarsky cut in abruptly: "Michael, we are a newspaper. . . ." The meeting ended with several of the editors still wondering if Parks "got it."

McKeon's words were the last straw for the staff, too. Three hundred people signed a petition questioning the paper's integrity and demanding an apology from management. As the petition circulated, Downing apologized to a meeting of senior editors. The publisher blamed her own "fundamental misunderstanding" of editorial principles. She said she had not told Parks of the profit-sharing part of the deal.

The *Times* finally published a story the next day, Thursday.

That afternoon Downing and Parks met with the hostile staff at a meeting that overflowed the cafeteria. This was raw stuff for the *Times*, far more angry and confrontational than anyone can remember seeing before. For more than two hours, until after 5 P.M., well into the witching hour for a morning paper, the staff demanded answers not only to the Staples affair but to many other fears and complaints that had been mounting.

Downing began the meeting, humbling herself before the crowd. She was crestfallen and emotional, her face beet red as she offered her "profound apology." She acknowledged she had put the paper under a "horrific cloud."

"I am responsible," she said.

There was no let-up from the staff. Some questions bordered on insulting. Downing was asked if she'd consider going back to school to learn journalism.

"This is a major, major mistake, but I am publisher of the *L.A. Times* and I am staying the publisher of the *L.A. Times*," she said. "The question is how do I come up the learning curve faster."

Reporter Henry Weinstein, a Berkeley-educated lawyer, rose to face the Stanford lawyer. Weinstein is known as a man who "keeps people honest" with his almost old-fashioned demand for purity and rectitude. He had written his speech.

"I've been here 21 years and I've never seen anything like this," he began. "Anything so horrendous, anything that has galvanized the staff in such a way." The executives who made the deal had crossed the Rubicon and somehow had to be brought back across the river, he said. Taking the blame publicly was admirable on Downing's part, he said, but McKeon's comment incensed him.

"We are not promotional vehicles," Weinstein pronounced.

The applause was the loudest, most sustained of the day. The weekend did little to calm things. The staff wanted an investigation. Parks resisted. David Shaw, the media critic, had volunteered but been rebuffed. The *L.A. Weekly* printed Parks' rationale, which only made things worse: "We know what happened. I don't see anything more to discover."

Now a second petition circulated, demanding the investigative story. Staffers lined up to sign it. Reporter Ken Reich announced he wanted his grandchildren to know he'd signed it. Boyarsky added his name. Most of the Washington bureau, including Doyle McManus, joined.

Each day seemed to produce another trauma. But what happened next was one of those moments in newspapering that few will ever forget.

"It was like nothing I've ever seen before," Dwyre says. "It was out of a movie. A newspaper movie. Like yelling, 'Stop the presses!'"

Otis Chandler could restrain himself no longer. On Wednesday, November 3, he called in and dictated a long letter to Boyarsky. He wanted the city editor to read it to the staff and post it on the bulletin board.

"I took this down like rewrite," Boyarsky says. "When I hung up, someone said, 'Was that who I think it was?'" Boyarsky nodded. He edited the letter and faxed it back. Otis made revisions and returned it. The process went on all afternoon, until 5:30.

Parks asked Boyarsky not to read Otis's letter in the newsroom. Boyarsky wouldn't budge. "I have to," he told Parks. "He's the man who created this paper."

"OK," Parks relented. "Just don't stand on the city desk when you read it."

Boyarsky read the letter to "somber silence," as the *Times* itself described it the next day. Then the cheers exploded.

Chandler said "sadness" was the one word that capsulized his feeling about events at the *Times*. "I am sad to see what I think may be a serious decline of the *Los Angeles Times* as one of the great papers in the country," he wrote. He called the *Times* employees "abused and misused" and the Staples decision "unbelievably stupid." He then took a direct shot at Willes and Downing. A great newspaper cannot be maintained, he said, when both its top executives "have no newspaper experience at any level."

Pictures of Chandler materialized all over the newsroom. His letter hit the Internet. It was retrieved at *Newsday* and flew around the newsroom to the delight of reporters whose dreams had been dashed in Gotham. Times Mirror's Eastern papers did not go easy on the story. The *Baltimore Sun* said the affair left readers "questioning the integrity and credibility of the newspaper itself." The *Times* was "reeling from an ethical controversy," *Newsday* wrote.

Tim Rutten was assigned to write the story for the *Times*. For it, Willes declined comment. But Downing didn't. Her statement landed on Roxane Arnold's desk late in the day. It said, "Otis Chandler is angry and bitter and he is doing a great disservice to this paper and that's too bad because when he was publisher, he did wonderful things. It's too bad when some people get old, they get so bitter."

Rutten looked hard at the sheet of paper and decided to edit his publisher. He cut the last sentence. It went too far. He consulted with Parks. Parks agreed. Few in the *Times* newsroom knew what had actually happened. But the rawness of the quote that did make the paper cost Downing dearly. Even her supporters were aghast. Why make it personal? Her newsroom had protected her from only part of herself.

Parks was also faring badly. Finally forced to reverse himself, he assigned Shaw to do the definitive investigation of the fiasco. He tried to do it with good humor in a situation that had none. He left a slip of paper on Wolinsky's keyboard, stamped with a red rubber stamp that Shaw once gave him as a joke. It said: PARKS CHANGES HIS MIND.

As 1999 neared an end—ten years from that unusual toast in which David Laventhol had said it had been a good year but he was glad it was over—a lull finally settled over the newsroom. No such toast would be made this year. People were waiting for the next shoe to drop. But they could glimpse the near future—the paper's redesign due in April, with a news space cut of 7 percent (making the decade's loss more than 25 percent) . . . the attrition of sixty-five more jobs . . . a travel-budget cut.

The subject of Otis had come and somewhat floated away. Many said they were thrilled he had spoken but were not sure he had really helped the situation. Willes was so angry he could not contain it in public for weeks afterward. Otis had gone surfing a long time ago now.

Still . . .

"Otis will forever be an icon around here," Bill Dwyre says. "He was a publisher who was a newspaper guy. He weighed in in our hour of need. . . .

"It's not that I wouldn't follow Mark Willes or Kathryn Downing. But Otis is Otis. In my career there's been nobody like Otis. I came here as a pimply-faced kid from Milwaukee, Wisconsin, and they made me sports editor and suddenly I'm in this giant place, not ready to be here, but given a chance. This is Patton out there, and you want to go out and get on the tank and ride with him. If Patton comes back and says let's go, there is one more mission, you go with him.

"He said the integrity of the newspaper and journalism has to be first and foremost. For all of us, that is a message we thought was slipping away. And here was our guy, pounding on the table from afar, saying, 'God damn it, let's get our priorities straight.'"

7 The Staple Center affair was part of a broader erosion of journalistic ethics, by no means confined to the L.A. Times. After the scandal broke in Los Angeles, Editor & Publisher magazine surveyed newspaper executives around the country for their reactions. A majority of the publishers who responded to E&P's survey (51 percent) said the revenue-sharing deal was an "acceptable" practice. Even many top editors—a disheartening 19 percent of those responding—called the deal acceptable.

One in three of those surveyed said it was commonplace for American newspapers to have "promotional ties or revenue-sharing arrangements" with people and institutions their reporters cover. Bob Hall, publisher of the Philadelphia Inquirer and Philadelphia Daily News, was quoted as saying that the Staples Center incident had been overblown, and that "there isn't a newspaper in the country that isn't sharing revenue with someone they cover in some form."

The survey asked about other common kinds of ethical violations as well, such as bending the news to favor advertisers. One in four publishers said they saw nothing wrong with asking reporters "to include advertisers in a story," and one in five said it was acceptable to kill or hold a story "that might negatively portray an advertiser."

Another study, conducted in early 2000 by the Pew Research Center and the Columbia Journalism Review, reinforced those findings. When researchers questioned three hundred journalists, both local and national, in various media, one in five said they had faced criticism or pressure from their bosses after producing or writing a piece that was seen as damaging to the company's financial interests. About one in four said they had voluntarily softened the tone of stories or avoided certain stories altogether out of fear that their bosses would object.

About the same time this study came to light, another newspaper scandal hit. Timothy White, publisher of the Hearst Corporation's San Francisco Examiner, testified in court that he had offered Mayor Willie Brown favorable editorial treatment if Brown would support Hearst's controversial purchase of the San Francisco Chronicle. As the Examiner's newsroom exploded in anger, White disclaimed his own testimony and the paper ran an editorial protesting that its pages were free "of any horse trading for favors from politicians."

All of this bespeaks an ethical crisis in journalism, fueled from the top. What was rare about the Los Angeles Times affair was that, in the end, the protests of its reporters and editors had an impact. However, before the Times could recover from the Staples Center *revelations, it was rocked by another surprise. In early 2000, the* Times *and its parent company,* Times Mirror, *were purchased outright by Tribune Co., a Chicago-based media chain. With this acquisition, Tribune Co. became the third largest newspaper chain in the country in circulation, with nearly 3.7 million copies sold on weekdays and nearly 5 million on Sundays. It suddenly owned eleven daily papers instead of four, and twenty-two television stations instead of sixteen. It had become the largest media company in four of the nation's five most populous states—California, New York, Illinois, and Florida.*

The purchase led to the ouster of Times Mirror's tarnished CEO, Mark Willes, and to the replacement of the Times' *publisher, Kathryn Downing, and its editor, Michael Parks. But a new set of uncertainties arose. Tribune Co.'s flagship paper, the* Chicago Tribune, *had lessened its commitment in recent years to national and world news, two areas in which the L.A.* Times *excelled. Furthermore, Tribune Co. had an entirely different newspapering philosophy, based on a media concept, popular on Wall Street, called "synergy," which the new owners promised to introduce at the* Times, *the* Baltimore Sun, Newsday, *and all their other newly-acquired properties.*

Synergy is a process by which several businesses, under a single owner, reinforce one another, making the combination more lucrative than the sum of its separate parts. It may take many forms. When the Disney company makes a movie like The Lion King, *publishes children's books about it, and sells Lion King toys, clothing, and memorabilia in its retail stores, that is synergy. When the Australian media baron Rupert Murdoch uses his newspapers, magazines, movie studio, and book publishing empire to promote his financial and political interests on a global scale, that is a darker kind of synergy.*

Tribune Co. has lobbied hard for a loosening of the legal restrictions on synergy in the media. Specifically, it has lobbied for an end to the Federal Communications Commission's ban against a company acquiring newspaper and broadcast outlets in the same market. The ban was imposed in 1975 to prevent the domination of local news by a single owner. Exceptions have sometimes been granted, but lately the newspaper and broadcast industries have pushed the FCC to scrap the cross-ownership rule entirely. Tribune Co.'s purchase of Times Mirror *was a direct challenge to the rule; the company was deliberately acquiring newspapers (*Newsday *in New York, the* Times *in Los Angeles, and the* Hartford Courant *in Connecticut) in cities where it already owned TV stations. In Chicago, the company owned*

TV and radio stations as well, but that ownership pre-dated the FCC rule and so was grandfathered in place. In purchasing Times Mirror, the company seemed to show confidence (or perhaps it was gambling) that the FCC would not force it to divest any of its overlapping properties. Media analyst John Morton wrote that the deal "may finally bring to a head the issue of cross-ownership of newspapers and television stations." He added: "Maintaining the cross-ownerships in Los Angeles, New York and Hartford is of course key to the success of the Tribune-Times Mirror merger."

Some other chains also own newspapers, radio stations and television stations in the same city, plus online news operations. Some are beginning to share news reports among these media outlets, cross-promote their programs and publications, and sell multimedia advertising package deals. Media General, Cox, MediaNews Group, and Belo have taken a serious interest in this approach. Dean Singleton of MediaNews told Forbes *magazine, "I don't think television standing alone is that great a business. I don't think radio standing alone is that great a business. I'm not sure Internet is that great a business. But all this put together creates a dynamic business. The one last piece is cross-ownership."*

Tribune Co, exploits cross-ownership more systematically than any other newspaper chain, and if its strategy succeeds, and the government does not intervene, other companies will surely follow. In May 1998, in the first article of the State of the American Newspaper series, Ken Auletta described the Tribune Co. as it existed prior to its Times Mirror purchase.

Synergy City

By Ken Auletta

I T WAS A LONG DAY at the annual PaineWebber Media Conference in New York, in December of 1997—a mind-numbing procession of men in dark suits, with wall charts, overhead projections, spreadsheets, and supplements in sheafs. But it was a big occasion, nonetheless: a chance for

America's newspaper companies to show off to Wall Street. One after another they trotted by, like thoroughbreds emerging from the paddock.

For the New York Times Co. and its young chairman, Arthur Sulzberger Jr., there was a prime slot to tell assembled analysts and managers that his company meant to "enhance society" with journalism of the highest order. Other entries preened for the buyers: Gannett, Times Mirror, Knight Ridder . . . strong runners all.

And there in the middle of the pack came four men from Chicago's Tribune Co. They wore dark suits that might have come from the same rack. None of them bore a well-known name: There was the chairman and CEO, John Madigan; the publishing president, Jack Fuller; the broadcasting president, Dennis FitzSimons; and the top financial officer, Donald Grenesko. Their company wasn't the largest, their newspapers weren't the best-read. But that didn't matter—because Tribune had a story to tell . . . and it was just the story Wall Street wanted to hear.

In charts and appendices, they showed a company that owned, at that time, four newspapers—and sixteen TV stations (with shared ownership of two others); four radio stations; three local cable news channels; a lucrative educational book division; a producer and syndicator of TV programming, including Geraldo Rivera's daytime talk show; a partnership in the new WB television network; the Chicago Cubs baseball team; and new-media investments worth more than $600 million, including a $10 million investment in Baring Communications Equity Fund, with dozens of Asian offices hunting out media investments. Tribune's profits were sailing past $600 million a year, and its stock price, as of that December morning, had soared to 58-3/4.

There was an internal logic and consistent language to their talk: Tribune, said the four men, was a "content company" with a powerful "brand." Among and between its divisions, there was "synergy." Whenever there was a bleak number on offer (say, Chicago Tribune circulation down 4 percent), it was coupled with a cheery number (ad revenues up 5 percent). Last year the publishing division brought in more than $430 million. And CEO Madigan said that broadcasting and education revenues would grow roughly twice as fast as newspaper revenues. The year 1997, said finance chief Grenesko, had been "a truly great year—a fitting way to celebrate our 150th anniversary. . . . We expect to set several new records this year in revenues, earnings and cash flow. . . ."

It was a well-scripted, well-rehearsed performance, thorough and thoroughly upbeat. And the word "journalism" was never uttered, once.

THE TRIBUNE CO. may have lacked the stature of the *New York Times* or the cachet of the *Washington Post*. And it was still more than two years away from acquiring Times Mirror, a purchase that would catapult it right up there with Knight Ridder and Gannett, the giants of the newspaper industry. But Tribune had already become a prototype for the cutting-edge newspaper company of the future. Tribune's profit margins, not Gannett's, lapped the industry. Unlike most newspaper companies, which are reliant on print, its non-newspaper revenues accounted for more than half its profits. Its newsrooms were multimedia models, with robotic cameras, digital audio and video equipment, and a central command desk shared by editors from TV, cable, the Internet, and radio. Without the bombast of Mark Willes of the *Los Angeles Times,* Tribune had already done, quietly, what Willes was loudly promising to do: it had lowered the wall between news and business. Here, journalism was *content.*

Executives—and editors, too—went on about *synergy* and *brand extension,* about how their individual companies were not mere newspapers, broadcast stations, or Web sites, but *partners* and *information providers.*

On the surface, the Tribune Co. was a quiet, established firm that took no chances. For all the outward magnificence of the Tribune Tower on Chicago's Michigan Avenue, with its carved inscriptions from Abraham Lincoln and encrusted stones from the Parthenon and Colosseum, the carpets inside looked industrial; the furniture could have come from a Holiday Inn. The extremely unfamous executives upstairs didn't swashbuckle.

But the dull, gray uniform was a deception. The Tribune Co. swung from the trees.

The four newspapers it then owned—the flagship *Chicago Tribune,* the *Orlando Sentinel,* the *Sun-Sentinel* of Fort Lauderdale, and the *Daily Press* in Newport News/Hampton Roads, Virginia—enjoyed 27 percent profit margins. State-of-the-art color printing plants had allowed the papers to shave costs, eliminate composing rooms, and target dozens of zones for news and ads. Its newsrooms were the first to blur the lines separating print, TV, radio, and Web sites. Its sixteen stations put the company in second place among TV group owners, with operations in eight of the top eleven markets. In partnership with Warner Bros., Tribune owned one-quarter of the expanding WB Network, which boosted the ratings of Trib stations and reduced programming costs, and one-third of the cable TV Food Network. Tribune Entertainment had become a major producer and syndicator of television shows. And don't forget the Cubs, who didn't win much but did provide free content for Tribune TV, radio, and cable.

In Tribune's diversification, perhaps most startling—and telling—was its embrace of the new media that many newspaper executives still regarded with fear and bewilderment. (When the *Tribune* readied a front page exclusive on the Chicago police superintendent's friendship with a felon, the news appeared first in its online edition.) Tribune was miles ahead of other companies that moved early into the electronic realm, including Knight Ridder and Cox. An early investor in America Online, Tribune owned 1.5 percent of this 11 million-customer behemoth. Together the two companies created Digital City, which vied with Microsoft's Sidewalk to offer online guides to restaurants and entertainment in cities across America. Again with an eye on Microsoft, Tribune started CareerPath, the country's largest online classified effort, in partnership with various other publishers. Another arm of the company, Tribune Ventures, had invested in an astonishing array of start-ups, including Excite, the Internet navigation network; StarSight, an electronic TV program guide; Peapod, an online grocery shopping service; and CheckFree, the leading electronic payment processing system. And it wouldn't stop there. "We are spending $40 million on new Internet-related stuff in 1998," said Grenesko, up from $30 million in 1997.

Overall, the company generated annual revenues of nearly $3 billion. And the cost of new online investments was more than offset by a 1997 pre-tax gain of $188 million when Tribune sold stock from its Internet investments. Many publishers were already insisting they were in the information —not the newspaper—business. But Tribune had moved money, not just its mouth. "This is a strong company that looks to the future, not the past," said Robert Pittman, the president of AOL.

At Tribune, "synergy" is the mantra. "It's all over the company," said Madigan, the tall, silver-haired and bespectacled chairman and CEO. "It's just gotten to be a way of life." Synergy, Tribune-style, occurs in the Washington office, when James Warren, bureau chief for the *Chicago Tribune*, and Cissy Baker, bureau chief for Tribune Broadcasting, attend one another's story conferences. Synergy occurs when Baker feeds the same TV story to her sixteen stations . . . when a TV or radio station, or twenty-four-hour cable news channel, or one of the online publications, uses a story from the Tribune newspapers . . . when Tribune reporters "extend the brand" by appearing in different media . . . when the Cubs help transform WGN-TV into Chicago's sports mecca . . . when the WB Network saves Tribune TV stations $8 million a year in movie expenses . . . when the Florida papers share sports or legislative coverage . . . or when Digital City on AOL advertises beachfront real estate from the *Sun-Sentinel*'s classified ads.

Synergy has its limits, but at Tribune they're not business limits. They're often matters of taste. Most stories that Jim Warren's D.C. bureau produces are deemed too long, complicated, and verbal—too serious—for Tribune TV, whose stations tend to favor all the news that bleeds. "If all the TV stations want is live shots from the Marv Albert trial and I'm not even covering it, there's no middle ground," says Warren. Though each of the three non-Chicago papers has at least one correspondent in the D.C. bureau, they normally pursue stories with local angles. The papers get almost all their national and international news from wires.

For the study of problems that beset American papers at the close of the century, Tribune is a lab-perfect culture. All the great questions of the business have been asked inside Colonel Robert R. McCormick's splendid old tower:

Can newspaper circulation grow dramatically? (No, say the Tribune people: Growth must be found in other venues.)

If Tribune papers get 38 percent of revenues from classified ads—and an even larger share of profits, says Grenesko—can this precious franchise be saved? (They're working at it—online.)

Is old media dead media? (Old media is "flat," they say.)

Does the future of news lie around the world, or around the corner? This battle, too, has been fought in Chicago, and a winner crowned. The colorful old Colonel, who ruled the paper from 1911 to 1955, affixed this phrase to its masthead: "The World's Greatest Newspaper." He thought its domestic and foreign bureaus eclipsed those of the *New York Times* (which, in the Colonel's view, was a pinko paper anyway). Although Madigan professes great respect for those who risk harm to pursue stories overseas, his business heart lies elsewhere. "The emphasis on local news has been increased tremendously," he says. "The effort is to drive the paper down as much as we can and to get as much local news as we can."

The company has also fought the battle between Wall Street and Main Street, the inherent conflict between shareholders and subscribers. Tribune executives focus unapologetically on their stock price. Grenesko says that every August each business unit is asked to sketch proposed revenues and expenditures for the next year. In September an eleven-person operating committee reviews these figures. The committee usually bounces them back, insisting that spending be held down and numbers be presented again in November, before seeking Tribune board approval in December. What criteria do committee members employ to determine that the first sketch is unrealistic? They do it, says Grenesko, by carefully talking to Wall Street and gauging its response. "The operating committee decides the goal—say, $2.40 a share." Then, he says, they tell the divisions, "This is what Wall Street is expecting from you."

What if Wall Street is unrealistic?

"They have not been unrealistic," says Grenesko.

Even apart from TV and new media—at the Tribune papers themselves—the editor in chief rarely presides at the daily page one meeting. The editor's gaze is fixed on the future, on new zoned sections, multimedia desks, meetings with the business side, focus group research . . . on extending the brand, or opening new beachheads in affluent suburbs. "I am not the editor of a newspaper," says Howard Tyner, fifty-four, whose official resume identifies him as vice president and editor of the *Chicago Tribune* (he would later become senior vice president of the company). "I am the manager of a content company. That's what I do. I don't do newspapers alone. We gather content."

Perhaps, as Tribune's financial success suggests, the newspaper company of the future will not be a newspaper company. Or as executive vice president James C. Dowdle has told Wall Street analysts, "We believe that content alone will not be enough as the Web develops. It will be more than words and pictures. It will be audio and, most important, video. Customers want the whole package. And pretty soon they're going to want it on demand. Tribune is the best-positioned media company to do this." Boasts David D. Hiller, senior vice president for development, "We believe we are building the media network of the twenty-first century—the next NBC."

But at what cost to its newspaper franchise? The *Chicago Tribune*'s circulation, like that of most metro papers, has been slipping for years. It stood at about 658,000 as the twentieth century came to an end. More ominous to some is a perceived decline in that venerable paper's editorial quality. In 1997, *Time* magazine wrote about the most compelling newspapers in America—a subjective exercise, to be sure, that even *Time* hadn't tried for thirteen years. Still, it should be noted: In 1984, the *Chicago Tribune* ranked solidly on the magazine's ten-best list. In September 1997, the *Trib* wasn't even mentioned in the discussion.

E NTERING THE NEWSROOM of the *Chicago Tribune,* your eye is drawn to a massive multimedia desk, around which are arrayed editors from WGN-TV, WGN radio, ChicagoLand TV (or CLTV, the twenty-four-hour local cable news channel), the Tribune's Internet edition, and the Chicago Digital City affiliate . . . all working together to disseminate news around the clock. Behind them looms a 26-by-24-foot TV studio, with an elevated set for an anchor and three cameras. In most companies, a Berlin Wall separates the different media; at the Tribune, all media units report to David L. Underhill, vice president for video and audio publishing. "The goal of our unit," says Underhill, a former engineer and broadcast executive, "is to be a synergy group. I love the word. It implies working across group lines."

This breach of group lines was first achieved at Tribune's Washington bureau, housed on the second floor of an office building at 1325 G Street NW. The sixteen-thousand-square-foot newsroom was converted in 1995 to a joint facility for print, TV, radio, and online. "We are the first bureau to combine newspapers and broadcasting into one newsroom without a wall," says Cissy Baker, a former CNN producer. "Everyone knows each other. Every day, Jim Warren knows what we're covering."

Warren, the *Chicago Tribune* bureau chief, is an intense and thoughtful man who came to the paper in 1984. He's best known in Washington for his campaign against celebrity journalists who accept pay for giving speeches to organizations they cover. But on this December morning he's talking synergy. Shortly before my visit, the Tribune ran a joint-byline piece by print reporter Frank James and TV reporter Shirley Brice about a three-day conference on Web pornography. "There's an example of added value," Warren says. "We turned out a newspaper piece and a TV magazine piece."

He ticks off other bureau synergies. Every Sunday night he and national correspondent Michael Tackett air a one-hour radio show for WGN. Warren orchestrates a weekly *D.C. Journal* for CLTV. National columnist Clarence Page, who has an office in the bureau, is a commentator for WGN. When Warren's thirteen reporters break stories, the Tribune's TV stations interview them in the newsroom. Stations also use reporters as commentators.

TV exposure provides subtle synergy. For Washington reporters who aren't from the *New York Times* or the *Washington Post,* the most common frustration is not getting noticed. "One of the big problems for a paper like us is getting your calls returned," says Page, whose political and social commentaries won a Pulitzer Prize in 1989. "That's one of the reasons I came down here." It's also one of the reasons he appears on TV shows like *The NewsHour with Jim Lehrer* and *The McLaughlin Group.* Page's calls get returned. "I attribute that to my tireless propensity for self-promotion," he says with a smile. "I'm kind of Mr. Synergy."

Warren has often ridiculed the Washington talk shows, but he himself became a regular panelist on *Capital Gang Sunday,* a former CNN shout-fest. "You have no illusions about the frustrations of not being read here," he says. "But to me that's been a challenge. To us it's a reason to try and take a more combative stance toward Washington and the culture." He says he was recently invited to a private party whose host was Washington insider Robert Strauss. "I'd never met him. Why was I invited? It had to be TV."

But even in the *Tribune*'s multimedia newsroom, synergy has its downside. For all the fanfare, Baker has only three full time reporters, and each averages a single story a day. She concedes that on most subjects they "don't have an opportunity to become well-versed." They're also limited in the kinds of stories they can pursue. "The Tribune stations are dedicated to local news," says Baker, who tells me that Denver's 10 P.M. newscast is typical—three minutes a night for national and international news. New York, Chicago and Los Angeles might use "a bit more," she says. Today, the big story she'll pitch to her stations is, again, smut on the Web. "The Internet story is an instant local story," she explains. "Viewers have children, and they have computers."

The grim synergy/exigency calculus is much the same at CLTV. The cable news effort began in January 1993 and now employs 146 souls in a squat, glass-walled office building in suburban DuPage County. What viewers get is News Lite: seven live thirty-minute segments a day, with regular weather and traffic spots. Reporters can update stories seamlessly because studios are being made fully digital. But the seven segments are repeated continuously to fill twenty-four hours. "I'm just proud of the fact that we are not sensational," says Barbara Weeks, the general manager. "We try and present straight news." But there are only five to seven reporters on an average day. By 5 A.M., when the first newscast airs, there is one working reporter; by 8 A.M. there are two. "We can only spend an hour or two on a story," admits Bill Moller, a reporter and anchor who is troubled by this superficiality. Once again, synergy is a goal. WGN radio contributes traffic reports. The *Trib* provides Alicia Tessling, who prepares cooking recipes for cable as well as the paper. The *Trib*, in turn, plugs her cable appearances.

Although 1.7 million cable viewers get CLTV, it reaches an average of only thirty-one thousand homes each hour. Nevertheless, advertising sales more than tripled in four years. And, said Weeks, by bundling the only local cable news channel with the number one newspaper in Chicago—not to mention the number one radio station, the number one independent TV station (which doubles as a cable superstation), the Chicago Cubs, and various online offerings—"any of the Tribune business units can get together and offer a super-synergistic effort. It's very compelling to an advertiser."

A company spokesman said CLTV tuned its first profit in 1999, and Dowdle, the executive vice president, predicted it would blast off in a few years, when technology enables cable to "multiplex"—that is, to multiply ads, just as the newspaper does, by selling zones. For an advertiser, TV becomes an efficient purchase when it can aim a rifle at a specific audience rather than hitting everyone with a shotgun. In "addressable advertising," the size of the audience often matters less than the ability to target it. "If we can regionalize the signals," Dowdle says, "and divide Chicagoland into five or six different regions, which could possibly correspond with our news-paper sections—Northwest, Southwest—we could then have information that would be relevant to the Northwest section. We could sell ads to the Northwest section. That's the upside of it."

For the moment, in all areas of the Tribune Co., synergy seems to herald "fill-in-ergy." If reporters help out on TV or radio, they enjoy the exposure —and the company benefits from their extra work—with no extra pay. If Jim Warren works harder, he really doesn't need a secretary, so he goes without. The bureau operates without its own copy editor. Warren says he has lost a handful of positions in recent years to expanded suburban cov-erage in Chicago. So now no one in the bureau covers the Pentagon; they fill in. Warren says the bureau has shrunk from seventeen people at one point to fourteen.

Tackett, who became a national correspondent in 1986, says he was told only once that he "couldn't go somewhere because it cost money." Still, he feels the squeeze: "I'd like to see more people hired here." Ernie Cox Jr., a top *Trib* photographer for four decades, told me just before his recent retirement, "I'm not able to travel as often as I used to. . . . I travel nowhere unless I can get in a car and cover it. I used to get on a plane and cover anything up and down the West Coast. Now they just use the AP." When President Clinton came to Akron, Ohio, for a town hall meeting on race relations, the *Trib* wasn't there. It published a front page account by James Bennet—of the *New York Times.*

Cost-cutting has trimmed the *Tribune*'s once-vaunted network of bureaus. The paper went from eleven domestic bureaus and thirty-two correspondents in 1987 to six bureaus (Washington, New York, Los Angeles, Atlanta, Denver, and Springfield, Illinois) and twenty-three corre-spondents in 2000. Overseas bureaus were trimmed from eleven to nine —offices in Toronto, Manila, and Berlin were shuttered, although Johannesburg was added. Plus, the Moscow office was reduced from two reporters to one. (The *New York Times,* by contrast, maintains twenty-three foreign bureaus.)

Tackett, for one, sees advantage in a homier *Tribune.* "I don't have to worry about a bureau chief who fought in the last war sitting over my shoulder and telling me what to do," he says. Tackett goes out of his way to praise Warren, as do others, for refusing to "bigfoot" his minions and snatch the best assignments. "I don't have people in Chicago looking over my shoulder. You have fewer layers." Reporters also say they appreciate not being pigeonholed. "I'm the New York bureau chief," says Lisa Anderson, "but I just spent one month in Africa doing a team report. I've had the luxury of only writing three stories since May. Why? Because I'm part of a team of 12 working on a series." That team traveled throughout Africa, South America, and Asia to investigate child-sponsorship agencies.

In fact, raw figures show the *Trib* staff hasn't shrunk at all. In the last decade, the number of full time editorial employees has risen from 613 to approximately 700. And it's no mystery where the troops are headed. For example, there's that glass-walled office amid the parking lots in DuPage County. . . .

WITH FEWER THAN 200,000 customers in the city proper, the *Trib* doesn't have the largest circulation in Chicago—the *Sun-Times* does. But the *Tribune* has been the paper of choice for Chicago's vast Republican suburbs since the days when Colonel McCormick branded Herbert Hoover a closet leftist and raged against the "crackpot socialism" of the New Deal. Those suburbs are still the heart of the *Trib*'s 654,000 daily and one million Sunday circulation—and the place where affluent readers entice advertisers.

Last year, to shore up a circulation slide in the western suburbs of DuPage, the former fox-hunting country where the Colonel used to reside, bureau chief Terry Brown was dispatched to direct a platoon of 10 reporters and three photographers who bivouacked in the CLTV newsroom. The office also got a beefed-up sales and circulation staff of about 160. In Schaumburg, another wealthy western suburb, another circulation drop drew another new Trib army—40 correspondents.

"One of our goals is to get more involved in the community," says Brown, a former editorial page writer and *Wall Street Journal* reporter. In his office overlooking the CLTV parking lot, Brown is newsroom casual— no tie. He's one of four lieutenants who help command this suburban outpost, along with one executive for advertising, one for distribution, and one for promotion. They all report to the DuPage general manager, or "mini-publisher." Brown says the team has undertaken extensive market research, primarily focus groups, to find out what readers want. What he has learned, he says, is this: "They don't think of us as their local paper. The

Tribune has the reputation of being aloof and arrogant." Brown talks about how the *Trib* must become "more visible" and "more friendly." The DuPage executives are even discussing sponsoring Little League teams.

But isn't there a conflict between being "more friendly" and the demands of independent journalism?

"I think you can be both," Brown says. "You can be aggressive and yet not be aloof."

It's in the suburbs where some *Trib* reporters most fear a breach of the wall between church and state, but in fact the wall has been chipped at everywhere. The *Trib*'s managing editor, forty-two-year-old Ann Marie Lipinski, along with corporate marketing executive David Murphy, head the paper's "branding committee." Together, they sit in on reader focus groups to determine, in the words of *Tribune* publisher Scott C. Smith, "what they should be writing about." Smith quickly adds, "Now, we don't substitute a popularity contest for journalistic judgment." But he insists on "a balance." And Lipinski, who won a Pulitzer in 1988 for investigative reporting (and was to become Tyner's successor in 2000), doesn't camouflage her business intent. "I'd like more people buying the newspaper," she says. "Certainly increased circulation is either 1-A or 1-B of this project." She sees her forays into marketing as a learning experience, an opportunity to reach beyond the confines of the newsroom. "I don't think research, a priori, is a bad thing—that's what you do when you do interviews," she says. "The objective is not to conduct a poll on which five stories should be on page one tomorrow. Readers expect us to make those decisions." But she adds, "I put some stories in the paper that readers suggested." In a 1997 focus group, for example, as the crisis with Iraq was building, she heard a reader blurt, "No one's explained to me what this son of a bitch has. Can he bomb me?" Lipinski promptly ordered up a story on the actual military and terrorist threat posed by Saddam Hussein.

DuPage bureau chief Brown, now in his early fifties, bears the credentials of a traditional journalist. "One reason the editor of the newspaper asked me to come out here," he says, "is that I am an old-timer, and I can stand up to advertising people and can say, 'Look, we are not going to print what the advertiser wants.' Yet I'm softening up. This is going on in the industry. You see it at the *L.A. Times*. The editorial department of the *Chicago Tribune* was the least-understood part of the paper. We wanted it that way. We wanted to protect our turf." But thumb-in-your-eye defiance has to change, he says, because newspapers are fighting for their lives and need better communication between business and editorial, not to mention with the community. "I have a better understanding, or at least empathy," for the business side, he says. "If we do a special dining guide that our advertising people sell a lot of ads against, they'll say, 'We're not trying to control content. We just want to know if you're going to be writing about a certain restaurant.' I don't see anything wrong with them wanting to know about the product—God, I'm talking like this, talking about product! But I have no problem as long as they don't make requests about what I write or when."

Isn't there danger of pressure to assure a friendly review?

"I would be very troubled if I saw advertising guys talking to my reporters," Brown answers. "That's where I draw the line." But Brown is operating in an environment that favors teamwork and cooperation. If the old newsroom culture was too cynical, the fear is that it will be replaced by an environment whose imperative—from the business side, from market research, from the community—is to be too friendly.

The church-state issue intensified at the *Tribune* as its focus grew increasingly local. The paper publishes eight zoned editions, and the number will likely rise dramatically within the next few years. There is widespread concern in Chicago that the *Trib* has become a suburban paper. U.S. Rep. Jesse Jackson Jr. (D-Ill.), who praises the paper for "being very fair to me," nonetheless observes, "I didn't realize until I went to suburbia that oftentimes they don't read the same paper I do." What they're missing, he says, is news from another planet—from the heart of his district on the South Side of Chicago, for instance, where eighteen shopping malls have closed and the sagging economy stands in grim contrast to the robust growth in affluent suburbs. "I wish the *Tribune* wasn't just catering to those who are doing well."

Hank DeZutter, a Malcolm X College journalism teacher and cofounder of the Community Media Workshop, says this about today's *Trib:* "Now it's like a baseball team. It can move. It doesn't have the passion for Chicago that it had, as bad as it was. I don't think it cares about the city." Clarence Page doesn't share that assessment, but he still worries. "What bothers me is that we have a Northwest section story and we keep it only in the Northwest section of the paper. What troubles me is when we ghettoize. . . . It happens all the time."

This criticism is sired by a perception, shared by many *Tribune* reporters, that editors are fixated on local news. "It is more difficult to get national and international stories on page one," grouses a Washington correspondent. Adds deputy managing editor James E. O'Shea, "One school of thought thinks we ought to be intensely local. My view is that we ought to be more regional. By that I mean a broader newspaper." He reached this conclusion after watching his former paper, Gannett's *Des Moines Register,* constrict its focus from statewide to central Iowa and lose nearly 200,000 subscribers from historic circulation highs. "The people in Iowa bought the *Des Moines Register* not to get intensely local news," O'Shea says, adding that readers were proud of the paper's scope and reputation. He fears Illinois consumers will turn to the *New York Times* for national and international news, and to local papers for local news. Thus the *Tribune* might get squeezed.

The *Tribune* recently lost its foreign editor, Thom Shanker, to the Washington bureau of the *Times.* After five years in Moscow and two in Bosnia, Shanker served only one year as foreign editor. He told associates he saw the writing on the wall: The number of bureaus was shrinking, the church-state barrier in the suburbs had become a picket fence. Although Shanker wrote a farewell letter extolling the editors' commitment to "excellence" and asserting that his move was "less about leaving the *Tribune* than about joining the *Times,*" he was, in fact, more depressed than he let on. Like others in the newsroom, he thought the paper had suffered an identity crisis. As a member of the national staff puts it, "The paper isn't sure anymore whom it is serving."

Or perhaps it is sure. When I ask the publisher, Scott Smith, to respond to the criticism that the paper is retreating from national and international news, he praises his far-flung staff and says he respects that view. "But the economics are not with that. The *New York Times* has economics that work for them in that regard."

Newsroom critics detect the dreaded voice of a "bean counter" in Smith's response—a complaint at the core of the 1993 book by former *Tribune* editor James D. Squires, *Read All About It! The Corporate Takeover of America's Newspapers.* The "blueprint" for the newspaper company of the future, wrote Squires, was drawn by former Gannett chairman Al Neuharth, who gobbled up newspapers, slashed costs, shortened stories and generally operated as if his principal audience was Wall Street.

But Lipinski, who joined the paper as a summer intern in 1978 and, save for a Nieman Fellowship, has never left, disputes her former mentor. "I feel like I'm working for a paper that's vastly better than the one I joined," she says. "The paper was relatively mediocre then. What Jim is describing is the fashionable criticism. It's very hard for me to balance that criticism with what I know my tools are. . . . If I thought quality didn't matter here, I wouldn't stay."

It is hard to argue that the *Tribune* is not a better paper than it was when Colonel McCormick, like William Randolph Hearst, whimsically ordered up stories and used the front page to ridicule or punish foes. Yet the paper that the Colonel called the World's Greatest is clearly not that. It is not the same paper that in 1947 was the first to have at least one reporter on duty every minute the Senate or House was in session. It hasn't covered the White House with the same intensity as it did under Squires. The current paper has weaknesses that can be noted at a glance. The Sunday magazine and book review are painfully thin. The vaunted international coverage is sometimes thin, as well. Although the October 4, 1997, paper contained a page one story from Moscow on the joint space mission, the few inside pages of overseas news were filled with wire copy, with the exception of one *Tribune* short from Havana. Arts and entertainment reviews almost always run a day late (e.g., a Monday opening will be covered on Wednesday). These specific nits, however, are subsumed by the larger criticism that the *Tribune* is, well, weaker.

"In some ways you're seeing a newspaper not quite as good as it was five years ago," says Jon Margolis, the *Tribune*'s national politics writer for twenty-two years. He left the paper in 1995 to write books. "When the bean counters took over," he says, "they hired people who had no memory." The absence of memory became so acute that the paper called back Margolis as a consultant for the 1996 presidential election. He and other alumni can point to a series of changes in service of the bottom line: There has been a delayering of editors; the paper no longer hires reporters after a three-month tryout, but employs "associates" who remain on probation a full year; the paper lost many experienced reporters, all hired in the '70s—Margolis, Eleanor Randolph, Harry Kelly, Jim Jackson—that it didn't replace. "In the last seven to eight years," Margolis says, "you could count on the fingers of your hand the number of established reporters they've hired. There's not much bench strength." As a consequence, he says, the worst effects are yet to come. "To the extent that Squires is right, it's more prospectively. You can see a slight weakening. Not because people are not good, but because there are not enough good people."

The *Tribune* has many strengths, including a seriousness of purpose that prompted it to pour enormous resources into investigating the tragic rash of deaths among Chicago children in 1993. In December 1995 the *Trib* published an eleven-part series exploring the ordeal of modern Africa. In June 1996 it exposed inadequate medical supplies aboard the nation's airliners, a shortcoming more lethal than crashes. The paper often carries snap-to-attention writing, such as Charles Leroux's profile of eighty-two-year-old Bernard O'Halloran, whose debilitating strokes separated him from Agnes, his wife of sixty years. The sports section is readable and feisty, the TV criticism pungent and apt. Its editorial page, under former *New York Times* editorial writer N. Don Wycliff, doesn't have the bite of Wycliff's former page. But he says proudly that the *Trib*'s page is "contrarian." It opposed the independent counsel law that so bedeviled the Clinton White House, pushed for elimination of Illinois's teacher-tenure laws, and lashed Israeli prime minister Benjamin Netanyahu, "whose reckless and provocative behavior has jeopardized the chances for peace"—a blunt stance that could not be found in the *Times* or *Post*. In elections, Wycliff ruefully concedes, the *Trib* is still plagued by knee-jerk Republican instincts. In the 1996 U.S. Senate race, he says, the *Tribune* couldn't turn fast enough and wound up supporting Al Salvi, a Republican who was "way far out there." Tradition, he believes, triumphed over judgment.

The *Trib* is rightly proud of John Kass, who took over the late Mike Royko's page three column. The son of a Greek grocer from Chicago's South Side, Kass is a college dropout who joined the Merchant Marine and worked as a butcher before becoming a newspaperman. For ten years he covered City Hall for the *Trib*. The competition to fill Royko's slot was ferocious, and the choice of native Chicagoan Kass, says Thom Shanker, "spoke a lot for the paper and how it didn't forget its roots."

Here's the beginning of a column Kass wrote about an alderman who was forced to resign because he enriched himself and friends of Chicago's mayor:

> Ald. Patrick Huels spent a lifetime as a loyal appendage—and only a week as an infected liability.
>
> So on Tuesday night, with the political health of Mayor Richard Daley at stake, Huels finally was removed after several painful days of sawing.
>
> The Bridgeport alderman is not the first to be amputated, and he won't be the last. It's the way of politics. But despite the operation, the bleeding won't stop.
>
> Something happened between Daley and his city this week that simple damage control and public relations spinning won't fix. . . . There's money being made at City Hall for the mayor's close circle of fat-cat friends who eat no-bid contracts and sweetheart deals.

There's a freshness to Kass—the kind of freshness sorely missing these days from Bob Greene's columns. (Come the third week in November, Greene is in Dallas, so he fills his space with rumination on the death of JFK. . . .) In time, Kass's name, like Royko's and Studs Terkel's, may become identified with Chicago.

But what about the news—the hard information that Alderman Huels used his public office to benefit his private security firm? That wasn't the

Tribune's story. The *Sun-Times* broke it. Not only was it first, the feisty tabloid also skinned the culprits with a populist, throw-the-bums-out crusade. When the *Trib* finally weighed in on the story, it was in a manner perhaps symptomatic of why it got beat. Critics call it a simple lack of passion. The *Trib* already had two reporters exploring the mores of the City Council, so they used the Huels scandal as a springboard for in-depth, contextual pieces illuminating aldermanic culture—and explaining why that culture condoned Huels's behavior. More Socrates than Patrick Henry, the *Trib* was so busy telling readers "why" that critics say it almost forgot about "what" or "who."

"The *Tribune* has withdrawn from the investigative journalism business," says Michael Miner, media columnist and senior editor of the *Chicago Reader,* an alternative weekly. "Instead of an investigation designed to nail someone, we get long studies of poverty. Their investigative reports are meant to help us understand, not change anything. A lot of the fun is drained out of the *Tribune. . . .* The *Tribune* is not in the pelt-bagging business anymore. It would rather commune with the bear."

Miner has a theory on why the *Trib* is fixated on "why." He links what he sees as a vice to what others see as the virtues of the man at the top: the president of Tribune Publishing, Jack Fuller.

Fuller has his share of august newspaper credentials—he won a Pulitzer Prize as editor of the *Trib*'s editorial page, and succeeded Jim Squires as editor in 1989. Now he oversees all four *Tribune* papers. But his resume also features interesting "outside" experience. He got his J.D. from Yale Law School in 1973. He served two years as special assistant to the U.S. attorney general in the Ford administration. He has lived on both sides of the barricade —which no doubt contributes to his tendency to see four sides to every issue. Fuller says that from his former view in the Justice Department, he saw "a disconnect between what I was observing and what the press was reporting. It was fascinating how right the press was on so many facts that people tried to hide—and how wrong they were about people's motivation."

At the *Trib,* the bearded Fuller is perceived as an intellectual. Books form small mountains on his desk and fill the shelves behind him. He writes his own books, too, including a philosophically challenging entry on newsroom ethics, *News Values: Ideas for an Information Age.* The book roams easily from Greek and Roman philosophers to the Reformation and the Founding Fathers. Along the way, Fuller picks up, examines, doubts, and finally dismisses many of journalism's platitudes. Fuller, for example, rejects the totem that journalists are meant to "comfort the afflicted and afflict the comfortable." The statement "makes sense," he writes, if it means journalists should report on the suffering of the poor and "have the courage to tell unpleasant truths about the powerful. . . . But it also can be an invitation to bias." Should journalists always afflict the comfortable, even when they do no harm? "Should they afflict them simply because of their comfort? And what about the afflicted? What if telling the truth to and about them would cause them discomfort?" To critics like Miner, this is Fuller blather: "The man is drenched in his philosophy, which is scrupulous to a fault."

In his office at the Tribune Tower, Fuller is still dismissing easy truths—for example, the charge that the newspaper has turned its back on its hometown. "We still devote more inches to the city of Chicago than anyone else does," he says. But he adds that a newspaper must balance reader interests. "If you're in Lincoln Park," he says, mentioning a pricey Chicago enclave, "are you interested in who the sheriff of Cook County is? Some things are universally important, and some things are not."

Fuller has plenty of allies in the newsroom. The growing interest in suburban news, says two-time Pulitzer winner William C. Gaines, "hasn't detracted from anything that I've seen." Gaines joined the paper as a police reporter in 1963 and is its investigative ace. He says the paper is as good, and hard, as it ever was. "We always have large projects going. I see the editorial department expanding." The *Tribune* is not without scoops: It forced Chicago police superintendent Matt Rodriguez to resign after revealing his brother-like friendship with a felon; it spotlighted police abuse on the front page; it revealed how some immigrants were assumed guilty until cleared by drug tests. Likewise, columnist Kass rejects the notion that the *Trib* was somnolent on the Huels scandal. "In other words, let's have some more Gotcha!" he snaps. "We got beat. It was a good story. We've beaten them. That's the ball game. You don't need all this intellectualizing about it."

But Fuller is eager to join the debate. He wants his reporters to be explainers, not hunters. "I'm not sure this newspaper can justly be accused of being too polite," he says. "If anything, the journalism of today is too often fixed on finding the culprit. I believe there are culprits, and we should find them and get them out of office. I believe we were spoiled by Watergate to believe every ill of society can be explained by one man. It's jejune. But I don't think the real purpose of journalism is jejune. The influence I'd love to have is to say our job is to get as close as we can, every day, to an accurate depiction of how the world works, without being afraid to point fingers, and yet not feel we have to."

Some at the paper would trade Fuller's cool musing for some old-fashioned heat. There would have been hell to pay under Squires, they say, if the *Trib* got beat on a corruption story. Columnist Page praises the paper's explanatory journalism but says, "That place is like an aircraft carrier. It's a very large operation. It needs strong leadership at the top—a go-for-the-jugular instinct. I haven't seen that instinct since Jim Squires and Bill Jones." Jones was a young Pulitzer-winning investigative reporter who became managing editor. He died of cancer in 1982.

When Squires was editor, through much of the '80s, shouting in the newsroom was common. People who made mistakes feared for their jobs. "The *Tribune* is a place where there is lots of excellence, but no one yells at you if you don't achieve excellence," says a former *Trib* reporter who asked not to be identified. "The *Tribune* is putting so much of its effort into synergy and brand." When Squires left, says a veteran *Trib* reporter who also requested anonymity, "passion walked out the door." Squires may have been explosive, "but so was Colonel McCormick. It sure helps to have a strong personality at the helm."

Lipinski makes a point of saying that there was a "dressing down—but not in the center of the newsroom." And no yelling. Her boss, Tyner, concurs. "There's not been a lot of screaming since Squires left," he says. Tyner's arm sweeps toward the newsroom, just outside the bay window of his office. "If you went around here and talked to folks," he says, "what you'd get is, 'We don't want to be flashy.'"

For his part, Squires is sticking to the critique in his passionate and acerbic book. Now raising horses at his farm outside Lexington, Kentucky, he praises Fuller and Tyner as good men who deserve credit for not tarting up the news. But today's *Tribune*, he insists, lacks "energy and passion." He links this failing to his book's larger theme, the corporatization of news. "The newspaper has always been relevant to the lives of people when it had passion," he says. "What it's trying to do now is keep up its profit margins. That's different. You're looking at a good newspaper, a newspaper with talent and serious people at the top, like Jack Fuller and Howard Tyner. But they are existing in a different world. I'm not as concerned about the survival of the newspaper as I am about the survival of journalism. What the *Tribune* is today is what every big newspaper is to its owner—a franchise. It's viewed differently than newspapers used to be viewed. We used to think of it as a quasi-public service to inform people about what they needed to know: Who's cheating whom? . . . What disease is lurking? . . . What government is wasting their tax money? . . . Journalism's job has always been to educate people. Today the owners view it as an information franchise whose job it is to make money."

FOR SEVERAL MONTHS I subscribed to the *Chicago Tribune* and the other three newspapers that fly the Tribune Co. flag. A few impressions hit me immediately. First, the three sister papers get their national and international stories from the wire services and other newspapers—though rarely from the *Chicago Tribune*. This frustrates *Trib* reporters, who wonder what became of synergy. Alas, Chicago is an hour behind its colleagues in Florida and Virginia. "Usually they don't get us stories on time," says the *Sun-Sentinel* managing editor, Ellen Soeteber, who came from the *Trib* three years ago and is widely credited with bringing new energy with her.

A second impression is that these are essentially local papers, probably better than most in their mid-range circulation categories. (The *Fort Lauderdale Sun-Sentinel* daily circulation in 1999 was 258,000; the *Orlando Sentinel*, 260,000; and the *Daily Press* in Newport News, 93,000.) Tribune acquired the Florida papers in the mid-'60s, the *Daily Press* in 1986. When comparing the *Trib*'s acquisitions with Gannett's, Fuller pointedly says, "Our signature is running good newspapers, and when we buy a newspaper we make it better."

Although the smaller papers don't publish as much investigative or enterprise reporting as the *Tribune,* you can still find exemplary work. The Orlando paper undertook a months-long investigation of Central Florida's overcrowded schools, a series that helped provoke a special session of the state legislature. Nor did Orlando editors censor TV critic Hal Boedeker when he eviscerated the monotonous coverage of Central Florida News 13—the *Sentinel* and Time Warner's jointly owned twenty-four-hour cable news channel. The Fort Lauderdale paper exposed Florida's sex entertainment business. The reporter on that six-part series, thirty-four-year-old José Lambiet, who arrived two years ago from the *New York Daily News,* marvels, "They left me alone for six months!" Nor did editors flinch when he wrote a sidebar on the paper's practice of taking ads from sex services. Lambiet wishes the *Sun-Sentinel* did as many whistle-blowing stories as the rival *Miami Herald;* he says the *Daily News* was "more dynamic to read" and adds, "We're kind of boring." But he's proud of his new paper. "We think more about what we do. The *News* just slaps things in the paper. They did a sex series in the *News*—it took them a week to do. An editorial meeting at the *News* was like a gang meeting. Whoever yells the loudest gets the story. Here they think things through a bit more."

In Virginia, the *Daily Press* has run tough editorials blasting Pat Robertson and the National Rifle Association. And when Oliver North ran for the Senate in 1994, it published weekly editorials headlined "Ollie's Lies." Publisher Jack Davis sounds like the *Chicago Tribune* editor he once was, citing these editorials among his proudest achievements. "We lost maybe hundreds of subscribers who were mad at us for our weekly insistence that Oliver North was not a trustworthy person," he says.

A third impression is that there are notable weaknesses in the Tribune papers. In Orlando, with a market heavy on young service workers (courtesy of Disney World, Universal Studios, et al.), the *Sentinel* seems light on government reporting. Publisher John Puerner says his audience wants mostly sports, classifieds, and entertainment listings. At each of the papers, half the front page is locally generated, but their A sections invariably brim with bylines from other sources. For example, a randomly chosen Fort Lauderdale edition ran forty stories in its twenty-eight-page main section. Only two came from the *Sun-Sentinel* itself; thirty-eight were from other newspapers or wire services, and that was not unusual. All five columns on the op-ed page were syndicated.

Fort Lauderdale's editor is Earl R. Maucker, a neat, mustachioed man of fifty who tends to speak in cliches ("Nothing succeeds like success!"). But he is thoroughly up-to-date on Tribune Co. philosophy: "This is, in all honesty, a reader-driven newspaper." Maucker says he wants readers to be "comfortable." And they won't be if the "newspaper breaks on the doorstep" because it is "heavy" with government and investigative news. The result of this ethic can be seen across the company: All three sister papers feel light, at least by metro standards.

It doesn't take a Wall Street whiz to notice another characteristic of Tribune papers: financial health. Unlike many city newspapers, they are located in vibrant economic enclaves. The Orlando paper monopolizes its region. Only 15 percent of its readers, says editor John Haile, read a second newspaper. The *Sentinel* reaches 37 percent of all potential households, 55 percent on Sunday, according to Puerner's figures, and offers advertisers 140 zones—one reason he cites for revenues growing 25 percent over the past four years. Haile prides himself on the fact that he thinks like a publisher as well as an editor, and he frets about inroads Cox might make into this market. Cox already owns nearly half the *Daytona Beach Journal,* plus Orlando's top TV station and a cluster of radio stations. But the *Sentinel,* he knows, has a sizable head start.

In Fort Lauderdale, the *Sun-Sentinel* owns fast-growing Broward County. No longer the mecca for college students on spring break, this has become an affluent residential area, more like Beverly Hills than Coney Island. The *Sun-Sentinel* has more competition than its brethren in Orlando—from Cox's *Palm Beach Post* to the north and Knight Ridder's *Miami Herald* to the south—but it has better penetration numbers.

Reflecting more affluent, more news-conscious readers, 44 percent of potential subscribers receive the paper daily, and 62 percent on Sunday, says publisher Robert J. Gremillion. Adds editor Maucker, "People would die for the kind of problems I've got!"

In Virginia, the *Daily Press* lost circulation when it raised its price a few years ago (a mistake publisher Davis says he would not repeat). He says circulation has stayed flat for the past ten years, but revenue has increased "dramatically." The *Press*, like its sister papers, has state-of-the-art printing presses that allow later deadlines and zoned editions. Plus, all three papers operate without unions, affording them more freedom to manage costs. And, like the *Chicago Tribune*, they have redefined how they do business.

Indeed, this is yet another characteristic of Tribune papers: a business culture that permeates every edition. Across the company, editors and publishers express a common devotion to editorial independence. No doubt this is genuine. No doubt Fort Lauderdale's Ellen Soeteber is correct: "In some ways these pressures were worse in the old days. It was more small town, and the newspaper was part of the local power structure." She concedes there's always a risk when the wall between business and journalism is lowered. "But less of a risk than before the corporatization of newspapers —which has allowed them to be more independent of the local power structure."

A financially strong corporate owner offers protection, adds Jane Healy, managing editor of the *Orlando Sentinel*. She won a Pulitzer in 1988 for a series exposing the downside of unchecked development. "Developers pulled advertising, and the publisher didn't flinch," she remembers. "I never even heard about it. That's a benefit of a healthy newspaper."

On the other hand, corporatization brings a new and, sometimes, too-cozy culture. In October, the *Sentinel* stripped a story about the start of its twenty-four-hour cable news operation across the top of the front page: "Local news channel debuts tonight." The *Daily Press*, on election day, plastered its front page with a notice to "Visit Digital City Hampton Roads tonight for updates on the governor's race" and to watch columnist Jim Spencer on WAVY-TV.

With passion, Orlando's Haile speaks of the need to preserve the wall between business and news because "the newspaper trades on its credibility." But Haile is a reasonable man—someone who loves his job, sees himself as an entrepreneur and takes pride in being open to change. So he adds, "Too many journalists seem afraid to confront the future. It's almost as if we deal with new media that somehow journalists will make the wrong decision about where you draw the line. I think you ought to have more confidence in yourself." The *Sun-Sentinel*'s Maucker goes further. "It's all attitude," he says. "You don't have to declare there are no walls. We've had project teams since I got here. There's always been a belief here in a team approach. . . . There are no walls. There shouldn't be any walls."

Does this mean, I ask, that someone from ad sales could call his editors?

Well, it's okay to call him, Maucker says, which is what most editors would say. But then he goes further: It's okay for an ad manager to call his bureau chiefs too.

At Tribune papers, the lingo of market research fills the air. People talk of setting up "joint task forces," of "listening to readers." Says Haile, "We have to rethink how we define news. My newsroom may not be in sync with what readers think. For example, if no one in my newsroom is interested in Puerto Rico and my readers are, we are in trouble." The editor, like the publisher, must bring a business sensibility to his mission. Haile welcomes the paper's cumbrous research into what readers want. "You've just got to try and keep ahead of them. We have to have some relevance to them. If they have no interest in government and politics, we have to find out what they are interested in." Ask publisher Davis to cite the strengths of his Virginia paper, and he immediately answers, "It knows its market." Fort Lauderdale's Soeteber says, "We're oriented to our readers."

To track readers' desires, editors attend two monthly focus group sessions, a common practice at the four papers. Giving readers more of what they want, Soeteber insists, "is not dumbing down the news. It means what issues are most meaningful to their lives." Maybe. Or it might also be true, as James O'Shea, the *Chicago Tribune*'s deputy managing editor, tartly observes, that most readers don't know what they want. "If I go to buy a suit," he says, "I don't go and say, 'I want a brown suit.' A newspaper is the same. You don't know what you want when you pick it up."

Finally, one notices that each Tribune property sees itself as an information company, not just a newspaper. Each has a multimedia desk. Each has an online newspaper and a Digital City guide on AOL. (Orlando also offers a Black Voices site.) Each has a TV broadcast partner or a twenty-four-hour cable news partner. And, except for Orlando, each has a radio partner.

Indeed, the *Sentinel,* says publisher Puerner, is "a regional media holding company." He sees his newspaper in the pivot, with a variety of businesses rotating about it: three magazines, including *Magic Magazine,* a joint publication with the Orlando Magic basketball team; a direct-marketing company, Sentinel Direct, which sells the newspaper's database to advertisers and direct-mail firms; a sign company, Sentinel Signs, which manufactures banners and storefront signs; a market research firm, Sentinel Tele-Services; Sentinel Classifieds, a company that bundles newspaper, online and magazine classified ads; and Sentinel Printing, which produces TV books and other publications. The mission is one-stop service for customers, be they readers or advertisers. "It's like mountain climbing where, as you go up, you have to secure yourself and keep moving up the rock," Haile says. "We know about technological change. But as you go up you have to find some place to secure yourself."

This climbing entrepreneurship is touted in every newsroom. Editor Davis of the *Daily Press* says, "The whole energy level of the newspaper has picked up. You feel you are reaching a bigger audience, having more input, with hardly any more work." Reporters at the four papers sometimes express annoyance that they're not paid for these extra appearances. But they welcome the occasionally larger audiences and the sense of riding the wave of the future. "I feel we're in the process of carving out our place with technology in the marketplace," says Doreen Christensen, who has worked at the *Sun-Sentinel* for eighteen years and currently edits its TV section. "I view it as my job to assure that the newspaper has a place in that new marketplace, and making sure that I am not left behind when the train leaves the station."

There is less mention of the downside: resources and attention being siphoned from the papers. In Fort Lauderdale, publisher Gremillion tells me that some money for multimedia is coming out of the newsroom. But there is an advantage, he insists, when other media provide "a promotional vehicle to brand" the newspaper. These promotional platforms reach nonreaders. They also, he says, save marketing dollars because they are "free" advertising. It all dovetails neatly with the mission of the Tribune Co., which corporate literature describes as "an information company" seeking "to create leading branded content."

OVER THE COMPANY'S 151-year history, three men loom largest: pioneering editor and Lincoln champion Joseph Medill; his grandson, Robert McCormick, who reigned—the only word for it—for more than four decades; and Charles Brumback, who was CEO just from 1990 to 1995, but whose passions dominated the company throughout the '80s and, to a large extent, still do.

The vituperative, jingoistic, FDR-bashing *Tribune* of Colonel McCormick was both biased and lively—troglodyte and risk-taker, abuser of free speech and champion of it. In his engrossing biography *The Colonel: The*

Life and Legend of Robert R. McCormick, Richard Norton Smith dissects and celebrates the "complexities of this lifelong maverick cum pillar of the establishment, whose *Tribune* reflected America as in a funhouse mirror. 'I contain multitudes,' Walt Whitman had written. So did Colonel McCormick." The Colonel's *Tribune* branched out into radio in the '20s (WGN, for World's Greatest Newspaper) and television in the '40s, before either was popular. It was the first to initiate color printing, and among the first to build a paper mill and introduce a Sunday newspaper.

McCormick's *Chicago Tribune* was a family-owned enterprise that reflected the boss's every whim. It wasn't until years later under the tenure of editor Clayton Kirkpatrick that the paper gained respect for its rising independence—the summit being in 1974, when it published a forty-four-page supplement containing the Watergate tape transcripts and called for Richard Nixon's resignation. In the '70s, under CEO Stanton R. Cook, management was centralized and professionalized. In 1983, Cook steered the company to Wall Street and its first public stock offering, just at the start of the Reagan-era boom market. But the regal Cook—who looked like a CEO from central casting, with flowing gray hair, dark suits, and wing tips—may be remembered most for spotting Brumback, a short, bald, pear-shaped, penny-pinching accountant who wore baggy sports jackets and short-sleeved shirts, and who was busy shutting off lights at the *Orlando Sentinel.*

Brumback was Orlando's business manager when Cook anointed him the paper's acting general manager in 1976. Sensing his own limitations, Brumback enrolled in a one-week crash course run by the American Management Association. "I knew enough to know I really didn't know what professional management was all about," recalls Brumback, who still has three of the textbooks from the course. Taught by management consultants, as well as current and retired CEOs, the retreat gave him a framework and showed him how to plan, how to decentralize management without yielding control, how to seek synergies, and, most of all, how to create a "climate" of professionalism and risk-taking.

Brumback dispatched his own managers to the same corporate boot camp. He got rid of Orlando's creaky letterpresses and invested in an automated offset plant. He poured money into marketing, sliced costs, and generally set everyone around him on edge. Brumback adopted a crude refrain: "Look to your right. Look to your left. One of you will be gone next year."

An early computer buff, Brumback owned one of the first Apple computers. He became convinced that the microprocessor would transform business. On the subject of technology he was an evangelist. In interviews with business-side job candidates, he'd ask if they could type without looking at the keyboard. He encouraged his managers to take computer tutorials. "You got to get your hands on it," he'd beseech, warning that those who feared or ignored technology did so at their peril. He sought out new businesses, new technologies, that could multiply his assets. John Puerner recalls joining Tribune as a financial analyst in 1979, and as part of his initiation being dispatched to Orlando. "I was inspired that Charlie had created a new-media test bed. He was exploring how newspaper content could be redistributed in many forms."

The same year Brumback became general manager, James Squires, then thirty-six, was sent to Orlando to edit the paper. The two men forged a close union. Squires toughened news coverage; Brumback stiffened the bottom line. Both attracted Chicago's notice. "By 1981," says Squires, "the *Chicago Sun-Times* was still the best-read newspaper in Chicago. [Consultant] Ruth Clark and her pollsters were still telling the *Tribune* that their readers were dying. It seemed that the *Sun-Times* was growing in the suburbs, where the *Tribune*'s strength had always been." The publisher of the *Sun-Times,* James Hoge, was "running a hell of a show," Squires says. In 1981, CEO Cook chose Brumback to become president of the *Chicago Tribune,* but kept the publisher title for himself. Brumback joined the board of directors of the parent company, and in 1982 he would lure Squires to Chicago to edit the flagship paper.

Brumback was scared. "Orlando," he recalls, "is one of those magical markets where our mistakes don't show." In Chicago, there was no room for error. And he fretted that he had no experience dealing with unions— a gap that, indeed, would haunt him later.

But Brumback did not act scared. He knew there was growing competition from television and computers for readers' leisure time, as well as competition for ad dollars from TV and direct mail. So he moved quickly to control costs, the first way he could address the "appallingly low" single-digit profits. His first target was the costly hodgepodge of 250 distributors who had muscled agreements to deliver the paper. "We didn't know who our customers were," Brumback says. "I couldn't advertise a price for the *Chicago Tribune* on television because I didn't know what the distributors were charging." He agreed to pay $45 million "to buy back something we never sold." With the help of computers, Brumback collected the names of subscribers, allowing him to bill and use direct mail.

Meanwhile, *Tribune* trucks were fighting daily with tunnels to the Tower, narrow loading bays and Michigan Avenue traffic jams. Brumback supervised completion of a $250 million, twenty-one-acre printing-plant complex—called Freedom Center—with water, rail, and expressway access. "Cook's strategy was to improve the productivity of the organization," says Brumback, who recalls finding the equivalent of forty-seven hundred full time employees when he arrived at the *Tribune*. With a term that butchers use for rich, fatty meat, Brumback explains, "We had a lot of 'marbling.'" With Cook's concurrence, Brumback took up his knives.

In all, he would slice one thousand slots from production areas, and about seven hundred more from editorial and other departments. He attacked church-state divisions by installing staircases connecting the newsroom, on the fourth floor, to the ad and business departments, on the second and third floors. He consolidated back-office functions, such as payroll and human resources, for all divisions. Cuts rarely occurred all at once, or exclusively through layoffs. Newsroom cutbacks were less glaring because he relied on attrition. Brumback de-marbled mid-level editors, researchers, receptionists, secretaries. And when in 1985 the paper's typographers went on strike, Brumback broke the union by hiring temporary replacements who became permanent, and trimmed 250 more jobs.

Brumback was hugely unpopular. Many reporters thought he cared more about technology than journalism. Page remembers that when Brumback visited the Washington bureau, he was only mildly interested in news. "But when I told him I just bought a new computer, he was really excited by that, and asked lots of questions." A *Trib* editor recalls, "He was mean to people. He didn't care much about people and their hurt. He would say things that were cruel." Yet that same editor, who asked not to be identified, marvels at Brumback's prescience: Those surgical cuts in the early '80s spared the *Trib* the turmoil and anxiety—perhaps the even more traumatic cost-cutting— that occurred at Knight Ridder and Times Mirror in the '90s.

From Orlando, Brumback brought another insight to Chicago: Profit margins were determined not just by cutting costs, but by revenue growth. By offering color and thirty-two zones, he reached new advertisers who wanted inserts aimed at specific neighborhoods. By building a computerized database and starting a direct-mail company, he could advertise to *Trib* readers and nonreaders. Years later, says Timothy J. Landon, vice president for strategy and development for Tribune Publishing, the company would generate $10 million in revenue (and 25 percent profit margins) just on niche magazines that carry information about cars or real estate, as well as classified ads. The *Tribune* also makes money printing the *New York Times'* Midwest edition and distributing it in Chicago. In 1999 the paper's operating profit margin stood at 29.2.

Says Scott Smith, "The key is the total revenue per subscriber, which is the highest in the industry" at about $1,000 a year.

Brumback brought a third insight, says Landon, who joined the paper as a twenty-one-year-old intern in 1985. "If you've got the cash flow you can afford to take chances," he says. "That came from Charlie." The same year Cook brought Brumback to Chicago, he lured James Dowdle from Hubbard Broadcasting to lead the Tribune's diversification into electronic media. At the time, Tribune owned TV stations in Chicago (WGN), New York City (WPIX), and Denver (KWGN). Under Dowdle, the company would expand from three to sixteen stations. Dowdle and Brumback were soulmates their first six months in Chicago, sharing an apartment in the John Hancock tower. Dowdle remembers coming home late and watching the rumpled Brumback bang away at something called a personal computer, a machine that at the time was still a novelty.

Brumback banged away at work, too. As Tribune president, he told executives that if they learned to use a computer the company would buy them one. John Madigan, who was then the chief financial officer, recalls, "Charlie was tightfisted. But on computers he was very liberal. That created a comfortability and familiarity. . . . A lot of Luddites saw the light quickly."

When Cook took Tribune public in 1983, there was new capital for investment, and new discipline. It was a way, says Brumback, to impose on the company the scrutiny of shareholders, who could reward or punish its performance—to a point. Like other family-owned newspaper companies that sold stock (the New York Times, the Washington Post, Dow Jones), Tribune protected itself by insuring that control stayed in friendly hands. Today, the not-for-profit Robert R. McCormick Tribune Foundation, whose shares are voted by current and retired company executives, controls 18 percent of the common stock; employees, who enjoy a generous stock benefit plan, hold all the preferred stock.

Brumback, whose influence had long since eclipsed his titles, was named chief operating officer of the parent company in January 1989. He was promoted (over John Madigan) to president and CEO in August 1990, succeeding Cook. Brumback immediately set out to change Tribune's traditional corporate culture. In 1991 he initiated quarterly management retreats for about fifty top executives. "He said, 'I want this to be a more entrepreneurial culture,'" recalls Orlando's Haile. "I said, 'Charlie, no one believes you. We've been a cautious newspaper company.' But it started a cultural process that really changed the Tribune." (At a 1997 management forum, one hundred Tribune executives spent a day at the company's education publishing subsidiary in Washington state, and another day at Microsoft.)

And Brumback initiated something else: a year and a half of intense weekly strategy sessions among the top five executives, a group he called the development committee. Its twofold mission would have fateful consequences. The committee sought ways to grow, which would prompt a focus on new-media investments. It also meant to rethink investments that showed slow growth.

Tribune was already trotting on the electronic track. In 1989, while other companies clamored to invest in Prodigy and CompuServe, Tribune was the first outside investor in Steve Case's fledgling Quantum Computer Services, exchanging $5 million for 10 percent ownership of what would become America Online. As Brumback gathered the reins of the company, electronic investment was spurred to a gallop. These investments were very much aimed at Tribune's new audience: Wall Street, which punishes anyone who's said to be in "yesterday's business." That threw a baleful light on two of the Tribune's grandest old investments. Even before Cook and the board chose him as heir apparent, Brumback had warned that the future of the company's Canadian paper mills and the *New York Daily News* would have to be resolved.

The Canadian plants were the best in the business, but paper mills need almost constant upgrading at huge cost. Newsprint was becoming a more competitive commodity, reducing its profitability at the same time that the Tribune could buy paper cheaply elsewhere. Brumback and his committee decided to sell the Canadian mills. As for the tabloid *Daily News*—well, that was more complex.

Another grandson of Joseph Medill, Joseph M. Patterson, founded the *Daily News* in 1919. The feisty "Picture Newspaper" grew steadily until, by 1949, it was selling 2.5 million copies a day, more than any other paper in America. But by the '80s, after decades of inefficient management and union corruption, the *News* was losing readers and ads, and was saddled with featherbedding contracts and an antique printing plant. The *News* was sucking cash from the parent company. In 1981, under Cook, Tribune made a deal to sell the *News* to Joe L. Allbritton. But at the eleventh hour, Allbritton claimed he hadn't been told of the financial liabilities imposed by union contracts he would inherit. When the Tribune refused to indemnify him against those potential costs, the deal fell apart.

But Brumback and the development committee wanted resolution; in the boss's words, they would "fix it or get out." "Charlie was determined to be bold," recalls Smith, who was then senior vice president for finance. To fix the *News*, Tribune managers imposed new work rules and had the *News* hire the same law firm that advised them during the 1985 Chicago strike,

King and Ballow, led by attorney Robert Ballow. Brumback thought they were hiring a "labor expert" to calibrate a careful strategy. But the strategy turned out to be short on care. Instead of isolating some mob-linked or racially gerrymandered blue-collar union—and walling off the white-collar Newspaper Guild from the strife—Tribune lumped all ten unions together. *News* workers became convinced that the company wanted to rid the paper of unions, and in 1990 they went on strike. With Brumback's sanction, the *News* hired replacement workers. There was violence. The mayor, the governor, the New York business leaders—even Cardinal John O'Connor—supported the unions.

Unlike Chicago, where the *Trib* was powerful enough to bust a strike, in New York the police sided with strikers. They did not arrest those who broke the law to impede replacement workers. Trucks were vandalized, "scabs" beaten up. The *News* was struggling to publish every day, but no one seemed to care. Most news dealers wouldn't sell the replacement *News*, and those who would found few buyers. This went on for months. New Yorkers sneered at the rubes from Chicago—The Gang That Couldn't Shoot Straight. "No question we underestimated the control of the streets of New York," says Dowdle, who attended daily strategy sessions. Looking back, Smith says, "did we miscalculate things? . . . Sure." But he insists that failure stemmed from Tribune virtue: Company managers were simply "eternal optimists. We really did believe we could do better in New York."

They did worse . . . and worse. The Tribune pegged *News* operating losses at $114 million for 1990. By the time they sold the *News* to the fly-by-night British baron Robert Maxwell in March 1991, the red ink was at flood. "Over the decade," says Smith, "we lost something over $500 million."

Brumback, for his part, says, "I don't know what we could have done differently." He rejects the notion that his strategy didn't pan out. "It did work," he insists. "Our strategy was to fix it or get out." They got out.

By the end of 1991, even though Tribune owned six TV stations, four radio stations, and the Chicago Cubs, and even though it had made a handful of new-media investments, two-thirds of its revenues still derived from newspapers. Brumback was determined to reduce this reliance.

In 1992 the *Chicago Tribune* became one of the first newspapers to publish an edition online. In early 1993 it was among the first to establish a local twenty-four-hour cable news outlet, CLTV. Both efforts would be replicated in other cities where it owned newspapers. Starting with the investment in AOL, the company staked a series of new-media ventures, often joining with the powerhouse Silicon venture capital firm Kleiner Perkins to bankroll start-ups like Excite, a navigation system to roam the Internet.

Brumback stepped down as CEO in May 1995 and was succeeded by Madigan. By contrast with the short, bald, gruff Brumback, Madigan was Wall Street smooth, with silver hair and a ready smile. If Brumback was the former infantry lieutenant who led the charge up a hill, Madigan, a former investment banker at Salomon Brothers, was more the stylish general staff man. But like his predecessor, Madigan was determined to change the business mix. He was preoccupied with the Tribune's stock price. "This is a company with a lot of momentum," Madigan told shareholders at the annual meeting in May 1996. "But we're not satisfied with our stock price performance over the last several years." The price was then 70–3/8 a share. (The stock would split two-for-one the following January.) Wall Street still perceived the Tribune as too dependent on print.

So Madigan accelerated Tribune's investment in other media, expanding into software, education publishing, and multimedia. He bought into the start-up WB television network. Then in July 1996, soon after the federal government relaxed restrictions on the number of broadcast stations a company could own, Madigan announced a blockbuster acquisition: For $1.1 billion, Tribune would buy Renaissance Communications' six TV stations. With one stroke, Tribune now reached into one-third of all broadcast homes in the nation, and 70 percent of cable homes, courtesy of superstation WGN. By the beginning of 1998, Madigan finally could boast that half of Tribune's revenues came from sources other than newspapers.

What do you like, I ask John Madigan, about the *Chicago Tribune?* Seated at a tiny wooden conference table in his modestly furnished office, Madigan answers slowly, with evident care. "The overall coverage is very good," he tells me.

And what does he admire about his other three papers?

"I don't read them regularly," he says. "I do when I go there."

It's hard to know whether Madigan is being coy or polite; as CEO, perhaps he doesn't want to criticize by omission those he neglects to praise. Or is he someone who pays more attention to numbers than the journalistic product that generates those numbers? When I ask about the police-blotter news so prominent on his TV stations, he says, "I can't regularly watch those stations"—though he surmises that "our newscasts are a better quality than that."

Tribune has maintained profit margins because the company has inventively found ways to generate new revenues. But if newspaper profits can't keep pace with those of broadcasting, entertainment, educational publishing, and new media, won't Wall Street thump the laggard papers?

That's when journalists want to hear that the CEO loves his papers—and is willing to sacrifice a few margin points to maintain their luster. Although Madigan, when asked, will answer that the media business holds a special trust because it provides information and helps shape public attitudes, he's not much for speeches about the World's Greatest Newspaper.

"I like the blend of local, international and national factors," he says of the *Trib.* "It's packaged well. There is an effective use of color and formatting. I think it's the best-looking paper there is."

This prompts another question that's heard in Tribune newsrooms: Does the company believe in newspapers? Within management ranks, from Madigan on down, the question is dismissed as ludicrous because it assumes that newspapers are static. Tribune regards papers as vessels to carry the company wherever it seeks to go. "The newspaper is at the center of what we do," says Orlando's Puerner. "And it will remain at the center. And everything else we do is complementary."

(At the time of these interviews, this newspaper-centered strategy was crimped by the fact that Tribune owned only four papers. The proclaimed synergies with local broadcasting, cable, and online seemed to require more than that. Jack Fuller admitted as much when he told me, "Our problem is that we don't have enough of the top 30 cities. No one does." Each of the big newspaper chains, Fuller said, had vulnerabilities: Gannett had only one metro in a top market, the *Detroit News*—although it was soon to acquire a second, the *Arizona Republic* in Phoenix. Knight Ridder was excluded from the nation's three largest markets, as was Cox.

(Tribune had been trying to acquire more papers, bidding in 1997 for Disney's newspapers and for the *Minneapolis Star Tribune,* among others, but in every case it had been too "disciplined" to pay top dollar. It finally found a solution to its problem in 2000, though, when Times Mirror became available. This stunning $8 billion acquisition—the largest merger deal in newspaper history—gave Tribune a total of eleven newspapers, including such trophies as *Newsday,* the *L.A. Times,* and the *Baltimore Sun.* Furthermore, the deal multiplied the opportunities for synergy by giving Tribune both a newspaper and a TV station in each of the country's three top markets: New York, Los Angeles, and Chicago.

(However, Tribune still wasn't home free. Under the cross-ownership rules of the federal government, a company may not own both a newspaper and a broadcast outlet in the same market—unless the company did so before the rule came into force, as is the case with WGN in Chicago, or unless the government finds a public interest in waiving the rule, as it did when Rupert Murdoch was allowed to rescue the *New York Post.* The Federal Communications Commission, so far backed by the courts, has ordered Tribune to choose between its Fort Lauderdale paper and TV station WDZL. The FCC let a March 1998 deadline lapse in that case so it could review the cross-ownership rules; those rules were still under review as this book went to press. If the company means to prosper from multimedia synergies between newspapers and TV stations, the rules will have to change. Tribune and some other media companies have lobbied intensely to make that happen.)

Another obstacle, which all newspapers face, is falling circulation. In the past decade, overall newspaper circulation has dropped 10 percent, a trend most analysts expect to continue. Madigan considers himself a realist. He says he'd be satisfied to hold circulation flat. But he frets, "We know young people are less inclined to read than their parents."

And what effects will newspapers feel from the Internet? Unlike with a newspaper, online users can "customize" their news, get it instantly, and get it free.

The other electronic menace to newspapers—Brumback identified this early on—is the efficient way classified ads can be presented online. Buying a home across the country? An online classified can show you color pictures, offer endless details, and send you to the right realtor. Want a new job? Online listings can link you to desirable openings in other states. Nationally, classifieds are a multi-billion-dollar market. Grenesko says they represent 46 percent of Tribune's newspaper advertising revenues. If electronic competitors reduce newspaper market share from 80 percent to, say, 50 percent, ad rates and profit margins would be decimated.

That's why Tribune has put so much effort into Internet classifieds. With the Washington Post and Times Mirror, it started CarPoint. And Tribune has a connection, CareerPath, with seven other publishers (representing 70 papers) to target employment ads. In their worst nightmares, Tribune executives see Microsoft extracting chunks of the classified market. But as is true with online news, Microsoft is thin locally. Landon sounds like a combat commander when he declares, "Our whole bet is to neutralize Microsoft's positioning, and then force it down to local ground wars."

Technology is compelling newspapers to fight these multiple-front wars. The Internet is likely to siphon off more customers, as will interactive television. With greater bandwidth, TVs or computers will be able to summon not just text but audio news and full-motion video. Tribune sees not only challenges here but opportunities. Because electronic links will allow companies to collect data on the interests of each customer, says Jeff R. Scherb, Tribune's senior vice president for technology, "you may get to the point where zones can be your house." Scherb believes the role of newspapers and journalists will change when consumers can interact and retrieve more information than papers provide. "I don't think ink on paper will ever be replaced," he says. "It's hard to surf the Web and find things you don't expect. You have to go looking for things." Still, he considers a decline in the printed page inevitable.

In his office at the McCormick Tribune Foundation, in the Tribune Tower, Charles Brumback looks up phone numbers, checks his schedule and exchanges e-mail, all from a wireless Palm Pilot. At his desk, he's equipped with the computer equivalent of a souped-up car. He subscribes to technical publications and changes his equipment frequently. But he has not changed his view that Tribune must flourish as a multimedia company. In the future, Brumback says, the "successful company is going to be the table of contents to the Internet."

I ask Brumback to describe his proudest achievement. "We really are today recognized as a successful information and entertainment company," he says. "I think we've applied technology to our products, to news, in a way that makes the end product much more interesting. We have people who are not afraid of the future. We have some middle-aged editorial types who just came to life."

One of those middle-aged types is the raspy-voiced columnist John Kass, forty-two years old and the father of twin boys. He is comforted by Tribune's extraordinary efforts to probe and prepare for a different future. Kass recounts the time he worked on a small daily, when the steel company in town announced sudden and massive layoffs. "People were saying, 'They should have understood the steel business had changed.' It was a good lesson for me. I try and put aside for changes. Those guys weren't prepared. What we're trying to do is prepare for the future so that the company can continue."

In preparing for that future, it may be that the greatest obstacles will be not technical but cultural. There is an inherent clash between the culture of business, which is to maximize profits, and the culture of journalism, which wants to maximize coverage. If circulation doesn't grow, business pressure will push money out of newspapers to somewhere else. At the same time, the tools to measure readership become more refined. "One of the great, and terrifying, things about the Web is that everything is measurable," says Hiller, the Tribune's chief strategist. Whether readers prefer horoscopes to international news, sports to science, gossip to government —all this can be quantified, he says.

So what happens when an editor's judgment collides, as it will, with market research? If readers say they prefer horoscopes to foreign news, I ask Hiller, won't there be pressure to drop foreign news?

"People really do want a quality editorial experience," he says. "On the open Web is chaos and madness. What we do as a newspaper is bring some coherence." Pressed, however, he responds, "I think, ultimately, the market works."

Meaning what?

"I think, long term, you get in trouble not giving the public what it wants."

And if it wants horoscopes?

"Then I'd give it to them."

As it happens, it's in Chicago's western suburbs where you find perhaps today's most extreme experiment in marketing-generated news. Here Copley has augmented its daily newspapers with a free weekly whose "community" is a Zip Code—indeed, its name *is* a Zip Code, *60504*. Its news content owes less to what journalists think than to what market surveys say the public and advertisers want. The result seems less a newspaper than an electrocardiogram.

At a well-run company like Tribune, where managers and editors alike speak of "quality," "credibility," and all the other heartfelt words that suggest they understand they have no product without good journalism, the problem is not executives who intend to do harm. The danger is inadvertent harm. Journalism is an act of faith. It is not concrete, like a balance sheet. Readers spend their money and time on the faith that journalists strive to learn the truth and don't cut corners. Journalists place their faith in the words of Abraham Lincoln—words etched into marble at the Tribune Tower's splendid entrance: "Let the people know the facts and the country will be safe."

8 | In Lord Thomson's Realm

By William Prochnau

A LITTLE MORE THAN one hundred miles northwest of the Washington Beltway, in the fishhook of western Maryland, Breakneck Hill looks down somberly on Interstate 68 where the highway cuts through one of the first low passes into Appalachia. Neither the hill, a 1,872-foot sentinel for the mountains ahead, nor the crushed-granite slash of the humpback pass is likely to occasion a postcard home. But they constitute a powerful natural barrier. It is here that you pass out of the East and into the rest of the country. It is here that you also pass out of the orbit of Washington and all its inside-the-Beltway dither—out of the orbit, for that matter, of the *Washington Post*. On one side, the *Post* still sells a handful of copies. On the other, it effectively sells none.

At a pass-through like this you also leave behind the world of modern mega-journalism and all the attendant hullabaloo that has relegated the media to the level of used-car salesmen and congressmen in the eyes of the American public. The gentleman pumping his fifty cents into the newsrack in the town ahead is not concerned that his local paper is scandal-driven at the expense of "real news." Packs and paparazzi are not issues to him; made-up columns and borrowed quotes and unnamed sources are hardly on his mind. You are leaving the orbit of reporters who "analyze" their own stories on nightly TV at fees that would cover the salaries of a couple of their colleagues—and entering one where Kris Baker rises before the sun to walk the cops beat in Logansport, Indiana, at $9.36 an hour.

The other side is not all Norman Rockwell.

Instead, the issues shift to salaries like Baker's while absentee owners often take 30 cents—or more—out of every dollar that comes in to newspapers once locally owned. The nitty-gritty issues are "advertorials," as one reporter calls them—buy an ad for your new hamburger stand and we'll run a story about it, too. About ads that have invaded what some consider the sanctity of page one. About the merging of editorial purity into marketing and selling. About a dozen ways to milk every last dime out of the "product." Getting married? Let us sell you a wedding announcement. Dead? Let us sell your kids an obit.

For the purposes of this journey the little hump in I-68 creates one other significant barrier—the almost impenetrable wall between two small-town newspaper monopolies, the *Hagerstown Herald Mail,* owned by the Indiana-based Schurz group, and the Thomson chain's *Cumberland Times-News,* nestled down in the hollow just ahead. It creates that invaluable monopoly turf.

Old Roy Thomson never visited this place. But, as the penultimate newspaper monopolist, he would have loved it. The mountainous geography around Cumberland pens in the kind of territorial stronghold out of which he mined one of the least known but most astounding newspaper fortunes—and showed others how to do it, too.

Thomson was one of the most unlikely newspaper barons in the checkered history of a colorful business. A Canadian, he was halfway through his life before he ever dipped his fingers into printers' ink. A backwoods traveling salesman, he had peddled auto parts, radios, refrigerators, and washing machines in the gold fields of northern Ontario, barely staving off bankruptcy. He was almost forty years old, at the height of the Great Depression, when he first dusted the cobwebs off a used printing press in Timmins, Ontario. For $200 down he began an empire knowing nothing about journalism except that, as he later put it, news was "the stuff you separate the ads with."

Thomson's formula was so simple others soon mimicked it: Carve a lot out of a little. He scooped up small-town dailies and dished out the least costly product he could sell. One early shell-shocked publisher, sitting in on the first meeting after selling to Thomson Newspapers, watched as the new budgeteers ordered that newsroom pencils be issued one at a time. "God help us if they ever discover there are two sides to a piece of toilet paper," he muttered. A modern-day Thomson editor marveled, "Roy Thomson could squeeze the last drop of copper out of every penny." In 1993 even Thomson's chief executive officer, quoted in one of the chain's few respected papers, Toronto's *Globe and Mail,* conceded that the company penny-pinched its way to "cruddy" newspapers. Quality was never a hallmark of a Thomson sheet—and employees of family-owned local papers blanched when they heard the Thomsons were coming.

Still, at its height in the early 1990s the empire owned 233 small and medium-sized newspapers (daily and weekly) in the United States and Canada and another 151 in the British Isles. Along the way, the old man had picked up a title that would have been the envy of any media baron: Lord Thomson of Fleet. Today his publicity-shy son, Kenneth, who runs the far-flung Thomson Corp. as it expands aggressively into cyberspace, is said to be one of the richest men in the world. Estimates of his net worth run as high as $21 billion.

This story will take you on a journey through small-town America and to some of its newspapers—first down the hill into Cumberland; then deeper into Appalachia to Fairmont, West Virginia, and the *Times-West Virginian;* and up into middle America to Logansport, Indiana, and the *Pharos-Tribune.* Mesa, Arizona, which once would have fit the group nicely but is now a booming suburb of Phoenix and home of the Tribune, will be the anomaly on the journey.

All belong to Thomson. But the trip is not in search of "cruddy" newspapers. Most small-town papers, once family-owned stalwarts with a mystical standing in the American way of life, have been gobbled up by chains now. It is not easy to tell a Thomson paper from its small-town neighbor up the road. Nor is Thomson the corporation it was just a few years ago. It has—and this has raised some eyebrows about its confidence in the future of the commodity that made it rich—reduced its daily newspaper holdings by two-thirds and moved into the ethereal realm of the Internet. As of this writing, Thomson's newspaper profile in the United States consisted of forty-nine dailies, a mere shadow of its former self.

Some analysts say Thomson is spooked. Thomson executives insist they are in the newspaper game to stay but are tired of being a "laughingstock" and will make money with journalistic quality in the future. This trip will help you be the judge of that. It is surely a new idea.

A T THE BOTTOM of the hill in Cumberland, Lance White, the managing editor of the Times-News, is grumpy. The 4:45 P.M. news meeting in his little office in the corner of the newsroom is almost over and, for White, it is a weak news day. The Middle East is coming apart again, President Clinton is wallowing in further developments, and the best White can muster is a cleanup story about a three-day-old unseasonable snowstorm.

"We're heavy on wire," he says.

"Letdown after the storm, I guess," shrugs his city editor, Debbie Meyer.

White grunts. His is the lament of almost every small-town editor in the country. He is understaffed and the news formula for hometown papers now is local, local, and more local. An hour from now, 143 miles away at the *Washington Post,* the Middle East and Clinton stories will be the good raw meat of the high-powered news meeting. Not here. "They've got TV for that," White says of his readers. "It's not our role."

Still, reluctantly, White yields today on the Middle East. "We'll lead with it," he instructs his night news editor, John Smith. "But I want a four-column package on the snow, above the fold." He kicks Clinton inside to page two. "Do we have an ad on page one?"

Thomson's president, Stuart Garner, a Brit seasoned in the hurly-burly of Fleet Street, where front-page ads are commonplace, recently opened up his U.S. covers to allow ads stripped along the bottom—at prime rates. The big takers have been car dealers and jewelry stores. The move raised a stink in the industry and at least briefly reinforced the image problems Garner says he is trying to correct. *Editor & Publisher* headlined that Thomson had broken an "unspoken taboo" against front-page display advertising in U.S. papers.

The news meeting is breaking up and Meyer makes one last bid: "We have the municipal election in Friendsville coming up Tuesday. This is just about the last chance."

"What about the thumbnails?" White asks.

"Got one," Meyer replies. "Not the other."

"Well, that's that, I guess," White waves her off. "Can't run a thumbnail sketch of the mayor if we don't have one of his opponent."

Smith tries to suppress a half-grimace, half-smile. Somebody has screwed up. Profiles of Mayor Spencer Schlosnagle of the nearby hamlet of Friendsville, population 611, are hard to pass up. The mayor's shenanigans are so notorious that he and Friendsville have been profiled nationally. Schlosnagle has been convicted twice for indecent exposure and just keeps on getting elected.

With a circulation of thirty-two thousand, medium-large for Thomson, the *Cumberland Times-News* has an editorial staff of thirty-two. But that includes part-timers and clerks. White's core staff, in addition to his editors, is nine reporters, three photographers, and four sportswriters. It's a thin stretch, especially in a place like Cumberland. The paper's downtown office is eight miles from the Pennsylvania border and walking distance to West Virginia. Consequently, just the governmental jurisdictions that a good paper should cover—three states, a half-dozen counties, several towns and municipalities, many school districts—far outstrip the staff's means. So much so that White no longer covers meetings of any kind on a regular basis.

White, forty-five, has been in Cumberland four years. He joined Thomson with only mild trepidation. Born in a farm town in Illinois, his career history is all too typical. Small-town editors lead gypsy lives. They move around like ball players in the minors. He has been with two papers that went out from under him and came here from the *Tribune-Democrat* in Johnstown, Pennsylvania. "I didn't have many qualms," he says of his move. And he has had few regrets. He understands the game. It is bottom-line. White says he has had virtually no editorial interference, or second-guessing, from the corporation. But the bottom line, of course, affects everything.

In early 1997 White and every editor in the chain had a mean bottom-line decision to make about Thomson's Washington bureau, a fourteen-person operation that dispensed localized federal news throughout the group. Up till that time the cost of the bureau had been carried by the corporation. Suddenly, Thomson announced that the costs would be allocated on a paper-by-paper assessment schedule. The announcement was made after approval of each paper's annual budget. The bottom line was already in and the proposed assessment for Cumberland was $21,042.38.

White waves his hand toward the little newsroom outside his office. Near the center pole his police reporter, forty-nine-year-old Jeff Alderton, is clearing off his desk to make room for John Smith, who has just emerged from the news meeting. Alderton, who works days, and John Smith, who works nights, share a desk and make the handoff at five. An Edna Buchanan book occupies the upper right-hand drawer. It stays there, a claim staked.

"What was I going to do?" White asks. The assessment was not much shy of Alderton's annual salary. "Trade a reporter for three or four stories a month out of Washington?"

White did what half the Thomson editors did immediately, with many others following soon thereafter. And what the corner-cutting corporation clearly wanted its editors to do, being saddled, as it saw itself, with a $1.4 million Washington budget that it no longer wanted to pay. White pulled his paper out and the bureau began a fast crumble.

The next morning in Cumberland the fading snowstorm is boxed four columns above the fold, with photo; the Middle East leads, one column on the right; and Clinton's problems have edged their way back into a bottom-of-the-cover strip (no ad today). Slow indeed.

In the newsroom Jeff Alderton dons a sporty topcoat and hat, steps out the door of the *Times-News* building onto Baltimore Street, hikes over the bridge at Wills Creek and strides uphill toward the historic Allegheny County Courthouse. This is a town that can say without hyperbole that George Washington slept here. He was stationed here during the French and Indian War and fought the only battle he led before the Revolution. He lost.

Alderton is as mild-mannered as Clark Kent, and Cumberland dapper, wearing a tightly clipped mustache and looking every inch the cops reporter. Walking the street with him becomes a nonstop greeting. *Hi, Lew,* he nods. *Hi, Jeff.*

Alderton is a hometown boy, having graduated in the same high school class as the police chief and the *Times-News* publisher, Ronald J. Monahan. A veteran of eighteen years at the paper, Alderton was a late starter. He began working there full time at thirty-one, the newspaper becoming his escape into a new and exotic life. Until then, he had been running a local convenience store. The circumstances give him a special reverence for his job and a clarity about its traditions that could not have been better instilled at Columbia. The circumstances also give him the frustrations of romantics in an impure world.

The walk is at my request, the bestowal of a professional courtesy. He doesn't walk his beat much anymore, and that clearly causes him some chagrin. His official title is public safety and general assignment reporter. That means he covers the cops in all the jurisdictions mentioned above. He also covers the courts and the fire departments. Plus general assignment. In the other world, it would have been as if someone had told him to cover the Middle East and Africa and do features out of Europe in his spare time. Filing twice a day, of course.

Before leaving the office, Alderton showed me the latest technological advance in cops coverage. A fax machine. He shook his head slightly. Edna Buchanan remained shut away tightly in the desk drawer, unable to see this besmirching of her craft.

For years he did his job the way thousands of cop-shop reporters had before him, hoofing it to the station each morning and pawing through the wire basket of scrawled, often misspelled police reports written in the graphic lingo of cops describing their town's unseen life at night. And like generations of reporters before him—only the truly and sadly overprivileged few could avoid a stint on cops—he always expected the next sheet to produce the gem: the delicious details on the holier-than-thou city councilman who had wrapped himself around a blonde and his Chevy around a telephone pole in last night's revel.

But now there are too many rap sheets for one reporter—eight hundred reports a week from the police alone, he says. Not to mention the fire departments and the hospitals and the courts. A fax machine, a small mechanical abomination delivering up police-selected reports on departmental press-release stationery, written like little news stories by a public information officer. He shakes his head again at the very thought of it.

"I'm not naive enough to think they give me the whole deal," he says of the police who now choose the reports to send him. "They do their editing, too. It's not the best scenario." It's the bottom line.

The *Times-News* is not an unusually timid paper. It runs all domestic-violence arrests. It has a policy of running all driving-under-the-influence arrests and appears to stick by it. A state delegate recently turned the town upside down trying to get her grandson's DUI killed—to no avail. A local official sideswiped two cars after an extra nip or two and read about it the next day. Makes a lot of people mad. Small-town newspapering is not metropolitan newspapering; it's up close and sweaty. White takes it for granted. "If the publisher gets arrested tonight, we'll run it. On page one." Then he grins. "Suppose that means me, too."

Still, beat reporters, even mild-mannered ones, run on angst. Even in a monopoly town the anxiety claws at the gut with the fear that the guy from the radio station, the woman from TV, will get it first. Alderton is no exception, and one day he could take it no longer. He headed into the managing editor's office and burst out that he'd been given so much ground to cover that no one could possibly do the job properly. White, with his immutable budget, could only reply, "Well, that's the way it's going to be." Alderton was so frustrated he asked his boss to walk the beat with him and see for himself. White said okay. But he never went. And Alderton never asked again. "There was just nothing that could be done," he says now.

Bottom line.

When I first saw Lance White a few weeks earlier, he was building a house of cards at Disney World.

The occasion was Thomson Newspapers' 1998 Readership Development Conference, the kind of meeting that seems to be the wave of the future— or more accurately, the wave of the present, even the past. The newspaper business forever sees the Gauls at the gate.

There is a wonderful story about Roy Thomson working up to a full head of steam almost a half-century ago. At a 1952 meeting of Canadian Press, Canada's wire service, a fellow publisher wallowed in a long lament about the future of their endangered business. "Circulation is down . . . TV is killing us . . . radio newscasts steal our stories . . . labor demands are endless . . . costs are rising . . . advertising revenue is falling." According to Braddon Russell in the biography *Roy Thomson of Fleet Street,* the gloomy discourse continued for ten minutes before Thomson spoke. "Want to sell?" he asked. He owned twenty-one papers at the time.

All these years later, the lament is louder than ever. *Nobody reads in a visual age . . . cable TV will kill what commercial television did not . . . the Internet sounds the death knell . . . downhold and downsize. . . .* Until you read the profit statements—20, 25 percent, and more, for papers large and small.

Thomson was the first to utter the classic phrase about discovering "a license to print money." In truth, he was talking about a television station and only over the years did the words inevitably get bent to the printing-press business that made him wealthy. But even in the raw avarice of the '90s, the numbers are staggering. Just to be sure, I asked Frank Wood, the publisher of the *Times-West Virginian,* if his paper's 28 percent profit margin means what I think it means. "Oh, I think so," he grinned. A dollar in the front door, 28 cents out the back. A funeral for newspapering? It would draw more stretch limos than lined up for Elvis.

Maybe that's why no one saw irony when a professional motivator had sixty-eight Thomson editors and sixty-five Thomson circulation managers —"circulators," they are called—building houses of cards in the meeting room just up the street from the Magic Kingdom.

The purpose of the Readership Development Conference was to get editors and circulators working shoulder to shoulder in the higher interest of selling those newspapers. So, teetering at every table was a playing-card skyscraper, held in place by girders of paper clips and, most of all, a new togetherness. "See!" exclaimed MaryAnn McWilliams, who bills herself as a "newspaper improver" utilized by Gannett, Times Mirror, and dozens of others. "See what you can do by working together!"

If the editors felt ridiculous, they had no idea how lucky they were. At other conventions, according to a Thomson house organ, executives "dropped eggs from balconies, jumped out of trees and haggled for beads and poker chips." All this presumably stone sober. Such mysteries in the ways of molding minds and moods have become part of the corporate culture of a new age. Rumors ran rampant recently that the new motivators had the editors of one of the nation's most powerful newspapers running around with lampshades on their heads in the interest of reducing their egos to size and bringing them into the real world, wherever that is.

As for tearing down the walls between the newsroom and circulation, Thomson Newspapers had made sure that its editors and circulators came to Orlando well prepared. Before arriving, the conferees spent several days in role exchanges at home—editors riding the motor routes and taking the "kicks" from angry subscribers, circulation managers sitting in on news meetings and page one planning. The pivotal panel session was called "They Lived to Tell the Tale." The opening comments from Harry Brown, the director of circulation from the *Winnipeg Free Press,* went right to the point. "I would like to say to my editorial colleagues: Don't be afraid about losing your virginity, don't worry about selling your soul."

Then the panelists bared all. At the *Times Recorder* in Zanesville, Ohio, managing editor Kim Margolis let circulator Todd Jones make all the decisions one week. Jones put a sewer story on page three and ran a photo of naked mannequins. Circulation went up.

At the *Daily Times* in Salisbury, Maryland, editorial's preference for a Clinton pronouncement about telling no one to lie gave way to a local auto accident. In Kokomo, Indiana, according to the *Kokomo Tribune*'s single-copy manager, David Johnson, the experiment "changed the culture in the newsroom." Johnson told about an old newsie staring him down: "We ain't ever going to let you into those meetings." The news hand was wrong. "At first it was like walking into a freezer," Johnson recalled. "Now I walk through the newsroom and they ask me what is doing well and what isn't."

"How Far Do You Go to Sell Newspapers?" highlighted the afternoon seminars, with subheaded questions: "Does a newspaper have to be 'serious' to be taken seriously? Does 'serious' have to be dull?" The organizers put together an inspired grouping: Terry Quinn, editor of the *Daily Record* in Glasgow, Scotland; Carl Sessions Stepp, a journalism professor from the University of Maryland; and Alan Geere, executive editor of Thomson's new entry in the suburban field, the *Tribune* of suburban Phoenix.

Quinn, who claims the highest household penetration level of any newspaper in Europe, has already told the conference that circulation and editorial are "joined at the hip" at his place. Now he describes a phenomenon more common than most newspaper editors are inclined to admit, although it has twists not familiar to the assembled Thomson crowd. "I live a very isolated life," he is saying, "driven to work every day in a limousine . . . to very pleasant surroundings. People bring me food." He can't get a sense of the real world from his journalists; they, too, have isolated themselves. But his circulators are out in the field, taking abuse but meeting folks who know what is right and wrong in his newspaper. Listening to his circulators brings him into the real world.

The Anglo influence at this conference is omnipresent. Stuart Garner presides, injecting trendy, sometimes gimmicky, Fleet Street ideas into the tired Thomson formula he wants to change. The corporation moved its headquarters from Canada to Stamford, Connecticut, in 1994, but Kenneth Thomson, still chairman of the board at seventy-five, won't leave Toronto. Even the Canadian editors carry themselves with a somewhat lordly manner, some of them running larger and far more nationally relevant papers than their U.S. counterparts.

Geere, forty-three, is also British. Garner's paladin, he is a self-described hired gun brought in to get the Mesa operation up and moving aggressively in its suburban war against the Arizona Republic. An immensely joyous man, he runs on a mix of adrenaline and ideas, good and bad, both of which will become yesterday's news without cheers or tears, a new set having by then erupted. He is here until December 31, 1999, when his work visa expires. His only regret after a year in the U.S. is that people find him intimidating. ("Everywhere I go I am surrounded by a sea of mildly antagonistic faces," he tells me.)

Now he exults about his Mesa experience: "We have fun day and night! We're not wrapped up in winning awards! We used to be a fancy-pants newspaper that tried to be like the *Washington Post*." But no more, he says. "I don't want to be a guiding light for society." Recently, he sent a young reporter out to interview moviegoers emerging from the political satire *Wag the Dog*. All went well until an elderly man, three times the interviewer's age, began chasing the reporter down the street, scolding, "You're the problem! You're the problem!"

Meanwhile, the professor is lecturing. Stepp tweaks current wisdom about newspapers that try to be "the reader's best friend." Then he adds, "The day is not far off when newspapers will have to pump much more into their newsrooms."

So far Garner, as host, has been mostly rah-rah with his troops, a prerequisite of leadership at Thomson Newspapers. It is not easy to constantly be the butt of the worst of the fish-wrap jokes. "We're now being talked about in this industry big-time," Garner has pronounced. "Believe me. You are now part of something very successful. Be proud of it."

But now Stepp jars Garner to his feet and, from the audience, the Brit complains that journalism schools are not turning out the kind of graduates he wants to hire. "Should news groups run their own training schools as a replacement for journalism schools?" he asks. Garner is not the first news executive to complain that journalism schools don't prepare reporters for the real thing, but the idea of training schools—essentially trade schools—is very British. The Brits here find American newspapers mostly dull and American reporters mostly pompous and lazy. Garner is no exception.

Stepp temporizes: "Maybe some of both." Then he rises to the bait. "I shouldn't say this," he says, "but it's not us [in academia] who are putting out the dull newspapers."

Afterward, Garner approaches Stepp with half an olive branch. "I'm sorry to invite you down here and then put that to you that way," he says.

Stepp shrugs and Garner continues. "But some of our editors are very upset about it. They just have to retrain everybody."

Later, in the hallway, I ask Garner what that exchange was all about. He takes to the subject with renewed passion.

"Well, I *am* thinking about it," he says. "Take high school graduates, or young people from 18 to 22, and put them into a training school for six months. The Thomson Editorial Training Center. That's what we did in Britain. We taught them, but they mostly learned by doing. We taught Pitman shorthand until they could take 100 words a minute. We taught them how the cops work, how the city works. A heavy chunk of it was on media law. We had 22 laws restricting what journalists could and do write. Defamation. But we didn't teach libel, nothing on libel. Or ethics. We didn't teach anything at all about ethics. I imagine old Carl there spends a year on that."

Briefly Garner sidetracks to his first job under a "thoroughly unpleasant" boss who turned out to be a "tough but empathetic mentor," a legendary British editor named John Brown Lee. "We got our pay each week in a brown envelope, cash, and the first week he shouted my surname and tossed my envelope so it landed on the floor between us. 'Get it on your hands and knees,' he said. 'That's all you're worth.'"

Terry Quinn is listening with a big smile. "And that has been Stuart's management philosophy ever since," he interjects.

Garner glares a grin back that says, Quinn, this outsider standing next to me better turn out to have a good sense of humor. But Garner is on a roll now and he pushes on.

"The bottom line was that we got young, enthusiastic reporters who were excited and gave us what we wanted. Now journalism schools. . . ." He makes a disparaging face. "Kids are coming in with their heads filled with the wrong stuff. I have a nephew, 17, desperate to become a journalist. 'What should I do?' he asked me. I said, 'Go to Serbo-Croatia if you want. Go to college if you want. But don't do journalism.' They come out of there writing learned treatises on women's studies or something . . . social issues, politics, and . . . liberal, whew.

"A professor in England came up to me one time and said, 'Isn't it a shame that they are all writing about the royal family and Diana?' My God. The only people you are interesting is the readers. Young people come out of journalism school feeling they are doing God's work, that they have a mission to save the world.

"I'm not against civilizing reporters. But as a news editor"—unlike most of Thomson's top executives, Garner spent most of his career in the newsroom—"I had to expect every reporter who worked for me to do three stories a day. Editors complain to me that they want more staff. I look at the record and I say, 'Look, only one story a day.' How can they want more reporters?"

It rained six inches in three days in Orlando. But a good time was had by all.

BACK IN CUMBERLAND, John J. "Jack" McMullen is telling me about how his and a co-owning local family came to sell the *Times-News* to Thomson. The year was 1986, the height of the small-town gold rush. Roy Thomson's secret had been out of the bag for years and chains competed to smother the dwindling number of local owners in cash. "I've never told anyone how much," McMullen says. "It was an ungodly sum."

McMullen, the publisher, had no desire to sell. But the family ownership, divided among a third-generation group of heirs, the only one of whom had any interest in running the paper being Jack McMullen, was ideally set up for a buyer. To the others the money simply looked too good. McMullen was outvoted. Thomson asked if he would stay on in the interest of continuity and he said he would. The staff was terrified. So were the town fathers. McMullen wrote a reassuring editorial: "You will have the same paperboy. When you come in to pay a bill, you will talk to the same person." But they would not have the same publisher. Two months after the deal a different Thomson man showed up on a Monday and said the new publisher would be there on Thursday. "Don't go out bad-mouthing us," the Thomson man said.

"Newspaper quality is such a subjective thing," McMullen says. "I've tried to be silent about it. People are always asking me what I think about the paper. Still. And I say that it would just be sour grapes. But I guess from that comment alone you can gather that I don't like everything I see. Page one was never for sale. Nobody got charged for an obit or a wedding."

Still, the changes in the newsroom came slowly, in other areas a lot quicker. "Ad rates went up immediately—way up—and all the advertisers were howling," continues McMullen, now sixty-five and practicing law. "You couldn't jump ad rates that way with home ownership. Your neighbor would never talk to you again."

In 1986 the paper was still a morning-evening combo with two staffs "that fought like cats and dogs," McMullen says. That went soon; probably would have anyway, he acknowledges. But the news staff now is smaller than either of the combination papers, he says. Most of the reductions came by attrition. The paper just didn't hire anybody.

"If there were a Pulitzer Prize for the bottom line, they would get it." He laughs but not with mirth. "Benign neglect" is the way he describes policy toward the newsroom. "The publisher comes in and says, 'Do what you have to do, don't get me in trouble, and that's it.' It's as if the old truism about journalism—that the newsroom is not a revenue producer—bothers them. I mean, actually bothers them. It's as if they don't understand what the whole idea is."

INTERSTATE 68 WEST out of Cumberland pulls hard uphill through Frostburg, where Lance White lives (he can't get to work in a tough snowstorm), then on through more natural barriers, past the home of Mayor Spencer Schlosnagle and across into West Virginia. All told, it is sixty-nine miles from Cumberland to Fairmont, home of the *Times-West Virginian.* Hard miles to a hard town.

Theresa Haynes is hot-footing it down Adams Street toward the Marion County Courthouse. She has two bylines above the fold this morning, including the banner, and now this is another busy day, a normal day. A grand jury is bringing indictments, the sheriff wants new high-intensity lighting around the jail, having been embarrassed by another escape, and the ground is dropping out from under her.

Fairmont is a tough old coal town trying to come back from rocky times. The framed front page in her publisher's office tells the old story in deck after deck of big, black headlines:

78 Miners Entombed in Farmington No. 9 After Blast Rips Workings; 21 Escape Underground Holocaust; Fire Growing in Intensity, Keeps Rescue Teams on Surface

The black dust from the once-rich mines has dug into the very face of the town's skyline, making it look like a gritty black-and-white photo on the sunniest day. Eighty mines once snaked mile after mile beneath the town. The last of them closed three years ago, a starker tragedy, most think around here, than decades of grim deaths. But that's history. Haynes deals with today's news, the first draft of history, as they say, and today's news is that parts of town are settling in on the collapsing cavities. The Catholic church slipped a few years ago. Now a house is sinking, too, but the state contends this one has nothing to do with the mines. Haynes landed the chore of checking it out, although she's not sure why. Lord knows she has enough to do covering the cops, the courts, and the county commission. No fax machine here.

At twenty-three, Haynes is the youngest reporter on the *Times-West Virginian* staff. She arrived from West Virginia University's journalism school last year at a college graduate's entry-level $336 a week and went straight to obits and night rewrite, then to cops. She is good at it, deceptively shy, maybe intentionally so, and tenacious. She also has one of the strongest qualities of a natural reporter: She is not afraid to ask a dumb question.

"What's with this DUI?" she asks the sheriff's clerk innocently, reading from a puzzling report she'd pulled from the tray of overnight misdeeds.

"A dee-VEE-eye, honey," comes the reply. "That's an expired vehicle inspection."

Haynes shrugs and plows on, taking notes on a man who tried to steal a car but couldn't get it started and an irate girlfriend who trashed her boyfriend's apartment by dumping all the food in the bathtub, smearing ketchup on the walls and filling his bed with dirt.

Then it's on to the sheriff's office for the mandatory "What's goin' on today?" She learned early that not all the stories are in the overnight reports. The best story of her young career came after the same question. The sheriff was "just plain bummed out" about a 911 call that the operator referred to the state police instead of his office. The call dealt with a rape in a convenience store. The sheriff had a man just a minute away. But the state police had to roust an officer from bed and, in the delay, the rapist got away. "It became a big issue that went on for days and days," she says. "We even gave it a name: The 911 Go Mart Case."

A quick stop at the Marion County Commission. The clerk is reading four single-spaced legal pages of unsettled estates, the county's last call for folks who were born broke and died broke. Haynes catches up on marriage licenses and then heads back to the office.

"At first everybody was friendly, but now there are a few who aren't," she says, reflecting on a job she likes. "You can either be friends or do the news."

Suddenly, she does a shy mimic of the new managing editor's first staff meeting: " 'Well, hi there, I'm going to redesign the paper by the end of the month, and everybody on the staff is going to produce a story a day.' " Haynes was taken aback by the last part. "I guess everybody wasn't," she says, deadly serious. She had thirty bylines last month.

Actually, Andy Prutsok redesigned the paper, wrote new design guidelines and began a weekly column in his first month. With a circulation of 15,900, the *Times West-Virginian* is the largest paper Prutsok, thirty-seven, has ever worked for. He also came out of West Virginia University—most of the staff did—with dreams of "going to the big city and being an ace writer." Instead he landed at a weekly and worked his way up to papers in

Cartersville, Georgia, and Hopewell, Virginia, and finally Mena, Arkansas, before getting this break. Here he has a staff smaller than Cumberland's but a luxury to him—seven reporters, two photographers, and four sports-writers.

"I suppose everybody out there is bitching about salaries," he says, gesturing toward the newsroom. "They ought to see what people were getting paid in the South—and the whole town was getting that kind of money."

Actually, the staff doesn't bitch that much, considering that grousing is an art form in newsrooms. The pay is terrible. A journeyman works his way up to $450 a week, maybe a few bucks more after a dozen years. But low pay is the curse of small-town newspapering, hardly peculiar to Thomson, although the chain has a deserved reputation for putting a registered trademark on the practice. Despite that, morale is unusually good in Fairmont. The newsroom has a chatter to it, like the dugout of a pennant-chaser: "This is a great story! George used the word 'draconian' in it. Everyone in town will know that one!"

The paper is small-town solid—maybe even good, such judgments, as McMullen says, being subjective. The publisher, Frank Wood, has stiffed the trend toward charging for obituaries and weddings. "We discussed it," he says. "But it's the only time most people get their picture in the paper and it just feels like adding insult to injury in a town that is struggling so hard to recover." What would it do to a 28 percent margin? Lift it to 28.02?

Almost everyone in the newsroom from Wood on down has his or her personal Thomson story—that moment of sheer panic during a takeover or that is-it-too-late anxiety attack after taking the job.

Wood was working at the *Register-Herald* in his hometown, Beckley, West Virginia. The paper had been on the market for awhile. Some heavy hitters, including the *New York Times,* were rumored to be interested. He was out of town when the word came out of nowhere that Thomson had made the buy. He called a friend in advertising. "Who is Thomson Newspapers?" Wood asked. He had never heard of the chain. "You don't want to know," came the reply. "I have heard nothing but horror stories."

Marlo Verrilla, the lifestyle editor who came to Fairmont eighteen months ago, tells a similar story. "When I came here, I didn't even know it was a Thomson newspaper. That might have made a difference. They had a terrible reputation. One of my friends heard and said, 'God, how could you?'"

The business editor, George Hohmann, has been in and out of Thomson papers three times. His first experience, not long out of journalism school in the early '70s, was jarring but apparently not indelible. He became editor of Ohio's tiny *Piqua Daily Call,* circulation about eight thousand. "I walked in," he recalls, "and I was immediately told that we had to reduce the staff by three and I got to choose the three. It was awful." He lasted eight months, then quit and spent a year recovering in Europe.

But for each there is a second half to the story. Thomson turned into a career for Wood—he says he found that if you make the numbers, "they leave the running of the paper to the publisher in each community, figuring he understands the place."

Ask Verrilla if she likes her job and the answer is an unwavering yes. She likes small towns, the mood in the newsroom and the elbow room—a side benefit of benign neglect. "They let you write longer," she says. "I get 20 to 30 inches for my features." (She does three a week, and for two days she edits the club news and food page.) "Once they gave me 75 inches. A photographer and I followed coon-dog puppies as they were raised and trained. Nine months. We took the front and back pages of the lifestyle section."

Hohmann ducked out to Europe and took another eight-year interlude, this time in the rare-coin business, but the narcotic of the newsroom, even a Thomson newsroom, always drew him back. "I don't think there is ever any doubt that they get their money's worth out of us," he says. "But what worries me is not the Thomsons." He gestures toward a monitor where a reporter is cruising the Internet. "What worries me is that we are all going to wake up some morning working for the telephone company."

Andy Prutsok, coming from Mena, had no doubts. Like any new boss, he is driving the reporters harder than ever. But they like him. He pushes them to improve themselves and he often does it with that most useful of tools—a sense of humor.

"An ideal page one?" he responds to a question. "Sex, drugs and rock 'n' roll." He wears just a wisp of a smile. "I have no qualms about compelling folks to buy the paper. But I guess ideally it would be a good local story that's not a government meeting." It's the new mantra. No government. No meetings. But the rookie, Theresa Haynes, still checks out the Marion County Commission as the unclaimed estates are read.

Prutsok's new column can be keenly satirical. An unusual bill introduced by a West Virginia state legislator inspired a recent one. The roadkill bill, they called it. The proposal would allow West Virginians to keep road kill for food if they hit it with their own cars. For Prutsok, a native, it was too rich to pass up. He wrote a column of one-liners suggesting bills that would give similar aid to West Virginia's image. Placing a luxury tax on shoes gives you the idea.

Prutsok, in town only six weeks, comes into the office a few days later looking sick. "I had my dog poisoned last night," he says, and you can tell he's trying to convince himself it had nothing to do with his job. He has two small children.

"He was a barker. I kept him in the garage. The cops said maybe he ate antifreeze. But I don't have any antifreeze." Who knows. Small-town newspapering can cut pretty close to the bone.

ABOUT THIS TIME *Forbes* magazine publishes its annual list of the world's richest men, and it causes, as Thomson editors and publishers describe it, "the groan heard throughout the empire." Kenneth Thomson has made it back into the top ten after a one-year dip to sixteenth. Quietly, the executives on the front lines complain that *Forbes* has changed the rules on them, reducing the list to the "working rich" and thereby eliminating such stalwarts as the Sultan of Brunei and his $40 billion or so. Thomson comes in at $14.4 billion. The only North Americans he trails are the Microsoft boys, Bill Gates and Paul Allen, the Walton family, and Warren Buffett.

"Every time he makes the list a copy goes up on the staff bulletin board," says Gary Omernick, publisher of the *Herald Times Reporter* in Manitowoc, Wisconsin, who admits that he breathed a sigh of relief during the year of the dip. "But you know what someone once said," Omernick adds. "The function of newspapers is to inform souls, but the role is to make money."

In approaching the story of the Thomsons and their empire it is important to understand that there really are two stories about each—the story about old Roy, the legend, and young Ken, the heir; and the story about the original empire and the successor realm, a part of the tale that is still playing out.

There is no doubt that Roy and Ken were chiseled out of the same Scottish hardwood gnarl. But, after that, they differed in almost everything but their unrelenting need to squeeze a buck out of all they touched.

A barber's son who quit school at thirteen, Roy Thomson approached life and money like a riverboat gambler, once uttering a line straight out of a casino addict's handbook: "I buy newspapers to make money to buy more newspapers to make more money." He brought the value of the dollar home to everyone in the family when, visiting Italy, he dispatched postcards home to his grandchildren by surface mail. Air-mail stamps cost too much.

The media empire began almost by accident—or necessity, depending on your point of view. But it began with a radio station, not a newspaper.

Two years before buying the newspaper in Timmins, Ontario, Thomson was going broke trying to sell radios to the gold miners. So he bought the local radio station, pumped it up with piano music and local commercials, lots of local commercials, until people damned well had to buy his backlog of receivers. From that moment on, he described his favorite music as "the sound of radio commercials at $10 a whack."

Still, he was a man of joy, "an animated cash register," someone said. The two characteristics—joy and the cash register—reached an apex in 1959, when Thomson parlayed his successes into the purchase of the *Sunday Times* of London, adding the *Times* of London shortly thereafter, and was rewarded with a peerage: Baron Thomson of Fleet of Northbridge in the City of Edinburgh. It was some march from Timmins. Thomson began to enjoy himself thoroughly. He met with world leaders and cut deals with the famous. Once, in the Kremlin, he met Nikita Khrushchev, who asked him what good all that money would do him. "You can't take it with you," the Soviet premier said. "Then I'm not going," Thomson replied. He became still richer in a North Sea oil partnership with billionaire John Paul Getty, a man also fond of one-liners. "A billion dollars is not what it used to be," Getty said. Thomson was undeterred. "Paul's richer than I am," he conceded. "But then, I'm six months younger than he is."

By the time Thomson died in 1976, at age eighty-two, no one was quite sure what he was worth—except plenty. "I'm as rich as my credit," he always had said. His will was disguised in legalisms and totally unrevealing. But analysts concluded Roy Thomson had fallen just short of the empire's first billion.

The son who took over was fifty-three years old, although Kenneth Thomson had been running the North American newspaper division for almost twenty-three years. As the Roaring '90s began and Kenneth approached seventy, he was still being called "young Ken" or, by his detractors, who were not few, "Lord Silverspoon." Of all the often legitimate abuse heaped on Kenneth Thomson, these were the least fair. Ken Thomson had spread the empire onto all continents but Antarctica and headed for cyberspace. He owned an airline with forty jumbo jets, Britain's largest package travel company and the majority holding in the Hudson's Bay Co. Next came what *Maclean's*, Canada's national magazine, called perhaps the world's "largest media oligarchy," daily newspapers with a total circulation of more than 4.5 million and a kind of Tinkertoy set of magazines and weeklies and newsletters and directories—"an incredible 40,000 other editorial products," the magazine wrote. His net worth had passed the Gettys and the Rothchilds, and he seemed likely to bequeath his heirs a fortune twenty times what his father had bequeathed him.

What he had done for the craft that provided the seed and much of the substance of his incredible riches was not as impressive. Most of Thomson's horror stories—the "awful-awfuls," one executive calls them—occurred under the leadership of Kenneth Thomson and his hirelings.

In her book *The Thomson Empire,* Susan Goldenberg noted that employees at some of the small U.S. dailies began rebelling with bitter strikes. In 1979 the workers at the tiny *Valley Independent* in Monessen, Pennsylvania, went out—and would remain out fourteen months—to move Thomson off a journeyman's salary scale of $190 a week. That same year the newsroom hit the bricks at the *Oswego Palladium-Times* in New York. A reporter named Carol Wilczynski, who ran a one-person bureau in a small neighboring town, complained, "If I wanted supplies, I had to go to Oswego and would be handed one pencil. We weren't allowed to buy reporter shorthand books but instead were given scrap paper."

In Canada the awful-awfuls were still worse. On the same day in 1980, Thomson suddenly shut down the *Ottawa Journal,* laying off 375 employees, and Canada's other major chain, Southam Inc., put 370 people on the streets by closing its *Winnipeg Tribune.* The simultaneous shutdowns gave Thomson a monopoly in Winnipeg and Southam a monopoly in Ottawa. The moves so outraged the Canadian government that it filed conspiracy charges against the two companies and formed a royal commission to investigate them. Thomson and Southam were eventually acquitted, but the commission recommended a breakup of Thomson. "Its small-town monopoly papers are, almost without exception, a lackluster aggregation of cash boxes," said the report. But time had passed and politicians don't take on publishers —witness the Newspaper Preservation Act in the United States.

The deepest scar in the Thomson legacy came in the company's handling of the suddenly jobless Ottawa employees. Southam immediately set about trying to find its Winnipeg people new jobs. But Kenneth Thomson did nothing but offer a billionaire's strange, almost otherworldly, advice: "Each one has to find his own way in the world." Throughout the '80s Thomson Newspapers maintained profit margins of up to 35 cents on the dollar and salaries a notch above poverty level.

Kenneth Thomson developed quite differently from his father. He never quite seemed to get the joy out of his money; never, as Roy did, hopped aboard his yacht, with its pseudo-snakeskin walls, and sailed off for impromptu dinners with Lord Beaverbrook in Bermuda; never impulsively bought a newspaper like the old *St. Petersburg Independent* in Florida so he would have a place to moor his boat. Most telling of all was his handling of the company's—and, at that time, journalism's—twin crown jewels: the *Sunday Times* of London and the *Times* of London. To Kenneth

Thomson the newspapers ate money instead of produced it—"just a drag on profits," he complained. He sold them in 1981 to a new colonial entering the game, Rupert Murdoch. Kenneth withdrew into a deeply private, almost reclusive life.

"The smartest thing those who have more than anybody else can do is not to flaunt it," he said in a rare interview with Peter C. Newman for his 1991 book on the Hudson's Bay Co., *Merchant Princes*. "It's resented and it's in terribly bad taste. It shows a poor sense of priority."

Thomson married a beautiful woman, a model named Marilyn Lavis, and they had two sons and a daughter—David Kenneth Roy, Peter, and Lesley. Marilyn cut her husband's hair to save the barber's bills. They lived in a twenty-three-room Georgian mansion in Toronto's tony Rosedale section. But when Newman visited it, he found the mansion dark and rundown, the drapes still those hung by the original owner. The Thomson family usually ate dinner in the kitchen to save on electricity. The family had difficulty keeping maids, the wages it paid to domestic help were so low.

Still, Thomson was no Howard Hughes. He reported daily to his office on the twenty-fifth floor (the public elevator runs to twenty-four) of the downtown Thomson Building. There he was surrounded by his other passion —a collection of paintings by the Dutch-Canadian artist Cornelius Krieghoff. Always the monopolist, he has owned as many as 204 Krieghoffs, virtually all the artist's output. Art critics noted that this might be a tribute to the quality of the nineteenth-century Canadian landscapes, but it also was a convenient form of price-propping for tax write-offs when the Thomsons donated an occasional canvas to a museum.

Lord Thomson declined to be interviewed for this article. The refusal was courtly and revealing. The Project on the State of the American Newspaper "promises to be of great value to the American newspaper industry and to Thomson Newspapers," he wrote, offering all possible cooperation except an interview. For a moment he almost revealed an unusual touch of romance about his multibillion-dollar corporation's founding in printers' ink.

"The first step in the creation of what is now the Thomson Corporation was taken by my father in 1934 when he bought his first newspaper in Northern Ontario—the *Timmins Weekly Press*," he wrote. "Almost miraculously in those Depression days he managed to buy the paper for $6,000— $200 down and $200 per month. Thomson Newspapers has gone a long way since then. We are proud of their quality, both as vehicles of public service and as sound business operations. The two are invariably interlinked."

The words about Timmins were touching, the town and the paper, one would think, corporate icons. But the empire's origins had already been extinguished by the bottom line. Susan Goldenberg visited the isolated town in her researches in the '80s and found the *Press,* by then a daily, in total disarray, the look of it Dickensian. Blue paint peeled off the news-room walls, torn pieces of plastic served as window blinds, reporters in a computer age still pounded away at wounded typewriters. In 1996 the *Timmins Daily Press* passed out of the Thomson fold like a ship in the night, sold quietly with a group of expendables. If the queen of English-language journalism, the *Times* of London, couldn't survive Thomson's bottom-line economics, how could the *Daily Press?* Emotion paid fewer dividends than front-page sewer stories. The founding paper was dis-missed without even a note in the corporation house organ, the Thomson News, which handled the obituary as part of the sale of fourteen unnamed Canadian papers "east of Thunder Bay, Ontario."

"They don't have an emotional bone in their body," says Bill Sternberg, Thomson's former Washington bureau chief, who now works at *USA Today.* Sternberg spent seven years building up the bureau, then saw it gut-ted in one night over dinner at the J.W. Marriott Hotel, the staff to be told in the morning. The bureau had only two reporters in 1998, one writing for Thomson's Arizona papers, the other for the Wisconsin group. "Just look at Timmins. They sure had enough money to have kept the paper for sentimental reasons. But they didn't. They don't have sentiment and they don't have ideology. The ideology is dollars."

By the time of the bureau upheaval, however, in January 1997, both the overarching Thomson Corp. and Thomson Newspapers had moved into a dramatically new corporate era.

Historically, the newspaper business has been remarkably recession-proof. Fortunes were made off screaming headlines during the Great Depression and, despite constant hand-wringing, the business had a Wall Street reputation for holding up throughout the periodic recessions since the end of the Second World War. The recession of the late '80s and early '90s was startlingly different.

A look at the arc of Thomson's newspaper profit margins since 1987 gives a perfect illustration:

1987: 33.9 percent	1993: 15.7 percent
1988: 31.2 percent	1994: 17.2 percent
1989: 29.3 percent	1995: 17.3 percent
1990: 24.4 percent	1996: 15.6 percent
1991: 20.0 percent	1997: 17.6 percent
1992: 17.6 percent	1998 (first half) 17.5 percent

Profit margins of 15 percent and up would not throw most companies into shudders of fear. But it did Thomson, as it did some others in the newspaper industry. The recession dug deep and lingered. Had the golden goose finally died? The statistics could prove almost anything—circulation shrinking, advertising down in a market filled with high-tech competitors, people not reading. The situation was made to order for the same woe-begone speech to which Roy Thomson had responded four decades earlier: "Want to sell?" But this time it was a Thomson who said "Yes."

Over the next half-dozen years, the company would shed nearly two-thirds of its daily newspaper holdings worldwide. From 1995 through 1998 it sold some 60 of its American papers. *Why We Must Transform Our Business,* blared a special "Transformation Now" issue of an in-house publication. Thomson was still buying—big. It was just buying differently.

The Thomson Corp., as publicity-shy as its owner, had always maintained an almost ghostly low profile in the corporate world—ignored by Wall Street because its stock was traded on Canadian boards (the corporation is publicly owned but 73 percent of the public is the Thomson family), and barely visible even within the newspaper industry. Ashtabula, Ohio, and Opelika, Alabama, do not draw much scrutiny. But then, as *Maclean's* magazine described it, Thomson began "moving through the corporate jungle with the stealth of a giant anaconda, sloughing off newspapers like old skin and gobbling up database companies in huge bites."

The hugest bite came in 1996 with the $3.4 billion purchase of the West Group, a Minnesota giant with ten thousand Internet databases in the legal field. Two years later Thomson sold its British travel group, airline and all, and pocketed $2 billion. Analysts looked askance at the West price; some said it was twice the true value. But that was straight out of the proven Thomson formula: Buy high and start milking. West, says Thomson, was paying a profit in its second year.

By the time all the billions had gone back and forth and the dust had settled—at least, the company said it had settled—the Thomson Corp. had transformed itself into a $6 billion colossus for the Information Age. Understand this: The product was *information,* not news; or, at least, information with a minor in news. Thomson now sold data—data to lawyers, data to doctors, data to bankers and accountants and securities advisers, data to anyone who needed data in the age of data.

The information could be as dull as the old newspapers. But if you were a lawyer who needed a court decision, a pharmacist who needed a quick hit on drug cross-reactions, a car repairman who needed an auto-parts list, Thomson was the information peddler for you. How about the specs on an Aegis guided missile destroyer? All yours, for $1,000 and an online subscription to *Jane's Fighting Ships,* part of the Thomson portfolio. Information turned to gold as surely as those $10-a-whack commercials and that stuff that surrounded the news. Lord Cyberspace, they now called the son of Roy. In 1997 all that information sold for $4.77 billion, with a profit of $1.25 billion. Just like the old days.

Meanwhile, what was left of the U.S. newspaper group had altered dramatically, too, in large part because the face of small-town America was changing. The Wal-Mart Effect, newspaper analyst John Morton calls it.

If American newspapers had yielded to the voracious appetite of the chains, so had American retailing. Home Depot ran the local hardware stores out of business, Office Depot the downtown stationery stores. Wal-Mart drove under small businesses right and left. The changes eroded the small-town advertising market in an irreversible way. National firms used national advertising companies and they didn't focus on Opelika, either.

"There's no such thing as national advertising in local papers anymore," says publisher Frank Wood in Fairmont. "We don't get airline, liquor, tobacco—any of it—the way we used to. A Detroit ad for Ford comes now through the local Ford dealer if it comes at all." Looking at the ad-news ratio in small-town papers brings the phenomenon into stark relief. The ratio used to be 60–40—60 percent ads, 40 percent news. Any local newspaper that can get 40 percent now considers itself riding high. But the 40 is ads.

"In effect, the Wal-Marts became national advertisers, too, not entirely but to some extent," Morton says. "Why advertise [locally] when everybody knows you are there and you are the only game in town?"

At the same time, a bold new player in American journalism, *USA Today,* enhanced the Wal-Mart Effect. At first it drew snooty scoffs from the media elite and didn't abscond with that many local customers. But it came sneaking into Thomson towns with all that color and circus makeup and a bold weather map straight off the tube. The news, at least at first, may have tasted like airline food, but it was far better fare than Thomson was serving.

The quality problem deeply embarrassed many Thomson executives. It wasn't easy for a CEO, as the Thomson Corp.'s Michael Brown did in 1993, to call one of his most public products "cruddy" and concede that "Thomson Newspapers has a reputation well-deserved for very poor quality." Brown was nearing retirement and trying to steer the corporation through drastic change. It now considered advertising-based publishing too vulnerable to economic cycles. Subscription-based publishing—those databases and the heady future of the Internet—became its new rap. As for newspapers, once Thomson's raison d'etre, the dilemma was daunting. To stay in at all, Thomson had to shape up *and* cut costs.

The corporation looked for the cost answer in something it called Strategic Marketing Groups—or clustering. The idea doomed the far-flung empire. No more lonely outposts. Now the goal was to cluster half a dozen properties in one tight region. The press in Logansport could also print the paper in Kokomo (conveniently gutting the union in Kokomo as well); the advertising manager in Anderson could oversee the accounts in all of central Indiana. Larger advertisers could make regional buys at discounts, partly neutralizing the Wal-Mart Effect.

By 1998 Thomson had reduced itself to nine clusters in the United States, plus a handful of still vulnerable "floaters." Thomson was not the first to try clustering, but it was among the first to bet its future on it. Soon most chains were in the game, with a wild flurry of sales and swaps and players to come. They were like kids with old bubble-gum cards: I'll trade you three Pennsylvanias for a Wisconsin and a Maine.

Improving editorial quality without spending money was a more formidable task. "We saved $200,000 in pressroom waste in central Ohio," rah-rahed Ellen Stein Burbach, vice president for readership development, at the Orlando conference. "If you can do that, we can put two more editors or reporters out there." From the looks on their faces, few of the editors in the room saw staff expansion in their future.

Still, newsroom improvement became the clarion call under the man running Thomson Newspapers during much of the upheaval, Richard J. Harrington. He was an unusual patron. An accountant, he had never worked in a newsroom and described himself as "a marketer and salesperson who can count." But not all analysts were convinced that Thomson intended to stick with newspapers. In its 1996 annual report, Thomson boasted that "advertising represents only approximately 10 percent of our total revenues." Some viewed the retooling as a way of dressing up the newspapers' profits for a richer sale down the line.

Still, when Harrington moved up to replace Brown as head of the parent group in 1997, he immediately hired a man with twenty-four years of experience in newsrooms—albeit all on the other side of the Atlantic. Hints that Thomson saw light in the British way predated the arrival. As early as 1993, a Thomson newsletter that provided monthly performance prods to its newsroom chiefs heralded:

Bold, Brash Newspapers Sell: We Could Learn a Few Things From Our British Counterparts

The chance arrived with Stuart Garner, fifty-four, the former managing director of two British newspaper chains and a man who has worked at virtually every job in a British newsroom.

Dispelling rumors that Thomson secretly intended to abandon the newspaper business came high on Garner's list: The upheavals of the '90s made the Thomson Corp. "unequivocally an information and publishing company," he insisted in an internal memo, and that should lay to rest "any lingering suspicions that Thomson is getting out of newspapers."

Garner is a cocky fellow with sprightly ideas. In the field, however, the reaction is mixed. One reporter, angry about the escalating trend at his paper against covering "boring" government stories, blames Garner. "He doesn't understand the First Amendment, the Second Amendment or any of the amendments," the reporter complains, although, in fairness, the trend had invaded newsrooms long before Garner came ashore. Bill Sternberg, the former Washington bureau chief, calls him a "very bright, sharp guy," but worries about his lack of background in gut issues for the American press. Garner, he says, "strikes me as someone who doesn't know what he doesn't know." But his editor in Manitowoc, Gerald Guy, just grins and points to Britain's invasion of American magazines and its inroads into New York publishing. "One if by land, two if by sea, three if by Thomson," he says.

Actually, the best insights into Stuart Garner may be in far-off Mesa, Arizona, in the low, stucco-dreary suburbs of the flat valley east of Phoenix. There Thomson Newspapers is trying its most adventuresome and out-of-character experiment.

THE DRIVE TOWARD Thomson's new suburban enterprise, the *Tribune*, is string-straight into Mesa through an endless bazaar of sun-bleached and sand-blasted one-story buildings—two stories would be a skyscraper. Local entrepreneurs tout their wares in tried and true fashion: Lulu's Taco Shop ... Metropolitan Mattress ... PETsMART ... Airtouch Paging ... Payday Loans Checks Mortgage Senior Day.

The newspaper office is two right turns off Main Street, at 120 West First Avenue, a modern brick building that is an unexpected testament to permanence and lined in front by newsracks. Harry Caray is dead and you discover it in seventy-two point: *So Long Everybody,* the trademark words of the grand old man who broadcast major league baseball for a half century and Chicago Cubs games for sixteen years. Caray was a folk hero here, for Mesa is the spring training ground for everybody's favorite loser.

It is not quite 8 A.M., a thoroughly uncivilized hour for a morning publication, and the newsroom already is abuzz.

"To hell with e-mail!" comes sudden thunder from the corner. The accent is British neighbor boy, steam-pressed only slightly by several years of overseas living. This is Alan Geere's way of calling the first meeting of the day.

Phil Boaz, thirty-nine, the city editor, who had been lost in his story budget, finds Geere angled at him ominously over a video display terminal.

Boaz was here when Thomson Newspapers arrived two years ago. The irrepressible, unyielding Brit showed up shortly thereafter. "At first we thought we had one foot in the grave," Boaz will tell me later of the Thomson development. Of Geere: "A lot of us wondered, 'When is this son of a bitch going to leave?' We knew he was going some day. Now I think we will regret it. I am a convert."

Not so with everybody. "A lot of people show a lot of affection for Alan," says one of his reporters, who requests anonymity for reasons that seem fair. "But Alan's a company man. If he was a first sergeant in Vietnam, he wouldn't be a grunt sergeant. He's the guy who sends you out. He knows who is promoting him."

Thomson picked up the five East Valley papers—Mesa, Scottsdale, Chandler, Gilbert, and Tempe (also served are Ahwatukee and Apache Junction)—from Cox in 1996. The package also included a floater in Yuma, Arizona, the hottest place in the country if not the hottest deal. Thomson merged the suburban papers and prepared for war with the *Arizona Republic,* the Phoenix metro whose reputation often suffers as much as Thomson's. So far, most of the shots have been over the bow. But the changes inside the building on West First have been dramatic nevertheless.

Gone is the old meandering suburban pace. The *Tribune* has a snap to it now, an unpredictability as well. It is far more metropolitan than other Thomson papers—it covers major league baseball. But readers also awoke one morning in July to, of all things, an all-good-news edition—right down to the logo, the *Good News Tribune.* The harsh realities of the news day were not allowed to spoil the event. A burning cruise liner off Miami demanded its place. The headline became: *All Aboard Survive Cruise Ship Fire.* The changes have been pure Geere, a man so full of contradictions and energy and ideas and push—"He has people running around like rats on amphetamines in a coffee can," says one—that he totally dominates the scene.

"I'm a hired gun, simple as that," Geere says. "You hire me, I'll go." One hire took him to Romania, where the European Community sent him to instill Western journalistic principles in newsmen and women emerging from the dark. Early on, he sent ten reporters out to cover a fire at a chemical factory and they came back with ten different stories. "I knew I was in trouble," he says. "They had all made their stories up. No official had ever talked to them in the old Romania, so this is what they had always done. I failed miserably."

Geere has not done that here, although sometimes the endless spew of ideas is the bane of his troops. He has sent reporters out into the street, with photographers, to interview women about the contents of their purses. To the reporters' looks of *you're kidding*, his return stare says: Don't you get it? If you can do that, you'll be able to knock on the door of a woman widowed only an hour.

"At first, I thought we were going to be an English tabloid," says Boaz. "But that wasn't it. He was teaching us."

Whether the eclectic thoughts of Alan Geere are an advance for the cause of good journalism is your choice as well as mine. The *Tribune* is still more meringue than pie.

The 8 A.M. meeting is a dawn patrol, with Boaz deploying his first troops—"launched" is his term. By ten the day's work is serious and the outlines of tomorrow's paper take form. Geere and his editors have moved to the conference room, where no news meeting is conducted without the phone hookup to the Scottsdale bureau. Scottsdale is the plum in the group—chic, upscale, so rich with advertising dollars that its zoned edition is done artfully enough that most locals think it is a separate paper. Since Orlando, the meeting doesn't go on without the circulation director. Mike Romero is smart enough to hang back from the table just a bit.

The meeting takes on an Alan Geere buzz. There's pie today. News.

A follow-up on a messy freeway fatal has a good Arizona twist. "The kid's father is in the witness protection program," Hal DeKeyser, the Scottsdale editor, rasps over the speaker phone. "Don't know what we are going to do about that. . . ."

Bob Satnan, the news editor, is antsy. Washington is threatening to go to war with Saddam Hussein again. Let's get past this Mickey Mouse stuff. . . .

Boaz: "We've got a 79-year-old man, he went out to pick a grapefruit in his yard before bed. They found his truck burned out this morning. He had been forced to use his ATM. They're dragging the canal. . . ."

Satnan: Iraq . . .

Boaz has an Arizona bright: A good Samaritan found a thousand dollars in a purse and walked it back to its owner. Who stiffed him.

Satnan: War . . .

DeKeyser by phone: A holdup man has stolen fifty-seven Rolexes from a Scottsdale jeweler.

Jim Ripley, the managing editor: "What does a black-market Rolex go for? Ten percent?"

DeKeyser: "I dunno. We're checkin'."

Geere has been listening silently. Now he interrupts, backtracking: "Do we have a clue from the police about the missing man? You know, 79-year-old man goes out to pick grapefruit, never seen again?"

The words clatter across the table like direct orders from Patton. By the end of the day two reporters and Boaz himself will knock on the widow's door—training pays off. Geere will drive to the scene himself, purely out of curiosity. "God, it's a green house," he says. "No one will pick a grapefruit from that tree again. Was it pink or white?" By morning the story will become the page-one centerpiece with two color photos, two maps, and words from the widow. Iraq will be below the fold.

As the news hands leave the room, Geere motions to Romero to stay behind—a holdover from Orlando. He's going a mile a minute now, wants to set up a promotion with Arizona's new major league baseball team, the Diamondbacks. And then Iraq. He goes so fast he sometimes seems to lap himself. "We need to get ready for this war. Who are we going to sell to? Where are we going to make some money?" He hits the brakes like a truck in a red-light intersection. Romero doesn't get the pregnancy of it. Make money off the war. Geere has run right over his foot. And he knows that I know that he knows. Suddenly, I think that he may be the only person in two months who realizes what I have been doing. Listening. Reporting. Writing things down. The chores they all do. Joan Didion's classic line about reporters runs through my mind: "People tend to forget that my presence runs counter to their best interests." He clearly has a similar thought—and I feel bad, *good grief.* This effervescent man has caught me up in his whirling orbit, too. Then I watch his face change, fatalistically. *Sauce for the goose.* . . . And he moves quickly on, a man full of an adrenaline mix of ideas, good and bad, soon to be yesterday's news, no cheers or jeers. He also is the only one in two months who invites me home for dinner.

GEERE LIVES OUT a desert road, up a desert cul-de-sac to a solid American house with a patio that's just about a hacker's drive down a dry desert fairway. It is a Sunday afternoon and, incurable, he shouts not-always-welcome coaching to the golfers as they skitter by, some with shots that ricochet dangerously near. The address—on Western Skies Drive—

seems chosen for the friends back home in Essex, where he started this work at age eighteen, taking names at funerals.

Geere cooks dinner and talks about the craft. He can be philosophical in every direction of the compass. Conventional wisdom is not his forte. But these days when editors tend to be the most conventional people in town, he is, if nothing else, refreshing.

"A lot of people don't understand what is going on because the world is moving so fast," he begins. "We are hooked on instant deadlines, filing stories on the Internet Web site because we can't get it off the press till tomorrow morning. Papers are all going A.M. for various reasons, yet working women don't have time to read a paper in the morning. Working women are absolutely time-starved. So they read it when they come home from work. So we are filing stories on the Internet to get an even break with the electronics and, in reality, nobody has time to read it till 24 hours later anyway."

Or: "British newspapers are so different. Fewer staff. Produce more. Work on six-month contracts. Journalism is not viewed as a calling. You're only as good as your last story."

And then he enthuses: "Newspapers have been so good to me. I've lived the most exotic life, like a sports star. I go places, I do things other people can only dream of. No one owes me anything. This business has given me everything."

He knows he can be gone at any minute. "I'm only here for as long as I'm good." Then he'd hire on somewhere else or go back to writing, freelancing, spinning for a living. He made a good living at that, too. He describes the freelance piece that earned him the most money of all:

"It was a story about a man who cracked walnuts with his bottom."

Back at the office the next morning, circulator Mike Romero tries to look into the future. Suburban journalism in this kind of area is hard work. The place is booming, transient, a winter sun-lover's economy, with a powerful metro that is spending millions trying to protect the growth area around its core. Romero has to deal with a "churn" of 130 percent a year—that means 130 percent of his subscribers turn over each year. You get, you give, you get back. It's all very costly. The cost of one churn is $17.50. With an average yearly circulation of 96,000—it soars to a high of 118,000 in the winter—the churn rate alone can cost the *Tribune* several million dollars.

Romero thinks Thomson is giving the *Republic* a run for its money. And, indeed, the *Republic* has been diverting troops as well as dollars to the suburbs. The metro is holding its own in and around the Phoenix city line, including a still-strong grasp of prosperous Scottsdale, but its position weakens as the sprawl moves east into the desert—Tribune country.

"We've got 45 percent penetration in Apache Junction," he says, then grins. "But that's halfway to New Mexico."

Romero, like any good circulation man, knows how to grub for readers. He works the trailer parks, works the trailer park owners to work the "snowbirds," the retirees who flock here with the sun. Almost 40 percent of the *Tribune*'s readers are snowbirds. He has to go for them anew every year.

"By tax day they are gone," Romero says wistfully, "and this becomes a very dead place heading into a hot summer."

FIFTEEN HUNDRED MILES to the northeast, which places you pretty much in the heart of the country, Thomson has no walls to tear down. When the receptionist at Logansport's *Pharos-Tribune* says, "Just a minute, I'll see if she's here," that is exactly what she means. She can cast her eyes right over advertising and circulation to the newsroom rows. The office of the Pharos-Tribune is one medium-sized room.

Arriving in Logansport, Indiana, which requires you to cross the Wabash River where it intersects with the Eel, is about as close as you can come to stepping into yesterday. That's the way the *Pharos-Tribune,* circulation twelve thousand, looks at it, too. Proudly serving the farm counties of Carroll, Cass, Fulton, Miami, Pulaski, and White, this Thomson paper has the look of a weekly that comes out daily and Sunday, printing every gram of news to do it.

"People complain there is no good news in the paper," says Margo Marocco, fifty-six, who has reported here for thirty-three years. "I have never understood that. The fact that babies are being born, people are getting married, the school board is meeting—that's all good news and it's all in our paper."

So it is—along with column after column of calendar events, hospital notes (even admissions are news), funeral notices, area briefs, and columns that pitch the past: "Where Are They Now?" and "Time Traveler. "

Marocco is a copy editor who also handles the wire. After all these years, she has opinions—and one is that she just can't understand the newspaper's new policy on obits. Charging people—$53, at that—in their moment of grief. "That didn't go over well at all, I'll tell you. We've had some pretty strange results, too. I mean, people have been survived by their dogs."

What would happen if the mayor died?

"Now, I hadn't thought of that one." Marocco's face turns from a frown to an impish smile, no offense to His Honor. "Fifty-three dollars, I guess."

This place marches to a far different drummer than the one pacing the Alan Geeres. Thomson bought the *Pharos-Tribune* in 1995 during the Strategic Marketing Group shuffling. Most of the reporters think the paper has been playing more softball since then. The executive editor and publisher, Dollie Cromwell, a whiz-kid arrival at thirty-three, is immensely popular but an unabashed booster. "The city council and the school boards have internal conflict," Cromwell says. "Everybody knows it. I don't want to feed the fires." But, if you are willing to get up very early in the morning, the way farm folk do, you find that all is not lost. That's when Kris Baker, twenty-one years old, moving double-time in her jeans and running shoes, starts the cop-shop run—6 A.M. in the summer, 6:30 in the winter.

Baker ran out of money and was forced to drop out of communications school at DePauw University after a year and a half. Now she uses her Thomson salary—she got a second-year raise to $9.73, an increase of 37 cents an hour—to repay her school loans and continue with night classes at nearby Indiana University at Kokomo. Her aspirations point toward the big city, but she is staying for the time being. Her father, who is into soybeans and corn and is now "doing cows and pigs," has been ill. It's not a good time to move on.

She flutters through the reports, pencil in hand—not a big news day, even by Logansport standards. Car hit by egg, reads one complaint; carpenter's level stolen off the roof of the Hard Times Custom Cycle, reads another. The egg caper will not make the paper. The stolen carpenter's level will, as will the damage that Frederick T. Weese did to his wheel and bearings hitting a pothole near the train tracks.

"Anything else?" Baker asks crisply after getting to the bottom of the basket.

"Nope."

Baker wears a shield of farm-girl shyness. But there is no straw in her hair and the disguise is as good as the one worn by her unknown soul mate in West Virginia, Theresa Haynes. "Sometimes they just withhold them," she says as she moves down the hall. So she lays booby traps behind her, almost invisible pencil marks in the corner of each report. Every few days she goes back through the old reports, thumbing the corners till a corner comes up unmarked. Gets her best stories that way.

POSTSCRIPT: *In early 2000, as this book was being edited for publication, Thomson Corp. confirmed the suspicions of many when it announced it was getting out of the newspaper business, at least in the United States—shedding all forty-nine of its U.S. dailies, plus dozens of weeklies, plus all but one of its Canadian papers. The company said it would concentrate resources instead on Internet-related services. It sold nineteen of its U.S. dailies to Gannett, seventeen to CNHI, and the rest to Media General, MediaNews, and a few other companies.*

9 *The quality of a newspaper depends, more than anything else, on its owners. When a chain is owned by financial investors whose sole concern is profits (Journal Register or Gannett, for example) its papers are often inferior. If a newspaper is independently owned, it may be excellent (the* St. Petersburg Times*) or dreadful (the* Daily Oklahoman*) or somewhere in between, depending on the commitment and talent of its owners. The same goes for a newspaper chain. Because the Thomson family owns 73 percent of that company's common shares, its papers could have been as good as the family wished to make them. What was missing was the desire.*

Of course, an owner's commitment may change over time. In the 1950s, under Norman Chandler, the Los Angeles Times *was an embarrassment, shamelessly promoting the Chandler family's interests while savaging its enemies. But when Norman's son, Otis, took control, he made the* Times *responsible and distinguished. Advance Publications, owned by the Newhouse brothers, Si and Donald, let its papers languish for decades, but in the 1990s a number of the company's papers improved considerably—the* New Orleans Times-Picayune, *the* Newark Star-Ledger, *and Portland's* Oregonian *in particular.*

Most of the best American papers have a third type of ownership. These were originally owned by a family that "went public"—that is, raised capital by selling stock—in such a way that the family retained operating control. The "voting shares" of the New York Times Co., for example, are held by members of the Sulzberger family, while the "non-voting shares" are traded on the New York Stock Exchange, and a family member who wants to sell shares must first convert them to non-voting stock. In this way, the Sulzbergers evade the tyranny of Wall Street. The Washington Post Co. has a similar stock structure, with the Graham family holding the voting shares.

Although independently owned newspapers are shrinking in number, chains with voting and non-voting classes of stock continue to thrive. Dow Jones & Co., McClatchy Newspapers, Pulitzer Publishing, Lee Enterprises, Scripps Howard Newspapers, and Media General all have this type of ownership. And as with privately owned papers, the difference in quality depends on the commitment of the controlling family.

A.H. Belo Corporation is a company that has not abandoned quality in its quest for profits.

Giant

By Roy Reed

LARRY MCMURTRY'S OLD Texas Rangers would not have much patience with Texas these days. Augustus McCrae would cast a baleful eye around Lonesome Dove, planted now no doubt with a thousand acres of office cubicles, and shake his head over the loss of amplitude. His laconic friend Woodrow Call would say to hell with it and strike out for Montana.

Even the Texas language has changed. Rangers are now a baseball team in a metroplex, and Cowboys are a soap opera searching for the Super Bowl. The verb "to wildcat," as for oil, is now as rare as "no sir" and "no ma'am."

With all the shrinkage in style, it is gratifying to find Texans who still think big. Giants are still at work down here, if you know where to look, in spite of all the urbanizing, modernizing, and taming of the Texas spirit.

One of them can be found smack in the middle of downtown Dallas, sitting on the top floor of the Belo Building on Record Street. Robert W. Decherd, the man who has, quite abruptly, turned the A.H. Belo Corp. into one of the nation's most important media enterprises, would be easy to miss if you caught him away from his lair. He wears glasses, quiet neckties and quiet suits, and if he were somewhat younger than his forty-seven years you would call him gangling. His shoes look Italian, but you don't ask. There's a coat of dignity about him that you don't violate with such an impertinence unless you really have to know.

But he is a giant, all right, even if he does fly like a scared quail at the mention of the word. Only a fellow with the brash confidence of the pioneer Texans could have mounted his unlikely nag, the *Dallas Morning News,* and run the *Dallas Times Herald* clean out of town. And now this unlikely conqueror has started moving into distant territories. As a result, rival companies that didn't even know they were rivals a few years ago are casting watchful eyes toward Dallas, wondering what Belo will do next. Those of us who have despaired over the downward drift of American newspapers in recent years are watching Belo for another reason. Here, it appears, is a business institution bent on proving that it can do well by doing good.

After a huge outlay in 1997 for new properties, which drove earnings down slightly, the company still had a net profit of $83 million on total revenue of $1.25 billion. In 1999 the net profit was $87 million on total revenue of $1.4 billion. Under Decherd's guidance, Belo has bought seven daily papers since 1995, although it put three of the smaller ones up for sale again in 2000. In a separate move, the *Dallas Morning News* has converted its zoned edition for Arlington, Texas, into a stand-alone daily paper to provide a buffer against the *Fort Worth Star-Telegram*. The *News* also has bought a profitable weekly at nearby Colleyville, Texas, and is running it as a separate enterprise. The largest and most prestigious of the acquisitions is the *Providence Journal*, the New England institution that became a daily newspaper during the presidency of Andrew Jackson. Others include the *Press-Enterprise* in Riverside, California, and the *Record-Chronicle* in Denton, Texas.

Belo's early promise as a newspaper chain seems to be based on two radical ideas promoted by Decherd, the company's chairman and CEO. If they prove profitable in the long term, they could prompt some second thoughts about newspaper publishing in the United States.

First, Belo leaves the local editors and publishers in their jobs when it buys a paper. Contrary to a trend among chains in recent years, Belo's philosophy is that these managers know more about the community and the newspaper than some hotshot sent from corporate headquarters to show the locals how to run things for a couple of years before moving on to a better job. There have been a few exceptions, but in those cases the papers sought help from Dallas. Managers on the scene are given remarkable freedom. "Run it as if it were your own paper," they are told.

Second, Belo operates on the theory that if mediocre journalism makes money—as it demonstrably does—good journalism will make as much or more, over the long haul. Underlining the emphasis on journalistic values, Belo looks for publishers with newsroom backgrounds. Where that is not practical, it trains its publishers to think like news people.

Decherd's philosophy seems to be working. Early indications are that the newly acquired papers, most of them already well-regarded, will become even better. And the *Dallas Morning News*, which a generation ago was considered a pariah in newspaper circles and was in a sullen slump in parts of its home state, has become one of the top papers in the United States, by one measurement the ninth largest paper. In 1997 *Time* magazine included it in a list of ten papers "worth watching." Once a narrow-minded instrument of right-wing politics, it has become a disseminator of non-ideological information on a broad range of the American scene. The people who run Belo say they intend to operate their new papers on the same principles.

Belo is a publicly traded company firmly controlled by a single family. Thanks to a stock ownership arrangement that makes it very difficult for ordinary shareholders to dictate policy, Belo can concentrate on long-term growth instead of short-term profit.

"We're making at least as much money, and I believe we'll make more money in the long term, than if we ran these businesses just for margins," Decherd tells me in one of two lengthy interviews in his quietly appointed office high above downtown Dallas. It is a remote aerie, but Decherd's amiable engagement makes it seem anything but isolated. He sits in shirt sleeves, relaxed, thoughtful, deliberate, but not too serious. "We are convinced," he says, "beginning with our directors, that you can achieve greater financial and business success by having extraordinarily good journalistic products."

Belo's growth has gone virtually unnoticed outside media circles, Wall Street, and the cities into which the company has expanded. The average American might not know how to pronounce the company's name (it's BEE-lo), much less identify its business. But that's changing, due in part to Decherd. He is doing for the company at the beginning of this century what a famous ancestor did for it at the turn of the last: He has transformed the *Morning News* into the most powerful journalistic voice of the Southwest, and made himself into a figure of interest and influence far beyond Texas.

A S A BOY, Robert Decherd was aware around the family dinner table that his father was part of the city's great newspaper dynasty, that Great-Grandfather George Bannerman Dealey had been the force behind the *Dallas Morning News,* that the city had named a plaza after him. But the boy felt no particular pressure to become a newspaperman. That might have been because his father, H. Ben Decherd, a talented, able man, was not allowed to run the company. He had the job of board chairman, but he never became chief executive. Never mind that he was an obvious choice. Speculation was that he simply had the wrong last name. Everybody knew that Dealeys ran the *Morning News.*

It was young Robert's interest in sports—he was co-captain of the football team at St. Mark's private school in Dallas—that led him to write for the school paper. Once on the staff, he discovered there was more to a newspaper than the sports section. He ended up as editor in chief.

Sent off to Harvard to study history, he made the same progression at the *Harvard Crimson:* sportswriter to news reporter to president of the paper. Decherd was the first Texan to run the *Crimson.* From Cambridge, he also worked as a stringer for the *New York Times.* David Gelsanliter, the author of *Fresh Ink,* a book about the *Morning News,* quotes a friend from Decherd's Harvard days as saying that this serious young man was "the only one of us who didn't smoke dope," and remembering him as "20 going on 35."

Decherd got hooked on journalism. He went straight home to Dallas after graduation in 1973 and enrolled in the management training program at the *Morning News.* He spent much of it in the newsroom, where he felt most at home. His youth raised eyebrows among those who didn't know him well. Here was a kid fresh out of liberal Harvard, a place more congenial to pinko Kennedys than to he-man Texan conservatives like some of his Dallas family. There surely was some internal worry, perhaps even suspicion, about a man who didn't carry the Dealey name becoming poised to take over the business one day.

Suspicions notwithstanding, it soon became obvious that here was a mature and capable individual. His elders noticed especially that he was good with figures, a rare quality in a newsroom.

Decherd was on the editorial page staff for a while, but all along he was developing managerial skills. Joe Dealey, who had succeeded his father, E.M. "Ted" Dealey, as head of the company, was impressed partly by the way Decherd helped thwart a pressmen's strike in 1974. Gelsanliter in *Fresh Ink* describes how the young man, after volunteering for the assignment, worked eighteen hours a day scheduling press crews and manning the telephones. It gave Joe Dealey a glimpse of the toughness his kinsman was about to exhibit with more momentous assignments.

In 1976 Decherd and his sister—happily named Dealey—came into control of the largest block of Belo shares when the family trust that owned the company expired. That gave Decherd the clout to win a seat on the board of directors, and he began to assert his influence. At his suggestion the company hired Jeremy L. Halbreich, an acquaintance from the *Harvard Crimson.* Halbreich joined as a management trainee and seventeen years later would become president of the *Morning News.*

By 1979, only six years after returning from college, Decherd was vice president for administration. At the time, the board was considering taking the company public. Decherd was asked to oversee the transition. Then came his most daunting assignment—figuring out how to deal with growing competition from the *Dallas Times Herald,* the city's longtime afternoon paper which was gradually converting to all-day.

Times Mirror, then a vigorously expanding media company with money, vision and talent, had bought the *Times Herald* in 1970, and in less than a decade it had almost caught up with the *News* in Sunday circulation. With newfound vigor and a way with a big story, the paper had shaken the more somnolent *Morning News* to its core. More troubling yet, Belo reasoned that it was only a matter of time before the *News* would be battling the *Times Herald* head-to-head in the morning. Dallas was a large and growing city, but it could not support two daily papers forever. Newspaper fans from out of state were predicting that the *Times Herald* would be the survivor. More than a few hoped so.

It was 1980. Decherd, having been promoted again to executive vice president of the newspaper, was just twenty-nine years old, an age when many men are just thinking of getting a steady job and settling down. Instead, he was being asked to steer his company's fortunes in a major newspaper war.

If he was intimidated, Decherd didn't show it. Indeed, as he mulled Belo's predicament with the *Times Herald,* another problem arose that he recognized as an opportunity. Tom Simmons, who had been with the *Morning News* for forty-nine years, was retiring as editor of the paper, and it fell to Decherd to find a replacement. In the context of the coming battle, he knew this would be one of the most crucial decisions of his entire career. In the same situation, most publishing executives would hire a search firm or solicit candidates through back-channel networks. Decherd, not yet thirty, went on a journey.

For eight months he crisscrossed the United States. He interviewed dozens of people, both candidates for the job of executive editor and others in the business who might give advice. Decherd had specific qualities in mind for his "perfect" editor. He wanted someone hard-nosed, energetic, quick to see stories and to make reporters see them. He avoided practitioners of advocacy journalism, which was still in some vogue at the time.

Mainly, though, he looked for something more than an editor. Several first-rate editors were interviewed, but most held, to some degree, the usual newsroom prejudices against the business side. "One of the purposes of the search," Decherd says now, "was to find not only a person who had the capability of sharpening the focus of our news and editorial efforts, but could grow into the role of publisher. . . . You can't be sure that the person you select is going to grow into that role, but we wanted to find someone who was inspired by the opportunity to work through the editorial track— the news and editorial track—to the top of the organization."

All the contenders Decherd interviewed were newspapermen—all but the one he would hire. Eventually he was led to a short, tough native

Kentuckian, a veteran Associated Press employee who hadn't worked at a newspaper since his first reporting job on the *Ashland Daily Independent* back in the '50s.

Decherd knew almost at once that he had found the right partner.

"T HE DIFFERENCE BETWEEN Burl Osborne and everyone else I met," Decherd tells me, looking back on that odyssey, "is that it was clear he understood how the entire newspaper operated. He had a very strong news and editorial background. But by sense of personality and his own instincts, plus his experience in the Associated Press, representing the AP to publishers, he had developed a very keen awareness of how the advertising, marketing, distribution and production requirements, or aspects, of a newspaper support the editorial mission. And that's rare among journalists. And among the group of very distinguished men and women I met, he had a stand-alone instinct for it."

Burl Osborne, then forty-two, was managing editor of the AP. Tough-minded and relentless, he was the first in his family to go to college. After that initial reporting experience, he had spent twenty years with the AP in Kentucky, West Virginia, Ohio, Colorado, Washington state, Washington, D.C., and New York.

He was smart—and quick-tempered. Osborne was a head shorter than Decherd, which led inevitably to Mutt and Jeff jokes around the company —but never to their faces. Decherd's dignity held such familiarity at bay. With Osborne, what held people back was a suspicion that he'd punch them in the nose.

Decherd made clear that Osborne's first priority was meeting the challenge of the *Times Herald*. He brought to the task his combative instincts and a shrewd mind for analysis. He knew the *Times Herald* was gaining. He had to figure out why. As it happened, an extensive reader survey commissioned by Decherd and Halbreich a year or so earlier had uncovered two main weaknesses in the *Morning News:* business and sports, subjects that around Dallas might better be called obsessions.

Osborne started with his business report. A second round of surveying had concentrated on Dallas CEOs, who had taken hours of their time to tell interviewers just how poorly both papers were covering their field. The *Morning News* business staff hovered around eight people, including the editor. Items usually ran on a single page inside the sports section. This in a city where banking, investments, and real estate had edged out ranching and farming decades ago.

"Dallas is a city that eats, drinks and breathes business," says Cheryl Hall, a *Morning News* columnist and former business editor. "Everything that is here is a business. . . . The Dallas Cowboys were successful because [the team] was a successful business. . . . It's a big city, but it also has kind of the same intrigue of a small community where people gossip and care what each other is doing."

One of Osborne's first moves, with Decherd's approval, was to increase the newsroom budget by 50 percent, from $6 million to $9 million. Much of that went into hiring reporters and increasing salaries, which had been embarrassingly low. (Hall went to work on the business staff in 1972 for $95 a week. She was making less than $400 a week as assistant business editor when Osborne arrived in 1980.) The increase in pay did more than boost morale. It enabled the paper to hire experienced reporters and editors who otherwise wouldn't have given the *News* a second look. In the business section, Osborne doubled the size of the staff virtually overnight. He shifted assistant city editor Bob Mong to business editor, a signal that something big was afoot since Mong clearly was an up-and-comer. Today he is executive vice president of Belo's publishing division.

Mong set about reorganizing coverage of the city's businesses, their leaders, and their workers. He hired new reporters and moved others from the city desk. Southern Methodist University's business school held special classes in business and finance so reporters could operate and write with authority. Authority: that was the aim of the revitalized coverage. The paper started its first separate business section, Business Tuesday, in late 1980. "It took the city by storm," recalls Jeremy Halbreich. "The *Times Herald* never got around to matching it. And I knew and Burl knew and a few others knew that was a strategic error on their part that they never recovered from."

Hall was promoted to business editor in 1982, the first woman to hold that job. The staff was up to seventeen by then. When she moved out to write a column ten years later, the staff numbered almost forty. Her reporters broke the news of the bankruptcy of Braniff Airways in 1982, for which the paper was a Pulitzer Prize finalist. The paper had two business reporters covering the Falklands war. "It was a money war, as so many wars are," Hall explains.

A business reporter, Steve Brown, reported in 1985 that Dallas had millions of square feet of new office space with too few tenants to fill it. When the city's real estate bubble burst the following year, some blamed Brown, the messenger. One reader sent him a hammer and a box of nails and said, "Why don't you just finish the coffin?" (Not everyone saw Brown's reporting as bold and aggressive. Some said he and the *Morning News* had watched in silence for most of two years, reporting little or none of the overbuilding until it became too obvious to ignore.)

In later years, the *Morning News* expanded its business coverage abroad. For a while there was a Canadian bureau for business news. Now the paper covers Asia and Mexico assiduously. It has three reporters based in Mexico City.

Hall says she has worked for two different papers, both at the *Morning News*—pre-1980 and post-1980. She has no doubt who gets the credit for the improvements. "If the recorder wasn't on," she says in an interview, "I'd say Burl is God."

OSBORNE MAKES AN unlikely deity, but there is no doubting his extraordinary drive and pride. He was reared in the Baptist church, which was always a little déclassé; a Baptist kid had to work harder to prove himself. Then there was the health history. His father died of lung cancer. Burl's own health was gravely threatened in his twenties. He was diagnosed with nephritis, a kidney disease that would have killed him without dialysis. After two years on the life-saving machine, his mother donated a kidney for a transplant. The surgery was successful, but sixteen years later Belo's physicians would size up Osborne as a poor health risk and recommend against hiring him. Decherd overrode them.

Years later Osborne would need another kidney transplant. The donor this time was his brother. Today Osborne brushes aside questions about his health with a joke: "The last time I was in, they said, 'Well, we have good news and bad news. The good news is, this kidney thing is never going to kill you. And the bad news is, something will.' I'm essentially normal. I'm certainly healthier than I have a right to be and probably above-average health for my age."

Osborne would channel his determination into the continued improvement of the News. After beefing up business, he turned to sports. Halbreich remembers it this way: "If we feel we need to totally remake a section, and in this case it's sports, where's the first place you're going to start? We need to find a great editor, okay? I can have all sorts of slick marketing to advertise to the community. I can have great solicitation programs. But unless we're going to get a great editor and sometime soon have a great product to deliver, we're not going to fulfill our mission. And that's when Burl and others identified Dave Smith."

David L. Smith came in 1981 with a national reputation. He had directed the Boston Globe's acclaimed sports section for most of the '70s, and he was at the Washington Star when Decherd and Osborne beckoned. "They said, 'Think about what it would take to make this the best sports section in the country,'" Smith recalls. "And I came back and gave them budget figures, personnel figures, told them how much space we'd need at the start." Decherd and Osborne obliged. There were twenty-one people on the sports staff in 1981; ten more were added immediately. By the late 1990s there were seventy.

With that many reporters and editors, Smith can overwhelm a story. He sent thirty-five people to cover the Super Bowl the last time the Dallas Cowboys played in it. The 1996 Summer Olympics in Atlanta rated twenty-one staffers. The 1998 Winter Olympics in Nagano, Japan, was staffed by nine. Sports Day, as the section is called, has won numerous awards. The Associated Press Sports Editors—Smith is a founder and past president—has consistently named it one of the nation's top ten sports sections. Smith himself won the prestigious Red Smith award in 1990.

Osborne had a theory. If the *Morning News* made a splash with sports coverage, the paper's sports reporters would talk about it in their travels around the country. Word would get back to newsrooms everywhere that the *Morning News* was a good place to work.

For whatever reasons—improved sports coverage is probably one—the paper has attracted good people from prominent papers. Denise Beeber, the news editor, worked at the *Dallas Times Herald* and the *Los Angeles Times* before being lured back to Dallas; Charles Camp, the business editor, had worked at the *Wall Street Journal;* Lois Reed, the assistant managing editor for administration, was hired from the *New York Times;* Keith Campbell, assistant managing editor for the news and universal desks, came from the *St. Petersburg Times;* Ricardo Chavira, assistant managing editor for national and international news, was a correspondent for *Time* magazine; Stuart Wilk, managing editor, had been assistant city editor at the *Milwaukee Sentinel* before the *News* hired him as night city editor in 1980; and Gilbert Bailon, vice president and executive editor, came to the *News* in 1986 after working as a reporter for the *Fort Worth Star-Telegram,* the *Los Angeles' Daily News,* the *San Diego Union,* and the *Kansas City Star.*

One of the few top editors who was not hired from a nationally known paper was Ralph Langer. In 1981 he was editing Washington's *Everett Herald;* Osborne plucked him out and made him his managing editor. He became executive editor in 1983. In 1991, when Decherd fulfilled his intuition by naming Osborne publisher, Langer became the top person in the newsroom and added senior vice president to his title. Today, Langer (rhymes with *ranger*) is editor and executive vice president.

AFTER BUSINESS AND SPORTS, Osborne's team set out to beat the *Times Herald* on local news. "Local" meant everything from city hall to Austin to southern Oklahoma. Dallas exploded beyond its official boundaries years ago. The metropolitan area that it now shares with Fort Worth covers a part of northern Texas that is almost one hundred miles long and one hundred miles wide. The freeways blur with commuters and commerce twenty-four hours a day. You no longer have to go downtown to see skyscrapers; they pop up right across the suburban landscape. Beyond geography is the Texas way of looking at things. Thus, a resident of Dallas—like a resident of Houston, San Antonio, or Austin—reasons that his city *is* Texas.

Osborne adopted that view. Under his prodding, the *Morning News* gave new scrutiny to government and public policy as far as the shadow of Dallas could be seen in his mind's eye—to the Rio Grande, the Panhandle, El Paso . . . even across the Mexican border.

Well-written features were played on page one. Immigration became a running story, and there seemed to be new sensitivity to the interests of Spanish-speaking residents. African Americans received more attention. One thing missing from Osborne's front pages was crime—the daily shootings, knifings, and robberies that some papers still emphasize. He told Gelsanliter, "We see our newspaper as a member of the family— coming into the house before breakfast, before you've had your first cup of coffee, when you may still be a little grumpy. Tone of voice is important then. There is seldom a need to shout."

Osborne and Decherd's people saw themselves as fighting for their paper's life. The corporate attitude at the competitor seemed less focused and perhaps, until it was too late, less concerned. In time, the *Morning News* strategy worked. The *Times Herald* lost its momentum, then began to lose ground. By 1986, the circulation of the *Morning News* stood at 390,000; the *Times Herald* had fallen to 245,000. Times Mirror gave up and sold the paper to Dean Singleton for $110 million in cash and notes. (Times Mirror also agreed to finish a $45 million plant expansion.)

Decherd thought Singleton paid too much and brought too little capital to compete. Singleton also suffered from bad timing. He bought the *Times Herald* shortly after Dallas had gone into recession because of a drop in oil and real estate prices. He cut one hundred jobs, closed four bureaus, and shut down the Sunday magazine. Meantime, he further extended himself by buying the *Denver Post* and the *Houston Post*.

Singleton bailed out in 1988. He sold the *Times Herald* to John Buzzetta, a former employee of Singleton's MediaNews Group. By this time the *Morning News*—agile, strong, rich, and locally controlled—was outpacing its rival by two to one, not only in circulation but in ad lineage. It was publishing more full-run classified advertising than any other American paper. The *Times Herald,* meanwhile, continued to cut costs. Then in 1989, Belo outmaneuvered the new owner and got exclusive rights to the Universal Press Syndicate's service, depriving the *Times Herald* of Doonesbury and other popular features. That was the last big blow for Buzzetta. He closed the paper in 1991 and sold the assets to Belo for $55 million. The *News* picked up more than half the other paper's readers.

The recession that helped to finish the *Times Herald* visited the *Morning News* as well. But Decherd and his people held fast. In spite of a serious dip in earnings, the company continued construction of an expensive printing plant at nearby Plano, an investment that would pay off handsomely in efficiency and improved looks of the paper. Decherd and Osborne were tempted to cut the news staff; they refused. They were tempted to cut the newshole to save on production costs; they refused.

"We took a hit," admits Osborne. "However, when that recession ended, we had a state-of-the-art printing plant. We had our staff intact. We had our newshole. We came out of it like gangbusters. So, we felt pain and we cut costs, but we tried not to cut where it would hurt the quality of the relationship with readers or the quality of [the editorial product]. And, you know, we don't feel heroic about that because it wasn't fun. But the fact is that we had choices to make, and we made them, and as a result I think we're stronger today than we would have been if we had done it otherwise."

Had anyone done an autopsy on the *Times Herald,* one other cause of death would be noted. Halbreich, president of the News, talks about it. "We [at the *Morning News*] were all local, and this was before Belo was even public. And so when we decided we were going to invest two, three million dollars in the product in these various initiatives over the next calendar year, we just did it. Obviously, Robert and others were involved in that decision-making process, but we just did it. When [the *Times Herald*] decided they wanted to do something or needed to do something, they obviously had to go to L.A., beg, borrow and steal, and by the time they got back, we were three months down the line. So we had some great, great advantages there."

Will Jarrett, a former editor of the *Times Herald,* confirms this. He told Gelsanliter, "If we wanted to try something new, we'd have to go back to the mother ship in Los Angeles for approval. It sometimes took weeks for us to get a response. Whenever the *News* saw an opportunity, they could turn on a dime."

There was another problem with chain ownership. "If Times Mirror sent some bright person to the *Dallas Times Herald*," Halbreich says, "either in a newsroom position or in a business position, they rarely came here with the sense that this was where they were going to make their career. They came here with the notion that if I can sort of earn my spurs in a short period of time, then I'll be promoted maybe to *Newsday* or back to Los Angeles. When those of us at the *Morning News* came to work for the *Morning News,* we came with the commitment that this was where we were going to have our career."

The deal to buy the rival's assets had to be approved by the Justice Department. To help persuade antitrust officials, the then-president of Belo, Jim Sheehan, promised that the *News* would offer a more diverse range of opinion. It has made good on that. The editorial page is a bastion of centrism, just a whisper to the right but nothing like the days when it was the bullhorned voice of the most conservative elements of Texas. The latter got a glimpse of the change some years ago when the *News* turned against apartheid in South Africa. The editorial page raised eyebrows further when it began talking about the environment. It shocked the conservative hard core when it came out for a state income tax and hiring gay police officers and even said good things about gun control. Then it started calling for diversity in local government—meaning, give Latinos and African Americans more of a voice. It enraged many conservatives by standing up for abortion rights, although in a qualified, limited way. It has made up for that somewhat by criticizing President Clinton for what it perceived to be shortfalls of character. Yet even here, the tone was less vituperative than the commentary of the *Wall Street Journal* and the *New York Times.*

Before Decherd and the tightening of standards, right-wing opinion occasionally leached into the news columns. A notorious example was a series the *News* published in the early '60s purporting to expose the Young Men's Christian Association of Austin as a hotbed of hippies and leftists. The series was titled "YM(?)A." That prompted an editorial in the student paper at the University of Texas headlined "Dallas Morning (?)."

On the twentieth anniversary of the Kennedy assassination, the '60s political climate of Dallas was described by Stanley Marcus, chairman emeritus of Neiman Marcus, in his weekly column for the *News:* "There was a spirit of hate in Dallas then—in the strong Republican districts in North Dallas where people believed they had the only true and revealed truth and could not conceive of any pluralism in society. They were abetted by this newspaper. The *Dallas News* was the one instrument that could have refuted that point of view, but it didn't. It just aided and abetted it."

UNDER DECHERD AND OSBORNE, the paper won three Pulitzer Prizes during the last five years of its competition with the *Times Herald*. One was for photography. Two were for reporting: an investigative piece on subsidized housing and an in-depth look at an airplane crash. Three more Pulitzers would come during the three successive years after the *Times Herald* closed, two for investigative reporting and another for photography.

In late 1994, the paper assigned two top investigative reporters, Howard Swindle and Dan Malone, to one of the most ambitious projects it had undertaken in years. As assistant managing editor for projects, Swindle had supervised three Pulitzer-winning stories. Malone had been involved in some of the paper's best investigative stories, including the Pulitzer-winning effort on police abuse of authority.

The pair started a reporting project that the paper later described as the first in-depth national survey of death row inmates. The research staff and the writers, assisted by several outside authorities on legal matters, drew up a survey of seventy-five questions. It was mailed to death row inmates in thirty-five states. It was answered by 603 condemned people. More than 100 others sent letters and other documents. The reporters interviewed more than three dozen inmates. The resulting series appeared in 1997, more than two years after research had begun, in four installments. It was a revealing, intimate, and chilling portrait of the most violent Americans and the system that deals with them.

Local and regional reporting continue to be strong, especially in the seven counties of the metro area. The *News* has become the paper of record in dozens of surrounding towns. It regularly breaks stories of wrongdoing by officials. Health, science, and social problems get lavish attention, not just at home but wherever in the United States the story leads. The paper was consistently ahead of the pack in reporting the legal troubles of the tobacco industry in Texas. It has bureaus in the capital city of Austin and three other Texas cities: Houston, San Antonio, and Tyler.

The paper keeps a bureau in Oklahoma City, which is a little more than two hundred miles from Dallas. In 1995, when the Alfred P. Murrah Federal Building there was bombed, the *Morning News* practically treated it as a local story. From the day of the bombing through the trials of Timothy McVeigh and Terry Nichols, the paper's expenses for coverage were more than $200,000, said executive editor Bailon. Added editor Langer, "We had five or six people on the road for weeks and weeks at a time." One of the stories, an exclusive report that McVeigh had confessed to a private investigator, was controversial. Some thought it would prejudice McVeigh's trial. Langer said editors believed the story was of national importance and that "we were obligated to publish it."

A large percentage of all news stories are staff-written, even those from abroad. The paper has bureaus in Washington and Los Angeles. It has five fully staffed foreign bureaus, in Bangkok, Cairo, London, Mexico City, and Panama. The editors are especially proud of the paper's coverage of Mexico, which Ricardo Chavira, the assistant managing editor for foreign and national reporting, considers the best in any American paper.

Staff correspondents produce authoritative stories on economics and politics from Asia and Latin America. Many are played on page one, especially if they go beyond breaking news and explain why Dallas readers should pay attention. And there's been a new emphasis on good story-telling in recent years.

Page one typically has five to seven stories, half usually local and the others from Washington and elsewhere. The newshole inside the first section is divided more or less equally among national, international, and state news. The Austin bureau reports on state government with rigor and frequently with style. In a story outlining the questionable past of two brothers in the private prison business, Christy Hoppe wrote, "Both have done business with so many state leaders that their Rolodex looks like a ballot sheet."

People in the newsroom point also to Doug Swanson, Steve Blow, and David Flick as especially good writers. Flick's features appear often on page one. Swanson often writes backgrounders on serious topics. Blow is probably the best local columnist on the paper except for the veteran sports columnist Blackie Sherrod, who moved to the *News* from the *Times Herald* in 1985 and has a national reputation for insight and acerbic wit. One or two of the other columnists seem plodding.

Political analysis is scarce, but managing editor Wilk contended that's not a bad thing. "You can get at it through good reporting," he said. The editors are alert for signs of editorializing. The adjective "posh" in front of "Highland Park house" will draw a warning note to the reporter. "We want colorful writing," Langer said, "but what we don't want is writing that tells people what we think about them. . . . The best writers have the least problems."

The paper's writing is generally clear and straightforward, if not always sparkling. It is still called the Morning Snooze in some circles, but that is wider of the mark than it might once have been. Paula LaRocque, the writing coach and an assistant managing editor, works full time training reporters and wrestling with writing problems, a Sisyphean task. She rolls her eyes when asked about a couple of strained leads on Super Bowl stories. Two days later, in a feature on fashions, I count twenty-eight words in an introductory clause before I get to the rest of the lead.

Perhaps the main criticism of today's *Morning News,* which one hears from people inside and outside the newspaper, is an echo of its past: that it is too respectful of the city's business establishment. One person tells of the time Robert Crandall, the longtime head of Texas-based American Airlines, exploded at a *News* business reporter over a humorous and seemingly inconsequential story. Crandall banned the reporter from the airline's premises. Osborne, who is well acquainted with Crandall, talked him into letting the reporter back in. The person who tells the story, who is not associated with the *Morning News,* cites it as an example of back-scratching among fellow members of the upper crust.

Another source who wishes not to be identified—also not a *News* employee—says the top officers of a Dallas-based corporation a few years ago went over the head of a *News* reporter who was investigating the company's stock decline on Wall Street. They met with senior editors and were assured that the editors would take a close look at the reporter's story. The source does not know whether the editors toned down the piece, but he says what appeared in print was not as tough as had been expected.

Reporters at two other news outlets say the *Morning News'* coverage of the Texas savings and loan scandal of the 1980s was thorough in some regards but tended to emphasize actions by Washington regulators rather than those of the local figures who caused the scandal. Some of those figures were highly regarded in the Dallas business community until they went to prison for such activities as using company money to buy beach houses and hire prostitutes. The same men stole hundreds of millions of dollars that had to be made good by the federal government. One of the competing reporters puts it this way: "Everybody who is somebody in Dallas is on somebody's bank board. There's no way you can do a story [like the savings and loan scandal] without hanging someone important."

Langer, with his customary calm, dismissed the idea that the city's business leaders have undue influence with Belo, even though the company's board includes some of the most prominent business executives in Dallas.

In the old days, it was common knowledge that eight or ten leaders of the Citizens Council (no relation to the disreputable white citizens councils that once struggled for racial segregation) made decisions affecting the entire city, and Belo was definitely represented on the council. This small club could get an arena built or a new road pushed through. But Langer said the Citizens Council no longer controls Dallas because political power has been dispersed.

Dallas voters approved a large bond issue in 1998 to build a new sports arena, and some in the newsroom saw the paper's handling of the story as yet another example of supporting the business leadership that wanted it. Langer said this notion was likewise untrue, and probably was floated because word got out that Osborne was interested in the story. "There are people in the newsroom—any newsroom I've ever been in," Langer said, "who see sacred cows where no one can hear a moo."

C URIOUSLY, the history of the *Dallas Morning News* begins not in Dallas but in Galveston. The paper was a spinoff of the *Galveston News,* which was started in 1842 when Texas was a republic and that port community was its primary city. It was not until north Texas began to develop after the Civil War that the *News* saw fit to open a branch office in the little town of Dallas.

By then, the paper had long been the leading editorial voice of Texas. Its first owner of substance, Willard Richardson, was an influential figure in pioneer Texas. He was a political enemy of Sam Houston. They fought among other things over secession; the editor was hot for it. He also stood up for slavery. When he died in 1875—outlasting the hero of San Jacinto by twelve years—control of the paper passed to an equally strong-minded younger man, Alfred Horatio Belo.

Colonel Belo had gone to work for the paper in 1865 fresh from battle. He had led a regiment of his fellow North Carolinians through much of the fiercest fighting of the Civil War. He was just twenty-six when Lee surrendered, and he was reluctant to quit fighting. Settling in Galveston and working for Richardson was a suitable compromise. The *News* continued a kind of war throughout Reconstruction as it led a five-year campaign to wrest political control of Texas from "the alien, the scalawag and the thief."

As Colonel Belo got his passions under control, he shifted the paper steadily toward the more impersonal journalism that would characterize American newspapers for most of the coming century. The emphasis on news instead of opinion paid off. At one time in the 1870s, the *News* claimed a daily circulation of eight-thousand, double that of any other Texas paper.

For the *Galveston News,* sending hundreds of copies of the paper to north Texas by railroad every day got expensive. In 1882 Belo ordered George Bannerman Dealey, a twenty-three-year-old mailing clerk, to scout out a location for a separate edition of the *News.* When after long study Dallas was selected as the home of the new paper, Dealey was named its business manager.

The *Dallas Morning News* put its first papers on the street October 1,

1885. To demonstrate that the new paper would be more than a shadow of its parent in Galveston, Colonel Belo moved his own family to Dallas. The paper quickly established itself as a spokesman for business and economic development. The railroad magnate Jay Gould was its friend. When workmen struck the Texas railroads in 1886, the *News* called them conspirators and subversives. Its news columns might be reserved for facts, but the editorial page continued to deliver strong opinions, just as it had under Richardson.

Populism, which ran strong among Texas farmers during the last two decades of the nineteenth century, was a favorite target. So was communism. A proposed commission to regulate railroads in the late 1880s was branded "an insidious form of communism." At the same time, the paper championed numerous civic improvements and public works. In the growing city of Dallas, Dealey led movements to clean up the town and make it healthier; to build a new railroad station, better streets and bridges, and a system of parks; to make city government more efficient; and to establish a city plan that would permanently shape Dallas's development.

Colonel Belo gave George Dealey responsibility over all departments of the paper in 1895. When the old man died and the company passed first to his young son and then, after the son's untimely death, to a succession of Belo relatives, the middle-aged general manager quietly continued to guide the paper. He finally assumed the title of company president in 1920, a generation after he had taken de facto control.

Three years later, the company sold the *Galveston News* and cut its last tie to the paper that had sired it. It was now a Dallas outfit and on its way toward becoming the dominant journalistic voice of the Southwest.

As the Belo heirs dispersed and died, it became prudent to reorganize the company and look to its future. The last direct heir to control the newspaper, Jeannette Belo Peabody, took the lead. She greatly admired Dealey. With her encouragement, he arranged financing and bought a controlling interest in the company in 1926. Dealey could have given the business any name he wished. He chose to honor the memory of the old warrior who had hired him fifty-two years before. It remains the A.H. Belo Corp.

In the '20s the paper led the fight in a cause that could have killed it. After World War I, the Ku Klux Klan spread west and north from the Deep South and became a potent political force. It captured local and county offices across much of Texas. A friend of the Klan was elected to the U.S. Senate from the state in 1922. The *Morning News* fought the organization from the start. Part of its reasoning would sound strange a generation later.

Explaining why the Klan was not needed, an editorial said, "White supremacy is not imperiled." The paper reported the organization's violence from around the nation. Anti-Klan leaders were sought out and interviewed. Editorials spelled out the Klan's violations of the constitutions of Texas and the United States.

The KKK fought back by boycotting the *News* and spreading the false rumor that the paper was owned by Catholics. Advertising declined. Circulation fell off. A cash surplus of $200,000 was wiped out, and some of the company's real estate had to be sold to pay the annual dividend to the heirs of Colonel Belo. But the Klan's power was ebbing. It ran one of its members for governor in 1924 and lost, thanks in part to the determined opposition of the *News*. George Dealey some years later would call the fight against the Klan "perhaps the most courageous thing the *News* ever did." Part of the credit went to his son E.M. "Ted" Dealey, a political analyst on the staff of the *News*. Ted sensed that the Klan was weakening and urged his father to come out strongly against the organization's last bid for statewide power.

Ted Dealey became president of the company in 1940, and his reputation would be quite different from his father's. Ted Dealey once said to President Kennedy at a White House luncheon for Texas publishers, "The general opinion of the grassroots thinking in this country is that you and your administration are weak sisters. We need a man on horseback to lead this nation and many people think you are riding Caroline's tricycle." He allowed the paper to run a John Birch Society ad attacking Kennedy on the day the president was killed in Dallas.

The man who runs Belo today is three generations removed from George Bannerman Dealey. If Robert Decherd keeps his great-grandfather's philosophy alive in the Belo corridors today, there is one big difference in their circumstances. Whereas Dealey had to satisfy a small band of family members, Decherd runs a public company with stock traded on Wall Street. Satisfying more than ten thousand impersonal shareholders is a far different challenge.

How has Decherd handled it?

Mainly, he has stuck determinedly to his notion that journalism is a valuable commodity that can be sold without trivialization or insult to customers' intelligence. And he has gone out of his way to see that the business side of his papers is ruled by news values. He says, "I have an extremely strong bias in favor of people with news and editorial backgrounds playing influential roles" in the company. He thinks it unfortunate that the business offices of the media generally have so few people with journalistic backgrounds.

Indeed, at a time when many journalists worry about a breach between news and business, Belo's innovative approach is getting national attention. Two years ago the paper started conducting workshops for business executives and employees. Editors, some from other Belo papers, teach the classes. The discussion leader is from the American Press Institute. Circulation and advertising people and others are challenged to think like reporters and editors. They talk about what makes news, developing sources, ethics, writing on deadline, making up pages, using graphics. They are asked to understand the sensitivity of newsroom people to pressure from the business side.

In short, the editors teach the business folks how news people think and feel. I remember getting my first exposure to that at the feet of Professor Frank Luther Mott at the University of Missouri School of Journalism. It took two semesters. The *Morning News* crams it into two and a half days, and maybe it works. I met a couple of business executives who got misty-eyed talking about their new appreciation of the newsroom. The paper also reverses the process, bringing in editors and reporters to listen to business people.

In addition, for more than fifteen years the paper has had daily meetings of the top officers of news and business. "We talk about absolutely every aspect of the newspaper," Halbreich says, "just to keep everybody aware of what's going on. We talk about new product activities, we talk about coordinating with production, we talk about new marketing initiatives, we talk about human resources policies that affect everybody. It's where we coordinate the newspaper. And so literally every morning of every work day for this many years, this key group, our absolute senior group of staffers, are hearing from Burl, from Ralph, from me, how we're running the newspaper. And they hear and understand how we're making decisions and why we make them."

Halbreich says it would be insulting to reporters and editors to suggest that they might be compromised by such close association with the business side. "Our advertising folks are not going to come up with some harebrained ideas that impinge on the objectivity of our news reporting," he says. "They're just not going to do it."

THE TIP-OFF that Tuesday, January 27, 1998, was not to be a routine day for my extended visit at the *Dallas Morning News* was a box at the top of that morning's front page. A story about President Clinton and Monica Lewinsky had been pulled from the paper after one edition, the box said, because the source for the story had backed away from it. The flawed report had said that a witness had seen the President and the intern in a "compromising" situation. When the source backed off, about midnight Washington time, it was like throwing a bucket of water on a computer. The paper stopped in its tracks. Top editors were called at home. The news desk rebuilt the whole first section to accommodate all the gyrations.

Everybody was understandably grumpy the next day, and grumpiest of all was Ralph Langer. It was he who had written the box explaining what had happened. By mid-morning Tuesday, he had already held a series of meetings and long-distance phone conversations. His normal good humor was not much in evidence. Downstairs in the newsroom, reporters and editors stood in clusters, muttering and cursing. Emotions ranged from disbelief to bafflement to acrimony. Everybody wanted to know more.

In forty-five years of journalism, I have never seen a greater display of anger and shame from editors and reporters who saw the integrity of their newspaper threatened by a mistake that should not have been made. That outpouring of concern told me more about the quality of the *Morning News* than any of the impressive statistics I had been given about circulation, advertising, profits, and journalistic prizes.

Long before the Lewinsky story, the *Morning News* had strict rules aimed at fair play with sources. For example, in a page one investigative piece, the target of the story had to be given a chance to reply, and his denial or explanation had to appear on page one, even if the denial pushed more interesting material onto the jump. The *News* had definite rules on anonymous sources, too. First, on any story that might cause legal problems, the reporter had to "Mirandize" the source (an allusion to the Supreme Court's decision requiring police officers to tell suspects of their rights). That is, the source had to be informed that he or she would be protected from identification until it became clear that the newspaper was in legal peril and that its financial condition was in jeopardy as a result of publishing the information, at which time the source would be asked to come forward. Second, information from an anonymous source had to be vital to the story, impossible to obtain another way and confirmed by a second source.

It was this last rule that the *News* violated in reporting the Lewinsky story. As a result, on January 27, 1998, the lead article in the paper's first edition began, "Independent counsel Kenneth Starr's staff has spoken with a Secret Service agent who is prepared to testify that he saw President Clinton and Monica Lewinsky in a compromising situation, sources said Monday."

Shortly after midnight Eastern time, the Washington bureau called Dallas with a desperate plea to pull the story. The source—only one, as it turned out—had backed off and had notified the reporter that his information was inaccurate. Besides appearing in the early edition, the story had already been posted on the paper's Web site. It also had been broadcast on radio and television across the country and picked up from the wire services by other newspapers. The editors killed it minutes after the call from Washington. For later editions they substituted the page-one box explaining what had happened.

The top editors and reporters and sub-editors involved spent all the following day trying to establish what had gone wrong. Then on Wednesday, Langer stood before a meeting of more than two hundred grim-faced newsroom employees and reported his findings. He answered tough questions for about an hour. He wrote an op-ed piece for that Sunday's paper explaining to the readers what he had already told the staff. The information had come from "a well-connected Washington lawyer who said he had inside knowledge of the story."

Then the problem: "Later Monday, a misunderstanding between the Washington bureau and the Dallas office led some editors to believe, wrongly, that the story had been confirmed by a second, independent source."

He concluded, "What happened last week should not have happened. Because of a misunderstanding at one point and a breach of our policy at another, we were left without the security of strong and independent confirming sources. Such a situation has never happened here before, and we will see that it doesn't happen again."

No heads rolled, but there were hard feelings toward those who had embarrassed the paper. Some in the newsroom predicted that the paper's entries for that year's Pulitzer Prizes would get less serious consideration because of the damage done to the paper's reputation. For whatever reason, no *Morning News* stories were among the finalists in any writing category— not even the stunning series on death row inmates by Swindle and Malone. The paper had a single finalist, Joseph V. Stefanchik, for photography.

There was a footnote that left the sensation of a stubbed toe for some in the newsroom. The anonymous source got back to the reporter a day after his backtracking and said, well, his information was not all wrong. What he had described as a "compromising" situation, he said, was actually just "ambiguous." Langer wrote, with a hint of anger, "It is unlikely that a story describing 'ambiguous' behavior would have received national attention, let alone ended up on the front page of the *News*."

DESPITE AN OCCASIONAL MISSTEP, the *Morning News* has done many things right, and continues to do so. Its hiring policy, for example, emphasizes diversity. When Langer went to work for the *News* in 1981, the newsroom had about 220 employees; three were minorities. Langer and Osborne sent out word that every pool of candidates for an opening had to include a solid representation of minorities. Not only that, the hiring editors were told to start looking beyond Texas. The newsroom had only a handful of people from elsewhere, and Langer thought the paper would profit by some geographic broadening.

The policy has worked. The paper's 520 newsroom employees are from all over the map, and 17 percent of them are minorities, mostly African American and Hispanic. Gilbert Bailon, executive editor and vice president, is Hispanic. In racial and ethnic terms, the *Dallas Morning News* has one of the most diverse newsrooms in the United States.

Women are numerous in the newsroom, but less so in the top editing jobs. Half a dozen hold mid-level jobs ranging from deputy managing editor to city editor. Rena Pederson, the most visible woman on the paper, is editor of the editorial page and a vice president of the company. She has a national reputation among editorial writers and has won numerous awards. She is a member of the Pulitzer Prize Board.

Salaries are competitive. Reporters start at $30,000 to $35,000 a year. Top reporting hands and mid-level editors earn up to $70,000 and above. There's not much turnover. Walt Stallings, the forty-four-year-old A.M.E. for metro news, is typical. He has been at the paper since 1975. "It's definitely a destination paper, and it didn't used to be," he says. The management, in fact, is starting to fret over what Stallings calls "the graying of the newsroom."

Of course, such transitions are easier to accomplish when you've got a cash engine like the *Morning News*. Although Belo doesn't reveal the earnings of individual properties, Halbreich said the Dallas paper's operating profit margins run in the low-30s, a remarkable performance (and one more commonly achieved at papers of considerably less distinction). *Editor & Publisher* ranks it tenth in circulation among American dailies, with 490,249 copies sold per day. Its Sunday circulation of 781,959 is seventh in the country.

The paper is hefty. A typical weekday edition has about 112 pages of news, 56 pages of classifieds (it has the largest classified section of any American paper), and a color pullout of advertising. The daily weighs about a pound and a half. The Sunday paper needs a young burro to carry it.

Steady profits from all divisions put Belo in a position to expand. The first large opportunity opened up in the mid-'80s when Belo learned that Dun & Bradstreet wanted to sell its Corinthian television group of six stations. Decherd swallowed hard and laid out $606 million. Belo now had television stations from Virginia to California.

The company continued to grow. By February 1995 it had added television stations WWL in New Orleans and KIRO in Seattle, pushing Belo's reach to 8 percent of the national audience. This bite cost $272 million.

Decherd swims for exercise and relaxation. He began to swim a lot in those days.

Belo also bought a number of other newspapers in the 1990s, including the *Providence Journal* in Rhode Island and the *Press-Enterprise* in Riverside, California. The company paid about $170 million for the *Press-Enterprise*. But because of the *Providence Journal's* huge broadcast holdings —nine television stations, scattered from Seattle to Charlotte—it came at a steeper price: about $1.8 billion in cash and stock. Robert Decherd, forty-five years old and showing a hint of gray, was swimming furiously as that deal went down.

Those additional stations ensured a generous flow of cash to support the company's expansion. Belo added a television station in San Antonio and another in St. Louis (in exchange for the new Seattle property). It combined its print and broadcast facilities in Washington into one of the capital's biggest news bureaus, and pursued the formation of a statewide Texas cable news channel. (By the end of the decade, Belo would have eighteen television stations reaching 14 percent of U.S. television households, including such major markets as Dallas/Fort Worth, Houston, Seattle/Tacoma, and Phoenix.)

In the midst of all this, the *Morning News* scrapped its twice-a-week edition for Arlington and converted it into a separate five-day-a-week paper with its own publisher and staff. Arlington, situated between Dallas and Fort Worth, has a population of about 300,000 and is home to the Texas Rangers baseball club. The *Fort Worth Star-Telegram* had had its own paper there for years.

B ELO ALSO PICKED UP a scattering of smaller papers during the middle and late '90s, including the *Gleaner* in Henderson, Kentucky, on the Ohio River. In explaining why he sold to Belo, Walter M. Dear II, head of the family that owned the Gleaner, said: "In looking ahead, our No. 1 concern was how well our successors would treat our communities, our people and our readers and advertisers. . . . Belo fits best in meeting this concern."

That's what Howard H "Tim" Hays said, too, when he parted with his Press-Enterprise, the Riverside paper his father bought into in 1928 and which Tim himself edited for more than fifty years. But when he had to face the fact that no one in his family, or in those of his two brothers, would succeed him, Hays quietly looked around for a buyer. His old friend Tom Winship, longtime editor of the Boston Globe, said good things about Belo. Marcia McQuern, Hays's publisher and his successor as editor, knew Burl Osborne and Bob Mong through the American Society of Newspaper Editors. She liked them. Belo was encouraged to buy a minority interest.

There were "two or three other possibilities" for buyers, Hays says, but he increasingly liked what he saw of Belo. McQuern and others are convinced that Hays could have got considerably more money from another big media company if he had put the paper up for bids. As she says, "The family left a lot of money on the table to sell to Belo."

McQuern stayed on as editor, publisher and president of the Press-Enterprise Co. She had handled almost every editorial and reporting job on the paper and had been state and political editor, then city editor, at the *San Diego Union* and assistant metro editor at the *Sacramento Bee*. She has been a Pulitzer Prize juror four times. Until April, she was a member of the board of ASNE. She is the first woman to be publisher of the *Press-Enterprise*. She is funny and, according to her new boss, Osborne, "very candid."

According to McQuern, the Riverside employees knew next to nothing about Belo and its methods before the Dallas company came on the scene. "We didn't even know how to pronounce it," she says. "We called it Bellow."

Early indications were encouraging. Newsroom people detected almost no changes in policy. They also learned that their benefits and pay were being increased somewhat. Still, a certain skepticism was in the air when, in February 1998, Robert Decherd made his first visit since the ownership change. He met with a sizable group from the newsroom. The first question carried an undertone of hostility. People were upset over the handling of a certain complex aspect of their retirement plan. Decherd apparently was unaware of it. "I'll find out and tell you as soon as I can," he said. Minutes after the meeting, Dallas was being instructed to get an answer. The problem was defused before the end of the week.

The staff liked the rest of what he had to say, especially this: "We can't edit from a distance. You don't want corporate people here telling you what to do. We don't know what's going on in Riverside." He shrewdly did not over-promise anything. When a copy editor said the paper sure could use a new computer system, Decherd agreed and said the "prospects are good." Another chronic complaint is that the newsroom in the rambling old building has no windows. A new facility is planned sometime soon, but for now, Decherd said, he might arrange to send a window from the *Dallas Morning News*. The staff laughed. They liked this guy.

Things were less sunny for Belo in Providence, a continent away from California in every sense.

At one public forum a local patriot suggested that the Journal company was "selling out to the devil dogs from Texas," implying that pillage and rape would surely follow. Two members of the Metcalf family, whose ancestor bought a share of the paper more than a century ago, took out a full-page ad while the deal was being consummated. "We mourn the sale of the Providence Journal Company to A.H. Belo," it said. "The news of this transaction was a complete shock and greatly upset us; but more importantly, we are saddened by the loss of the independence of the newspaper and what that has meant for well over 100 years to the citizens of Providence and the state of Rhode Island."

Reaction in the Providence newsroom was hardly less muted. A famously outspoken reporter there, Brian Jones, had bought a few Journal shares against the day when he might want to rise in a stockholders' meeting and speak his mind. That occasion came in early 1997 when the stockholders were called together to discuss the offer from Belo.

"No matter how high-minded the rhetoric that has surrounded this sale," he told the gathering, "the truth is that what is happening here this afternoon is a tragedy, it is wrong. It is wrong because when the paper loses its local control and community roots, it will not have the same connection, the same intensity, the same willingness to take risks and to spend money, which are important ingredients in excellent local journalism. It is wrong because the *Providence Journal* is as much an institution in Rhode Island as Narragansett Bay, Brown University, crooked politicians, gangland slayings, frozen lemonade and the Independent Man. . . . It is wrong because desires for personal wealth and gain have been elevated above public service."

Stephen Hamblett, the publisher and chairman, took criticism inside and outside the paper. Even the man who sold him cigars unloaded on him. He looked Hamblett in the eye and said, "You've sold this institution. It's our paper!"

Signs of skepticism and hurt pride remain in the city, which after all was two hundred years old before Dallas was even a farming settlement. A businessman who deals regularly with the *Journal* says many business and professional people felt betrayed when it was sold. (The paper's management, ever aware of the citizenry's proprietary attitude toward it, had said it was not for sale.) The businessman says with some hesitation that he has not noticed much change—yet. "But the expectation is that the other shoe has not dropped yet. There's still fear that change is coming." The rumor mill had lumped Belo in with other media companies of less savory reputation. "The *Journal* was always committed to the community," he says. "What we heard was that Belo did not have the same kind of mentality, that it was more interested in the bottom line."

When Decherd and Osborne first visited Providence, they left an understated message: Watch what we do. Wait five years and see whether we told the truth. What they've done so far has defused much of the suspicion. They installed Belo's retirement package, which turned out to be richer than the *Journal*'s for older employees. They encouraged some aggressive new ideas for heading off a circulation slide. Most important to the newsroom, Belo made no attempt to alter the way the paper covered the news.

A year after his stockholders' speech, reporter Jones sounded like H.L. Mencken in the famous rehearsal of his remarks applying for admission at the Pearly Gates: "Gentlemen, I was mistaken." He said things had not turned out the way he feared, that he had seen few changes "except the Belo logo on our paychecks and time cards." He had gone to Dallas and had been favorably impressed by the *Morning News*. At home, the *Journal* was still doing serious reporting.

But Jones also was mindful of a warning from Ben Bagdikian, the media critic, who told him, "Watch their second year. They're all on their good manners the first year."

The lingering anxiety is easy to understand. The three or four years before the sale to Belo had been unsettling to the employees. The afternoon edition of the paper, the old *Providence Bulletin*, had been shut down after years of decline. (The morning paper was then renamed the *Providence Journal-Bulletin*, but this July the paper dropped the Bulletin from its title.) The Sunday magazine, the *Rhode Islander*, a source of pride for a long time, had been laid to rest for the same reason. That saved $750,000 a year. Then the Journal Co. went public and opened its shares for sale beyond the handful of old families who had owned them for generations, a boardroom-full of Metcalfs, Sharpes, Danforths, and Wilmerdings. On the heels of that came a period of downsizing and cost-cutting. The number of full-time-equivalent employees dropped from 1,600 in 1986 to 1,140 a decade later. The news staff was demoralized by the departure of two or three of its ablest reporters. The cost-cutting led to speculation that the management wanted to make the company attractive to a buyer. When Belo came along, those suspicions seemed to be confirmed.

The managers and owners, however, had something else in mind until late in the game. They saw themselves as preparing the company to expand. The Providence Journal Co. had already positioned itself as a potential acquirer of more media properties, thanks to its profitable broadcast and cable holdings. By 1990, it had accumulated more than $500 million in cash to use for purchases, according to Forbes magazine. Hamblett was speaking openly of the company's ambitions.

Hamblett had known Burl Osborne for years through the same trade associations that had led the latter to Tim Hays and Marcia McQuern. Hamblett remembers getting a telephone call from Osborne one day in 1996.

"Do you want to sell your TV stations?"

Hamblett said he didn't. "Do you want to sell yours?"

There was a long pause, and Osborne finally said, "Well, I guess we understand each other." They laughed, but didn't quite forget the conversation. Later that year Hamblett saw Osborne and Decherd at a publishers' convention. They talked about "how we have this great commonality of interest," Hamblett recalls. He adds, a little wistfully, "And, you know, I would have liked to have acquired them. But that wasn't in the cards."

He told some of his board members about Belo's interest, and they said he had an obligation to hear them out.

Hamblett flew to Dallas that summer and laid down his conditions to Decherd: "That he would have to come up with some form of structure that guaranteed the autonomy of the *Journal* newspaper forever, and that he would have to come up with a price that would be, you know, a good, healthy selling price." Decherd met the conditions to the satisfaction of Hamblett and his board. The price was right, and the Journal kept its own board of directors to provide some measure of independence.

The vote of the shareholders was not in doubt; a controlling majority, including the widow of the last Metcalf to head the company, was in favor of the merger. But ill feeling from a sizable minority could have poisoned the atmosphere for years to come. Credit for helping to prevent that was given to Henry D. Sharpe, a retired member of the board and a grandson of Lucian Sharpe, who bought an interest in the company in the 1870s. Sharpe told the assembled shareholders that his father in passing on his shares of *Journal* stock had written in his will, "Treat this stock not as a financial investment but as a public trust."

He said he had been impressed by Robert Decherd. "You may be unhappy," he said, "but this company, of all the companies you could get in bed with, will come closer to providing the people of Rhode Island as much independence as they could aspire to have." He warned that if Belo were rejected, other takeover bids would come, and they would be increasingly tempting until the shareholders' greed would finally impel them to sell, and perhaps not wisely. Some who attended said that speech turned the meeting from hostility to acceptance.

The day the merger was to be announced in 1997, rumors swept the newsroom. Some said the paper was being bought by the *New York Times.* Some said the new owner was Disney. The big fear, one reporter confides, was that the *Journal* was being sold to Gannett.

In a matter of weeks, that reporter had special reason to be grateful that the buyer was Belo. Gerald Carbone followed the police to a local nightclub one night the previous fall. There had been a report—erroneous, as it turned out—of shots being fired. Shortly after Carbone arrived, police ordered him to leave. He asked to speak to a supervisor. Instead, the officers arrested him, charged him with "obstruction of justice" and locked him up for half the night.

Burl Osborne happened to be in Providence the next day. When executive editor Joel Rawson told him what had happened, Osborne said, "You're going to sue the bastards, aren't you?"

As it happened, they didn't. Instead, Belo authorized the *Journal* to hire the best defense lawyer in Rhode Island. The paper spent $50,000 to fight the charge and, in case it became necessary, to persuade the court that the obstruction-of-justice statute was unconstitutional. The constitutional argument was not necessary. The judge dismissed the charge and sent the cops packing. The message to the newsroom in that $50,000 defense was probably as important as springing Carbone from the hoosegow.

B ELO'S PERFORMANCE as it absorbs its new acquisitions and looks for more will be watched closely, both by the media industry and by Wall Street. John Morton, the media analyst and columnist, believes that Belo will probably succeed over the long haul in publishing good journalism and making money at it.

The company may run into problems in expanding, he says. He notes that Decherd's people have been reluctant to pay the high prices that some papers have commanded, and most of Belo's acquisitions have been bargains by today's standards. While that means Belo may lose some opportunities, shying away from extravagance keeps the company better able to afford the kind of improvements it likes to make when it does buy a new property.

Overall, Belo's profits don't equal those of some of the more bottom line-oriented companies, but Belo is hardly complaining. Its operating margin has hovered at or just under 20 percent for the last ten years. There were exceptions during the late '80s and early '90s when Texas was hit hard by an economic downturn. In 1999 it was 18.4 percent.

The broadcasting segment has accounted for most of the healthy margins, sometimes over 30 percent in years when the margin was poor in the newspaper publishing segment. In 1988, a tight year for the company generally, the operating margin for publishing was only 7.3 percent. That rose steadily after the economic downturn and in 1997 had reached 22.9 percent.

The company's revenues during the same period rose from $382 million in 1987 to $1.4 billion in 1999. Significantly, its operating cash flow almost quadrupled during the decade, from $102 million to almost $376 million. Cash comes in handy for buying newspapers, even if you're borrowing money for most of the cost.

Whether Wall Street will share the enthusiasm for Belo that old-fashioned newspaper people are demonstrating is not certain. One thing professional investors like about the company so far is its big holdings in broadcasting, Morton says. On the other hand, he says, after Belo's earnings softened in the late 1990s "there was a cooling of the stock."

Decherd is careful not to overstate his or his company's ambitions. The last time we talk, he emphasizes the importance of continuing to grow, not just for growth's sake, he says, but to maintain the company's strong competitive position.

I tell him it looks as if Belo is headed toward becoming a giant of the industry. I know better than to make it personal, but he's not about to bite anyway. He understands that gianting is high-risk work, whether you're competing for ready-built herds of rustled cattle on the Rio Grande, like Woodrow Call and Augustus McCrae, or writing checks for a billion dollars.

"Well," he says, receding into the wallpaper, "there's the giants and there's the big guys. Maybe we'll be a big guy someday. I don't think we're going to be a giant. Time Warner and Disney and those guys can have it. They're the giants."

10 | The Battle of the Bay

By Cynthia Gorney

JOHN CURLEY'S JIHAD SPEECH, which he found himself delivering impromptu to a roomful of colleagues at the *San Francisco Chronicle*'s 1996 all-day planning retreat, was so earnest and impassioned that as he finished, it seemed to him entirely plausible that someone might begin snickering or pelting him with crumpled sheets of paper. There had been some hilarity just a few minutes earlier, somebody saying *So let's sum up our conclusions, then,* and somebody else cracking *Our conclusions are that we have to keep the newspaper safe for the family's profit margin,* and amid the laughter and hooting Curley had risen from his chair, not wanting to lose the moment, not wanting the day to dissipate into wiseass reportery banter about the fractious rich people who still owned the *Chronicle.* Curley stood there until the room quieted down. He looked at the display easels with their big newsprint tablets scrawled up in marking-pen headings: Content Committee. Rewards & Incentives. Hiring & Training. Job Redesign.

Then Curley, who was the *Chronicle*'s sports editor and therefore not by job description inclined to deliver pronouncements of this nature, made his face serious and talked about going to war.

Extraordinary circumstances had brought them all here, Curley said. Not for thirty-five years had the competition for readers and advertising money appeared so formidable, the chief opponents so sumptuously armed. Across San Francisco Bay to the north, in Marin and Sonoma Counties, the rival papers were owned by Gannett and the New York Times; to the south, in the peninsula split crosswise into San Mateo and Santa Clara counties, Knight Ridder's *San Jose Mercury News* had tightened its lock on Silicon Valley and was continuing its northward press into long-held *Chronicle* territory. To the east, Dean Singleton's Alameda Newspapers group was flogging its dailies at annual subscription rates a fraction of the cost of the *Chronicle.* And now Knight Ridder had arrived en masse on the east side of the bay as well, scooping up five suburban dailies with its $360 million purchase of the privately held Contra Costa Newspapers chain.

"We're surrounded," Curley said. "For us this has got to be—a jihad. Because unless we take this up, we're going to be pushed into the sea."

Pushed into the sea, that was actually the way Curley phrased it, and the moment the words came out of his mouth he was struck by the deep improbability of the whole tableau: the rented conference center, the written-up tablets on the easels, the editors and reporters draped companionably over sofas and armchairs, and the sports editor exhorting them all to holy war. John Curley had worked at the *Chronicle* for fourteen years, most of them spent in the fraternal isolation of the sports department, and aside from the occasional inspirational speech to beat writers or his assignment desk he had never gotten publicly worked up about the Future of the Paper; no one did, that was the point about the *Chronicle,* and it required a veteran's tenure at the newspaper to understand why an event as conventional as a newsroom planning retreat might feel so dramatically out of character.

The *Chronicle* didn't *do* retreats. The *Chronicle* didn't plan, not in the big-time way that ambitious modern newspapers plan. The *Chronicle* didn't invite reporters and managers to spend the day talking and arguing and thinking large thoughts. The *Chronicle* certainly didn't retain management consultants to shake up the proceedings by playing a booming recording of "Leader of the Pack" while the executive editor strode in wearing a bandanna and sunglasses and a motorcycle jacket. Since the current executive editor of the *San Francisco Chronicle,* a young *Chronicle* lifer named Matt Wilson, is a soft-spoken bow-ties-and-plain-suits man whose thin unlined face generally makes him look like an underaged computer whiz, this particular bit of theater had provided a moment of high comedy earlier in the day, but Wilson had been a good sport about it, doing his best to stride, a gait that does not come naturally to him, and holding aloft the plastic tricycle that had been handed to him as a prop. The message was as plain to Curley as he supposed it was to his assembled colleagues in the meeting room: Hey! Wake up. We're in trouble here.

That was why Curley said what he did, and why the reaction in the room interested him as much as the somewhat unsettling fact that he had said it at all. No one laughed at him. Susan Sward, a city room veteran widely regarded as one of the toughest and most capable reporters in town, was gazing at Curley with sober, consuming interest; Carl Hall, the ardently pro-union reporter serving as president of the Newspaper Guild local, was listening with what appeared to be unfeigned respect. "There weren't even any stifled giggles," Curley says. "Which you've got to take as a good sign, right? There wasn't a hint of: What a jerk, what a management stooge. And people's eyes were bright. I think they were looking for some-one to unfurl a banner."

Thus it was that a waterfront conference center on the northern lip of the bay became the launch site for the *San Francisco Chronicle*'s ambitious, edgy, and exceedingly high-stakes campaign to remake itself into a news-paper at war. The martial imagery was not dreamt up by John Curley; three months earlier, in June 1996, Matt Wilson had circulated an open call-to-arms memorandum declaring that the *Chronicle* was at risk of being beaten into submission by Knight Ridder and the other hostiles now massing around San Francisco Bay. "Our historical position of leadership is at serious risk," Wilson wrote. "Within a decade, Knight Ridder's Bay Area newspapers may have more readers than the *Chronicle.* . . . Circulation dominance will translate into advertising dominance. . . . In short, the *Chronicle* is in a war with the *Mercury News* and Knight Ridder. Whoever wins the war will become the Bay Area's dominant provider of news and advertising information."

It was not Knight Ridder alone that ought to be scaring the *Chronicle,* Wilson had written; online services and other stepped-up forms of com-petition were changing the nature of daily information delivery so rapidly that the *Chronicle* newsroom needed a radical overhaul if the paper was going to make any serious effort to keep pace. "CULTURE SHOCK," Wilson's memo read, and "THE CRISES," and "THE NEW ORGANIZATION." The Manifesto is what managing editor Jerry Roberts calls Wilson's 1996 war memo now, and when Roberts begins describing what's gone on at the *Chronicle* over the months since the Manifesto—the zoning, the regional columnists, the big-display enterprise projects, the business section expan-sion, the beefed-up high-tech reporting, the $1.5 million gamble on new bureaus and reporters in the suburbs—he, too, slips cheerfully into the jar-gon of a field marshal rousing the troops. Roberts likes to call Knight Ridder the Evil Empire. He uses phrases like "ground campaigns," describ-ing the *Chronicle* push into Knight Ridder-dominated suburbs, and "pin-cers movements," describing Knight Ridder advances up the flanks of what used to be *Chronicle* territory. He says: "I think they want to surround and squeeze us," and: "I think they want to turn us from a three-county paper into a one-county paper," and: "Well, basically, I think they want to take over the world."

Roberts busts up laughing when he gets to the Take Over the World part, but he and Matt Wilson and John Curley are all dead serious about the gravity of the enterprise. By contemporary media standards it's a rare and wonderful phenomenon we have going on out here, an actual big-time brawl for the daily attention of people who read newspapers. The expansion of Knight Ridder's Bay Area holdings has helped turn San Francisco into one of the few genuinely competitive markets in the country, with newspaper companies putting real money and editorial muscle into improving their papers.

And the real prize, as the mapping of the ground campaigns and pincers movements has demonstrated, is no longer the celebrated city itself. With a daily circulation of 475,324, the *Chronicle* is still the biggest West Coast paper north of Los Angeles, but almost three-quarters of those *Chronicles* are sold outside San Francisco, in the huge suburban market north, east and south of the city limits. Nine counties abut San Francisco Bay: That's six-and-a-half-million people; three-and-a-half million jobs; four dozen cities; six major newspaper owners; too many online news services to keep track of from one week to the next; and a spectacular amount of aggregate newspaper money. (One market researcher recently estimated the annual regional spending on recruitment classified advertising alone— that's just the newspapers, and just the employer ads, only one subsection of the lucrative classifieds business—at $200 million.)

The *Chronicle*'s circulation, amid this riot of potential readership numbers, had been dropping—from 487,000 in 1996 to less than 457,000 in 1999. And as Jerry Roberts commenced his third year as managing editor, a job he took on with some trepidation after a long career as a *Chronicle* political reporter and editor, he faced from one worrisome audit report to the next a set of challenges that may sound familiar to similarly embattled compatriots in other urban newsrooms. How does a family-owned paper beat back a behemoth like Knight Ridder? How does a metropolitan daily attract both central city readers and those desperately needed suburbanites who may be deciding their two-paper days are over? How does a cadre of editors and reporters who genuinely love their newspaper haul its large, unruly, famously somnolent self into the new era of grown-up competition for an increasingly distracted audience?

"It's just a lot of *work*," Roberts told me one day last fall, a particularly shoulders-sagging sort of day, when the circulation numbers were aggravating him and neither he nor his metropolitan editor had been crazy about the front page. "For a long time, when I was at the *Chronicle*, there was just this smug superiority: We're the big paper, it doesn't matter what we do, we don't have to try hard. And to change the culture of the newsroom so you do, you do want to beat the other guy, you are aggressive and you are competitive and you want to act competitive on every story, and to stand in front of my colleagues and say that stuff—you've got 300 skeptical cynics. And you have to try to convince them."

For this is part of the jihad, too, maybe the hardest part—this internal and external assault on a national reputation more than three decades in the making. The *San Francisco Chronicle* is a legendary newspaper, and no one in the newsroom has any illusions about what it's legendary for; there's not another paper in the United States that has the distinction of having been insulted for laughs in a movie meant to glorify the hard-working press. (The movie was *All the President's Men,* in 1976, and it was a throwaway line, but in certain circles it stuck.) "I knew it only from the reputation: 'Send it to the *Chronicle,*'" John Curley told me, remembering how the paper looked to him from a distance before he was finally persuaded to leave the *Los Angeles Times* in 1982 to take a *Chronicle* editing job. "I believe in the book it's 'Send it to the *San Francisco Chronicle.* They'll publish anything.' In the movie, it's 'Send it to the *San Francisco Chronicle.* They need it.' Not that we have *any* self-consciousness about our reputation, you understand."

Curley was drawing on the top of a notebook as he said this, his gaze fixed on the ballpoint hatch marks filling the left-hand corner, but he was smiling; he's part of the cadre. He's left the sports department and moved into a glass-walled AME office at the top end of the *Chronicle* city room, where he now spends his days fanning life into the rigorously competitive paper the *Chronicle* is working so hard to become. It's not that competition in itself is a novel idea at the *Chronicle;* San Francisco remains one of the few American cities with two mainstream dailies, and for a long time reporters at the *Chronicle* have paced themselves against their counterparts at the *San Francisco Examiner,* the Hearst-owned afternoon paper to which the *Chronicle* has been contractually bound by a joint operating agreement since 1965. The *Examiner* on its best days is a very good city newspaper, rowdier and faster-paced and more visually striking than the *Chronicle,* but since the *Chronicle* has four times the circulation and the revenue generated by both papers goes into a single pot, the *Chronicle-Examiner* rivalry is a playground spat beneath the shadow of the Evil Empire. "Jesus, if we think the *Examiner* is our competition," Curley said, "then we're in big trouble."

IN A HIGH-CEILINGED community hall in the East Bay town of Pleasant Hill, across the Bay Bridge from San Francisco and deep in the heart of the hard-fought suburban readership territory called Contra Costa County, thirteen *Chronicle* editors and reporters sat side by side at a long table one October evening, looking out a little nervously at the men and women who had come to hear what the newspaper people had to say for themselves. The event had been advertised in the *Chronicle* as a community forum in which the locals might meet in person the large new bureau now covering their county, and the paper had gone to some trouble to put on a nice show: A Mexican caterer dished out free plates of enchiladas and tamales, microphones had been placed in the aisles between the rows of audience chairs, and the newspaper people's table was decorated with a long bright banner that read "The Chronicle."

The words "San Francisco" were notably missing from the banner, and the sample metro section blown up for display also bore no reference to the city of San Francisco. The section's masthead read "Contra Costa," its center-piece story was about a championship Catholic high school football team based in the Contra Costa County town of Concord, and as the reporters took turns introducing themselves to the audience, half of them began by proclaiming their local roots—that's local as in born-in-the-suburbs, not shipped in from across the bay. Tanya Schevitz, the bureau's energetic young education reporter: graduate of the Concord public schools. John King, the thrice-weekly columnist for the Contra Costa section: born and raised in Walnut Creek, the county seat. Erin Hallissy, head of the new bureau and senior reporter in the crew: born and raised in Concord, a credential under-scored in the glossy four-page Meet the Staff brochures being passed around at the forum ("Our Contra Costa bureau chief is a lifelong resident with local roots that go back several generations").

Hallissy's picture was in the brochure, too, along with her e-mail and telephone number and a dozen comparable illustrated bios of her bureau colleagues. And when the *Chronicle*'s local news AME Linda Strean took her turn at the microphone, everything she said radiated sincere goodwill and the wish that the people of Contra Costa might guide the *Chronicle* in serving them better. "We want to know what you like, we want to know what you hate, and we really welcome your suggestions," Strean said.

Both Strean and the *Chronicle*'s regional editor, Vlae Kershner, had fought their way through the miserable late-afternoon commute out to Pleasant Hill from the *Chronicle*'s city room in downtown San Francisco. Jerry Roberts was supposed to be there, too, but he had been out sick that day, and for a while Roberts' nameplate remained on the *Chronicle* table, a small reminder of the seriousness of the paper's intentions: Here's nearly the entire editorial chain of command, from managing editor on down, showing up in your suburban community center to ask all forty-five of you—there were several rows of empty seats—whether the paper is doing a good enough job. The ad guys also stood and introduced themselves (the new Contra Costa bureau includes three full-time salespeople to attract retail advertising from local businesses), and a man from circulation got up to make encouraging remarks about "penetration" and "retention," and as I sat in a back row, eating my free enchilada and taking notes about new tactical weaponry in the war for territorial domination, I found myself thinking almost wistfully about Count Marco.

Count Marco was *Old Chronicle.* You have to be over forty to remember Count Marco, and to have grown up in a household where the *Chronicle* was delivered to the doorstep so that your mother could open the women's pages to Count Marco and begin pounding the table about what an idiot he was. The *Chronicle* had hired Count Marco in 1959—in real life he was a hairdresser named Marc Spinelli—to assume the voice of a fussy Continental aristocrat in a regular column that railed about "you American women," who Marco liked to complain were fat and whiny and insufficiently attentive to their husbands. ("I'll make a deal with you libido-orationists," read one typical Marco passage. "Do as I suggest and I'll go along with your bleats and pleas, even to the point of encouraging you to strangle femininity to death.") As actual newspaper copy it was ludicrous, but as *San Francisco Chronicle* material it was choice: arch, silly, flamboyantly uninterested in bourgeois sobriety, and aiming, I'm guessing, for precisely the sort of reaction it elicited from my mother, who loved being infuriated by Count Marco as much as she loved reading George Murphy's front-page stories about the scandal of English muffin redesign. The English muffin stories ran in 1969, when I was a teenager:

> A bakery blasphemy is abroad in San Francisco.
> Foster's English Muffins are being sold sliced.
> As everyone here knows, English muffins are never touched by a knife.
> "You must tear, tear," says the San Franciscan to the benighted visitor.
> Actually, the true English muffin devotee first takes the muffin whole and inserts the tines of a fork about the perimeter.
> Now, having achieved purchase, he takes thumb and forefinger (there are some two-handed muffin-tearers, but they are in the minority; mostly the one-handed approach is favored) and delicately separates the top from the bottom....

In a sense the whole paper was written in those days for my parents, who were literate, funny, well-traveled people who had moved to San Francisco because the city—that shorthand, The City, was and has remained the standard terminology around here—seemed to them unlike any other place they had ever been. San Francisco's visual appeal was famous, the crowded wooden-house-covered hills bathed in golden light and ringed on three sides by water, but the geography also helped reinforce a kind of exuberant self-absorption that Scott Newhall, the most famous editor the *Chronicle* ever had, understood exactly how to exploit. Scott Newhall is part of the reason the *Chronicle* became so terrible. But Scott Newhall is also part of the reason my parents and a great many people like them took such enormous pleasure in living in San Francisco, and to get this story right—to follow the sorrowful tale right down to the trough-bottom days of "Send it to the *Chronicle*"—you have to go back about forty-five years, when Newhall masterminded the last publicly declared Bay Area Journalism War, which Newhall won, and rather brilliantly, too.

Scott Newhall was named executive editor of the *San Francisco Chronicle* in 1952, when the paper was running a dismal fourth in circulation behind the *Oakland Tribune*, the *San Francisco News Call Bulletin,* and the *San Francisco Examiner*. The *News Call Bulletin* and the *Examiner* were both Hearst papers, but the *News Call Bulletin* was an afternoon daily; it was the morning *Examiner,* the flagship paper in the Hearst publishing empire, that Newhall decided to attack head-on. He had been at the paper for seventeen years by that time, not counting the stretch in 1936 when Newhall and his wife both quit their jobs, sailed out the Golden Gate on a forty-two-foot ketch, wrote cartoon-illustrated newspaper dispatches from the Mexican interior ("Horse Gets Colic, Bed Crashes, It Rains"), and finally came home with Newhall so sick from a bone abscess that American doctors amputated his right leg. After a while on crutches Newhall learned how to get around vigorously on a wooden leg, thereby adding to his aura. He was by all accounts an utterly charming and quick-witted man, fiercely opinionated, given to fits of impulse, and passionate about the sound of the writing on the pages he edited.

"His idea of a perfect headline on a mysterious murder of three people on Market Street, if that were to happen, would be: A Strange Occurrence at Night," recalls William German, the paper's longtime and now mostly emeritus editor, whose spacious carpeted corner office in the city room still contains a few items of Newhall vintage, like the massive leather-topped desk. "He took the cannon with him when he left," German says. "This guy was a complete wacko. But a very talented wacko. And probably right for the time."

The paper Newhall inherited from his predecessor, a high-minded visionary named Paul Smith, was often described by Smith himself as a West Coast version of the *New York Times*. It was stodgy, distinguished, and dense, and it was losing money. When Smith was relieved of his duties and replaced by the editor who had filed those dispatches from Mexico, the paper began what Newhall would later refer to as "a long trip back up": Newhall wanted the paper read, and read in greater numbers than the *San*

Francisco Examiner, and the come-on he chose was a front page that could not possibly be mistaken, by the time Newhall was finished with it, for any other front page in the United States.

Newhall's *Chronicle* sent Count Marco, accompanied by a real reporter who did the deadline work incognito from the back of the courtroom, to cover a sensational Los Angeles murder trial. ("Carole has changed the tint of her hair from sun bronze to copper tone. I consider this action an important switch indicating her present state of mind and perhaps her own future.") It ran highbrow limerick clues, most of them composed by Newhall's wife, Ruth, to the Emperor Norton Treasure Hunt, an annual citywide search for a buried $1,000 medallion. It carried a run of hugely displayed stories about a comedy writer's campaign to combat the moral disgrace of rampant animal nudity, illustrating one of the front-pagers with a drawing of suggested undershorts for cows. In 1963 the paper commenced its own civic campaign to improve the quality of San Francisco's coffee, accompanied by a lead editorial titled "Decent Coffee—A Basic Right."

> We have documented the shameful manner in which ignorant, money-grubbing, hole-in-corner restaurateurs of San Francisco crudely ravish this peer among brews. The offensive, long-simmering swill they pump out of their tarnished boilers is a disgrace to the city.

Easterners casting about for material with which to make fun of the *Chronicle* always come up with the coffee campaign, but they miss the essence of it: The essence was "swill." What other newspaper would use a word like "swill" to describe bad coffee in a front-page headline? (Just for the record, the famous and often slightly misquoted head was "A Great City's People Forced to Drink Swill." There was also "Coffee Horror," and "The Recipe for Horror"—it was a series, after all—and numerous sub-heads, like "4 O'Clock Varnish" and "Heady Brew.") The paper managed to be lyric, loopy, and unbelievably parochial all at the same time, a great private joke that San Franciscans liked to imagine only we really understood, and although professing outrage about the *Chronicle* became a popular civic pastime, circulation soared. On the day in 1960 when the *Chronicle*'s circulation made its first official surge past the *Examiner*'s, Newhall walked out of his office, according to the veteran *Chronicle* reporter Charles Petit, and cried, "Well, we've done it." Then Newhall ordered up champagne for the newsroom.

That David Perlman tells this story with such affection—he was there, and got his share of the champagne—is a testament to Newhall's ability to keep some dedicated newspapermen working pretty happily in the midst of the carnival acts. Perlman was then and remains today a nationally admired science writer (he's eighty, looks twenty years younger, and has no imminent plans to retire), and when I asked him whether he had minded watching his copy appear alongside pictures of livestock in boxer shorts, he smiled and adamantly shook his head. "Oh, no, it was too much fun," he said. Perlman learned to adapt his leads to the squiggly boxes, as did his junior colleague Charles Petit, who came to the *Chronicle* in 1972; the squiggly boxes were front-page wavy-line rules that flagged the reader to stories about sex or weird behavior, thus assuring extra attention on the newsracks.

"If you somehow got the word 'bizarre' into your lead, you got a wiggly line," Petit told me. "So I tried to find every way to do it. Science is perfect for that. I could slip the word 'bizarre' into a story about strange bacteria or weird plants or exotic diseases. They're all bizarre."

But by the time Charlie Petit got to the *Chronicle*, the paper had begun its slide into the post-Newhall era, and the joke was wearing thin. Before Petit left the *Chronicle* in 1997 to join *U.S. News & World Report*, the paper gave him a framed copy of the front page that ran on the August 1972 day he was hired; as we were talking Petit pulled it from a closet and gazed at it with fond resignation. "Look at this," he said. The lead was an Associated Press story about George McGovern. Lower right, a *New York Times* story about nuclear strategy; page middle, an AP Vietnam War story; and off-lead on the left, a squiggly box—150 WED AT MARIN RANCH. Illustrated, too: Marin County ranch ladies, in long skirts and bonnets, preparing for their Synanon-arranged group wedding. "The only thing we contributed was a goofball photo of a bunch of people getting married," Petit said glumly. "It's like being the best sitcom on TV. You're not *60 Minutes*. You're not *Nova*. But damn, you're funny."

The paper still had its strengths. Petit, like Perlman, was a dedicated reporter whose "bizarre" leads usually sat atop serious science and medical stories. The beloved Herb Caen, who had turned three-dot reporting into an art form no other newspaper was ever able to match, had defected temporarily to the *Examiner* but was now back home at the *Chronicle*, with the little San Francisco skyline logo that always ran above his column head. The *Chronicle*'s columnists and cultural writers were memorable, the sportswriters were very good, and the Two-Handed Muffin-Tearers school of newspaper prose still showed up from time to time to dress up the front page. But even on its best days, the *Chronicle* was an awfully fast read. "There *was* substance, but it was irrelevant substance, and it generally went for the gag," Petit reflected. "Serious journalists made fun of it. But readers liked it. It was amusing. It was a diversion from serious matters."

Part of the problem at the *Chronicle*—the heart of the problem, according to the standard modern-day *Chronicle* version of events—was the 1964 joint operating agreement that formally ended competition for the San Francisco morning newspaper audience. From January 1965 on, under the terms of the deal signed by the Hearst and Chronicle Publishing companies, a single jointly owned production facility would print, distribute, sell advertising, and manage circulation for both the *Chronicle* and the *Examiner*. The agreement closed the *News Call Bulletin*. It declared that the *Chronicle* would publish as a morning daily, that the *Examiner* would publish as an afternoon daily, and that on Sundays the joint facility would print a paper called the *San Francisco Sunday Examiner & Chronicle*, with most of the news sections to be produced by the *Examiner*. Editorially, the two papers were to function as "separate, distinct and independent newspapers," in the language of the JOA, but their business operation was now to become a single entity, collecting all advertising and subscription revenues and allocating any after-cost profits "to Chronicle and Hearst, in equal shares."

A fifty–fifty split, in other words—no head-to-head competition, everybody makes money together, and at the end of the day each side gets half the take. The deal was somewhere around the twentieth JOA in American newspapers, according to University of California at Berkeley law professor Stephen R. Barnett, who has written extensively about joint operating agreements, and opinions around here vary as to which entity was ultimately worst served by the terms of San Francisco's: the *Examiner* newsroom, suddenly stuck with the shrinking audience for afternoon papers; the *Chronicle* newsroom, stripped of any real competition and forced to watch half of every profit dollar tossed over the wall to the other guys; or the reading public, its one morning daily gradually losing interest in itself as the jolly war years gave way to something darker and more tedious.

Scott Newhall quit the *Chronicle* in 1971. People said the JOA had taken the fun out of it for him. His replacement was one of the *Chronicle* heirs, a distinctly uneditorly party named Richard Thieriot, and here we enter what in most *Chronicle* memories plays as the keep-your-head-down-and-try-not-to-think-about-it years, with the guiding light coming not from a brilliant wacko but instead from the designated scion in a family generally regarded as eccentric Republican skinflints. The *Chronicle* had been founded in the nineteenth century by DeYoungs—the brothers Charles,

Michael, and Gustavus started the *Daily Dramatic Chronicle* in 1865 (the title was prophetic; Charles was shot to death fifteen years later by the son of a politician his newspaper had assailed in print)—and when ownership passed in the early 1900s to the four DeYoung daughters, the family tree crowded up with their married names: Cameron, Tucker, Tobin, Thieriot.

Richard Thieriot was Michael DeYoung's great-grandson. When he arrived as editor, the publisher was still Richard's father, Charles DeYoung Thieriot, whose thinly smiling countenance still gazes out disapprovingly from an enormous portrait on the *Chronicle* boardroom wall. After his father died in 1977 Richard took over as publisher, too, which from the newsroom perspective seems to have replaced a mean, cheap, politically conservative boss with a cheap, politically conservative boss of largely undetectable personality. (The *Chronicle* was locally famous for its endorsements, which always appeared to have been shipped in en masse from the Twilight Zone: amusing liberal-leaning news content, deeply Democratic town, and every November you'd look for the CHRONICLE ENDORSES column and see this top-to-bottom lineup of right-wing Republicans.) Richard Thieriot rarely spent much time in the newsroom; his appointed overseer was Bill German, a veteran of the Newhall era, whose title was executive editor but whose job required a great deal of what one *Chronicle* writer described to me as "getting in the cage with Dick."

Since the metaphorical Richard Thieriot cage also contained the rest of the *Chronicle* heirs, who controlled the fortunes of the paper through both a seven-member board and what appeared to be a lot of heated family argument, this was regarded around the newsroom as deeply unpleasant duty. German was a gifted, incisive editor when he had actual copy in his hands, but the principal message he carried out of the cage, the sort of *leitmotif* of the post-wacko paper, was: No. No, too much money. No, we can get that from the wires. No, let's wait to see if the *New York Times* thinks it's a story. In a sense the Send it to the *Chronicle* insult—Jason Robards playing the *Washington Post*'s Ben Bradlee as Bradlee dismisses one exceptionally silly news feature proposal by snorting, "Send it out to the *San Francisco Chronicle*"—was misdirected, as German likes to point out: By the time this line was being repeated in movie theaters around the country, the *Chronicle* had given most of Bob Woodward and Carl Bernstein's Watergate stories almost exactly the same play the Post did. German is right about that; the paper wasn't silly anymore. It just wasn't very good. From time to time a new hire would arrive and take uneasy measure of the newsroom pallor: reporters writing novels at their desks, minimal enterprise, listless local government coverage, and the big No from the carpeted office in the corner. "On my first day, in my perky little AP way, I looked at the man at the next desk and said, 'What do you do here?'" Susan Sward told me; she'd come to the paper in 1979 from the AP bureau in Sacramento. "And he said: 'I'm waiting to retire.'"

Nonetheless the circulation figures stayed high for the *Chronicle,* propped firmly in place by the JOA. The *Chronicle*'s average daily circulation hovered around 500,000, while the *Examiner* struggled to maintain the 150,000 or so that seemed to be the most an afternoon paper could manage here even if it *was* subsidized by its own competition. (The *Chronicle* and *Examiner* shared a single circulation director, under the elegantly self-defeating terms of the JOA; technically this person was an employee of the San Francisco Newspaper Agency, which meant he was instructed, as former circulation director Steve Hearst put it, "to make sure one didn't grow at the expense of the other.") The readership territory spread out around the nine Bay Area counties and considerably beyond, as far as the circulation department was concerned: Every morning *Chronicles* were trucked east to Nevada and flown west to Hawaii, where it was a point of company pride to have the paper available at the finer Honolulu newsstands.

But that didn't mean the *Chronicle* covered the nine Bay Area counties, nor even that a working *Chronicle* reporter could necessarily have located them all on a map. Susan Sward has described the institutional ethos, during her inaugural years at the *Chronicle,* as Bored Urban Chic: We write about The City, which is all any sensible person could possibly wish to read. Herb Caen was the *Chronicle*'s anchor, for most people the merriest and most important read in the morning paper; his column created a mythic, gossipy, insular little town in which the suburbs—distant places like Contra Costa County's Pleasant Hill, or San Jose, which was growing so fast that its population would eventually overtake San Francisco's—were reserved for the occasional doofus joke. There were newspapers out in those suburbs, but they were rarely seen to matter, except as local shoppers or *Chronicle* farm clubs, and in the corporate offices at Fifth and Mission nobody seemed to be paying much attention to the growth itself, which was remaking the economic future both of the Bay Area and of its newspapers. The San Francisco Newspaper Agency, to put it in newsroom parlance, was missing the story.

"SLOW DOWN, John," David Rounds said from the rear seat of the black Mercedes in which three of us, me and two mid-level officials of the Evil Empire, were driving around the back roads of Contra Costa County. Rounds, a tall pale-haired man whose long legs made him look somewhat cramped even in the back of such a fancy car, is vice president for circulation for the Contra Costa Newspapers. John Armstrong, who was driving, is editor of the Contra Costa papers, and as he slowed down Armstrong nodded for my benefit toward the hills that stretched out to either side of his car.

These were bare hills, still, and quite beautiful in the Tuscan colors of northern California autumn: dry golden grasses, weathered fences, live oak trees, birds. Some beehive boxes stood unattended in an open field. In the distance, across the crest of the farthest hill, a convoy of construction vehicles stretched in silhouette against the sky. I was trying to come up with a word besides "gash" to describe the newly cut pit just visible at the far curve of the road, where a backhoe was spewing and lengths of thick sewage pipe lay stacked on the flattened dirt, but Armstrong had a more practical view of things. "Think of Danville," Armstrong said helpfully, which I knew, having spent some time earlier in the day with his newspapers' chief market researcher, meant: Think upscale suburban, college educated, both parents work, kids play team sports, Dad commutes, Mom is thirty-five to fifty-four years old and drives a Suburban (this is *detailed* market research; Knight Ridder paid for it). "Think of that mother with two point five kids," Armstrong said. "Lot of soccer moms in Explorers."

"Suburbans," I said.

"Suburbans," Armstrong said. He drove the Mercedes in silence for a moment, contemplating the imaginary newspaper readers crowding up both sides of the road. Rounds pointed out from the back that the plans for this particular section of the county call for fourteen thousand new residents, which all of us agreed would be hell on the local freeway but was the kind of number circulation directors pay a lot of attention to. "They're going to care about schools," Armstrong said, envisioning the newspaper pages opened in front of fourteen thousand breakfasts. "They're going to care about the environment. They're going to care about traffic, they're going to care about crime. But in addition to that, these are people who are going to want something more sophisticated."

They were going to want, in other words, The Only Paper You Need. This is the marketing slogan now driving the Contra Costa Newspapers, which have managed while the *Chronicle*'s back was turned to morph from sprightly but unthreatening little suburban papers into big good-looking dailies with sharp color and strong graphics and bylines out of Washington and Moscow and Tokyo. Some of these bylines now go on to read *Knight Ridder Newspapers* in tiny typeface, a detail that is likely to escape most of the morning BART commuters with their papers on their laps; all they see is a perfectly grownup-looking page one, probably a national story in the lead, one or two more Washington or international datelines somewhere on the page, and inside the kind of metro stories that suggest a staff doing conscientious local city council and zoning board duty: Antioch-Area Golf Course Proposal Put on Hold. Pinole Is Used to Study Hercules Police Merger. The papers have as much heft as the daily *Chronicle;* they use color photography more lavishly on every section front; they come with separate sections for business and features; they produce sober, beautifully illustrated pullouts on national topics like the Summer Olympics and the Starr report; and their sports staff follows major Bay Area teams around the country and pays serious attention to local high school athletics.

It's enough to give a *Chronicle* editor heartburn, which is a source of considerable pleasure for John Armstrong, who keeps on his office wall a large lapel button that displays the *Chronicle* logo beneath a bright red slash and the capitalized letters WE'RE GONNA EAT THEIR LUNCH. What looks at first to be a company poster on the opposite wall reads, "San Franciscans Don't Get It," but the epigram turns out to be lifted for amusement purpose from the competition: Armstrong had it copied from a *Chronicle* newsrack card, where the phrase was being used as part of the *Chronicle*'s ad campaign for its specialized new Contra Costa edition.

"It's a slogan I happen to agree with," Armstrong told me when we were back in his office at the *Contra Costa Times,* the flagship paper in the four-daily chain. He meant San Franciscans Don't Get It, which Armstrong had noticed me dutifully copying into my notebook, but he also meant The Only Paper You Need and We're Gonna Eat Their Lunch—it's been a slogany season at the Contra Costa Newspapers, where every reported slump in the *Chronicle*'s local circulation is regarded as uplifting news. The *Chronicle*'s much-vaunted Contra Costa County bureau, with its advertising campaign promising "news tailored to your hometown," is shrugged off by Armstrong as a hapless last-ditch effort by the bully across the Bay: San Franciscans, you will recall, Don't . . . et cetera. "They're late to the party," Armstrong said. "They're late to a market they've ignored forever. Now that the market's grown up, they want a piece of it."

A brief geographical digression is in order here, to explain more fully both the regional war maps and the significance of the territory at stake. San Francisco, as most people are aware, is positioned directly between the Pacific Ocean and a huge but narrow-mouthed saltwater bay. The city itself occupies the hilly northern end of one of the two coastal peninsulas that face each other at the entrance to this bay, which accounts for the fine urban vistas—grand expanses of water all over the damn place—but gives the resident population nowhere to go, should it wish to grow or give its kids a lawn to play on or shell out less than eight zillion bucks a month in rent, except out. Out means south, down the Peninsula (it's capitalized in the local argot) through Palo Alto and on toward San Jose; or north, across the Golden Gate Bridge and up into Marin County; or east, across the Bay Bridge, where the two big counties that fan back from the bridge's eastern end are called Alameda and Contra Costa.

Some of the most enticing Bay Area newspaper demographics, by which we mean not only large numbers of reasonably well-off people but more importantly growing numbers of reasonably well-off people, are in those last two counties. Growth studies around here are loaded with promising data about this particular swath of the East Bay: During the 1980s, for example, Contra Costa County added 103,000 new jobs, which put its job growth rate at 51 percent, more than twice that of the overall Bay Area economy. And in Alameda County, patches to the southeast along the Contra Costa border are among the fastest-growing population centers in northern California. It was the particular genius of Dean Lesher, the man who built the Contra Costa Newspapers chain, to see these demographics coming; indeed, Lesher had enough to do with creating these demographics, rampant pro-development boosterism and so on, that his newspapers came in for some vigorous drubbing even as they were raking in very considerable quantities of money. (The late C.K. McClatchy, of McClatchy Newspapers, once singled out the Lesher newspapers as one of the three worst chains in the United States. "The primary purpose of these newspapers," McClatchy declared in a 1988 lecture on the ways ownership can affect the quality of newspapers, "is to be ever-faithful cash cows for the owners.")

The Lesher corporate offices fired off an angry retort to that McClatchy remark in the form of a three-page small-type advertisement in *Editor & Publisher*, but on the evidence it would be hard to disagree with the cash-cow part. By the time Dean Lesher died in 1993 he had lived to be ninety and had made a *Forbes* magazine wealthiest-persons-in-California list, on which Lesher was ranked number four: estimated net worth, $360 million. He was a Maryland-born Harvard Law School graduate who made his newspaper money by homing in first on small, unglamorous California towns—the *Merced Sun-Star*, in the San Joaquin Valley, was Lesher's initial newspaper purchase—and then on small, unglamorous California towns that were about to make the transformation to San Francisco suburb. Eleven years after the 1936 opening of the bridge linking San Francisco to the East Bay, Lesher bought the *Walnut Creek Courier-Times*, a bi-weekly in a Contra Costa County town where walnuts really were the principal cash crop. Over the postwar decades the walnut groves gave way to suburban housing, and the *Contra Costa Times,* as Lesher renamed his little Walnut Creek paper, became the largest-circulation daily in a chain of Northern California newspaper acquisitions that at one point included ninety different publications, from suburban dailies to small-town weeklies to free shopping inserts.

Some of Lesher's newspaper purchases were less successful than others; his efforts to build a strong regional group around Sacramento never quite coalesced, for example, because he couldn't get his hands on the papers in certain key towns. But in Contra Costa County, where two commuter highways funneled people and jobs and developer money out to the land around Walnut Creek, Lesher bought up nearly every local paper inside county borders. His local dailies, weeklies, and shoppers kept a firm lock on newspaper advertising in this increasingly robust market, and by the '80s Lesher's Contra Costa newspapers had begun attracting suitors, none more keenly interested than P. Anthony Ridder, the future CEO of Knight Ridder Inc.

Tony Ridder had put in his serious training years in newspaper publishing less than an hour's drive south of Contra Costa County, down at the *San Jose Mercury News.* Ridder had started in San Jose in 1964, when the *Mercury* and *News* were still separate morning and evening Ridder papers; he was only twenty-four then, an heir apparent moving his way along in the chain his great-grandfather Herman Ridder had founded at the turn of the century. During his first years out of college Tony Ridder had worked at company papers in Pasadena, California, and Aberdeen, South Dakota, and when he was posted to San Jose, the *Mercury* and *News* were still the lackluster dailies in a small city that considered itself the poor relation to the famous place up north. ("Even here," Tony Ridder told me, 'The City' meant San Francisco.")

But Ridder stayed on in San Jose, becoming business manager and eventually publisher of the *Mercury* and *News* operation. And as the city flourished—not the capital-C city, but the city of San Jose, which had the good fortune to be located at one edge of the fledgling industrial area nicknamed "Silicon Valley"—so did the papers. In 1977, three years after Ridder Publications merged with Knight Newspapers, the new Knight Ridder headquarters in Miami sent San Jose one of its heavyweights, the former executive editor of the *Miami Herald,* Larry Jinks. With Jinks as editor, Ridder as publisher and the *San Francisco Chronicle* still gazing at its own navel—"I wish I really knew why we were so damn stupid about San Jose," the *Chronicle*'s Bill German told me somewhat mournfully—the

Mercury and *News* coalesced into what just about everybody around here agreed was the best paper in Northern California, lavishing attention and editorial resources on the high-tech phenomenon, which of course turned out to be, as they say, a story with legs. There was serious foreign and investigative reporting, too; the first of two Pulitzers came in 1986, for reporting from the Philippines (the second was to come four years later, for coverage of the Loma Prieta earthquake), and the paper opened bureaus in Mexico City and Tokyo, a signal of its swelling ambitions. And as the *Merc*'s circulation increased—200,000 in 1976 to 260,000 a decade later—the paper's readership area began pushing north up both sides of San Francisco Bay.

To the west, that meant steady encroachment up the Peninsula, into territory that had traditionally belonged to the *Chronicle*. To the east, it meant bumping up into southern Alameda County, where the *Mercury News*' circulation quadrupled over that same decade. And although he told everybody who asked that he had no interest in attacking the *Chronicle* head-on in San Francisco, Ridder had been keeping a close eye both on Lesher's Contra Costa papers, which he coveted for Knight Ridder, and on the neighboring Alameda County chain that belonged to the other irascible old man of East Bay publishing, Lesher's arch-rival, Floyd Sparks.

Between the two of them, Dean Lesher and Floyd Sparks had carved up most of the East Bay's local newspaper readership—and fairly neatly, at that, although Sparks and Lesher were said to loathe one another and perpetually snapped at each other's heels at the border towns. Sparks's empire was smaller than Lesher's, four dailies and a semiweekly shopper. Ridder liked them as potential buys, but not quite as much as he liked the Lesher papers; on their southern end the Sparks papers competed directly with the *Mercury News,* for one thing, inviting antitrust trouble. And Lesher's territory had more readers with the kind of income and education levels that look great on demographic brag sheets. ("These are the kind of people advertisers *lust* after," says one former *Contra Costa Times* editor. "These are people who can walk into the Jaguar dealer and write a check.") Sparks had a few pockets of the Jaguar people, but his papers also serviced a lot of the grittier working-class neighborhoods of Alameda County, and when Sparks finally sold his chain in 1985 to Dean Singleton, Ridder shrugged off the loss and redoubled his attention to the elder Dean.

"I would go up and meet Dean Lesher from time to time, as the publisher, without any corporate people," Ridder told me. "He'd talk about his plans to sell. He would tell me that if he ever got ready to sell, he'd contact me. And I would just stay in touch with him."

In 1986 Tony Ridder joined the Knight Ridder corporate operation in

Miami, but his interest in the Contra Costa papers never flagged. The word "synergy" was not yet in vogue among newspaper people, but that was more or less what Ridder had in mind: a profitable Knight Ridder–owned chain in Contra Costa County, a profitable Knight Ridder–owned paper in San Jose, and between the two a pooling of resources that might make more money for both even though Singleton's Alameda papers formed a kind of down-market buffer in the middle. "I knew enough about newspapers, and enough about markets, to think we could all work together," Ridder said. "We could sort of take one plus one, and get it to add up to three."

In 1989, when he was eighty-seven years old, Lesher appeared finally to have made up his mind. He called Tony Ridder in Miami, Ridder said. "And Dean says, 'Tony, I've decided to sell the paper.' Just out of the blue. 'I've decided to sell the paper. And you need to come out right away.' He wanted a bid from us in a week or something."

It was a terrible time for a rushed bid; a board meeting was coming up, Ridder had a thousand things to do, and he pleaded with Lesher for a delay. "But he said, 'Tony, I'm sorry. That's my deadline.'" So Ridder collected a half-dozen corporate guys, worked up a plausible purchase proposal, and flew out to Walnut Creek to spend the whole day talking to Lesher and studying the numbers. "The next morning Dean says, 'I need to talk to you alone,'" Ridder said. "He said, 'I couldn't sleep last night because I kept thinking about what life would be like after I sold it.' And he said, 'You know, Floyd Sparks died six months or so after he sold the papers.' He said, 'I'm convinced he died because he sold the papers. I'm afraid if I sell it, I'm going to die.'"

Actually Floyd Sparks had hung on for three years after selling his papers—Sparks died of cancer in 1988, at the age of eighty-seven—but Lesher's distress was palpable, Ridder recalled. Ridder tried to assure Lesher that Knight Ridder would welcome his involvement even after a sale, but that wasn't enough: "He said, 'No, I wouldn't have total control, it wouldn't be the same.' So we packed up and went back to Miami. And that was the end of that."

Dean Lesher never did let go of his newspapers. It was his widow, Margaret, and the Lesher trustees who finally clinched the sale, in the summer of 1995, after a prolonged in-house drama that included inquiries from the New York Times Co., Dean Singleton, Central Newspapers, and a group of *Contra Costa Times* editors who tried to buy the papers themselves and were left convinced that the deal had been greased for Knight Ridder from the start. "Knight Ridder was my first choice," says George Riggs, who has been publisher and CEO of the Contra Costa Newspapers —now organized as the *Contra Costa Times,* the *Valley Times,* the *San*

Ramon Valley Times, the *West County Times,* and a one-region-only daily *Contra Costa Times* insert called the *Ledger Dispatch*—since Lesher's death in 1993. "When I first told the board it was time to sell, I said, 'I think Knight Ridder is far and away the best potential buyer.'"

The reasons should be apparent to anyone, Riggs says: generous offer, highly reputable newspaper chain, and the powerhouse potential of a Contra Costa Newspapers–*Mercury News* alliance. This is the synergy of which people now speak with such reverence, and news coverage has something to do with it—the Contra Costa papers surely do look more comprehensive with those far-flung Knight Ridder stories out front. But when Tony Ridder talks about adding one plus one to get three, he has more in mind than joint reporting projects or shared news budgets; he's also talking about how much money you can make when numbers that once looked just okay can suddenly be added to each other to produce an entirely different effect. Here's one example: In 1995, as the Knight Ridder

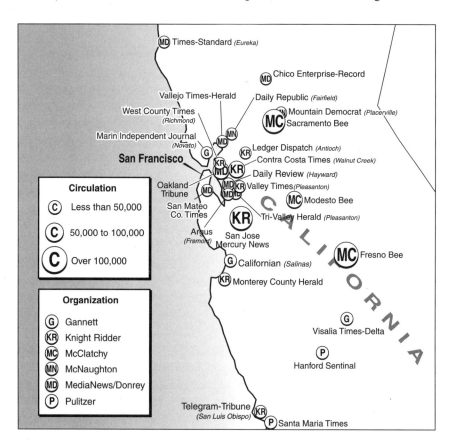

purchase was winding up in Walnut Creek, the Contra Costa papers were running at about 190,000 total daily circulation. The *Mercury News* was at about 280,000, and climbing. Add those totals together, draw a single gerry-mandered boundary around both readership areas, jog the western border east and south to exclude the *lumpen* cities serviced by Singleton's Alameda papers, and you have suddenly produced a new creation entitled the San Jose–Contra Costa Market, which comes with some very sexy Bay Area sta-tistics when the calculating is done the right way.

To those of us who grew up around here, the concept of something called a San Jose–Contra Costa Market is mildly jarring: One is a former scruffy town way down south, one is suburbs in the golden hills, and on a bad freeway day it takes an hour and a half to make the passage in between. But the synergy people think bigger than that. They see housing developments at one end, housing developments at the other, and the aforementioned freeway sprouting phylogenetically similar telecommuni-cations and software companies to either side. More to the point, they see one massive if weirdly shaped chunk of spending money. The city of San Jose is in Santa Clara County, which the high-tech industry has lofted to demographic prominence; there's plenty of poverty in Santa Clara County, but there's also enough money and new business to pull up those averages, and it's the big numbers that turn the heads of ad customers, both national and classified, who can see the usefulness of paying for one profligate group of newspaper readers instead of two or three.

Try this: Of the six most populous counties around the Bay, the San Jose–Contra Costa Market accounts for more than half the total popula-tion, more than half the total retail sales, and—marketspeak alert!—57 percent of Households w/EBI $50,000+. That's Effective Buying Income, for those of us who don't know advertising shorthand, and the statistic is from the current *San Jose Mercury News* & *Contra Costa Times* market presentation book, a spiral-bound volume whose illustration displays a *Merc* and a *Times* folded side by side but sort of overlapping, if you see what we mean. It's an expensive-looking booklet, on thick shiny pages, and the subtext is evident in its every graphic and demographic chart: "Separating the truth from the fog." "The Heart of High Tech." "The Industrial Exodus to Contra Costa County."

TRANSLATION: Forget the *San Francisco Chronicle,* and while you're at it, forget San Francisco, too. Tony Ridder is known for being a genial and non-pugnacious interview, despite his reputation as a ferocious business rival; he does not much stoop to publicly dissing the competition, and over two longish conversations I was never able to prod him into proclaiming that the *Chronicle*'s days of Bay Area domination were over. He was more keen to talk about "making these papers as strong as we can make them." From certain perspectives this is akin to collecting three of the four railroads on the Monopoly board and then discussing your plans for transit improvement, since over the last three years Knight Ridder has acquired not only the Contra Costa papers but also the dailies in Monterey, 120 miles south of San Francisco, and in San Luis Obispo, another 150 miles south of that. You can trace the Knight Ridder holdings in California now with a finger moving down from Walnut Creek: nice curved line, each marker separated from the next by a direct length of freeway.

The Monterey and San Luis Obispo acquisitions set off some elaborate speculation about just what Ridder was up to. The papers became Knight Ridder property in a 1997 swap with E.W. Scripps: two Scripps California papers, the *Monterey County Herald* and the *Telegram-Tribune*, for Knight Ridder's *Daily Camera* in Boulder, Colorado. Boulder is regarded as an exceptionally lucrative small-newspaper city, the kind of place a company might be unwilling to abandon unless some grand design were pulling it elsewhere, but Tony Ridder says the trade was initiated by Scripps, which also owns the *Denver Rocky Mountain News* and was locked in mortal combat against Dean Singleton's *Denver Post*. "They approached us about giving us Monterey if we would give them Boulder," Ridder told me. Ridder had always liked the idea of buying the newspaper in Monterey, he said; he had looked longingly at it back in the late 1960s, when he was still too green to have much sway with his corporate superiors. Even in those pre-synergy days he could see the logic of owning the two biggest papers along a one hundred-mile stretch of California—"I thought it would sort of help fill in the territory," he said—and when the *Herald* finally sold to Scripps in 1992, as Ridder put it, "I thought: 'Lucky them. I keep missing this at every chance.'"

Nonetheless Knight Ridder wanted more than a simple Monterey-for-Boulder swap, even though both papers run about thirty-five thousand circulation. "I specifically told them about San Luis Obispo, that *that* would have to be part of the deal," Ridder said. So Scripps, evidently intent on securing that extra fortification in Colorado, threw in the thirty-four-thousand circulation *Telegram-Tribune*. "Nice market," Ridder said. "And it's the next medium-sized market as you move south, down the coast."

Then, in the spring of 1998, Knight Ridder announced that the company's corporate headquarters was moving from Miami to a seventeen-story building in downtown San Jose. ("Knight Ridder people," Tony Ridder explained at the time, in a company press release, "simply must be immersed in the kind of futuristic and entrepreneurial thinking found in Silicon Valley.") Then in August, Knight Ridder announced that the company had bought the Hills papers, a ninety-thousand-circulation collection of mostly free weeklies, biweeklies, and shoppers that are tossed into driveways in some of the tonier neighborhoods of northern Alameda County. Ridder was studiously nonchalant when I asked him about the Hills acquisition; by Knight Ridder standards, the purchase price was chump change, he said—"between 5 and 10 million is as close as I'd want to go"—and if Knight Ridder hadn't bought the papers, he added, Singleton would have. "We compete with Dean Singleton fiercely in eastern Alameda County," Ridder said. "They were either going to go to him or to us."

It doesn't require much imagination to see a pattern shaping up here, what with Ridder fielding questions from the brand-new corner office in a granite San Jose skyscraper whose street-level outside wall is graced with giant steel letters that read *Knight Ridder*. It's hard to avoid the looming quality of the new corporate presence, and when I asked Tony Ridder whether he had designs on the northern end of San Francisco Bay, too— say a swap for a Marin or Sonoma County paper, thereby almost entirely surrounding San Francisco with the KR stamp—he hesitated for a second and then said, "No comment."

"No comment," I repeated, slightly rattled; I'd expected something more along the lines of, We're just making these papers as strong as we can make them. "I'd certainly consider it," Ridder said. "I have to tell you that when Santa Rosa was bought by the *New York Times*"—that would be the ninety-three-thousand-circulation *Press Democrat,* up in Sonoma County, sold to the Times Co. by the Finley family in 1985—"I was deeply disappointed. I mean, I had been spending a lot of time with Everett Person, who was the publisher. His wife was really the owner of the paper. And he had assured me that if he ever decided to sell it, he would call me. So after he sold it to the *New York Times,* he was very apologetic: 'I got this offer, I just couldn't believe how high it was, I accepted it.'"

The greater Bay Area still supports a long roster of papers that Knight Ridder doesn't own, in fact, including independents and alternative weeklies and the five Singleton papers, which Dean Singleton swears he has no intention of giving up. ("Not going to happen," Singleton said firmly, when I called him at his MediaNews headquarters to ask about the persistent rumor that he is poised to sell Knight Ridder his Alameda News Group papers. "One of our key franchises. Very dear to our heart.") For that matter, Tony Ridder has always declared that he had no plans for an attack on San Francisco itself—that there will be no *Bay Area Mercury News* or *Contra Costa and San Francisco Times.* "When I was publisher here, I used to have people in corporate who would come out and say, 'Now, the *Mercury News* is clearly the best newspaper, better than the *Chronicle,* better than the *Examiner,* so what you ought to do is just take over the Bay Area,'" Ridder said. "But that has never been my goal, to take over the Bay Area."

His goal, Ridder repeated patiently, was to make each regional paper as strong as Knight Ridder could make it. Newspaper analyst John Morton had suggested to me that perhaps Knight Ridder now regards Northern California as a kind of laboratory, one great experimental workshop in which the company can investigate various modern corporate trends in newspapering: synergy, clustering, new media, swapping, and freebie acquisition come readily to mind. But when I tried that out on Ridder, he replied with some asperity that "laboratory" suggested efforts that might not work. "We are going to make it work," he said.

And the nasty truth, were one to be assessing this prospect from behind a *Chronicle* executive's desk, is that in order to make it work Knight Ridder doesn't really need the city of San Francisco at all. So far most of the synergy between the Contra Costa Newspapers and the *Mercury News* has taken the form of an infusion of Knight Ridder money and expertise at the CCN headquarters in Walnut Creek, where corporate-dispatched people arrived, shortly after the Knight Ridder purchase, to lead the Contra Costa staff through a readership market study considerably more ambitious than anything ever undertaken during the Lesher days. Once they had gotten past the working-ladies-in-Suburbans phase and moved on to thornier questions of habit and taste—why do you buy this paper, what do you like in that one—one of the many things they learned, says the Contra Costa market research head, Don Olmstead, was just how big a percentage of their readership (including, presumably, those folks who put checkbooks in the Suburbans before driving to the Jaguar dealership) took the *Chronicle* in addition to their Contra Costa paper.

In the business this is referred to as "duplication," and it used to be considered a pretty ordinary suburban arrangement: one paper for the large news and big-city columnists, one paper for the police blotter and school lunch menu. But it made advertisers cranky, Olmstead told me. Why should they bother paying for Contra Costa Newspapers ads in suburbs where the *Chronicle*'s penetration was high enough for them? And there's another factor, too: Buying two daily papers costs more than it used to, even with the screaming price discounts now showing up as part of many new-subscriber campaigns, and there's all that reading and bundling and recycling to contend with. With harried two-worker families already distracted by television and the Internet, people are warier than they used to be about renewing that second subscription. "The *Chronicle*'s strategy has been to drive duplication in our market," Olmstead said. "From our point of view, now, it's just the opposite. You've got to drive duplication out."

You can see where this is going. "The issue is," Olmstead added, "can we make this paper attractive enough so it will become, for a substantial number of people, The Only Paper They Need? Five years ago I don't think you could make that statement, because the product wasn't there."

Now it is, or so Olmstead and John Armstrong would like to think, particularly after the Knight Ridder people guided them through a 1997 redesign that spiffed up the Contra Costa page fronts and consolidated the five local Sunday papers into one 202,000-circulation edition, with thicker, more elegantly packaged versions of the things people expect of a serious Sunday paper: book reviews, business, entertainment, world news. It's not been an entirely smooth transition—one hears complaints inside and outside the Contra Costa newsrooms about the papers abandoning their community identities—but all you have to do is scan the absorbed faces on one of the crowded morning BART trains to see what the *Chronicle* is up against if it means to hold the Evil Empire back. Don Olmstead has been working at Bay Area newspapers for twelve years now, five with Contra Costa and the previous seven with Singleton's Alameda News Group, and he reminded me that suburban papers had been sparring for readers and ad dollars long before Knight Ridder descended on Walnut Creek. "Wasn't that much different from now," Olmstead said. "Except that—to use the war metaphor—the guns got bigger."

SO THE *CHRONICLE* is shooting back. Some days you can see it all over the paper, some days you can't. Here's a *Chronicle* from early October of 1998, an ordinary Tuesday two years into the jihad: five stories on the front page, all of them serious, all *Chronicle* bylines, two from the paper's bureau in Washington, D.C., one a local enterprise story about the malfunctioning San Francisco transit system. Ten pages of staff-written business news, not including the stock listings, and not including the page one high-tech story describing the industry spillover out of Silicon Valley. Five zoned regional sections, four of them aimed directly at the suburbs, each featuring a different local columnist and showcasing, with accompanying graphic, the same thorough and well-written enterprise piece about the public school shortage of math and science teachers. "We fight on the air, on the land, and on the sea," Jerry Roberts told me drily that October day, as I was studying the little map that runs atop each of the new regional sections to indicate which suburban areas it's aiming for. "It's in some sense a defensive maneuver. *This far and no farther.*"

Roberts had already presided over three editorial meetings in a row that morning; there would be a fourth and fifth before the day was over, and from a corner of the crowded glass-walled conference room I had watched Roberts stand up, sit down, pace back and forth, crack jokes, roll up his shirtsleeves, squint at tacked-up newspapers, scratch his beard, rub his forehead, pull his glasses off, put his glasses back on, and write story slugs left-handed onto a giant planning board on the wall. Roberts and I had known each other for many years, in a collegial, fellow-reporters sort of way; he has friends in nearly every city room in the Bay Area, and it had taken me some moments to adjust to the sight of Jerry at the editor end of the table—the smart, cynical, battle-scarred political correspondent now trying simultaneously to choreograph a better newspaper, figure out just what it is those 475,324 people want to read, and worry about the 8,894 who went away this year, maybe because the competition is sucking them up, maybe because the subscription price increased, maybe because the coupon-printing company threw a snit about wanting lower rates and temporarily yanked all the coupons from the Sunday paper. When I asked Roberts about the circulation drop, he sighed and assumed his On the Record voice: "Circulation is extremely complicated, and it's difficult to pull out what's an editorial piece from what's a business piece. I remain convinced that the changes we're making editorially, in the long run, are the right changes to build readership."

He doesn't exactly know, in other words; nobody does, and in the meantime there's nothing to do but push on with the Change. That's how it's written, capitalized, in the multi-page newsroom memos that have issued over the last two years from Matt Wilson's office: the Change Project, encompassing Content Change, Special Projects Change, Values Change, Public Image Change, and a long list of other Changes that would sound preposterously ambitious if they had been presented to the city room by a pricey consultant. They weren't. *Chronicle* reporters and editors thought them up. For many months after the 1996 planning meeting at which John Curley delivered his pushed-into-the-sea speech, the *Chronicle* newsroom was lively with committees and subcommittees, staff people branching off into investigatory teams to interview their own co-workers, complaints and proposals piling up: "More pressure on slackers." "We need a better sense of political and social history of the region and county." "The competition provides more features for families and for young people to read." "Don't punish reporters by giving them more low-impact work just because they will do it well."

In point of fact the *San Francisco Chronicle*—which has won five Pulitzers of its own, by the way, three during the pre-Newhall years and two over the last decade (criticism, 1990, to architectural writer Allan Temko, and a 1996 special citation to Herb Caen)—had begun a concerted internal effort to improve the paper as far back as the mid-1980s, first with some aggressive new editorial hires, and then, to the relief of most in the newsroom, with the exit of Richard Thieriot. Thieriot was removed as editor and publisher in 1992 as part of a corporate housecleaning instigated by the younger and more liberal wing of the *Chronicle* family. His successor in the publisher's office, a retired Capital Cities/ABC executive vice president named John Sias, quickly established himself as a serious newsman intent on undoing the financial mess created by years of executive featherbedding and inept San Francisco Newspaper Agency management. And inside the *Chronicle* newsroom, the top editorial chairs shuffled with Thieriot's departure: Bill German's title was changed from executive editor to editor, despite the fact that at seventy-five he was past what would have been most newspapers' retirement age; and Matt Wilson, the paper's thirty-seven-year-old managing editor, was given German's job.

The ascension of Wilson raised some eyebrows around the paper, not because Wilson was personally disliked—he is by nearly all accounts a cordial and thoughtful person—but because he looks so spectacularly wrong for the part. Wilson bears a strong resemblance to the pictures one sees of the young Bill Gates, as *Chronicle* friends of mine have been observing to me for years, and by that they mean not only the boy-genius face with the wire-rimmed glasses, but the whole affect: reserved, cerebral, disinclined to use bad language, head full of numbers and data and systems designs. Wilson's father had been a longtime *Chronicle* editor himself, so in some sense Matt was primed for the life; his only actual reporting experience was as a Chronicle sports stringer in college, but he had been at the paper ever since, working his way up from summer copy boy to various editorial and computer systems positions, where he made a name for himself, as Wilson puts it, as a guy who could do a lot of different things pretty well. "There was always somebody better than me at any one thing, but I could do more things at a useful level of competence than most other people," he told me. "I wasn't the best headline writer, but I could write a headline. I wasn't the best copy editor, but I could edit copy."

What Wilson is extremely good at—maybe better than anybody else who has occupied that office, as it turns out—is assessing the long view, and not in the gut-driven Newhall fashion, but instead by doing his homework. He reads three-hundred-page regional planning studies. He composes newsroom-wide lists of goals and accomplishments, which seems a modest enough personnel tactic unless it's being introduced in a workplace where nobody has ever done such a thing before. He writes an upbeat, resolute, biweekly newsletter, which also includes job postings and ergonomic tips. And having read those three-hundred-page regional planning studies, he has been worrying about the suburbs since even before Knight Ridder bought the Contra Costa Newspapers; indeed, Wilson assured me loyally, much of senior management had worried about the suburbs, but nobody had felt moved to do very much about them when the across-the-bay competition still looked so puny. "That, in a way, had been our problem before," Wilson told me. "How could anybody take all that seriously the San Ramon Whatever-it-was as a single entity? You couldn't."

Which is not to pretend that the Change has proved a completely rollicking success. There are those pesky circulation numbers to contend with, for one thing, and the advance into the suburbs has been both costly and perplexing. In 1997 and 1998 the *Chronicle* added forty new full-time staff positions to the coverage of Bay Area suburbs—that's reporters, photographers, artists, bureau chiefs, copy editors, assigning editors, and an editor who spends all week coordinating the new servicey, listings-filled Friday sections, a completely different edition for each zone, which tend to display as their centerpiece some featury account of an admirable community effort. "The unqualified success has been the Friday sections," Roberts said. "There's a utility to them. That's the place where we can reach a level of localness that we can't get into the daily paper."

The daily regional sections, which are supposed to load metro news into a tailored-to-your-area blend of the immediately local and the area-wide, are more problematic. If you're really trying to convince Mrs. Suburban–driving Upscale that the newspaper printed in Walnut Creek is not The Only Paper She Needs, what do you offer her by way of a substitute? When she tells a pollster that one of her highest priorities is "local news," as newspaper readers so reliably do these days, what exactly does she mean? Does she want the results of the previous night's city council meetings (which in each of the Bay Area suburban regions might encompass ten or twelve city councils), or a compelling read out of some suburb down the road, or the old *Chronicle* great-columnists-in-a-quirky-paper package that Knight Ridder will never be able to deliver? "It's not an easy problem by any means," Roberts told me. "We cannot bring you the school board minutes from every district in Contra Costa County. But we told the reporters we didn't want a lot of meetings. We wanted scoops, and smart stories."

The art of landing those scoops and smart stories, with bureaus staffed at a fraction the size of the local competition's city staffs, still eludes a little more often than the *Chronicle* editors would like. The week I sat in on news meetings, the AME Linda Strean, a hard-working former *Examiner* editor whose new *Chronicle* jurisdiction encompasses all local news, was blunt in her dissatisfaction: The regional sections had lost their way over the previous weeks, she told one roomful of assembled editors. "We've been falling back on feel-good features instead of news," Strean said, to nods all around; that very day's paper had led two of the regional sections with a pleasant volunteers-help-repaint-rundown-suburban-high-school piece, as though this were the East Bay's pressing story of the moment.

It's not always that dour at the regional desk; some days' sections have considerably more bite to them, the education reporting is often terrific, and the paper now addresses commuting like the area-wide obsession it truly is. But it's vexing, trying to understand how best to look more local while the local papers are trying to look more sophisticated, and at the *Chronicle* the whole enterprise has been doubly frustrating by the Sunday problem. Until just recently, for all intents and purposes, there was no Sunday paper for the news departments of the *San Francisco Chronicle;* there was a big Sunday thing with a rubber band around it, but the only editorial sections the *Chronicle* contributed were an entertainment and book review tabloid, the TV listings, and a quasi-op-ed section called "Sunday," a gracefully written, gently paced collection of features and personal essays.

The rest of Sunday's editorial product, although many *Chronicle* subscribers never quite figured this out, was written by the *San Francisco Examiner.* The *Examiner* and the *Chronicle* maintained a feuding-cousins relationship that was fiercely cherished by both sides (each news staff took special pleasure in getting wind of some long-developed project that was about to appear in the other paper and immediately assigning a spoiler piece on the same subject). This meant there was no sensible weekend collaboration at all, that the *Examiner* would occasionally run Sunday pieces that appeared to duplicate the following week's story in the *Chronicle,* and that the whole we're-your-regional-paper effort vanished every Sunday, since the more sparsely staffed underdog *Examiner* pitched itself as the hip, aggressive voice of the city of San Francisco—"the un-*Chronicle*," as *Examiner* editor Phil Bronstein wrote in a staff memo.

If this split-personality flavor was mystifying to *Chronicle* subscribers, it was almost equally mystifying to *Chronicle* staffers, who were prohibited by legal contract from putting out a front-page news section in what was supposed to be the highest-impact paper of the week, the 578,541-circulation Sunday paper, which went down by more than nine percent, by the way—54,972 copies—from 1997 to 1999.

And that brings us nearly full circle back to the joint operating agreement, which every newspaper person in town agrees had turned into a life-support system for an afternoon daily that long ago lost the ability to breathe on its own. Frank McCulloch, a retired done-all California newspaper man many Bay Area reporters think of as the only certified grownup we know (McClatchy editor, *L.A. Times* managing editor, *Time* Saigon bureau chief, etc.), drew me a Bay Area map at his kitchen table one day, pointing a big black arrow at the squiggle that was the city peninsula. "That's San Francisco, surrounded by water," McCulloch said. "Look at the problem here. This area will support one newspaper, not two. The resources simply are not there."

POSTSCRIPT: *In the summer of 2000, a new order of battle arose in the Bay Area. Hearst, in a move to regain its old dominance in San Francisco, purchased the* Chronicle *from the DeYoung descendents. This ended the Joint Operating Agreement. At the same time, Hearst sold the* Examiner *to a local family, the Fangs, promising, however, that all of the* Examiner's *newsroom staff would be welcome at the* Chronicle. *William Randolph Hearst III, grandson of the chain's founder, said the merging of the* Examiner's *217 journalists with the 375* Chronicle *staffers would "create a kind of supernewspaper." These combined resources "should make the new paper the equivalent of the* New York Times *and the* Washington Post," *he promised.*

Meanwhile, Knight Ridder mounted a new attack of its own by launching a San Francisco edition of the San Jose Mercury News. *The* Mercury News *opened a San Francisco bureau, set out an additional two hundred newspaper racks in the city and began providing home delivery to San Francisco residents. In a letter to readers, David Yarnold, San Jose's executive editor, promised expanded San Francisco coverage, expanded regional and business coverage, and "more listings for the arts, entertainment and things to do than any other Bay Area newspaper."*

Susan Goldberg, managing editor of the Mercury News, *called the new confrontation "America's last, best newspaper war."*

11 | Independent Papers: An Endangered Species

By James V. Risser

IN NOVEMBER OF 1997, a week before Thanksgiving, nearly two hundred friends of Howard H "Tim" Hays gathered in a nostalgic mood at the Regency Club in Los Angeles. They were there to toast a distinguished journalism career and to ponder the demise of yet another independent, family-owned newspaper. Not demise in the sense of "stop the presses," but rather a shift in ownership of the type that has become the industry norm.

Since Harry Truman's first term, Hays had built the fortunes and reputation of his southern California daily, the *Riverside Press-Enterprise*—built it into a powerful, profitable and respected paper. But now Hays was eighty years old, and he had succumbed to the inevitable: He was selling his beloved *Press-Enterprise* to the A.H. Belo Corp.

Tim Hays was packing it in.

Sure, he'd hoped his sons or relatives would carry on, but none wanted to. He explored giving or selling the paper to Stanford University, his alma mater; family members agreed they weren't after the last dollar. He toyed with the idea of selling to a public-spirited non-journalist who would agree in writing to grant editorial independence. He even looked into employee ownership. But economics, tax laws, and assorted other difficulties frustrated all these efforts.

So Hays—a quiet man, never one to trumpet his considerable accomplishments—was both pleased and wistful at the center of that evening's homage, as he and his wife, Susie, greeted guests in the posh top-floor club overlooking the palmy Westwood neighborhood. The dinner and testimonial had been arranged by the leaders of California's newspaper industry, but true to Hays's common touch the guest list embraced Riverside friends, neighbors, and longtime subscribers.

After the roasted veal chop and Chilean sea bass, two titans of the business rose to pay tribute. Don Graham, the usually low-key publisher of the

364 JAMES V. RISSER

Washington Post, spoke effusively about how Hays had given Riverside "a wonderful, wonderful newspaper" and was "one of the great principled editors of his generation." Hays, he said, was "as sincere a friend of the reading public in his business policies as he was in his editorship." A half-century ago he led the way in publishing zoned editions to serve readers in nearby towns. He kept subscription costs down. And so as southern California grew, so did the *Press-Enterprise*—from a circulation of 18,000 when Hays started there in 1946 to 167,000 when he sold it.

Then the decorous Lou Boccardi, president of the Associated Press, took the podium. He extolled Hays's dedication to quality journalism and press freedom, including his willingness to spend the paper's resources (in other words, his own money) to fight passionately for "First Amendment values" in the pages of his paper, and in court. On two occasions Hays had taken cases involving press access to criminal proceedings all the way to the U.S. Supreme Court. He won both.

Tim Hays also began a local news council. He sponsored an annual public lecture by a nationally prominent journalist, a series now in its thirty-third year. Hundreds of journalists around the country treasured the little lecture reprint booklets that Hays mailed to them each year. He gave away millions of dollars to favorite charities and causes. He was president of the American Society of Newspaper Editors. He served on the Pulitzer Prize Board. The *Press-Enterprise* won the coveted public service Pulitzer in 1968, for exposing the corrupt court handling of property and estates of a California Native American tribe.

In short, Hays exemplified what a determined and principled newspaper proprietor can be. Yet at the close of his half-century at the *Press-Enterprise,* he had no choice but to sell to a corporate suitor.

Even then Hays was the faithful steward: He picked the best chain he could find. Indeed, no one at the dinner bad-mouthed Belo. Burl Osborne, head of Belo's publishing division, was even among the guests.

But it was Don Graham who made the point: When Tim Hays began at the *Press-Enterprise* shortly after World War II, three-fourths of America's daily newspapers were family-owned. Now, Graham said, owners of independent papers were "fewer than whooping cranes."

DEPENDING SOMEWHAT ON how you define independent papers, their number is now down to about 280, out of 1,483 dailies in the United States. Most of these are small. Only 12 independents have circulations exceeding one hundred thousand.

It's a given in the newspaper business that this vanishing act is lamentable. One reason why is that once upon a time virtually all newspapers were independents—we mourn what we were.

There's also an undeniable romance about them, in part because historically they've been platforms for our very own renegades, characters, and cranks, and still are. Only at an independent does a committed publisher advertise for "full Gospel" Christians to fill newsroom openings, as happened recently at the *Daily Times* in Farmington, New Mexico. Only at an independent paper like the *Manchester Union Leader* does a Nackey S. Loeb try to bend New Hampshire to her will with front page pronouncements. Only at an independent paper like the *St. Petersburg Times* does a Nelson Poynter decide to donate the whole shebang to charity. ("I've never met my grandchildren," Poynter once said. "I may not like them.")

Of course, a newspaper under independent ownership is not, by definition, a wonderful newspaper. An independent can be good, or not so good. Which is to say, it can emulate Tim Hays and spend more money on staff, thus producing a richer news product. It can ponder the problems of the community from the perspective of longtime inhabitants, instead of editors or publishers waiting for that next promotion to the next town. It can gulp hard in bad times and settle for lower profits without worrying that corporate headquarters will want cost cuts to appease the stockholders.

On the other hand, it can fritter away the journalistic opportunities that an independent franchise affords. Its connection to the community and to advertisers can be too close for vigorous journalism. It can take a quality-be-damned attitude and turn the paper into a cash cow for the owners, or into a commercial for their ideology. It can pay poverty wages and recycle pencils.

Or, it can be *really* bad.

In Tennessee some time ago, the owner of a small independent was looking for a new publisher. When one prospect asked to examine the books, the owner told him that wasn't possible; he could see the numbers if he took the job. "We're doing a respectable business," the owner admitted, "but we'd like to be doing even better." The man signed on, looked at the books—and blanched. The paper was already making a 38 percent profit.

In theory, then, when an independent falls to a corporation, its quality may plummet or improve, depending on who owned it and who buys it. Some get worse, a few get better, and most get homogenized.

But what about the country's remaining independents? How are they faring? How well are they meeting their own aspirations, not to mention ours? I visited six of them in early 1998, and a close, sustained reading of their news columns gave me an insight into the industry's own endangered species, and a chance to see what's actually different about papers that remain free of corporate tethers. The six were of varying sizes, varying editorial philosophies, and certainly varying quality.

Alabama's *Anniston Star* exhibits a combination of worldliness and strong leadership all too rare in a small newspaper. Oklahoma City's *Daily Oklahoman,* a good corporate citizen, nonetheless shortchanges its readers. Eugene, Oregon's *Register-Guard* is a true family operation, in the best sense of that now-quaint notion. The *Tribune-Review* has made Pittsburgh a two-paper town again, and it actually has more going for it than owner Richard Mellon Scaife's conspiracy theories. The venerable *St. Petersburg Times* may be the best independent newspaper in America. And the brand-new *Palo Alto Daily News,* an experiment playing itself out on the gold-paved streets of Silicon Valley, covers the news with zest, a sense of humor, plenty of gaps and . . . well, take one—it's free.

THE *ANNISTON STAR*

Nestled in hilly woodlands in the eastern part of Alabama, midway between the state's metropolis, Birmingham, and booming Atlanta, the town of Anniston rose from the rubble of the Civil War in the 1870s. Samuel Noble, a Confederate munitions maker, and Daniel Tyler, a northern military man with money, bought land, laid out a city and started up the Woodstock Iron Works. Anniston is a compression of "Annie's Ton"— ton for iron ore, Annie for Tyler's daughter-in-law.

The founders' inspiration was Atlanta newspaperman Henry W. Grady, the New South advocate who argued that a combination of southern know-how and northern capital could put the devastated region back on its feet. When the company town opened to the public in 1883, it was Noble who decided it needed a newspaper. But legend credits Grady with naming it. Sitting on Noble's front porch, watching the explosive glow of the foundry's furnace, Grady supposedly declared that the paper should be called . . . the *Hot Blast.*

A weekly at first, then a daily, the *Hot Blast* was bought in the 1890s by Dr. Thomas W. Ayers, a physician who owned a competing Anniston paper. But at the turn of the century he sold the paper and went off to China as a Baptist missionary. A son, Harry M. Ayers, later returned to Anniston, bought the *Hot Blast* in 1910, and two years later acquired the *Evening Star.*

He merged the two and picked a new, more dignified-sounding name, the *Anniston Star*. That was eighty-eight years ago, and the name change—"I kind of wished he hadn't"—seems about the only regret that Ayers's son, H. Brandt Ayers, has about his family's decades of newspapering.

Ayers and his wife, Josephine, have done well in Anniston. They live in a large, striking contemporary house, which they built at 1 Booger Hollow, on a hilltop overlooking town. They have a vacation home in North Carolina and they travel, but they're deeply involved in civic and cultural affairs back home. Josephine Ayers, for instance, started the prestigious Alabama Shakespeare Festival in Anniston (which later relocated to Montgomery). "We are rooted here," says Ayers, the *Star*'s chairman and publisher. "It's the one patch of Earth that we care the most about in the world. Everywhere I go, I see ghosts."

On the table in his comfortable study is a copy of Richard N. Rosenfeld's book *American Aurora*, about a radical Philadelphia newspaper of the late eighteenth century. Above the fireplace hangs a large and stern portrait of Ayers's father, Col. Harry Ayers, reminding the son daily of his heritage and mission. The colonel was "a Democrat and a Wilson supporter," he says. "Grandfather had been a Bryan man, and my father was always for the Democrats—including being an Al Smith man, which was kind of tough to be in this part of the world."

Courtly and proud, Ayers is an engaging storyteller with a hearty laugh—a small-town Southerner with a patina of sophistication. He graduated from the University of Alabama in 1959, worked at the *Raleigh Times*, and then went to Washington for the *Times* and other southern papers served by the Bascom Timmons Bureau. When his father's health started to decline, Ayers reluctantly abandoned the glamour of Kennedy-era Washington and returned to Anniston in 1963, where he has been ever since, save for a Nieman Fellowship at Harvard and a fellowship at the former Gannett Center for Media Studies.

Everyone in Anniston calls him Brandy, and few doubt his and the newspaper's commitment to good government, to the economic development of the town and to social equality. Ayers's few detractors think his real interests these days lie outside Anniston—they cite his connections to Washington and to Democratic politicians (he was an unofficial but frequent adviser to Jimmy Carter), his travels, his commentaries on National Public Radio, his membership on the Council on Foreign Relations—and that he affects aristocratic airs. That feeling is fed by the signed column he writes on Sundays, commenting on national and world affairs and sometimes alluding to friends in high places, as when he wrote in January about attending a New Year's Eve party at the home of former *Washington Post* executive editor Ben Bradlee.

Yet the column provides Anniston with a worldly view of politics and culture that it would otherwise not get, just as Ayers himself brings a touch of elegance to a somewhat gritty town. He's not unlike a benevolent baron, using his twenty-seven-thousand-circulation newspaper to inform, educate and guide the town's citizens, hoping to help them "solve their problems and realize their visions." He carries on the tone of social tolerance that has characterized the *Star* through much of its history, and he uses the paper to monitor local and state government, scolding them when need be. And in an age when newspapers are under pressure from competitors and supposed reader disinterest in traditional news, Ayers still believes that journalism is the answer.

So he spends more money on his paper than do many owners. A news staff of forty-five is one indication. That's about one and a half times the rule of thumb that calls for one editorial staffer for every one thousand subscribers. But the breadth and sophistication of the *Star*'s local coverage is likewise unusual. Ayers is obviously willing (though the paper's profit figures aren't made public) to settle for earnings well below the 20 percent or more expected of papers owned by public companies, and he has said as much.

The *Star* also has a healthy newshole. Ed Fowler, vice president for operations, has worked for chains where the aim was 60 percent advertising, but the *Star*, he says, averages 48 percent. "That puts a big obligation on me to justify the use of that newshole," says executive editor Chris Waddle, noting that the paper has an op-ed page, two pages of comics, a Sunday comment section, and a book page—features often missing in smaller papers.

"This company's profitability demands are much less than other papers I've worked for," Fowler adds. "Our ad rates are almost one-third less than comparable competitors, and we don't try to maximize profitability. Our owners look more at getting a fair rate of return. That attitude is one of the reasons I'm here." Subscription costs are also low—$10.75 a month for seven-day delivery. Circulation slid from a peak of about 34,000 in 1990 to about 29,000 when I visited there, to 27,400 in 1999, according to *Editor & Publisher*.

While Waddle and Fowler handle the editorial and business details, Ayers gently steers the *Star*'s general course from a large first-floor office only steps from where the locals place ads or buy back copies. His office walls are lined with political and journalistic mementos. Among these is a photograph of a meeting he had with Gov. George Wallace. No admirer of the *Star*'s liberalism, Wallace inscribed the photo, "No big problems we can't settle—that is if you see it my way."

Today Ayers's own assessment of the paper is that "we know local news is our franchise, and we're doing a good job on that. Sports is a strength, but we may be overdoing it. The A section is too weak in national and international coverage."

An examination of the paper over several weeks supports that critique. The weekday front section is often just eight pages, and since it contains some of the better local stories as well as the editorial page, the space for national and world news is scant. On the other hand, the paper carries more non-local news, and a richer mix of it, than other papers its size. The stories tend toward the solid and contextual. Though young staffers come and go, veterans like education writer Judy Johnson cover important topics with skill and insight. Business coverage is strong and, as Fred Burger, a former business editor, says, "Covering business in a small town can often be difficult."

The paper trains young journalists from Ivy League schools and then dispatches them to larger papers and sometimes illustrious careers. One of the best-known alums is Rick Bragg, now covering the South for the *New York Times*. Born in nearby Possum Trot, Bragg got his start in Anniston—actually, at the company's weekly in Jacksonville—while still in college. He got the job after another student turned it down because he could make more money at the Kentucky Fried Chicken franchise. Bragg became a general assignment reporter for the *Star* and went on to win a Pulitzer for the *Times* in feature writing in 1996.

But at the heart of the *Star* is a cadre of longtime staffers who never left. One of these is Cody Hall, who has worked there almost fifty years in jobs from reporter to editor in chief. Now in semi-retirement as the paper's book editor, Hall dates "the modern *Star*" from when Brandy came home in 1963, raised the salary floor and started recruiting nationally. "It's been mostly fun," says Hall. "All these years, nobody has told me, 'Don't print this story.' In a small town, with all the pressures from advertisers and other people, that's amazing."

Joe Distelheim, who was executive editor from 1990 to 1994, says the paper's strength is its "tradition of wanting to do good journalism and big journalism. Some days its reputation exceeds its performance, but it has real flashes. It turns out big socko stories." He recalls that during his tenure, one report that stirred the community showed that local churches treated people with AIDS shabbily. Another package evaluated judges who were frequently reversed on appeal. "They continue to do big-picture things," says Distelheim, who left to edit the bigger *Huntsville Times,* a Newhouse paper. "Brandy is a pretty hands-off publisher, not interested in the details but seeing a mission for the paper, a kind of Don Quixote role." There was no formal budget, and "considerable resources for a paper its size," though Distelheim also remembers that the paper sometimes paid "skinflint" salaries.

Waddle and Fowler both tout the advantages of independent owner-ship but admit there are downsides. One is a reluctance to change. Another is an inability to keep up with technology, either because of cost or lack of expertise. They say the *Star*'s computer system is "clunky" and inadequate. Staffers grouse that only two slow terminals are available to access e-mail and the Internet.

As at any newspaper, staff morale rises and falls, and some staffers from bigger cities see the *Star* as somewhat parochial. Most, though, are proud of the paper's independence. A longtime features writer, Sue Vondracek, says the paper "has been fearless. People will ask Brandy not to put some-thing in the paper, but he doesn't go along." When advertisers threatened to pull ads over her stories, she says, the paper "never buckled, never."

Anniston being where it is, race has long been an issue, and the *Star* has, for the most part, been a positive force over the years—though Brandy Ayers readily acknowledges that his father, while taking a stand against the worst evils of segregation, "never got past separate-but-equal." Indeed, to this day some veteran journalists recall how the elder Ayers scandalized the 1956 ASNE convention with a rambling discourse on the races ("The con-suming desire of every Negro is to possess a white woman").

Still, the *Star* has tried to lead the community toward racial tolerance. In the early '60s, a Freedom Rider bus was burned in Anniston. Around the same time, Brandy Ayers helped organize an effort to find those guilty of the random killing of a black man, and he got three hundred Anniston residents to endorse a *Star* ad opposing violence. A reward offer led to the arrest of the killer, who was convicted by an all-white jury. "A racial mur-der has to outrage you," Ayers says. "You have to get involved; you have to stick the paper's neck way the hell out." In the '70s he helped bring blacks and whites together in a Committee of Unified Leadership to calm ten-sions in the schools, professionalize the police department and work for other reforms. "I doubt," Ayers says quietly, "that a manager from a corpo-rate newspaper somewhere would have involved himself so deeply."

Roosevelt Parker, a lifelong resident and the president of the local

NAACP, gives the paper credit. "Anniston race relations aren't as good as they could be, but the *Star* tries to promote them," he says. Nonetheless, Parker faults the paper for "not bringing all issues to the forefront for fear they will cause unrest," contending, for instance, that it's not adequately covering drugs, which he says are "destroying the community." And he says the *Star* was hard on the director of a community action agency, an African American, when he was accused of misdeeds, and more tolerant of another official, who is white, in similar circumstances. "Overall they do a pretty good job; I'd grade them a B-plus," says Parker, adding that "the white establishment sometimes comes down hard on the *Star* because they think it's too liberal on race relations."

Cleophus Thomas Jr., who writes reviews for Cody Hall's book page, is an attorney, a University of Alabama trustee and an African American. He assesses the *Star* as "progressive" and a paper to which "young people of ability are attracted," but not as liberal as its reputation. "I don't know that there's something warm and fuzzy about the *Star* that wouldn't exist if it was owned by Rupert Murdoch or Gannett," he says. Thomas says some blacks regard the paper as "authoritarian and repressive" and believe it "hounded" the last mayor, David Dethrage, from office. Dethrage, who is white, sometimes allied himself with two African Americans on the city council. The main issue on which the *Star* opposed him was his attempt to dismiss the city manager.

Executive editor Waddle, who says Dethrage behaved like a "pharaoh" and was out of his league as mayor, wrote a series of editorials attacking Dethrage, who ultimately spurned Waddle's compromise proposal on the city manager dispute. Dethrage says the paper was "biased against me and my administration. The paper wants a government they can control, and they have a monopoly on the news." The current mayor, Gene Stedham, is a fan of the *Star*. "They do an excellent job covering the council and city issues," he says. "They can make or break a politician. They probably elected me as mayor, frankly."

Ayers yearns somewhat for the days when the paper could cover the civil rights movement as a "moral crusade involving a great sweep of history." The movement has evolved, he believes, "into classic interest-group politics, with structures, agendas and bureaucracies." When the *Star*, "the classical friend of the black man," criticized a black anti-poverty leader for buying a stretch limousine with public funds, "I suddenly found myself the hero of the rednecks," Ayers says, "a very odd sensation."

Today the biggest local issues are, as in most places, economic. The dislocation that may result from the closing of nearby Fort McClellan has been the hottest topic. There's also, in Ayers's words, "the fact that 7 percent of the nation's obsolete chemical weapons are sitting there at the Anniston Army Depot, and we must rid the community of them." Waddle has taken on the weapons issue, traveling to military bases in Utah and editorializing for incineration of the chemical stockpiles as the least dangerous way to dispose of them.

Because of efforts like this, Anniston owes the paper more than it may realize. "I'm not really sure that most people here appreciate what they have in the *Star*," says Scott Barksdale, director of the Spirit of Anniston Main Street Program, which is working to rehabilitate downtown and to lure new business. "They will tackle any issue, they're not affected by advertiser pressure, and they don't avoid anything. They say in editorials when a problem is being mishandled or ignored. I've seen too many examples of other kinds of newspapers in small cities."

At Ayers's behest, Waddle is taking on a larger role at the paper. A Texas native, he went to college in Alabama and came to Anniston in 1982 from the *Kansas City Times*. Before he became executive editor, Waddle ran the editorial page, mindful of the admonition from Col. Ayers that still appears at the top of the page: "It is the duty of a newspaper to become the attorney for the most defenseless among its subscribers." Now he runs the news operation from a small office whose entire back wall is covered with a National Geographic map of the world. He is generally admired for his talents as an editor and for his commitment to the paper—though some regard him as an arbitrary manager, and there are whispers about his second-guessing subordinates. Clearly, though, Waddle has been anointed to carry on the paper's traditions: In 1998, when Ayers changed his title from editor and publisher to chairman and publisher, he named Waddle vice president for news.

When Ayers, who is sixty-seven, leaves the scene, there are no immediate heirs willing or capable of taking over. But he and his wife, their daughter, and their relatives have agreed the paper should remain independent. They have set up what they hope will be a self-perpetuating board to keep the paper out of corporate hands.

When "Alabama's largest home-owned newspaper," as the front page slogan reads, switched to morning publication in 1997, Ayers wrote a front page letter declaring, "We're not for sale—not for $50 million, not for $100 million." He went on to remind readers: "On Dec. 18, 1985—the date Dad would have been 100 years old—I promised him that, here on the front page. The promise still holds, Dad."

THE *DAILY OKLAHOMAN*

Four years before Oklahoma joined the union, twenty-nine-year-old Edward K. Gaylord, a newspaper business manager from St. Joseph, Missouri, came to the territory, prowled the still unpaved streets of dusty Oklahoma City and bought a minority interest in the fledgling *Oklahoman.* That was in 1903. By 1918, E.K. Gaylord had gained control, and his family has been running Oklahoma's largest newspaper ever since.

Today the *Daily Oklahoman,* circulation 201,892, and the *Sunday Oklahoman,* with 293,185 copies sold, constitute one of the country's largest remaining independents. Both paper and family have figured prominently in the development of the forty-sixth state, and their presence is apparent. One of Oklahoma City's downtown streets is named for E.K. Gaylord. At the large and impressive National Cowboy Hall of Fame, a bronze bust of Gaylord, a "founding benefactor," stands in the museum's Hall of Great Westerners. Special exhibits there are housed in the Edward L. Gaylord Exhibition Wing, named for E.K.'s son. Tens of millions of Gaylord dollars have been given to universities, hospitals, and dozens of charitable and civic organizations.

More recently, after the catastrophic 1995 bombing of the Alfred P. Murrah Federal Building in downtown Oklahoma City, the newspaper donated its former headquarters there—a vacant but classical 1909 building listed on the National Register of Historic Places—to the YMCA, whose own building had been severely damaged by the blast.

Clearly, the Gaylords have a sense of civic pride and an interest in the well-being of Oklahoma. At the same time, they have done extraordinarily well themselves. Large amounts of the family's wealth have been spun off into Gaylord Entertainment Co., which created the Nashville Network and Country Music Television and owns the Opryland Hotel in Nashville. In 1991, the newspaper itself was moved to a stunning, twelve-story black tower that rises from the flatlands in north Oklahoma City. "We now have by far the nicest newspaper facility in the United States," the general manager, Edmund O. Martin, boasted during the paper's 1994 centennial celebration. It would be hard to argue. With palatial paneled executive offices, an airy newsroom, and such amenities as a cafeteria, auditorium, fitness center, outdoor running track, basketball court, and lake, the *Oklahoman's* quarters are truly impressive.

It's not clear, though, that enough Gaylord money has been spent to make a better newspaper. Modest in size, the *Oklahoman* gets by with a small news staff—just under 150 full-timers, says the managing editor, Ed

Kelley, an Oklahoma native and staffer since 1975. He knows that's low for a paper the size of the *Oklahoman* but says he inherited staff limits when he returned from the Washington bureau in 1990 to take the top newsroom job.

Some papers this size have half again as many newsroom employees. On the other hand, it's not clear what the paper would do with additional reporters, given its relatively small newshole. Analysts point out that the weekday *Oklahoman* traditionally has had low household penetration in its market. Kelley is proud, though, that the paper covers the entire state and circulates in every county, and he boasts of its coverage of local news and sports. He says the suburban news, and the writing and editing in general, "certainly need to be better." And he cares about the paper's performance. "I want us to get to the point where we're not a pretty good newspaper," he says, "but a very good newspaper."

The paper's locally written stories often lack style and imagination. When the federal building was bombed, the paper did not publish an extra, but it did put together four- and six-page special sections every day for the next week. At the same time, the *Oklahoman* more than doubled the number of papers printed for street sales. More important, Kelley believes the paper helped hold the community together during a time of devastation and fear. The coverage cost about $1 million in extra pages, bigger press runs, and overtime pay, he says. The paper spent another $250,000 to cover the bombing trials in Denver, and the coverage continues. "This story will be for Oklahoma City like the Kennedy assassination was for Dallas," he says. "It will go on forever."

The paper's coverage won several awards but did not make the finals of the Pulitzer competition. In fact, rather surprisingly for a paper of its size and dominance, the *Oklahoman* has won only one Pulitzer, and that was fifty-nine years ago for editorial cartooning.

The paper tries to put six news stories on the front page each day, the usual mix being four city/state stories and two national/international. The paper uses AP copy "nine times out of 10," says assistant managing editor Mike Shannon, another native *Oklahoman* and a staffer for twenty-seven years. "We have a bias here that government needs to be watched. We watchdog state government and see how they're spending the taxpayers' money." Kelley and Shannon are hardly alone in believing that a paper's chief mission today—even the key to survival—is intensive local reporting. They may be right, but the trend is leading many papers to abandon intelligent and thorough coverage of national and international news. The *Oklahoman*'s selection of foreign stories is quirky at best. In 1998, when the United States was threatening to bomb Iraq and the Pope was visiting Cuba, the *Oklahoman*'s coverage was so skimpy that a subscriber would have been better served reading almost any out-of-town metro.

The paper seems most dedicated to urging a right-wing, anti-government conservatism on its not-always-receptive readers. The editorial page editor, Patrick McGuigan, says it forthrightly: "We're trying to change the political culture; we're trying to make Oklahoma a conservative bastion." Unsurprisingly, that dovetails with the longtime philosophy of the Gaylords, including E.K. Gaylord II, grandson of the founder and current president of the parent Oklahoma Publishing Co. He has written of the need for a "weeding out" of government employees with "socialistic ideas" and for passage of a state right-to-work law to help Oklahoma business. His father, Edward L. Gaylord, used to blast what he called "liberal bubbleheads" and once accused the notably down-the-middle AP of being leftist.

McGuigan, a longtime Oklahoman with a graduate degree in history, joined the editorial page in 1990 after ten years at a conservative Washington think tank, the Free Congress Foundation. He describes himself with cheerful enthusiasm as "a multi-issue conservative" and believes his page is "filling a critical niche" in a national landscape of liberal editorial pages. When the first stories appeared about President Clinton's sexual affair with White House intern Monica Lewinsky, McGuigan immediately published an editorial titled "Clinton Should Resign." Three days later, in a signed piece, he accused Clinton of "habitual immorality" and "a casual indulgence in fornication." Though the charges against the president were just beginning to be investigated, McGuigan was confidently saying, "He did it."

Aiding McGuigan are two full time editorial writers—one in Oklahoma City, one in Washington—and longtime editorial cartoonist Jim Lange. McGuigan says the page wants to "help people understand what's important in life," is "pro-free enterprise, anti-regulation," supports a strong military defense and favors conservative social values. "We're not buying into the gay rights agenda," he volunteers. "In fact, we don't use the word 'gay'; we use 'homosexual' and 'lesbian.' We get accused of being homophobe, but we're not."

Actually, the problem with the *Oklahoman* editorial page is not that it's conservative but that it's blindly so, simplistic and loose with the facts. When McGuigan's page went after the global warming treaty agreed to in Japan in December, 1997—labeling the U.S. role "Clinton's Kyoto Calamity"—it claimed, dubiously, that there is "growing doubt among climatologists about the human effect on atmospheric temperature change." When the AFL-CIO launched an advertising campaign in 1998 to promote union membership, the *Oklahoman*'s editorial said the ad campaign failed to disclose the "brutality, selfishness, fraud, corruption and intimidation" associated with unions. Disagree with union "bosses," the editorial concluded, and "your life may be in danger, your tires may be slashed and your family may be trembling in fear that you won't come home in one piece."

The city's alternative weekly, the *Oklahoma Gazette*, publishes letters attacking the *Oklahoman*. After the verdict in the bombing trial of Terry Nichols, the daily paper was editorially upset by the jury forewoman's criticism of the FBI. But a *Gazette* reader wrote that the *Oklahoman* itself had helped "sow the seeds of cynicism" by its "relentless knee-jerk harangue of almost all government."

The conservative message appears on page two in the person of Argus Hamilton. He writes what passes for a humor column, stringing together often tasteless one-liners on a variety of issues. In a 1998 column, he noted a popularity drop by President Clinton and wrote that "only Sonny Bono went downhill faster." When the Clintons got a male Labrador retriever, Hamilton wrote, "So far, they say the three-month-old puppy jumps all over every woman who walks into the White House. Monkey see, monkey do."

The man behind the message, E.K. Gaylord II, who has admitted that his true loves are horses, rodeos, and film production, now seems to have dedicated himself to running the newspaper. Just forty-one years old, he pledged during the paper's centennial celebration in 1994 that "as long as I'm alive, this will be a privately owned, family-based company." Chances are it will remain independent and in the control of the Gaylords, who own most of the stock. E.K. II, as he's known at the paper, turned down requests for an interview, leaving it to general manager Martin to discuss the newspaper's finances and the family's views.

The *Oklahoman*, being a private company, does not announce its profit margin, but Martin says "we would far exceed the industry standard," which he says he understands to be a percentage in the mid-20s. "We do very well."

Asked about the *Oklahoman*'s virtues, Martin cites "the love and care and concern about the community and the state we operate in" and the fact that as an independent publication "we control our own destiny in the product we put out." The newspaper is "financially supportive" of local good causes and is "part of the community, like a bank or other major institution." The Gaylord family, he says, "has a commitment to the city and the state, and believes in newspapers."

The *Oklahoman*'s professed care for its community and state seems genuine. But unless it begins to spend more of its ample resources on staff, on more ambitious reporting efforts and on more lively writing, it will remain a journalistic underachiever.

THE *EUGENE REGISTER-GUARD*

A decade after taking the helm of the *Eugene Register-Guard,* Tony Baker can relax. He has successfully engineered an agreement among family members to perpetuate their longtime control of the paper, Oregon's second-largest daily, and in 1998 he presided over the move to a new and thoroughly modern plant.

The *Guard* (as it's known by all) is a seventy-five-thousand-circulation newspaper that's exceptionally close to its community. The paper is scrutinized, praised and criticized, but hardly ever ignored. The Baker family has owned it for seven decades. Alton F. "Tony" Baker III is editor and publisher, the third of his immediate family to lead it. Baker's cousin R. Fletcher Little is general manager. Another cousin, Richard A. Baker Jr., is information systems manager. Cousin Bridget Baker-Kincaid directs corporate and public relations. Cousin David H. Baker serves the newsroom as assistant managing editor. Cousin Carol Little Johnson is a classified advertising sales assistant. Tony's sister, Susan Baker Diamond, is the Newspaper in Education coordinator.

Tony's grandfather, the original Alton F. Baker, son of the general manager of Cleveland's *Plain Dealer,* struck out for the West in 1927 and bought the sixty-year-old *Guard* in growing, still raw Eugene. Three years later he purchased the competing *Register* and merged them. He ran the combined paper for the next thirty years as Eugene grew from a timber and college town—home to the University of Oregon—into a diversified city. He became a civic force, and today the largest public greenspace in Eugene, running for two miles alongside the Willamette River across from downtown, is named Alton Baker Park. Upon his death in 1961, he was succeeded by his son, Alton F. "Bunky" Baker Jr. After Bunky retired more than twenty years later, it was his brother Edwin's turn. Five years after that, Tony Baker took over.

When the paper completed its move to a new $40 million facility in north Eugene in 1998, Baker said the expenditure demonstrated the family's commitment to maintaining ownership. "It underscores our long held philosophy that we believe the community is best served by a locally owned newspaper," Baker told *Register-Guard* readers in an eighteen-page section about the move. "It's the family's intention to continue to own and operate the paper in that manner for years to come. There's no question that if the family was interested in doing anything other than continue to own and operate the paper, it wouldn't be saddling itself with this debt load."

He wrote, correctly, that "there are not many family-owned papers our size . . . not many left at all." Because of family ownership, he explained, "we're able to make all the decisions here locally. . . . We don't feel the pressure from investors or stockholders, wherever they may be, to drive that bottom line on a quarterly basis. . . . There's pressure but we put that pressure on ourselves, because we make our own decisions about what we're going to buy and sell, the products we're going to produce, where we circulate and the setting of ad rates."

A brightly modern, cleanly edited newspaper, the *Register-Guard* puts a premium on civic duty and on trying to be the conscience of Eugene, as exemplified by its local public affairs news coverage and its thoughtful, moderately liberal, good-citizen editorial line. It wins deserved praise for its sports pages and its classy and well-displayed photography. A dozen times in the last two decades the *Register-Guard* has captured the Oregon Newspaper Publishers Association's highest honor, its General Excellence Award.

The paper's coverage of local news, especially government news, is persistent and aggressive, and stories are nearly always written with skill and style. The main section sometimes gives questionable front page play to local features and photos with little news value, squeezing out state, national, or world stories that deserve better play and would better serve Eugene's literate readership. But it doesn't omit those stories from the paper, and its overall report is complete, intelligently edited, and rarely dull.

Local coverage mostly adheres to the paper's written "News Coverage Philosophy," which states that "our professional role is civic observer, not civic booster." The paper does, however, involve itself directly as a contributor or backer in such community efforts as United Way and the construction of a downtown performing arts center.

Tony Baker candidly assesses the *Register-Guard* as not doing enough in-depth projects, needing to beef up literary and cultural coverage, and lacking sufficient reporting on outdoor recreation and on homes and gardens. So he has authorized four new editorial hires this year. The news staff now numbers about eighty full time and twenty part time people, says managing editor Jim Godbold. That's an acceptable, but not exceptional, staff size.

Baker says he intends to look at other news needs too, including strengthening the Sunday paper, which is sometimes thin and stints on local news. The Commentary section is solid, often provocative, and replete with intelligently selected pieces usually tied to the news. There's no Sunday magazine other than *Parade,* but that's not unusual these days. What's different is there's no television magazine either, because the *Guard* publishes its book on Saturday, believing it's of more use to people then. In fact, the Saturday edition is the biggest seller, at eighty-three thousand copies, because of the TV magazine. The paper sells about seventy-five thousand copies Monday through Friday, seventy-eight thousand on Sunday. It forces a seven-day buy on subscribers, and the extra Saturday and Sunday numbers come from street sales. Circulation has been flat for three years.

Although some young staffers use the paper as a training ground and move on to bigger newspapers, Tony Baker says "many people stay a long time because they like the paper and they like the community. We're blessed with a strong staff, a lot of people who are overachievers, who have more good ideas than we can put into practice."

Don Bishoff, a three-times-a-week columnist who holds forth concretely and pungently on local issues, is in his early sixties and has been at the paper for nearly forty years. Bishoff's columns sometimes take a different point of view on local controversies from the editorial page, but that doesn't upset most staffers, who figure it adds to the paper's appeal.

Editorial page editor Don Robinson has been there for thirty-five years and directs a staff of four, which he says is "certainly bigger than the chain papers of our size." They produce daily editorial and op-ed pages and a four-page Sunday commentary section that are admirable, thought-provoking, and well-read, judging from the many letters to the editor. The editorials are more rigorously reasoned than in many larger newspapers. Politically, Robinson says, the *Guard* is "largely centrist, but sort of moderately liberal." The paper endorsed Bill Clinton in both his presidential bids. Tony Baker's father, Bunky, still in charge during Ronald Reagan's presidency, insisted the paper endorse Reagan over Walter Mondale in 1984, but he initialed the editorial because Robinson and most of the staff disagreed with him.

A flap early this year involving the Eugene city manager, Vicki Elmer, illustrates the extent to which this paper engages in and promotes local debate. Near the end of Elmer's first year on the job, reporter Joe Kidd analyzed her performance. He concluded that she'd made numerous bad decisions and, by firing some key officials, had damaged City Hall morale to the point that her own executive team urged her to quit. The editorial page followed up with a strong editorial, "Elmer should resign," and said if she didn't, the city council should fire her. Then the paper granted Elmer space for a twelve-hundred-word reply, in which she defended her performance. But the city council took the *Register-Guard*'s advice and dismissed Elmer. Perhaps because the paper had prepared its readers, no one was taken by surprise and there was a minimum of civic trauma.

The paper suffered its own public embarrassment in December 1997, when the sports editor mistakenly quoted a black University of Oregon football player as saying that bowl opponent Air Force "had a good white defense." It turned out, as a tape recording showed, that he'd actually said "a good WAC defense," WAC being the Western Athletic Conference. This prompted a front page apology by Godbold. He offered "a full and complete retraction of the error," saying it had hurt the image of the university's football team and "the credibility of the *Register-Guard* in ways that won't be quickly forgotten." The player in question accepted the apology. "It was an awkward thing to go through," Baker admits.

Eugene being the kind of place it is, a liberal, activist college town where citizen debate is as much a way of life as drive-through espresso stands, not everyone loves the *Guard*. Some think it's too leftish and lives in the 1960s. Others believe it's turned too conservative. Some think it's gone soft. "A lot of people in Eugene are very critical of the *Guard*," says Fred Taylor, the retired executive editor of the *Wall Street Journal* who reads the *Guard* from 125 miles away in Coquille, where he owns the weekly *Coquille Valley Sentinel*. "But I tell them they just haven't read enough papers in other towns. The *Guard* is a very good medium-sized newspaper and one of the best of its size in the country that I've read, and I've read a lot of them."

Not to say he is without quibbles. Taylor says the paper's stories have grown shorter over time and lack detail for "political junkies like me," who he says are apparently expected to get the added information by phoning the paper's audiotext, GuardLine. He adds the paper "ought to look more closely at the university; they don't cover it very well." But Taylor volunteers that he's a stockholder of the competing *Eugene Weekly* and therefore could be "suspected of self-interest" in any critique of the establishment paper.

Another expert reader is Jon Franklin, who won two Pulitzer Prizes at Baltimore's old *Evening Sun* before coming to Oregon to write and teach. He calls the *Guard* "a rather good newspaper"—high praise from the curmudgeonly Franklin, who harbors strong doubts that newspapers will survive as a medium, at least in present form. Still, he finds the paper too buttoned-down, "very sober-sided. There's not a lot of joy. They take themselves very seriously." (Franklin has since returned to newspaper journalism at *Raleigh's News & Observer*.)

But whatever criticism one hears of the *Guard*, it's almost always offered in the context of overall admiration for a solid paper that, as Taylor says, benefits from local ownership and stable leadership. The *Guard*'s top brass may sometimes be too close to "the bankers and the developers," he says, "but that's maybe not as bad as a paper being run by floating editors and publishers from somewhere else."

Tony Baker plans to keep it that way. "The prospects for retaining family ownership are good," he says. "I've argued that what's good for this business is good for the family. We've kept pace with what would be considered a reasonable rate of return. We're not as profitable as the published reports of some publicly owned papers—we're not doing 20 percent; let's put it that way. But we're not poor either."

Twenty-one relatives, all direct descendants of founder Alton F. Baker, own the stock and constitute the board of directors of Guard Publishing Co. Five of them, including Tony, control a ten-year voting trust that began in 1987 and was renewed for another ten years. That arrangement stems from months of discussion among the family in the mid-1980s when Tony's father and uncle were retiring. Eventually the third-generation Bakers signed a document, pledging to their parents that "despite the problems and the tremendous amount of work ahead of us, we have decided we want to keep the *Register-Guard* in the family. We all have strong emotional ties to the paper and to Eugene. We know we've got a good thing here, and we believe we have the ability and the dedication to maintain it and to make it better."

The paper seems well positioned for the foreseeable future. Managing editor Godbold says the work force is stable, the new building and equipment are "state of the art," and journalistically, "what I hear all the time from Tony is, 'We want to do the right thing.'"

Such can be the mantra of the independent newspaper.

THE *PITTSBURGH TRIBUNE-REVIEW*

It's impossible in today's media environment to start a new daily newspaper. That's the accepted wisdom. But such rules do not apply to multimillionaire Richard Mellon Scaife, who is happily cultivating a new and growing daily in Pittsburgh. It's actually a spinoff of his *Tribune-Review* newspaper in Greensburg, thirty miles to the east.

Heir to the Mellon banking and oil fortune and reportedly worth close to a billion dollars, Scaife is a philanthropist of considerable generosity. But these days he's much better known as the funder of right-wing causes, some way off the chart of believability. He has long been a financial backer of the *American Spectator* magazine and other conservative critics of President Clinton. And it has been widely reported that Scaife money has benefited David Hale, a former judge who was an anti-Clinton witness in independent counsel Kenneth Starr's Whitewater probe.

But all that is about politics. What motivated Scaife to launch his Pittsburgh venture is a strong belief that a major city should have two newspaper voices. (At least that's the reason his associates give; although Scaife employs journalists, he doesn't talk to them.) He proved this once before in Sacramento, where he kept the underdog *Union* going despite a decade of negative cash flow. In the Steel City, events were put into motion in 1992 when a devastating strike prompted Scripps Howard to unload the *Pittsburgh Press.* Scaife tried to buy it but Scripps rebuffed him and sold the paper to the Block family, owner of the rival *Post-Gazette.* The family in turn closed the *Press,* and an incensed Scaife decided to rectify matters.

So he set up a newspaper office in the city's historic Station Square, a scenic spot on the banks of the Monongahela River that he'd earlier restored with more than $10 million in grants from his Allegheny Foundation. He began printing a Pittsburgh edition on his Greensburg presses, while starting construction of a $43 million printing plant north of Pittsburgh.

In October of 1997 the state-of-the-art plant, dubbed NewsWorks, opened and started printing Scaife's *Pittsburgh Tribune-Review* at the rate of about 35,000 copies on weekdays, 50,000 on Sundays. The Greensburg edition, whose slogan is "Worthy of Western Pennsylvania," circulates about 82,000 daily, 162,000 on Sundays. Even so, the combined Greensburg-Pittsburgh editions are dwarfed by the *Post-Gazette,* which sells 240,000 on weekdays, 417,000 Sundays. Scaife's startup news staff in Pittsburgh, nearly one hundred (the Greensburg edition has about the same number), is also small compared to the Post-Gazette's.

"Right now, for us it's not about making money," says David House, who came to Pittsburgh as editor from the *Corpus Christi Caller-Times.* "It's about providing Pittsburgh with an alternative daily. Here's a guy, Dick Scaife, who really wants Pittsburgh to have two newspapers. He was willing to put his money where his mouth is."

House says he took the job because "this is a privately owned newspaper and it's an exciting challenge." Newspapers owned by public companies, he says, are plagued by "a bottom-line philosophy and downsizing, with catastrophic results. That makes it tougher and tougher to perform." Over in Greensburg, a classic Pennsylvania mountain town, editor Tom Stewart agrees. "We were never forced to run on a shoestring here. We've always been healthily staffed. We can react quickly to things." The paper's conservative editorial policy "doesn't drive our news decisions," Stewart says. "We sit here every day and try to put out a good newspaper and cover both sides of an issue."

Still, Scaife's views clearly affect story play, headlines and overall tone. A few days after the Clinton-Lewinsky story broke, the papers' lead story, an AP piece used inside in many papers, explored why citizens weren't more disturbed. It was based on comments from William Bennett, Alan Keyes, Jesse Helms, and others from the right. The *Tribune-Review* headline read "Conservatives Ask: 'Where's the Outrage?'"

Much of the outrage, of course, resides in Scaife's bosom. A virulent Clinton opponent, he seems haunted by conservative conspiracy theories that drive him to publish bizarre stories about governmental intrigue and murder plots in Washington. Those stories—implying, for instance, that White House lawyer Vincent Foster was murdered, and that Commerce Secretary Ron Brown may have died from a bullet to the head, not in the crash of an Air Force plane in Croatia—color every judgment about Scaife's papers. Editors in Pittsburgh and Greenburg, forced to print the stories no matter what they might think, only shrug when questioned about them and try to change the subject.

The most notorious *Tribune-Review* stories have been written by Christopher Ruddy, a special correspondent who previously worked for the *New York Post* but was let go. Scaife's editors were reticent when questioned about Ruddy and the details of his hiring, but he apparently was given carte blanche to write and publish his stories on the front page of the *Tribune-Review*.

Stewart is the paper's liaison with Ruddy, who is based in New York City. "He's broken some controversial stories," Stewart acknowledges. "He's not assigned to go out and dig up dirt on enemies." Asked whether he believes Ruddy's stories about Ron Brown's death, Stewart demurs but says Ruddy has turned up some curious facts about a wound in Brown's head that could have been a bullet hole.

Ruddy's stories implying that Vince Foster's shooting death was made to look like a suicide have brought even more attention but have been thoroughly discredited, including by Kenneth Starr. (Although Starr says he has never met the megamillionaire, their names continue to be linked.) Even so, Scaife apparently believes the stories, having told the *Dallas Morning News* in a rare interview in 1995, "The death of Vincent Foster: I think that's the Rosetta Stone to the whole Clinton administration. There are just too many questions that have no answers."

Scaife's employ of Ruddy is of a piece with his financing of dozens of conservative organizations and causes, dating back to his $1 million contribution to Richard Nixon's campaign in 1972. One recipient of Scaife's largess is Pepperdine University. In 1997 the California university invited Starr to become dean of both its law school and a new school of public policy that the Pittsburgh conservative helped endow. Starr first said he would accept the Pepperdine offer; then, after a storm of criticism, he announced he would postpone his move. Then he said he would forgo Pepperdine altogether. (Another big financier of the Pepperdine public policy school is Edward L. Gaylord of the *Daily Oklahoman*.)

Edward H. Harrell, president of the *Tribune-Review* and the man in charge of both editions, claims not to know the details of the paper's arrangement with Ruddy. "He's a correspondent; he comes up with his own ideas," says Harrell, who runs company operations from an office in suburban Pittsburgh and consults with Scaife frequently. Harrell acknowledges the *Tribune-Review*'s ideology, but he says "no one ever points out that we run some liberal columnists, too." He cites the paper's use of Molly Ivins and Donald Kaul.

Trying to assess the Greensburg and Pittsburgh papers without taking into account the Ruddy portfolio calls to mind the old line, "Other than that, Mrs. Lincoln, how did you enjoy the play?" But the truth is, overall, Scaife's papers measure up well journalistically. In fact, they're quite good. Were it not for his extreme political agenda, Richard Scaife would be considered a respectable independent-newspaper owner.

The Greensburg newsroom supports a projects team that has published examinations of various state government programs gone awry, a look at problems in prison financing, a year-after piece on the relatives of those killed in a nearby airline crash, and a series on the Bill of Rights called "We the People." The latter, which the editors cite with special pride, ran for five days beginning July 4, 1997 and seemed designed to stir patriotic fervor. In February 1998, the paper published two lengthy front page stories about threats to individual privacy. All these projects were well-crafted and raised legitimate issues, but they possessed an edge that seems particularly suited to a Scaife-owned paper, with their tone of pro-Americanism, pro-individualism, and anti-government.

Says Sue McFarland, a news editor in Greensburg, "Our readers feel connected to the paper because Scaife lives in the community and has made contributions to it. He has a vested interest in the community and in the quality of life here." The *Tribune-Review,* she says, has a good reputation as "a place where you can grow and where you can tackle some meaty journalism."

Art McMullen, the general manager, says "technologically, we're way ahead of other places our size," leading the way, for example, in pagination. The Greensburg and Pittsburgh editions, which have nearly identical makeup, are clean in appearance, with a healthy newshole and a balance of local, state, national, and international news. The papers use color and graphics skillfully, and they share a fair amount of content. Although Scaife's operation is not as big, complete, or ambitious as the *Post-Gazette*'s, his papers would stack up well against many metros.

House, the editor of the *Tribune-Review*'s Pittsburgh edition, expresses great enthusiasm about his paper's future. "We can't go toe to toe with the *Post-Gazette* now, but that doesn't bother us." He figures the paper and the staff will keep expanding, as the capacity of NewsWorks, the new printing plant built in nine months, is 320,000 copies daily. Meanwhile, staffers at the old Greensburg office are nervous about their sister paper's ascendancy. The *Post-Gazette,* clearly not a disinterested observer, published a piece in October of 1997 saying some in Greensburg thought the Pittsburgh edition was overstaffed and a money drain, while Pittsburgh staffers thought the Greensburg operation wasn't providing enough stories.

But Scaife and his top people seem committed to both editions. With Scaife's deep pockets, that shouldn't be a problem. "Dick doesn't take any money out of the papers," says Harrell. And the profit margin? "We don't say. We're a private company."

Scaife has actually expanded his western Pennsylvania empire, purchasing three small dailies from Thomson and two dailies and a weekly from Gannett—all near Pittsburgh and Greensburg. The aim is to capture suburban readership. He's also begun to print the regional editions of *USA Today* and *Baseball Weekly.* Scaife has vowed to spend whatever it takes for up to a decade to make his Pittsburgh edition profitable. If he does, this mysterious conservative may outdistance the headlines to become an ever more influential journalistic force.

THE *ST. PETERSBURG TIMES*

In 1997, when the *St. Petersburg Times* uncovered shocking misconduct and possible fraud by the president of the National Baptist Convention

USA, it had a tricky story on its hands. Besides the usual concerns over fairness, proof, and libel suits, there was the troubling fact that the Rev. Henry Lyons was African American and a local minister. St. Petersburg was trying to heal the wounds of a violent racial disturbance that shocked the city the previous year and brought into question the *Times'* awareness of conditions in the black community.

Pursuing the Lyons story might well reopen the wounds. But the paper did not flinch. A team of reporters produced story after story. They reported that Lyons had used National Baptist Convention funds to help buy a $700,000 waterfront estate with a woman, Bernice Edwards, a convicted embezzler.

The paper said Lyons had drastically inflated convention membership lists and sold them to corporate marketers "for personal profit and political gain." More than $1 million intended for convention coffers had gone into a secret Wisconsin bank account set up by Edwards and used by her and Lyons for personal purchases. Plus, Lyons had received $350,000 from the Nigerian government while he was lobbying Washington to ease up on military rulers there. The stories were prominently displayed with headlines like "Lyons' Big Lie."

In 1998, criminal racketeering and grand theft charges were filed against Lyons, alleging that he and codefendant Edwards had stolen nearly $5 million and spent much of it on lavish living. The newspaper's aggressive coverage became one of three *Times* stories from 1997 to make it to the finals of the 1998 Pulitzer Prize competition. Only the *New York Times* and the *Los Angeles Times,* much bigger papers with much broader reach, had more finalists.

In the end, the Lyons stories didn't win, but another St. Pete finalist did. Thomas French's series on a three-year investigation into the murder of a vacationing Ohio farm wife and her two teenage daughters captured the feature writing prize. The other *Times* Pulitzer finalist was David Barstow, whose narrative piece about the proposed tobacco settlement was recognized in explanatory reporting.

And so it goes at the *St. Petersburg Times,* which many journalists consider the nation's finest local newspaper. The morning daily, with 366,000 weekday and 463,000 Sunday subscribers and apparently on its way to becoming the largest daily in Florida, displays admirably unflagging enterprise and tells riveting stories that rival the best in any paper or magazine.

It also has one of the most unusual ownership structures. Bought in 1912 by Indiana newspaperman Paul Poynter, the *Times* eventually was taken over by his son, Nelson, who ran it for four decades until his death in 1978. Nelson Poynter directed a newspaper that practiced good journalism (laced with a good deal of boosterism), pioneered in newspaper storytelling and in-depth reporting, and was socially progressive, opposing school segregation before any other major paper in the region. The *Times* led the way in cold type, color, and other technological innovations. But what Poynter did to ensure the paper's long-term independence was his most remarkable achievement.

In 1947, Poynter laid down his fifteen "Standards of Ownership," which his biographer, Robert N. Pierce, described nearly fifty years later as a kind of combined Declaration of Independence and Constitution for the newspaper. The first standard defined newspaper ownership as "a sacred trust and a great privilege." The fifteenth declared that a publication is "so individualistic in nature that complete control should be concentrated in an individual. Voting stock should never be permitted to scatter." Poynter also asserted that chain ownership doesn't ensure quality because the owners must worry about all the properties and thus show "diluted or divided" loyalty to any one paper. The fifteen standards were compressed later into ten.

He mistrusted even the usual course of trying to retain independence through family ownership. Eugene Patterson, the respected Atlanta editor who succeeded Poynter, recalls that Poynter believed the paper should go "not to family, but to professionals who recognize what the duty of the paper is." Poynter believed that a newspaper has "a public service role that can't be fully met if it's in group ownership," says Patterson, whose own view is that "the great plus of being an independent newspaper is that it frees you up to innovate and initiate, to try new ideas."

So Nelson Poynter gave away his newspaper. He set up an educational institution and willed the *Times* to it when he died. Today the renowned Poynter Institute for Media Studies operates training programs for print and broadcast journalists and sponsors forums on media issues at its downtown building beside Tampa Bay. It also owns *Congressional Quarterly* (created because Poynter wanted to track what his elected officials were up to) and *Florida Trend* and *Governing* magazines. Andrew E. Barnes, Patterson's successor, is editor and chairman of the *Times*. He also chairs Poynter and votes all the stock. When Barnes, fifty-nine, leaves, he will be succeeded in both posts by Paul C. Tash, now forty-three and the executive editor.

This setup is not likely to be duplicated elsewhere, most owners being disinclined to give away their newspapers. But what's just as striking about the *Times* is the overall quality of its leaders and staff, the verve with which they put out their newspaper, and their commitment to it as a great place to work. Barnes came to the paper twenty-five years ago from the *Washington Post*. Tash has spent his entire career there, beginning as a reporter in 1978.

Philip L. Gailey, the editorial page editor, was lured from the *New York Times* Washington bureau and presides professorially over more than a dozen editorial writers and columnists. In 1994, he freed up editorial writer Jeffrey Good for the better part of a year to research and write what amounted to an expose of Florida's probate system for settling estates. His work won a Pulitzer the next year. "We can choose to be as good as we want to be or as mediocre as we want to be," Gailey says. "The decisions are made right here in this building. If we were counting beans, how could we justify giving Jeff Good eight months to work on a project?" Gailey's editorial page is liberal ("progressive" seems to be the preferred word) and regularly endorses the Democratic presidential candidate in a circulation area that's mostly Republican.

Ruling this empire from an office atop the *Times'* handsome downtown building, Andy Barnes projects an enthusiastic and intellectual sense of what the paper is all about. He recalls that Poynter believed "a community needs a newspaper that loves it best. And Nelson talked about creating a newspaper where the decisions would be made by people who live in the community, on behalf of the community. He felt very strongly the division of allegiance that comes with remote ownership.

"It had the effect of creating a distinctive institution. The *St. Pete Times* is pretty quirky, in that we edit the newspaper very largely based on who we are and the wonderful response we get from the community, and we don't really have to wonder what does somebody think in Rosslyn or Miami or wherever," Barnes says, referring to the corporate headquarters of Gannett and Knight Ridder (although Knight Ridder's headquarters has since been moved from Miami to San Jose, California).

"It was the received wisdom when I got here," he continues, "that you serve first the readers, then the advertisers, then the staff, and all those are priorities. That really is quite powerful. The other distinctive thing is that not only are we independent, but we're private." During what Barnes calls the "unconscionable run-up" in newsprint prices several years ago, he had only to meet his obligations to the Poynter Institute. "I could fiddle with the profit margin and not have to explain it to anybody, and did," he says. "That had the effect of maintaining newshole and of not having—because of the exigencies of a quarter or a year—to undo what we'd spent five years creating."

The ratio of news to advertising at the *Times* runs about 60/40, the reverse of the rule of thumb. "Mind you, we're very careful about our profitability," Barnes says, "and we keep it very healthy." *Times* executives studied the question several years ago and decided they wanted operating profit "to be on the order of 15 percent. If it was going to be under 10 we'd damn well want to know why, and if it was over 20 we'd be doing something wrong."

Barnes well appreciates that his counterparts at public companies can only dream of such latitude. On the other hand, few of them have ever lived through the storm Barnes endured when Texas financier Robert M. Bass waged a furious effort to take over the *Times*. In 1988, Bass acquired a minority stake held by Nelson Poynter's nieces, who had been upset by the company's offer for their shares. After several bruising years—Bass accused the *Times* of being inefficient while the company painted him as a corporate raider with no real interest in journalism—the Poynter Institute paid the financier $56 million, thereby regaining all its stock.

Barnes says Nelson Poynter's motive for creating the institute, which is financed largely by the *Times'* earnings, was "to do good and to preserve the paper from having to be sold to pay taxes, and he was perfectly candid about that." The institute's president is James M. Naughton, the former executive editor of the *Philadelphia Inquirer.* A highly respected journalist equally well known for his love of pranks, Naughton delights in running Poynter's seminars and workshops. He sits at a desk in what's supposed to be the anteroom of the director's office because he has filled up the larger room with a full-size pool table.

Naughton, a man of demanding standards, finds little fault with the *Times.* It's "a writers' newspaper but well edited," he says. It's local without giving up national and international coverage, "covers the hell out of the legislature," is first-rate on enterprise and investigative work, and handles sports "exceptionally well." But he thinks the front section is often too small and says the paper needs to continue efforts to upgrade business coverage. The *Times* was "shocked and surprised" by the 1996 racial disturbances, Naughton says. "They'd tried to cover that community but hadn't really succeeded. But they reacted quickly when it happened, and they're doing better now. They're more receptive to learning opportunities than most newspapers."

Even so, readers take the paper to task for being too liberal or politically correct. Some in the black community still wonder if the *Times* understands their problems. And in 1998 Florida's Seminoles leveled some high-profile criticism of their own. The tribe claimed that *Times* staffers acted unethically in gathering information for an investigation of the Seminoles' casinos. The articles detailed the casinos' huge earnings and uncovered questionable finances and jackpot payments. Executive editor Tash defends the series as "a statement of our own journalistic findings" and accuses the Seminoles of engaging in deceptive public relations to try to obscure the facts.

Tash, like Nelson Poynter an Indiana native, joined the *Times* twenty years ago after earning a law degree from Edinburgh University in Scotland. He has been city editor, metro editor, editor, and publisher of *Florida Trend* magazine, and the *Times'* bureau chief in Washington. He believes the *Times* tries to guard against what he sees as two dangers of independent ownership: "isolation" from the ideas and expertise that can come from a group setting, and "complacency" that can be fed by a paper's economic security. "We're a better paper than we were 10 years ago," he says, "and we think there's a bright future for newspapers as long as they stay energetic and committed."

Tash treasures the paper's ability to make a decision quickly. In the 1996 campaign he wanted the paper to sponsor the vice-presidential debate. He told Barnes it would cost $500,000. At many papers, if the idea was even entertained there would have been "a huge bureaucratic review and attempts to justify" the expense, he says. "Here, we spent 10 or 15 minutes on the decision. I told Andy I thought we should do it, we discussed it briefly, and he said, 'Let's do it.'"

The news operation includes ten editions published in St. Petersburg and four other counties. The idea is to follow the area's growth and expand outside St. Petersburg, where population has declined slightly and where significant numbers of downtown businesses are shuttered. Half the paper's four hundred editorial employees work outside the main St. Pete office. The suburban editions are given their own name and identity, such as the *Clearwater Times* (followed in the mast by "An edition of the *St. Petersburg Times*"). Another edition is on the home turf of the *Times'* long-standing rival, Media General's *Tampa Tribune*. But so far, Barnes acknowledges, it has achieved only a 7 percent penetration rate in Tampa. The *Times* also supports a Washington bureau of four reporters, a Tallahassee state capital bureau of five reporters, a Miami-based Latin American correspondent, and another foreign correspondent who operates as a rover.

Staffers say morale is generally good and has improved since management listened several years ago to complaints of female and minority staffers that they weren't getting equal pay and promotions. It's clear, as numerous reporters and editors say, that most take pride in working for a paper with a strong commitment to journalism.

The paper has a Web site, although Barnes isn't much interested in it. Nor is he enamored of the civic journalism movement. "The idea that all journalism should be focused on participatory democracy is not how I think," he says. Still, Barnes is adamant that the *Times* be "very involved with our community," through its news coverage, letters to the editor and talking to readers. "My ambition for this newspaper," he says, "is that it can find ways to continue to speak to future generations of readers through vigorous discussion of topics that are of interest and importance to them." In that view, Barnes holds true to the vision of Nelson Poynter, whose one-of-a-kind organization seems to be working exactly as he intended.

THE *PALO ALTO DAILY NEWS*

In November 1995, three bold entrepreneurs from Colorado slipped into affluent Palo Alto, California, leased a vacant plumbing showroom, set up a few Macintosh computers and a satellite dish, and told the curious a vague tale about going into "electronic publishing." That remained their cover story until one day their plumber-landlords said, "We've thought about it, and we've decided you guys are CIA."

At that point, Dave Price says, he and his two partners decided they'd better come clean. They admitted that in a few days they would be launching a daily newspaper. The plumbers were so enthusiastic that they bought champagne to toast the new arrival.

"We started publishing secretly on December 7, a day which will live in infamy," jokes Price, the editor. "We didn't want to raise expectations by announcing that Palo Alto was getting a new daily newspaper and then have people see this little eight-page tabloid and say, 'What's this?'"

The first issue of the *Palo Alto Daily News* was, in fact, eight pages, written and edited by the three partners, with just one advertisement—from the plumbing company in whose former showroom the paper set up shop. The press run was three thousand copies, which were distributed free around town. By April of 1997 the *Palo Alto Daily News* was still in the plumbing showroom, with staff crammed into every nook. There were twenty-two full-timers, including a news staff of six headed by Price, and about thirty part-timers. The paper was up to eighteen thousand copies Monday through Saturday, and was typically running thirty-two to forty pages, with about two hundred ads, most from medium-sized local retailers. It's still free.

On its admittedly modest and eclectic terms, the *Daily News* is playing out an interesting experiment. It has taken the model of the free weekly— a concept that has gained widespread acceptance among readers and advertisers alike—and applied it to a daily. You're not supposed to be able to start a newspaper unless you have Scaife-sized pockets, so prohibitive are the expenses. But computers have put production on the desktop. And if you don't need an army of carriers or your own multideck Goss Metroliners, well. . . .

"Our belief is that a free newspaper, available where people shop and work, will do well," Price says. "The newspaper industry has been managed so badly that we have dying dinosaurs in a lot of cities. Independent and small newspapers are the future, and I don't think home subscriptions are the future of the newspaper industry."

Palo Alto, a picturesque Bay Area city of fifty-seven thousand, is home to Stanford University and many of Silicon Valley's newly rich. It had been without a daily newspaper since the *Peninsula Times Tribune* was abandoned in 1993 by its owner, the Tribune Co. In a classic case of newspaper mismanagement, Tribune had purchased two dailies, the *Palo Alto Times* and the *Redwood City Tribune*, and merged them. That was the first of two mistakes. Both Palo Alto (rich, mostly white, very high-toned) and Redwood City (middle-class, blue-collar, ethnically mixed) resented the clumsy amalgamation. The second mistake came when Tribune, to trim costs and appear more worldly, cut back on local coverage. The foolhardy aim was to compete head-on with the sleepy but dominant *San Francisco Chronicle* to the north and the surging *San Jose Mercury News* to the south.

Circulation plummeted, a Stanford graduate named Bill Johnson started the free-distribution and high-quality *Palo Alto Weekly*, and the downward spiral continued. By the time Tribune woke up to what it had wrought it was too late. The *Peninsula Times Tribune* had been so thoroughly run into the ground that no buyer could be found, and Tribune one day kicked the employees out, shut down the presses and locked the doors. Its building, on a prime block of downtown Palo Alto, has since been torn down and replaced by offices and townhomes.

The *Mercury News* has an excellent bureau on the Peninsula, and the *Palo Alto Weekly*, now published twice weekly, does admirable in-depth stories on local issues. Still, Price and partners Jim Pavelich and David Danforth—all of whom had run newspapers in Aspen and Vail—figured that Palo Altans missed their daily.

The new paper emphasizes local news, but it subscribes to the AP and carries a mix of local, state, national, and world stories. When water was discovered on the moon, the *Daily News* localized the news by featuring the role of scientists at the NASA research center in nearby Mountain View. "People see a tabloid, and they think 'alternative newspaper,'" says Price. "But that's not what we're trying to do. We see ourselves as more of a mainstream newspaper, a community daily newspaper."

The paper covers local government, business, and Stanford and high-school sports, and tries to stay on top of such hot local controversies as whether to ban noisy leaf-blowers. It carries a few comics, publishes a quirky horoscope ("Aquarius: Do creative things with paper clips today") and treats the news with cheeky irreverence. When the *Daily News* set up its own Web site in 1998, it announced the move on the front page with the headline "Newspaper enters 20th century—with just two years to spare."

The paper is printed at a job press in Hayward, across San Francisco Bay. Armando Mendoza, a *Daily News* employee, makes the half-hour drive to Hayward alone at midnight with the pages for the next day's paper, waits while the copies come off the press, then drives his loaded truck back and directs his small crew's distribution activities.

Readers find the paper in news racks in and around Palo Alto, and at stores and shops. The *Daily News* encourages retail advertisers to include a coupon for discounts on their products. That gives both the advertiser and the newspaper a way of measuring response, and Price says it's working. "Our circulation is not audited and I could probably give you any figure I wanted," he says. "But we know how many copies we're printing, and we know a lot more people than that read the paper. We find papers in our news racks that people have read while they're eating, and then they put them back in the rack with food stains on them."

Price says the *Daily News* became profitable in early 1997—"at least we're taking in more money than we're spending"—and he is enthusiastic about the paper's future. He likes to quote a local politician, who told Price that when the city's previous daily failed, Palo Alto "lost a mirror on itself."

THE JOY OF NEWSPAPERING, at least for now, is carrying the day in Palo Alto. That same spirit pulls along hundreds of other kindred, independent souls.

Michael Gartner, who edited two major metropolitan dailies—the *Des Moines Register* and the *Louisville Courier-Journal*—and then headed NBC News, is back home in Iowa having the time of his life running the *Ames Daily Tribune*, circulation ten thousand. In 1997 he won the Pulitzer Prize for editorial writing for his pungent observations on life in Ames and his critiques of its biggest employer, Iowa State University. He has made friends, and plenty of enemies. He shrugs off the latter, declaring, "You show me a beloved newspaper editor and I'll show you a shitty newspaper." What he likes most is knowing "the history and rhythms" of Ames. Running your own newspaper, he says, "you can make long term financial decisions, not short term ones where you always worry about quarterly profits."

Kansan Edward L. Seaton, who owns and operates the *Manhattan Mercury,* a paper originally run by his grandfather, agrees. At his 10,500-circulation daily with eighteen news staffers (more than the industry standard), "we're not publicly traded and we don't have the pressures that come with that. We spend what is required to cover the news." A small-town cosmopolite who has been honored for his work on behalf of press freedom in Latin America, Seaton was the president of ASNE in 1998.

There are other admired independents still afloat—papers like Vermont's *Rutland Herald;* Spokane's *Spokesman-Review;* the *Day* in New London, Connecticut; the *Albuquerque Journal;* the *Journal-World* of Lawrence, Kansas; and the *Free Lance-Star* of Fredericksburg, Virginia. But unless industry economics change drastically, and that's unlikely, independent and family-owned newspapers will remain a dying breed.

"There's a terrible inevitability to it," says Ben Bagdikian, who has monitored the shift toward concentrated newspaper ownership for fifteen years in successive editions of his book *The Media Monopoly.* "Families have offspring, and offspring have offspring, and things happen," he says. Heirs fight among themselves, or want greater financial returns than the family-owned paper brings them; eventually ownership gets diluted. "Of course, there were a lot of family-owned papers that were rotten," Bagdikian says. "But people like Tim Hays at Riverside and Nelson Poynter at St. Petersburg cared passionately about journalism. And their papers were founded at a time when the newspaper was a prestigious institution in town and the crown jewel among news media. A newspaper is not anymore the most glamorous and powerful property a media family can own."

As for Tim Hays, these days you won't find him in Riverside but in St. Louis, where his wife restores vintage homes. He's mostly philosophical about the 1997 sale of the *Press-Enterprise.* But he still holds to his belief that independence is more than a nice-sounding label. It's often the key to "quality and prestige taking priority over this year's earnings," he says, and to a newspaper with strong journalistic values and a bond with its community. With Riverside's low subscription rates and generous news staff, the paper's earnings as a percentage of income were never all that high.

But then that wasn't the point.

"I have fond memories of some of the family owners in California—the Knowlands; the McClatchys; the Chandlers; Tom Storke in Santa Barbara, who used his paper to fight McCarthyism. It was very gratifying to know those people and to assume that their children would carry on.

"The goal," he says, "was to turn out a paper that served a larger and larger audience and served them well. A newspaper ought to be owned by people in the community it serves."